NEW MEDIEVAL LITERATURES

New Medieval Literatures is a new annual of work on medieval textual cultures. Its scope is inclusive of work across the theoretical, archival, philological, and historicist methodologies associated with medieval literary studies. The title announces an interest both in new writing about medieval culture and in new academic writing. As well as featuring challenging new articles, each issue will include an analytical survey by a leading international medievalist of recent work in an emerging or dominant critical discourse. In order to promote dialogue, from time to time issues will include digests or translations of important new work originally published in languages other than English. The editors aim to engage with intellectual and cultural pluralism in the Middle Ages and now. Within this generous brief, they recognize only two criteria: excellence and originality.

Editors

David Lawton	Washington University in St Louis
Rita Copeland	University of Pennsylvania
Wendy Scase	University of Birmingham

Advisory Board

Jocelyn Wogan-Browne	Fordham University
Hans Ulrich Gumbrecht	Stanford University
Jeffrey Hamburger	Harvard University
Sarah Kay	University of Cambridge
Alastair Minnis	University of York
Margaret Clunies Ross	University of Sydney
Miri Rubin	Queen Mary, University of London
Paul Strohm	Columbia University
Christiane Klapisch-Zuber	École des Hautes Études en Sciences Sociales, Paris

Submissions are invited for future issues. Please write to any of the editors:

Rita Copeland,
Department of Classical Studies
University of Pennsylvania
202 Logan Hall
Philadelphia, Pennsylvania 19104, USA
Email: rcopelan@sas.upenn.edu

David Lawton,
Department of English
Washington University
Campus Box 1122, 1 Brookings Drive
St Louis, Missouri 63130-4899, USA
Email: dalawton@artsci.wustl.edu
Fax: +1 314 935 7461

Wendy Scase,
Department of English
University of Birmingham
Edgbaston
Birmingham, B15 2TT, UK
Email: W.L.Scase@bham.ac.uk
Fax: +44 (0)121 414 5668

For information about subscriptions and orders, guidelines for contributors, and contents of previous issues, please visit the NML website: http://artsci.wustl.edu/~nml/

New Medieval Literatures

6

Edited by
DAVID LAWTON
RITA COPELAND
WENDY SCASE

OXFORD
UNIVERSITY PRESS

This book has been printed digitally and produced in a standard specification in order to ensure its continuing availability

OXFORD
UNIVERSITY PRESS

Great Clarendon Street, Oxford OX2 6DP
United Kingdom

Oxford University Press is a department of the University of Oxford.
It furthers the University's objective of excellence in research, scholarship,
and education by publishing worldwide. Oxford is a registered trade mark of
Oxford University Press in the UK and in certain other countries

British Library Cataloguing in Publication Data
Data available

Library of Congress Cataloging in Publication Data
Data available

ISBN 978-0-19-925251-0

Printed and bound by CPI Group (UK) Ltd, Croydon, CR0 4YY

Contents

List of Illustrations

Mapping Performance

David Lawton

Volume 6 of *New Medieval Literatures* opens with Daniel Birkholz's extraordinary essay on 'The Vernacular Map' and closes with Bruce Holsinger's groundbreaking analytical survey, 'Medieval Literature and Cultures of Performance'; it is framed, that is, by issues of mapping and performance, and the frame proves of value in reading the essays between. The volume contains essays that challenge received boundaries, such as those between propaganda and writing that establishes the constitutive role of public service (Clementine Oliver); or those of discourse and subject position in determining the direction of scholarship on a topic as frequently visited as the sexuality of Chaucer's Pardoner (Alastair Minnis), or constituting the modern scholarly topic of heresy (Mark Pegg). Here are essays unafraid to represent their own hermeneutic work, finding their subject in the interplay between terms (commonalty and voice in the case of Emily Steiner) or temporalities (Birkholz, Larry Scanlon). Several of these essays, notably Suzanne Verderber's on *Yonec* by Marie de France, undertake virtuoso acts of rereading with self-conscious implications for the histories of reading and writing. A feature of the volume, indeed, is the amount of sustained work prepared to instantiate in its writing the subject it seeks to articulate; I am thinking of Birkholz on the vernacular map or Jeremy Tambling's relentless reading and theorization of the solitary Hoccleve, literally beside himself. The business of much of this work, overtly, is mapping; its mode, even its focus, is performative. And because the writers recognize their own performativity, they are led, long passages of synchronic study notwithstanding, to admit and conceptualize the diachronic. This volume of *New Medieval Literatures* has a reasonable chronological scope, from the twelfth to the fifteenth centuries, and by no means an exclusively English geographical or linguistic emphasis (see Pegg, Verderber); nevertheless, English literary history has a special and unusual prominence. It must be said that this is not a regular or respectful disciplinary move. The hope is that we may suggest reorientations, different ways not only of doing English literary history but also of defining the subject—which here becomes diverse movements between languages, modes, genres, readers, and spaces.

Maps are in vogue, not least in *New Medieval Literatures*, but I realize that I learned the meaning of 'mapping' as I use it here many years ago, in the early 1970s, from Elizabeth Salter. For her it was a preferred term—as a noun summarizing, in effect, three parts of her total project, entitled by her executors, after her devastatingly premature death in 1980, 'English and International' and by her, provisionally, 'an obsession with the continent'.[1] She took colleagues and graduates with her to Martel in the Dordogne, where she was attempting to set up a base: whatever our topics of specialization, she expected us all to share her fascinations with the history of the region, the planning of bastide towns, with the Hundred Years War and family conflicts, with macaronic religious drama, above all with troubadours and Cathar communities; and all these related back to the complex of interdisciplinary courses taught in the York Centre for Medieval Studies, of which she was founder and first director. Their interrelatedness, and its very concrete nature, were obvious to her, and she worked hard to foster the kinds of conversation that would make them more accessible to us (who came to York excitedly, in those early days, with training in smaller and tidier disciplines such as Middle English and Old French, sometimes in spite of headshaking by our abandoned mentors in these fields). So her practice included, first, an interdisciplinarity of such ambition and courage as always to be on the verge of overturning, then redefining, its subject; secondly, a sense that that multiple subject subsists in cultural transmission and what we now call cultural transfer; and thirdly, a notion of mapping that was not just a striking literary usage. In Elizabeth Salter's work, well ahead of the 'cartographic turn' and anticipating work that Brian Harley was yet to do, there is recognition that literary history is geographical in ways transcending identification of national or regional place. A reproduction of the Gough Map hung in her

---

[1] Elizabeth Salter, *English and International: Studies in the Literature, Art and Patronage of Medieval England*, ed. Derek Pearsall and Nicolette Zeeman (Cambridge, 1988), esp. xi–xiii and 1. 'Mappings' is the title of the third chapter of Elizabeth Salter, *Fourteenth-Century English Poetry: Contexts and Readings* (Oxford, 1983), 52–85, also posthumously published. I had the privilege of reading a draft of this chapter in manuscript in 1973. Nothing I say here detracts from the huge and inspirational role of Derek Pearsall in building the York Centre; I simply echo his view (often expressed and most recently published in his introduction to Sarah Rees Jones (ed.), *Learning and Literacy in Medieval England and Abroad* (Amsterdam, 2003), 1) that Elizabeth Salter was 'its true "onlie begetter"' and, in my view, the greatest medievalist of her generation–to whom, often through Pearsall's own efforts, much of the best modern work in the field is indebted.

office; one has only to remember how she uses it to ask where exactly Laȝamon did his reading, and what sort of community one might thereby suppose.[2]

Given the vocabulary we were later to acquire, we might have seen in Salter's practice a premature challenge to a text-bound notion of text or, indeed, an early recension of *mouvance*: a radical reading of texts in their specific and multifarious contexts, as social performances. This volume supplements the notion of mappings with that of performance—another current vogue that has recently come to flood, sweeping all before it in the manner, Holsinger suggests, of gay studies ten years ago. Holsinger's first move is to critique the 'rhetoric of the contemporaneous' in modern performance theories, whose 'unacknowledged subject', he argues, is 'history': 'Performance casts in miniature the dilemma of ultimate irrecuperability endemic to historical inquiry.' In historicized forms, performance becomes an alternative or supplementary way of conceiving the diverse movements that motivate Salter's mappings, and one that consciously does not follow modern generic or disciplinary boundaries: medieval drama, for example, is to be studied at the same time as music and liturgy, the visual arts, and rhetorical *actio*. Thus conceived, performance study is a powerful diachronic as well as synchronic mode, offering access to what one might call (after thick description) 'thick diachrony'; and it enables radical transdisciplinarity in the study of medieval cultures by helping us see that its subjects are not as our time-bound disciplines would conceive them. Holsinger's great example is medieval liturgy, which 'constitutes an inherently antidisciplinary field . . . embracing music, literature, theology, the visual arts, dance, drama, costume, pageantry, agriculture, and numerous other dimensions of medieval civilization in a material practice that impinges on nearly every aspect of cultural production'.

This move—from interdisciplinarity to antidisciplinarity, emphasizing synchronic specificity while recognizing a simultaneous need for a deeper, 'thicker', diachrony—is relevant to the essay preceding Holsinger's, Mark Gregory Pegg's forceful call to rethink the subject of medieval heresy. Pegg is concerned that we should not isolate the components of 'heresy', but see them as fully imbricated in cultural and material practice. He is concerned too that we recognize the acute local specificity of each instance, even if that should challenge the assumption of instantiation; he also asks that we should not be led by easy sympathy into

---

[2] *English and International*, 70; and see 'Mappings'.

becoming actors in our own scholarly performance. At the same time, Pegg therefore recognizes that the moments of our and others' reading must be weighed together with the objects of study; it is diachronic self-awareness, not denial, that will help us most. There is no easy exit from the 'intellectualist hall of mirrors'. At any rate, one might see Pegg's provocative essay as one agenda for mapping performances, and as a particularly vigorous call to antidisciplinarity.

The notion that the scholarly gaze constitutes or reconstitutes its object informs both the new cartography and recent hermeneutics. Daniel Birkholz considers both in his essay on 'The Vernacular Map'. His twofold subject is the small map of England found in the sixteenth-century manuscript Beinecke 558, which he argues derives from the thirteenth-century Gough Map, and with which it forms a double text, encompassing the medieval and the early modern. Birkholz explores the manuscript's contexts, not only its original owner—Thomas Butler, draper—but also later owners and readers, claiming for example that the Beinecke map would not have appeared antiquated until mapping practices changed later in the sixteenth century. In order to understand the manuscript, we need to appreciate the broader linking of its elements as a cultural system (medical, meteorological, historical, astrological, cartographic): cultural precisely because antidisciplinary—we must break out of our disciplinary histories in order to comprehend them. And this conjunction of interests, he argues, forms a mode for apprehending culture at the national level, and provides a model for vernacular literary history grounded in cartography. Given Birkholz's focus on 'the dynamics of our looking', the meeting of medieval and early modern is represented as a particularly complex map, for which in his view the term 'hermeneutic circle' would appear ludicrously, at least over-optimistically, simple. I would be tempted instead to resort, not for the first time, to Deleuze and Guattari on the rhizome.[3] Certainly, Birkholz's essay is itself necessarily rhizomic, tantalizing in its tracings of multiple and intersecting connections.

Under pressure of such complexities—of cultural forms deployed and redeployed—what might a literary history of cultural forms be like? Working in a century and language neglected (in Birkholz's view) by the dominant paradigm, Suzanne Verderber provides one model in her major essay on Marie de France's *Yonec*. Taking one detail of the text—the

[3] Gilles Deleuze and Felix Guattari, *A Thousand Plateaus: Capitalism and Schizophrenia*, trans. Brian Massumi (Minneapolis, 1987), 15.

shadow cast by the lover who arrives in the form of a goshawk, who will father the lady's child and slay her husband—Verderber establishes it as central not only to the lay but to its author's aesthetic, opening the way to Marie's negotiation between sacred and secular to make space for a truthful vernacular fiction. Marie clearly seeks to recall the annunciation—and its scene of reading and conception; yet this is not an antireligious move, though its direction is surely secular. Into the hermeneutic of the *integumentum* Marie interpolates the *simulacrum*, the 'perverse subject', manipulating received reading practices in order to reconcile the scriptural and the Ovidian: the metamorphic, polymorphous nature of the hawk-lover is aligned with the Eucharist, and becomes blessed against the fixity of the husband's body. Indeed, the lover's anomalous body is identified with the vernacular against the masculine fixity of Latin allegoresis. Verderber's essay ends with a case-specific reading of Lacan, relating the hermeneutic practices involved with the social forms flouted by Marie, especially of loveless and unequal marriage.

The phallus, its vernacular displacements, and an anomalous male body form an ironic bridge to Alastair Minnis's new essay on Chaucer's Pardoner. Minnis engages diachronically in the history of reading this compulsively fascinating figure. For him, modern readings claiming the authority of queer theory cloud issues of cultural differences between medieval and modern and paradigm shifts in notions of sexuality; he recuperates queer theory by appealing to it against the binarism of hetero- and homo-. Minnis also reacts against the spiritual allegorizing of some earlier readings that purport to prove the Pardoner a type of the damned; he is on the side of those who have emphasized the figure's enigmatic quality or mystery. Minnis offers instead an intensive scholarly focus on medieval sources, 'consideration of the Pardoner's deviant body in view of the range of conditions covered by "eunuchry" in Chaucer's day', and makes a culturally specific diagnosis: 'cold testicles'. This is likely to become an authoritative essay. Its effect is like that of a bold but subtle painting restoration, except that it reassures by offering not a newly fixed image but rather instabilities of medieval culture—medical discourse under literary redeployment, in mid-performance.

The Pardoner is not infrequently read as a distorting mirror of vernacular authorship; most strikingly, by Rita Copeland, as the embodiment of rhetoric.[4] Hence the bad faith in moving between secular and

---

[4] Rita Copeland, 'The Pardoner's Body and the Disciplining of Rhetoric', in Sarah Kay and Miri Rubin (eds.), *Framing Medieval Bodies* (Manchester, 1994), 138–59.

spiritual, and hence the necessary carriage of the fake, such as the relics and false documents the Pardoner bears. Larry Scanlon's essay on the *Clerk's Tale* concentrates on a scene of documentary forgery: the papal dispensation that supposedly allows Walter to divorce Griselda. Scanlon's essay also relates to Verderber's: these negotiations, which involve the truth of writing and reflexively of vernacular fiction, are related to unstable and developing ideologies of marriage. And Scanlon offers a new map in Birkholz's sense, giving a conspectus of several scenes of reading, medieval and modern. He shows that the slow transition of the story from Boccaccio does not support the notion of Chaucer as simply 'queering' Petrarch by means of irony; indeed, his conclusion on this issue recalls Minnis's on queer theory and the Pardoner. In modern times, Scanlon sets scenes of reading divided partly on disciplinary lines (English, History) against Caryl Churchill's *Top Girls*—in which Griselda is still seen as exemplary (as in seventeenth-century versions of the story). Then Scanlon proposes that the didactic is a form of desire, steadfastly diachronic: following Žižek, 'it seeks to recover from the future a replacement for what has been lost in the past'. The aesthetic, moral, and social pressure of the *Clerk's Tale* comes from its constituting a feminine space of the domestic for the display of spiritual virtue. This is not solely a textual issue, of course, but inseparable from the late medieval development of marriage as an institution marked, *contra* Duby, by the collaboration or collusion between canon lawyers and secular authorities (as the forged papal dispensation at face value suggests). Scanlon's essay is radically interdisciplinary, concentrating on 'interrelations among marriage, clerical regulations, and written instrument', and its diachronic reading reverses modern reading: 'For Chaucer and his audience, it was the Wife of Bath who spoke for tradition, and Griselda who represented innovation.' Chaucer's investment in the tale is at once ironic and ideological. If his interest in forgery is that of a bureaucrat, it is a distinctively medieval and narrativizing kind of bureaucrat: for whom the point of rules is the hermeneutic flexibility with which they are interpreted.

This may take us some way to perceiving interiority in the late medieval collaboration between bureaucracy and authorship. That relationship occupies the next three essays in the volume. In the first of these, Clementine Oliver writes a revisionist account of Thomas Fovent, whose *Historia*—an account of parliamentary proceedings at the time of the lords appellant—has been cast, in the terms of T. F. Tout's reading, as partisan and propagandist. Oliver argues for what seems to me an important and valuable distinction: what Fovent is doing is speaking for himself, and in so doing both voicing and appealing to 'public opinion'. Fovent is unlike authors of 'public poetry', as characterized in the classic essay by Anne Middleton,[5] because he does not seek to mediate; he is also unlike Thomas Usk, because he does not become entangled in 'the web of factionalism'. On the other hand, both in status and career, he is surprisingly like Chaucer; and Oliver uses Fovent's case to argue that concentration on Chaucer has distorted the history of late fourteenth-century authorship and reading of clerically produced texts and discourses. Far from needing to be supremely politic, Oliver argues, Chaucer only needed not to be Usk. Those seeking a wider audience for *The Canterbury Tales* might look again at Fovent and indeed at parliament, in which both Chaucer and he served; in a piece of diachronic mapping, Oliver shows how a 1641 translation of Fovent's work was used against Charles I. 'Fovent's public had a keen interest in parliamentary proceedings, and was hungry for vitriol. Fovent knew this because he wrote the *Historia* for people like himself. Fovent was a bureaucrat, not a partisan'.

The essay following, by Emily Steiner, presents an alternative way of conceptualizing what Oliver sees in Habermasian terms as public opinion. Steiner's subject is *commonalty*: how literally and figuratively English writers, poets, bureaucrats, and lawmakers sought in the late fourteenth century to perform collectivity, in parliamentary business, in civic politics (Usk again), and by writing itself (here Langland, not Chaucer). Such commonalty is neither a given nor a stable concept for, entailing a negotiation between a common good and social status, it exists only in performance, 'within the formulation of a vernacular rhetoric which blurs social distinction in its very fashioning of political structure'. Its most authentic literary mode, for Steiner, is allegory, whose very purpose in *Piers Plowman* is the rhetorical and intellectual figuration of commonalty in a kind of rampant antidisciplinarity: 'If poetic invention—allegorical puzzles, narrative incoherence, generic shifts—may be considered a type of response to medieval political life, Langland's allegory is itself the very process through which contemporary political structures come into being'. They do so noisily. If Oliver sees her essay as support for David Aers's now famous 'whisper in the ear of early modernists',[6] what Steiner hears is 'clamour', a collectivity of voices in which

[5] Anne Middleton, 'The Idea of Public Poetry in the Reign of Richard II', *Speculum: A Journal of Medieval Studies*, 53 (Cambridge, Mass., 1978), 94–114.
[6] David Aers, 'A Whisper in the Ear of Early Modernists', in Aers (ed.), *Culture and History, 1350–1600: Essays on English Communities, Identities, and Writing* (Detroit, 1992), 177–202.

commonalty subsists. A key contribution of her essay, in such highly documentary and literary contexts, is its foregrounding of a cultural notion
of *voice* as figuring both political and literary representation.

So much that has been of positive value in the preceding essays occurs
in Jeremy Tambling's reading of Hoccleve's *Complaint* as lack. Instead of
commonalty, there is the isolation of melancholia and mourning, 'a subject outside the circle—of his wits, and of his friends, and of those who
would give him social validation'. His voice, that would articulate the
centre, is decentred; it is neither entirely his (in part redeployed from
Chaucer and Langland even where most 'autobiographical'), nor is it
heard by those for whom he would speak. The problem is his madness:
how can his readers trust him when he announces his cure? 'What is an
autobiography if it admits that its memory has disappeared? What good
is it even if the subject says that its memory has come back? Can it remember not having a memory?' Tambling glosses Hoccleve's condition in
two ways: politically, as amnesia, it anticipates the modern state; generi-
cally, as madness, in C. S. Lewis's view, it is equivalent to allegory. But this
is not the fruitful allegory Steiner reads in Langland or that Verderber sees
manipulated by Marie de France to authorize her fiction. It is Walter
Benjamin's allegory, 'writing which knows that there is no more than the
ruin and the fragmentary'. However personal, the ruins are those of a culture—of a sacred text to which the faithful Hoccleve allows no free play,
and of the Lancastrian state: 'Hoccleve as the mad subject is a casualty of
unacknowledged usurpation, replicating in his own absence of work an
emptiness elsewhere'. In response, Hoccleve wants to obey, and fantasizes
a pre-emptive orthodoxy; but what he sees, in a scene of almost unbearably Shakespearian poignancy, is his own face in the mirror, estranged
from the social order and from his own health. Tambling juxtaposes this,
disconcertingly, with Deleuze and Guattari on 'faciality': 'the face is produced only when the head ceases to be part of the body'.

It is a relief to move from the horror of Hoccleve's orthodoxy to the
productivity implied by Pegg's polemic on heresy, and then to the free
play everywhere evident in Holsinger's account of performance.
It is tempting to read these movements in something like the terms
of fixity versus fluidity proposed for Marie's work in Verderber's essay,
or, for example, to set Hoccleve's face and voice alongside those of
the Pardoner as aspects of vernacular authorship. So many common elements run through these essays that one might well speak, in conclusion,
of closing the circle—except, once more, that it is a rhizome, and the concept of closure is therefore meaningless. The pleasure of reading this

volume will be in exploring, in mapping its various performances. The pleasure of writing these essays has had to do, I suspect, with working through the pressures that rhizomic structures place on the writing of essays. Antidisciplinarity and innovative writing go hand in hand. We learn that things are not where we thought they were, and join in ways we have to renew ourselves to see. The editors of *New Medieval Literatures* are always looking for new writing and new voices. We are proud to announce the award of the $1,000 prize for our second essay contest, won by Suzanne Verderber for her essay in this volume.[7]

Washington University in St Louis

[7] Shortlisted candidates, limited to current doctoral candidates or those within five years of the award of the Ph.D, were selected by the editors and read by one or more members of the Advisory Board. The competition was judged by Paul Strohm and Jocelyn Wogan-Browne, who had played no part in the earlier process. Our thanks to all concerned.

The Vernacular Map: Re-Charting English Literary History

Daniel Birkholz

I. Medieval Perspectives

Near the middle of a sixteenth-century English commonplace book now held at Yale University—Beinecke Library MS 558, a compendium of vernacular astrological treatises and household notes produced between 1547 and 1554—there appears a very curious drawing: curiously medieval, that is. A scroll-shaped cartouche across its top labels this composition 'The Map off Ynglonnd' (Fig. 1). Another cartouche along the bottom attributes the work to 'Thomas Buttlar', a name of frequent reappearance in this manuscript. Although the manuscript's overall contents bespeak an unusual context for a map such as this, and although, given Butler's signature, the work may be reliably historicized, neither this Tudor miscellany nor its oddly anachronistic rendering of 'Ynglonnd' have as yet received any critical notice.[1]

The lack of attention so far paid to Thomas Butler's map may (at least in part) be attributed to the perceived 'imprecision' of the piece—which is to say, the backwardness of its technical cartography, with respect to innovations the second half of the sixteenth century would see in terms

I am pleased to thank Pomona College and the University of Minnesota for the research grants making this essay possible. Also essential were the welcomes I received at the Beinecke Rare Book & Manuscript Library and the Cushing/Whitney Medical Library in New Haven, as well as at the Essex Record Office and the Museum of Harlow. I have benefited from feedback by Elizabeth Allen, Peter Barber, Diane Beck, Edward Copeland, Rita Copeland, Paul Dahlgren, Clark Davis, Catherine Delano-Smith, Paul Harvey, Patrick Jagoda, David Lawton, Julia Mickenberg, Pamela Smith, David Wallace and Robert Woods. Thanks, also, to audiences in Claremont, Austin, and Madrid; and for common-room conversations at Downing College, Cambridge. This essay is dedicated to the memory of Clark Davis.

[1] New Haven, Beinecke Library, MS 558. For a partial list of contents, see archive dossier. The map is on fos. 47^v–48^r. A dating of c.1547–1554 is derived from internal evidence (e.g. fo. 49^r's charts of reigns) and confirmed by extracts from datable contemporary treatises. For appearances of the Butler (alias Stallon) family name see fos. 4^r, 5^r, 42^{r-v}, 47^v–48^r, 61^r, and 63^v.

FIG. 1. 'The Map off Ynglonnd' by Thomas Butler, c.1554.

of map-printing and (especially) scale-based mapping practices.[2] In a related development, toward mid-century momentum began to gather
around the notion that a new, scientifically up-to-date map of the realm
ought to be produced. This was a drive fuelled in the short term by the
maps of George Lily (printed 1546/55) and Humphrey Lloyd (printed
1573), among others, but despite counting men like John Leland among
its advocates, the project did not reach full elaboration until Christopher
Saxton's Atlas of 1579.[3] Most important to note is that, over time, what I
shall call the 'regnal map'—the map of the realm or state, first at a
national, then an imperial level—would rise to a position of unmatched
prominence among cartographic images. Such a position has been maintained to this day, when territorial maps (the shapes of countries) have become images of the nation nearly unrivalled in their influence and
ubiquity, signs of the sovereign state *par excellence*.[4]

Conclusive evidence is not yet available to support the proposition that
in the Middle Ages (as is the case so unequivocally for later periods) there
existed any fully-fledged tradition of mapping the realm.[5] Yet however
little we know about early developments in regnal mapping, medieval
efforts in this enterprise nonetheless culminated quite spectacularly for
England—in the celebrated but understudied Gough Map (Fig. 2), a

[2] For useful overviews, see P. D. A. Harvey, *Maps in Tudor England* (Chicago, 1993), esp. 7–8,
and Sarah Tyacke (ed.), *English Map-Making 1500–1650: Historical Essays* (London, 1983). For a
dismissal of non-scale mapping ('the medieval school of pictorial representation of topography,
where precision is conspicuous by its absence'), see Marcus Merriman, 'Italian Military Engineers in Britain in the 1540s', in Tyacke, 59; but see also J. B. Harley, who argues in the same
volume ('Meaning and Ambiguity in Tudor Cartography', 32) that an 'apparently careless
delineation' of map-icons may '[connote] a set of values rather than a purely technical
backwardness'.
[3] See Catherine Delano-Smith and Roger J. P. Kain, *English Maps: A History* (London, 1999),
49–111 ('Mapping Country and County'), esp. 57–71. The literature on Saxton is extensive.
[4] On the relationship between cartography and the nation-state, see J. B. Harley, 'Maps,
Knowledge and Power', in D. Cosgrove and S. Daniels (eds.), *The Iconography of Landscape: Essays on the Symbolic Representation, Design and Use of Past Environments* (Cambridge, 1988),
277–312; John Pickles, 'Texts, Hermeneutics and Propaganda Maps', in T. Barnes and J. Duncan
(eds.), *Writing Worlds: Discourse, Text and Metaphor in the Representation of Landscape* (New York,
1992), 193–230; and David Buisseret (ed.), *Monarchs, Ministers and Maps: The Emergence of
Cartography as a Tool of Government in Early Modern Europe* (Chicago, 1992), esp. the essays by
Peter Barber.
[5] Very few maps of this sort survive; for what does, see G. R. Crone, *Early Maps of the British
Isles AD 1000–AD 1579* (London, 1961). The impact of the related tradition of geographical *description* of Britain—a feature of both universal and insular chronicles—should not be under-
estimated. Regarding this tradition during the sixteenth century, see Lesley B. Cormack, 'Good
Fences Make Good Neighbors: Geography as Self-Definition in Early Modern England', *ISIS*,
82 (1991), 655–61.

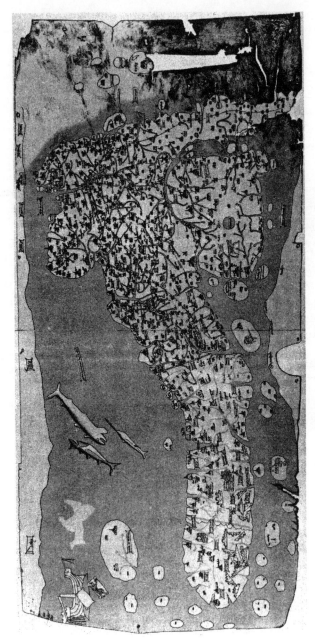

FIG. 2. The Gough Map of Britain, c.1360; prototype c.1280.

wall-map approximately 56×118 cm (2×4 feet) across whose extant copy dates to about 1360.[6] What makes the map in the Beinecke manuscript so compelling is that although this 18×26 cm production runs to only a fraction of Gough's size, and dates to almost two centuries later, there can be no doubt but that this is a copy or near relative of that elusive landmark of medieval cartography.

Here is not the place for in-depth examination of the Beinecke Map and its predecessor, but just a glance at our two maps will establish their family resemblance. Overall, Beinecke recalls Gough clearly in the shape, orientation, and framing it gives to the island of Britain. This basic correspondence compels increasingly the further we proceed in comparing details: the maps duplicate one another's place-names and topographical features, but share (most tellingly) a number of iconographic oddities.[7] The Beinecke Map's smaller proportions have left no room for the Gough Map's famous highway system; but fo. 47[r] (the overleaf of the left half of the map) contains a table setting out 'The ways from town to town unto London & the dystance in myls' (Fig. 3). This table's routes and distances correspond exactly to those registered (via Roman numerals and red lines) on the body of the Gough Map, with the occasional addition or alteration.[8] In the table's third route, for example, running from Walsingham to 'Waltham, and so to London', Beinecke adds the village of Puckeridge ('pukreh') between Barkway and Ware, whereas the Gough Map omits this leg of the thoroughfare. Puckeridge's appearance looks to be a detail of relevance. For beneath a chart recording 'what [moon] maketh full sea at many portes' (fo. 4[r]), another marginal signature spells out our manuscript's provenance: 'Thomas Butler', it reads, 'of Harlow in Essex'— Harlow being a town just a few miles away.

[6] For a facsimile reproduction and full description see E. J. S. Parsons, *The Map of Great Britain circa AD 1360 Known as the Gough Map* (Oxford, 1958). However, as B. P. Hindle comments (in a view that goes back to R. A. Pelham), 'it is likely that [the map] was originally compiled in about 1280, the extant copy being a later revision', *Maps for Local History* (London, 1988), 13; see also G. R. Crone, *Maps and Their Makers* (London, 1953), 7.

[7] Compare, for example, the icons for Mount Snowdonia in North Wales. For the relationship between these maps, see Daniel Birkholz, 'The Gough Map Revisited: Thomas Butler's *Map off Ynglonnd*, circa 1554', *Imago Mundi: The International Journal for the History of Cartography* (forthcoming).

[8] Beinecke's highway table includes a number of emendations of this sort, particularly in the area around Harlow, plus two 'new' routes (that is, highways not registered by the Gough Map) in the general vicinity. For a listing of Gough's roads, see Parsons, *Map of Britain*, 36–7. For discussion see Frank Stenton, 'The Roads of the Gough Map', in Parsons, 16–20, and B. P. Hindle, 'The Towns and Roads of the Gough Map', *Manchester Geographer*, 1 (1980), 35–40, among other publications. See Birkholz, 'Gough Revisited', for comparison with the Beinecke table.

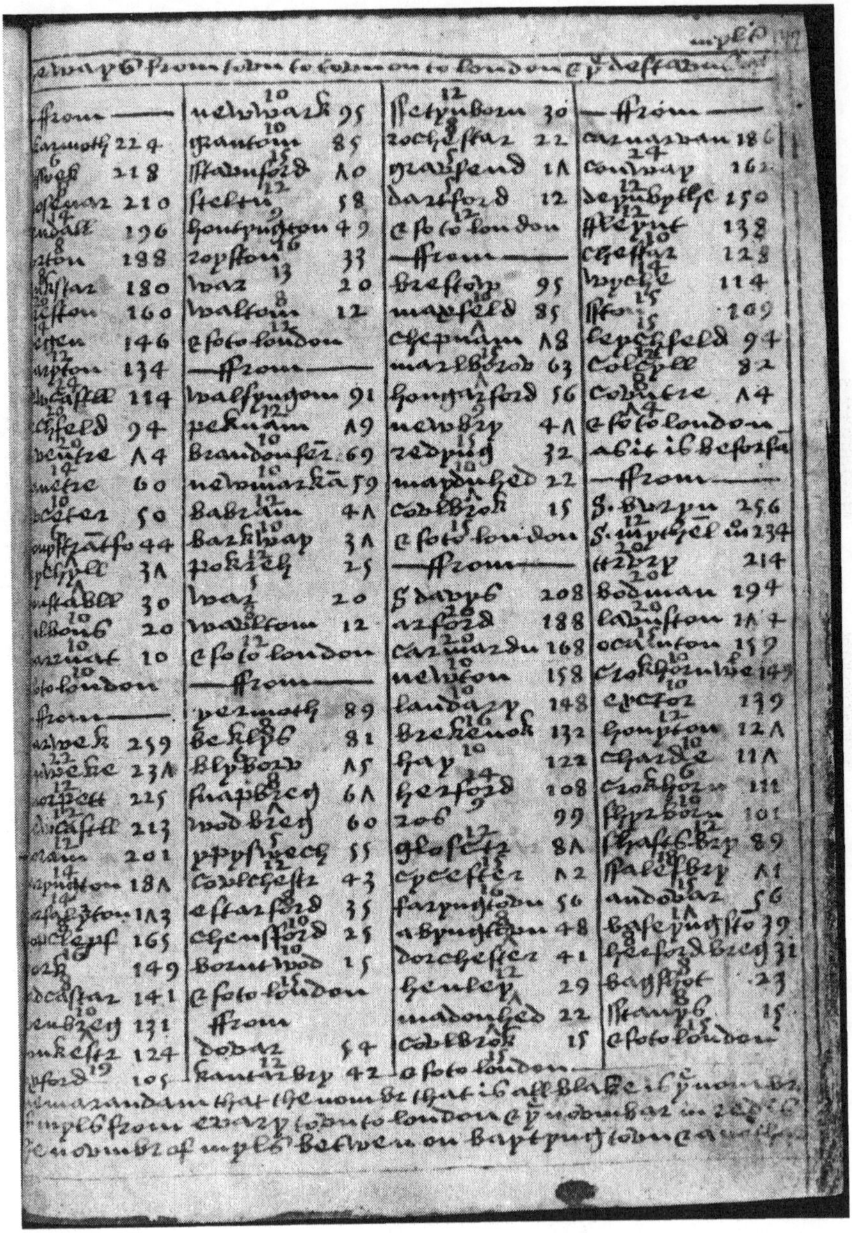

FIG. 3. 'The ways from town to town unto London'.

Highway data aside, the most prominent of these maps' shared features is the (gratuitous) inclusion on each of an elaborately drawn English warship. Gough's ship is appropriate to the fourteenth century, Beinecke's to the sixteenth; yet both come complete with lifeboat in tow, and are deposited in a similar location: upper-left corner, drifting inward upon the North Sea. This corresponding pictorial flourish should enforce the point of Beinecke's debt to the Gough Map sufficiently. It is likely that other versions, maps now lost, intervene between these two extant documents. Yet I am not interested here, ultimately, in determining the precise degree of these maps' formal resemblance, or in laying out the stemmatics of their relationship.[9] The crucial point is that to stumble upon Thomas Butler's 'Ynglonnd' in the midst of a set of Tudor astrological treatises and household notes is—for the practising medievalist at least—simultaneously to encounter, essentially to re-experience, this image's more famous but also more enigmatic forebear.[10]

There is thus a certain doubleness of vision now inherent in any viewing of the Beinecke Map—itself an artefact of the sixteenth century, but one to which we cannot help but bring a medieval perspective. This perspective has some advantages, especially when it comes to writing what Paul Carter has termed 'spatial history',[11] or when it comes to examining what might be called (as in this unique case) the dynamics of cartographic redeployment. The central work of this essay will be to characterize that particular act of redeployment which Thomas Butler performs when he reproduces the Gough Map's image (and corrects its road system data) in the pages of his heterogeneous manuscript. I should acknowledge here that I intend to conduct this investigation from a stubbornly medievalist standpoint. For one of my goals along the way to charting the implications of a map of England's appearance in Beinecke MS 558 will be to show that despite cartography's seemingly pronounced divide from literary culture and its concerns, premodern practices of mapping— map-making in an actual sense, not only the usual figurative sense (cartography as metaphor)—have much to offer contemporary

---

[9] Roger Mason of Oxford has, in preparation, a comprehensive stemma of maps related to Gough.

[10] That the Gough Map 'remains an enigma' has been observed most recently by Delano-Smith and Kane, *English Maps*, 48. Such an assessment has become traditional: see P. D. A. Harvey, *Medieval Maps* (Toronto, 1991), 78, who describes Gough's production context as 'wholly mysterious'.

[11] Paul Carter, *The Road to Botany Bay: An Exploration of Landscape and History* (Chicago, 1987), pp. xx–xxiii.

medievalism. This has become especially evident recently, in the wake of some provocative essays by anglophone medievalists on the interlocked issues of cultural periodization and literary history; nationalism and philology; but above all topography and historiography.[12] If it is true, as David Wallace predicts, that examination of the process by which the Renaissance paradigm imposed itself 'will assume increasing importance for medievalists',[13] so also, I would suggest, is it likely that premodern cartography will demand increasing attention. Because they constitute a peculiar order of document (e.g. as visual/textual hybrids) and because they possess a special authority as images (due in part to their activation of an at-a-glance epistemology), early maps are uniquely suited to negotiating between some of the present moment's most important critical categories.[14]

I have argued elsewhere that the Gough Map, whose prototype probably dates to the late thirteenth century, is a document that activates both 'geographic' and 'symbolic' modes of mapping in order to promote an explicitly royalist political agenda. Probably associated originally (in production and use) with the bureaucratic class known as 'King's Clerks', this is a text concerned to advance Edward I's programme of state consolidation and territorial expansion, his claim, based on the precedent of King Arthur, to a 'monarchy of the whole island' of Britain. The Gough Map's marked and measured routes in Wales (visible in Fig. 2) reproduce late thirteenth-century military and royal administrative circuits. Similarly, although in a different representational mode, the map's North Sea illustrations—the (wrecked) warship mentioned above, and a scene of battling sea-monsters beside it—speak directly, if allegorically, to the

---

[12] See e.g. James Simpson, 'Ageism: Leland, Bale, and the Laborious Start of English Literary History, 1350–1550', *New Medieval Literatures (NML)*, 1 (1997), 213–35; Jennifer Summit, 'Topography as Historiography: Petrarch, Chaucer, and the Making of Medieval Rome', *Journal of Medieval and Early Modern Studies (JMEMS)*, 30 (2000), 211–246; David Wallace, 'Dante in Somerset: Ghosts, Historiography, Periodization', *New Medieval Literatures*, 3 (1999), 9–38; David Lawton, 'The Surveying Subject and the "Whole World" of Belief: Three Case Studies', *NML*, 4 (2000), 9–37; and (most eclectically) Catherine Brown, 'In the Middle', *JMEMS*, 30 (2000), 547–74. For work on complementary themes, see John Dagenais and Margaret R. Greer, 'Decolonizing the Middle Ages: Introduction', *JMEMS*, 30 (2000), 431–48. For the suggestion that '[the] New Philology may have been launched as part of the longstanding academic rivalry between medieval and Renaissance scholarship', see Sarah Kay, 'Analytical Survey 3: The New Philology', *NML*, 3 (1999), 301.
[13] Wallace, 'Dante in Somerset', 38.
[14] See J. B. Harley, 'The Map and the Development of the History of Cartography', in J. B. Harley and David Woodward (eds.), *The History of Cartography*, vol. i (Chicago, 1987), 2–3.

Scottish succession crisis (the 'Great Cause' of 1290 & ff.) that Edward and his clerks came to use as a pretext for conquest.[15]

One question raised by the Beinecke Map might be how exactly the Gough Map's administrative and proto-colonial ambitions get reconfigured in this much later and much-reduced version of the image. There are implications to be found in Beinecke's decision to lop off Scotland (note the map's straight left edge), while this territory looms large for the Gough Map, both symbolically and topographically. Just having foundered (prior to Beinecke 558's compilation) was another attempt at dynastic/military annexation of Scotland: the so-called Rough Wooing of the mid-to-late 1540s, in which the English sought to compel Queen Mary of Scotland into marriage with young and sickly Edward VI.[16]

Such explicitly political questions are never *not* relevant to a representation of territory. However, the distinction between these maps lies not so much in their renderings of political space, as in their respective social emplacements. Because the Gough Map's first known owner may have acquired it through a government source (and indeed the map's content corroborates such a hunch), commentators have frequently proposed for Gough an official, metropolitan, and bureaucratic context.[17] By contrast,

[15] See Daniel Birkholz, *The King's Two Maps: Cartography and Culture in Thirteenth-Century England* (New York, forthcoming), esp. ch. 3: 'Of Sea Monsters, Salt and Sovereignty: Edward I and the Gough Map of Britain'.

[16] Merriman, 'Italian Engineers', 58; see also John Guy, *Tudor England* (Oxford, 1988), who notes that 'Scotland was crucial' to the schemes of the Lord Protector (the Duke of Somerset) who sought 'to assert Edward I's ancient claim to suzerainty; to unite the crowns; and to enforce the marriage between Edward VI and the infant Mary Stuart' (201–2); also Simon G. Ellis, 'The Limits of Power: The English Crown and the British Isles', 65, and Simon Adams, 'Britain, Europe and the World', 194–5, both in Patrick Collinson (ed.), *The Sixteenth-Century 1485–1603* (Oxford, 2002). Adams notes that 'The Rough Wooing' was a term 'actually coined by Sir Walter Scott'. Interestingly, Saxton's patron William Cecil was Somerset's apprentice in the matter of Scotland's 'incorporation into an English scheme of things, by means fair or foul' (precisely the territorial ambition of both Edward I's clerks and the Gough Map); see Collinson, 'Introduction', *Sixteenth Century*, 3–4.

[17] See e.g. Parsons, *Map of Britain*, 2, 15; R. A. Pelham, 'Early Maps of Great Britain II: The Gough Map', *Geographical Journal*, 81 (1933), 39; B. P. Hindle, 'Roads and Tracks', in L. Cantor (ed.), *The English Medieval Landscape* (Philadelphia, 1982), 196; and P. D. A. Harvey, 'Local and Regional Cartography in Medieval Europe', in Harley and Woodward, *The History of Cartography*, 493. See also n. 6, above. For the map's early history—prior to its acquisition by Richard Gough in 1774, and subsequent gift to the Bodleian in 1809—see Parsons, *Map of Britain*, 1–2, who traces its ownership through Thomas Martin to Peter Le Neve (d. 1731): 'Le Neve was in touch with government departments and had been appointed one of the deputy chamberlains of the exchequer, an office which he gave up in 1705–6. He would therefore have had the opportunity of obtaining it from an official as well as from a private source.'

the Beinecke Map operates within a more fully documentable world, but one less easily categorized. Beinecke's milieu amounts to whatever set of overlapping communities we can construct, whatever web of social and intellectual connections we can document or infer, for Thomas Butler and his book.

Unlike most of those who produced maps or otherwise dealt in geographical knowledge during these years, 'Thomas Butler of Harlow in Essex' was no gentleman scholar, whether an antiquarian (like Leland and Lloyd) or a scientist/surveyor (like Leonard Digges or John Dee). Neither was Butler a government clerk or an estate steward; nor yet was he the sort of technical craftsman—a ship's navigator or military engineer, say—who a generation later would have become a professional cartographer.[18] Evidence suggests that the author of the Beinecke Map may have frequented the Blackfriars shop of printer and instrument-maker Thomas Gemini in the early 1550s, and so maintained connection to the London scientific community of his day.[19] Yet if Butler grazed against this vibrant world of empirical endeavour, he does not, professionally speaking, appear to have been *of* it. Instead, Thomas Butler owned a woollen-shop—strange qualifications, for the man to whom we owe a reproduction of the apparently 'official' Gough Map.

Most of what can be ascertained concerning the figure responsible for 'The Map off Ynglonnd' derives directly from the pages of Beinecke 558, but equally fortuitous is that a copy of our protagonist's will (dated 5

---

[18] For cartography's links to various professions and a run-down of confirmed and potential map-makers in the mid-sixteenth century, see Delano-Smith and Kane, *English Maps*, 58–66, who stress that 'the link between maps and instruments was close', 60; see also Harvey, *Maps in Tudor England*, and Tyacke's introduction to *English Map-Making*. For military surveyors, see Merriman, 'Italian Engineers'. On the advent of professional surveying and a 'golden age of estate cartography', 1585–1615, see Peter Eden, 'Three Elizabethan Estate Surveyors', and William Ravenhill, 'Saxton's Surveying: An Enigma', both in Tyacke: 70, 76; 114.

[19] That Butler was familiar with the shop of Gemini ('one of the founders' of the English instrument-making trade, in which London enjoyed 'a virtual monopoly') is suggested not only by the scientific devices (quadrant, astrolabe) deposited within his London chest, but also by the fact that Gemini had printed the treatises by Humphrey Lloyd (*Almanack and Kalendar*, n.d.) and Leonard Digges (*A Prognostication of Right Good Effect*, 1553) whose extracts appear in Beinecke MS 558. For the world of London instrument-making, see G. L. E. Turner, 'Mathematical Instrument Making in London in the Sixteenth Century' in Tyacke, *English Map-Making*, 93–111. In 1556 Gemini printed Digges's treatise on surveying (*A Boke called Tectonicon*) 'at London in ye Blackfriers', describing himself as 'ther ready to make all the Instruments appertaining to thes booke'; see both men's entries in the *DNB* (xxi. 118–19; xv. 70–1), as well as R. T. Gunther's editions (*Ashmolean Reprints III–IV*) of Digges's *Prognostication* (Oxford, 1926) and *Tectonicon* (Oxford, 1927).

August 1556) has survived.[20] Thomas Butler had side-concerns in agricul-tural commodities, as well as a few leases to manage, but our sometime-cartographer was in essence a draper, whose rising prosperity in the second quarter of the sixteenth century appears to have afforded him op-portunity to pursue a set of amateur intellectual interests.[21] Butler oper-ated his woollen shop—located at 'Bromleys' in Latton, the parish adjacent to Harlow—with the help of his wife Elizabeth, who oversaw it following her husband's death before passing it along to their second son, Thomas.[22] In an exceptional first section (detailing items bequeathed to eldest son John), Butler's will reveals that he owned a number of scientific instruments, among them a quadrant, a 'great astrolabe that was wont to hang over the sphere in the hall', and a mysterious 'little clock called amometer'.[23] These devices lay collected in 'my chest standing at Lon-don'—a detail provocative in itself—which also held a second, more deluxe manuscript: 'my great written book with a boarded cover that Isaac wrote' (which is to say, *not* Beinecke 558, a modest, mostly autograph quarto).[24] So far, the milieu implied by Butler's will might seem suffi-

---

[20] Essex Record Office D/AMR 1/55. For a printed abstract see F. G. Emmison, *Essex Wills (England)*, vol. i: *1558–1565* (Washington, DC, 1982), 310 (#1002): 'Thomas Stallon *alias* Butler of Harlow, 5 August 1556' (proved, n.d.). See pp. xxvii–xxviii for explanation of editorial method. Interestingly, Emmison's volume was undertaken at the urging and cost of an American bene-factor, John B. Threlfall, two of whose ancestors are included. Although one fell before his period—this was, bizarrely, the very will I went looking for—Emmison 'used editorial license to include' it ('Preface'). For a fuller version of Thomas Butler's will, with others in the family (plus further documentation), see Threlfall, *The Ancestry of the Children of John Brooks Threlfall* (Madison, 1970), entries #15, 208, 7604, 3802. My thanks to Mr Threlfall for supplying this material.

[21] Despite a 'progressive decline in the importance of the small producer', nonetheless the English cloth industry overall was 'set on an upward phase of production', one which 'continued almost uninterruptedly until the 1550s'. Between 1541 and 1550 alone, wool prices doubled. See Peter J. Bowden, *The Wool Trade in Tudor and Stuart England* (London, 1962), 2, 5, 6.

[22] See Emmison, *Essex Wills*, 275–6 (#890) for 'Elizabeth Stallon of Harlow, widow of Thomas Stallon *alias* Butler of Harlow, 16 September 1557' (proved 26 Apr. 1559); ERO D/AMR 2. See Threlfall #7604 (ERO D/A BW 35/67) for 'Thomas Stallon of Latton, 13 September 1387' (proved 25 May 1590). On female drapers in the period, see Pamela O. Long, *Technology, Society and Culture in Late Medieval and Renaissance Europe, 1300–1600* (Washington, DC, 2000), 47.

[23] Emmison, *Essex Wills* ('Preface'), speculates that 'amometer' may be a variant of 'anemo-meter', an instrument for measuring wind-velocity, but not recorded in the *OED* until nearly two centuries later'. Building on this, Threlfall suggests that Butler may have had an early career as a navigator, but see discussion below regarding the Beinecke manuscript's relative disinterest in nautical matters.

[24] New Haven, Yale Medical Library, MS 26. See archive dossier for date (*c*.1551–4), descrip-tion, and partial list of contents. See Emmison, *Essex Wills*, p. xix, on the extreme rarity with which books (not to mention scientific instruments) receive mention in wills of this class, region, and period.

ciently rarified to explain an interest in cartography (largely confined to landowners and government officials in these years). However, in this document's second section—detailing shop implements earmarked for second-son Thomas—we enter another world entirely, this one as mundane and workaday as the other is intellectually sophisticated. Here Butler's will lists 'my press, my jack, my shears, my cutting board'—also 'my clock [probably for regulating workers' production of cloth], my joined chest in the shop, and a box of iron'.[25] This inventory of the tools of trade, and their careful assignation to one particular son (John converts his inherited leases and shop-wares into money), is a feature standard in Essex mercantile and artisan wills of the period.[26]

The self-conscious pendulation in Butler's will, between scientific paraphernalia for John and industrial stock-in-trade for Thomas, is matched by a similar bifurcation between the realms of the intellectual and the economic in Butler's commonplace book (a hallmark of this genre, it so happens).[27] Scattered among the Beinecke manuscript's astrological and meteorological items are expense figures and production accounts; an enrolment of rents; a list of prices for wheat, peas, herring, salmon, oil, malt, honey, and so forth; also charts on the measurement and cutting of cloth. Certainly there appears much potential for mobility in this context, social and professional. But nowhere is a sense of the *un*-refinement that *at least partly* characterizes Thomas Butler's immediate milieu better suggested than in a stray observation tucked toward the back of Beinecke 558. Plugging an empty line just above 'a help for mowltiplication' (i.e. a multiplication table), just below 'a rewll for dayly expenses for the day & the weke & the month & the year', and not far off from memos noting that 'thes be the 7 sciences' and 'thay be arts', is the book's most endearingly quotidian detail: the reflection that 'yt is good to kalf a kow'.[28] At a private, testimonial moment like this, we seem as far

---

[25] Long notes that textile workers in Flanders 'began to work according to the sounds of mechanical clocks' in these years, *Technology*, 45–6; but see also Carlo M. Cipolla, *Clocks and Culture 1300–1700* (London, 1962), regarding the clock's developing roles as status symbol and as a machine attracting 'more and more the inquisitive curiosity of scholars', 103, 57; also Long, *Technology*, 46. The will of Thomas Stallon *alias* Butler of Harlow mentions only this shop-clock (and the mysterious 'amometer') but Thomas the Younger (see n. 22, above) bequeaths 'my largest clock' to one son and 'my lesser clock' to another: both appear to be chamber clocks, as they are not listed alongside shop-items but grouped together, respectively, with articles of formal clothing and domestic furniture.

[26] See F. G. Emmison, *Elizabethan Life III: Home, Work and Land* (Chelmsford, 1976), 76.

[27] See David R. Parker, *The Commonplace Book in Tudor London* (Lanham, Md., 1998).

[28] Beinecke MS 558, fo. 65ᵛ; for production accounts and charts see fos. 63ᵛ–65ᵛ; 86ʳ–88ʳ, etc.

removed from the Gough Map's world, its king's clerks and programmes of conquest, as we are from the institutional apparatus that underwrote production of Saxton's Atlas, from its sponsorship by leading minister William Cecil down through the logistical support that was mandated at a local level.[29]

As we shall see below, Beinecke 558 is a book of considerable idiosyncrasy. Among much else it includes a herbal ('the Names and natures off herbes') and a Manual of the Astrolabe; extracts from contemporary meteorological treatises (by Lloyd and Digges); plus 'Judgments' and 'Sayings' compiled from standard astrological authorities: Almansor, Massahala, Zahell, Stoeffler. Especially evocative, and made all the more so by the inclusion of Butler family birthnotes and horoscopes, are a set of household astrological procedures: how to tell 'Whether a woman be with child or no'; 'Yff geste bidden shall come'; 'Whether a thefe be a stranger or no'; 'For one's brother how he doth'; and so forth.[30] All of this collateral data—that is, social information connectible to 'The Map off Ynglonnd' via Thomas Butler and/or Beinecke MS 558—makes the Beinecke Map's reproduction of the Gough Map's image of the realm, however faithful it may be in form and detail, arguably a cultural act of completely divergent implications. Holding aside the maps' discrepancies in size and setting, even just the sheer documentary particularity we can bring to Beinecke, as opposed to the speculation surrounding Gough, creates a profoundly different critical climate. The intense historicist focus it is possible to train on Butler's drawing, that is, as one in a constellation of grounded documents, cannot help but lend whatever 'social meanings' we generate for it, whatever interpretations we propose, an added (authoritative) heft.

On the other hand, to the extent that cartographic content *itself* contains meaning (i.e. generic meaning, meaning that can be inherited), we must acknowledge that these two maps remain inescapably linked, strangely blended. Just as, for example, the wills of Butler senior (1556) and of son Thomas (1587) throw mutual light on one another, so in-

---

[29] Ravenhill, 'Saxton's Surveying', 115. See also Richard Helgerson, 'The Land Speaks: Cartography, Chorography and Subversion in Renaissance England', *Representations*, 16 (1986), 50–6, for compelling analysis of 'Saxton's Atlas' as a composite production, subject to competing authorial claims (monarch, minister, patron, surveyor) and ideological uses (e.g. localist vs. royalist).

[30] Beinecke MS 558, fos. 81ʳ–82ᵛ; 22ᵛ–41ʳ; 1–5ʳ; 6ᵛ–15ʳ; 16ᵛ–22ʳ; 62ʳ–63ʳ; 66ʳ–85ᵛ. Family birthnotes appear on 63ᵛ, horoscopes on fos. 42ʳ⁻ᵛ. See dossier p. ii for alternate spellings of astrologers' names.

evitably do all details touching *either* the Beinecke Map *or* the Gough Map—distinct as incarnations but bearers of a shared genetic code—reveal insights potentially applicable to both texts (assuming appropriate cultural conversion), despite otherwise incommensurate contexts. If we acknowledge these maps as necessarily related—glimpsing Gough through Beinecke, approaching Beinecke by way of Gough—we are left viewing a kind of cartographic palimpsest, or medieval/Tudor double-exposure. Not so much two discrete historical texts as a single interwoven composite, such an image enfolds whole eras even as it stitches disparate moments and distinct interpretive communities together.

Among the many questions that are raised by this intertextual image—questions activated, to put matters baldly, by *my encounter* with the Beinecke Map *as a medievalist*—those concerning premodern cartography's relationship to historiography (and its competing methodologies) rank as most important, certainly in terms of setting up our later excursions. In a series of essays beginning some two decades ago, J. B. Harley laid out what he described as a new 'interpretive strategy' for the history of cartography. This new approach 'would involve a shift . . . from an emphasis on the making of the map artifact to [an emphasis] on its use and its reception within the society which created it'. Nowadays, few would dispute the proposition that 'social and cultural context go to the root of understanding' in cartographic (or for that matter literary) study.[31] Questions of 'use' and of 'function', in the context of a document's original setting—the world into which it was 'born'—have become central to the discipline.[32] Indeed, this is so much the case that the study of cartography might now be said to have become entrenched in a lateral-looking historicism, or what recently has been described (in the context of literary study) as 'the analytical model of a dense materialist synchronism'.[33] In other words, we have become all but obsessed—and I include myself here—with interdisciplinary horizontal archaeologies, with the communities in which a given text or map image first appeared and operated.

Traditional 'cartographic history', Harley argues, 'has tended to stop at

[31] J. B. Harley, 'The Iconology of Early Maps', in C. C. Marzoli (ed.), *Imago et Mensura Mundi: Atti del IX Congresso Internazionale di Storia della Cartografia* (Pisa, 1981), 33; Harley and Woodward, 'Concluding Remarks' to *The History of Cartography*, 507.

[32] Harley, 'Meaning and Ambiguity', 32, 30, 22. For a similar sentiment in the context of book-history (not map-history), see Roger Chartier (ed.), 'General Introduction: Print Culture', in *The Culture of Print: Power and the Uses of Print in Early Modern Europe* (Princeton, 1989), 1–10, esp. 3.

[33] Rita Copeland, 'Childhood, Pedagogy, and the Literal Sense: From Late Antiquity to the Lollard Heretical Classroom', *NML*, 1 (1997), 125.

the moment the craftsman steps aside and the image is born into the world'. But if 'this is where the *social history* of cartography begins' (emphasis mine)—with painstaking reconstruction of a map's 'precise cultural coordinates' and contemporary ideological uses—it must be said that in practice our 'social histories' of cartography don't always travel very far. They tend, rather, to stay frozen, in the fetishized moment of birth, or at best early infancy. Harley acknowledges periodically 'that the meanings originally attached' to map images were 'subject to change'.[34] And yet, even in his own careful work (not to mention in the field generally), such gestures toward an appreciation of the later lives of early maps remain underdeveloped. Like so many of us, Harley restricts his inquiry primarily 'to a consideration of the meanings which *contemporaries* may have ascribed to particular maps in the period . . . *when they were first created*' (emphasis mine).[35]

Now, in part because it remains divorced from any fully reliable display context (and hence from anything but a speculative socio-historical location), the Gough Map of Britain has long baffled critics for its spectacular divergence from the usual conventions of medieval map-making. As one early critic noted, 'the map is remarkable for its isolated position in the cartographic record'. Going further, some commentators have been inclined to suggest that in essence, this isn't *really* a 'medieval' map at all. Though its late thirteenth-century prototype appears to have been a contemporary of the Hereford Cathedral *mappamundi*, 'in conception'—so the received opinion goes—these maps are 'years apart'.[36]

It is not my goal to push too hard on the irony of this situation—in which the Gough Map, with its 'admirable accuracy',[37] is widely praised for being ahead of its time, while the Beinecke Map, unfortunate in standing on the wrong side of a surveying revolution, is effectively ignored for seeming behind the times. Still, it is worth noting that here we have one image felt to be, as it were, anachronistic twice over. At the outset of this essay I invoked the term 'medieval', perhaps a bit irresponsibly, and here again I toss around 'anachronistic' as if a cultural text's temporality (or placement in a given historical period) were a thing casually constructed rather than a matter of immutable, numerical fact. Yet come to

---

[34] Harley, 'Meaning and Ambiguity', 40, 23, 35.   [35] Ibid. 22.

[36] Parsons, *Map of Britain*, 4; Harvey, 'Local Cartography', 496; see also W. W. Jervis, *The World in Maps: A Study in Map Evolution* (London, 1936), 78, who describes Hereford as 'even more retrogressive than most' of its type; and G. R. Crone, *The Hereford World Map* (London, 1949), 10.

[37] Helen Jewell, *The North-South Divide: The Origins of Northern Consciousness in England* (Manchester, 1994), 107; also Parsons, *Map of Britain*, 7, 15; Hindle, *Local History*, 12–13.

that, actually this is more or less my point. It is also this essay's interpretive crux.

Considerable scholarship of late, especially in medieval literary studies, has addressed itself to issues of historiography and cultural periodization. In particular, scholars have looked to challenge the long-entrenched concept of a medieval/early modern divide—for this still-operative historiographical model, as James Simpson has said, is one 'according to which the "medieval" continues to figure all that is other to modernity, and in which the function of scholarship is to define and reaffirm "the medieval" '.[38] The original point of such identification and reaffirmation of 'The Middle Ages' and things 'medieval' was, as is now often remarked, to enable Renaissance cultural workers to 'see themselves as writing on the boundary of one, positive epoch, about another, negative period ending in the immediate past'. Two important figures for England in this respect are, first, John Leland, who in the 1530s and 1540s conducted a truly massive investigation into the realm's architectural and manuscript antiquities, producing along the way a detailed topographical survey; and second, John Bale, Leland's scholarly executor, who in the 1550s brought the voluminous notes comprising Leland's 'impossibly ambitious [project]' into a publishable order. Much as had Petrarch before them, Leland and Bale seek—and essentially this is 'the basis upon which Tudor historiography was built'—to highlight the brilliance of their own age, and to contrast that with the darkness of the past'.[39]

Yet although the medieval past may be 'consistently rejected as obscure' (as Simpson explains), 'it remains true that great figures need to be rescued from that obscurity'. Leland and Bale 'rescue their cultural heroes by describing them as wholly exceptional figures, almost miraculously capable of resisting the obscurantist culture of their period'.[40] The stakes involved in scholarly activity these latter days, as Henry Kissinger once helpfully remarked, are not perhaps so high. However, in the crucible of mid-sixteenth-century English politics, to engage in (and seek patronage for) projects of bibliographical and topographical surveying amounts to

[38] Simpson, 'Ageism', 213, 235; see also Summit, 'Topography as Historiography', 212.
[39] Simpson, 'Ageism', 217–18, 222; 218; Summit, 'Topography as Historiography', 212. See also Lawton, 'Surveying Subject', 33–7; May McKisack, *Medieval History in the Tudor Age* (Oxford, 1971), 1–25; and Howard Marchitello, 'Political Maps: The Production of Cartography and Chorography in Early Modern England', in M. Ezell and K. O'Brien O'Keeffe (eds.), *Cultural Artifacts and the Production of Meaning* (Ann Arbor, 1994), 22–4.
[40] Simpson, 'Ageism', 218; I have silently removed the parenthetical phrase '('nature repugnying')' after 'miraculously'.

something more. As Wallace says, it becomes 'a matter of crucial, nerve-wracking import . . . that those attempting to discriminate between hidden treasure and works of superstition—texts to redeem and texts to destroy—judge rightly'.[41]

It seems clear that the empirically oriented Gough Map, unlike such self-evident 'works of superstition' as *mappaemundi*, did indeed qualify for the English Renaissance as a 'text to redeem'. Here is a 'hidden treasure', a 'cultural hero' of a map if there ever was one—a document so successful at resisting the 'superstitious' and 'imprecise' medieval world around it that it could fulfil official England's need for a map of the realm for almost three centuries. Indeed, so usefully precocious was the Gough Map that Lily's 1546/55 Map of the British Isles 'represents little advance' on Gough, and appears partially to have been based on it. As Catherine Delano-Smith and Roger Kain have said, given that by the mid-century the various means were available with which to produce a new map according to up-to-date scientific principles, 'The question is, why did nothing happen about the systematic mapping of England until the 1570s'?[42]

My question for the Beinecke Map must be formulated differently: can we even see this image outside the filter imposed by that later programme of 'systematic mapping' embodied by Cecil, Saxton, and their printed Atlas of 1579? Later we will examine the climate of empirical inquiry that is incipient in the manuscript surrounding the Beinecke Map, its interest in astronomical and meteorological phenomena, in scientific instruments and the observational, computational, and prognosticatory practices they enable. What I want to highlight here, instead, is the inevitable eventual consignment to the trashbin of 'the past' of the image reproduced by Beinecke from the model provided by Gough—this map's characterization as 'medieval', its identification as a text to be rejected, and if not destroyed, then at least as one to be reclassified as antiquarian in nature, as 'curious', as something fit to be placed under 'house arrest' (to borrow Siân Echard's borrowed term, for the process by which the documents of the past are prepared for consumption by the present, in the controlled environment of our libraries, museums, and archives).[43] The

---

[41] Wallace, 'Dante in Somerset', 35.

[42] Delano-Smith and Kane, *English Maps*, 47–8, 63, 66.

[43] Siân Echard, 'House Arrest: Modern Archives, Medieval Manuscripts', *JMEMS*, 30 (2000), 185–210; Echard takes her operative term from a phrase in Jacques Derrida's *Archive Fever* (1994), 2. Regarding the term 'curious', see discussion below on the library of antiquary John Brand.

moment of this consignment to the past of Gough's vision of the realm, as an image backward looking, a thing medieval, a text opposed to modernity: this moment seems to have been deferred until perhaps the 1570s. At this point—with the full advent of surveying and of map-printing—we might say the Beinecke Map 'becomes' medieval, loses whatever claim it may once have had to representational currency, to a technical as well as a social 'accuracy'.

Close attention to the frameworks supplied by disciplinary histories—the various critical filters we now necessarily look through—is indispensable to any inquiry into an early map's (or other text's) multiple and changing social meanings. This is particularly the case if we wish to stage conversations that move diachronically, or vertically between periods, and not just synchronically, or across them horizontally. There are palpable pleasures to be had in a scholarship of 'dense materialist synchronism', as may become apparent as I continue scattering facts about my protagonist and his manuscript. Yet such an approach, attentive as it is to synchronic archaeologies, needs to be augmented by diachronic investigation—an examination not just of map genealogies and genres but also of our inherited critical paradigms. When we encounter the Beinecke Map of England now, whether in my illustrations or in Thomas Butler's manuscript, we cannot help but see it through the lens of what we 'know' about cartographic history—and indeed about English cultural and literary history more generally. It will be my goal in this essay to scratch a bit upon these lenses. For if we seek to uncover social meanings that are historically contingent yet 'subject to change', we need to examine the dynamics of our own looking as vigorously as we do the images we think we see.

II. Cartographic Afterlives

This essay began by examining the historiographical fate of Thomas Butler's 'Map off Ynglonnd' during the half-century after its production—how, on grounds of its seeming anachronism in an era dominated by printed maps and surveying, the Beinecke Map appears to have 'become medieval' in cartographic character. As it happens, with the erosion of astrology's cultural legitimacy following 1660, Beinecke 558's corpus of scientific texts—similarly—comes to constitute a literature newly 'medieval'. For with the Enlightenment Thomas Butler's astrological compendium becomes an artefact definitively outmoded, of sensibilities now self-evidently antique. In the 1550s, Butler's scientific and carto-graphic materials had both been current; then during the first century fol-lowing his death, even as the technical credibility of his map drained away, the overall cultural capital enjoyed by his astrological material will have been on the rise. Finally, once the claims to accuracy of both their modes had been undermined, Butler's map and the astrological treatises around it return to being coeval, contemporaries in inaccuracy and superstition.

Of course this isn't the end of the story. J. B. Harley's exhortation that we attend to the later lives of early maps deserves to be taken seriously not just for a landmark map like Gough, but also for a minor production like Thomas Butler's copy of it. To be sure, it is here in the realm of map *re-ception*—what Roger Chartier would term 'readerly appropriation'—that we are at our 'most speculative' in the history of cartography.[44] Yet to accept Harley's gadfly proposition—that the social meanings of a given map remain perennially 'subject to change'—is to accept a scholarly chal-lenge. By these standards, if we are to read a map fully and plurally, not just at a given moment but cumulatively, over time and from shifting per-spectives, we must seek to lay open the dynamics according to which such changes in cartographic meaning occur.

The critical risks here are substantial, but in looking to examine the afterlives of early maps, we do have certain tools to hand: the philological, the historicist, the bibliographical. Recent work on early textual cultures has emphasized that manuscript setting always plays a role in helping to direct reception. But just as an individual text's location within a particu-lar 'manuscript matrix' requires close analysis, so also, scholars have come to stress, does a codex's own physical and institutional setting, the arte-fact's emplacement itself, require interpretive consideration.[45] Put simply, books themselves have histories, between their initial production and most recent archive classification, and such lateral associations as their proximity to other volumes or ownership by specific individuals—we might say extrinsic factors—can impact on meaning as crucially as do the intrinsic qualities of their texts (e.g. webs of allusion and imagery, the-matic arguments, generic structure).

[44] Harley and Woodward, 'Concluding Remarks', 508; Roger Chartier, 'Texts, Printing, Readings', in Lynn Hunt (ed.), *The New Cultural History* (Berkeley, Calif., 1989), 154–75, esp. 156–7, 171; see also 'Popular Appropriations: The Readers and their Books', in Chartier's *Forms and Meanings: Texts, Performances and Audiences from Codex to Computer* (Philadelphia, 1995), 83–97; also 1–4.

[45] I have been especially influenced by Chartier; for 'manuscript matrix', see n. 87, below.

We know from his will that Thomas Butler's 'chest standing at London'—full of scientific devices and at least one manuscript, a 'great written book with a boarded cover'—passed to his eldest son John in 1556. A modest autograph quarto, Beinecke 558 rates no mention in Butler's will, although this is typical for such books. The first change in meaning Beinecke undergoes came early on in its existence, with the production of Yale Medical Library MS 26, a volume apparently designed to upgrade and replace it. Butler's illustrated and commissioned 'great book' reproduces almost none of his commonplace book's incidental material, but duplicates most of its scientific items, adding further medical/astrological material and presenting all in a lavish format that contrasts with the earlier manuscript's ad hoc layout and mixed-use character. The mercantile and industrial items that appear with particular density in Beinecke 558's later folios—expense figures, rentals, commodity prices, cloth-charts— are especially suggestive when placed beside a reference in second-son Thomas's will to 'certain writings' secured in a cupboard at the family woollen-shop.[46] The likelihood is that beginning with Yale Medical 26's production (*c.*1553) and then intensifying following Butler's death (1556), the Beinecke manuscript came effectively to function, for Thomas the Younger (who appears not to have shared his father and brother's interest in science), as more or less a 'shop-book', i.e. a tool of the cloth-trade not unlike the press, jack, shears, and cutting board Thomas also inherited. The Beinecke Map, in this early iteration of its 'social meaning', fills an explicitly professional (i.e. strategic planning) function, in that a good deal of any merchant-draper's activity lay in coordinating the movement of goods (that is, in commodity acquisition, production subcontracting, and distribution).[47] Obviously crucial to domestic wayfaring is the highway chart accompanying the map, reproduced from the Gough Map's 'national road system radiating from London'.[48] Yet insofar as wool constituted the early English economy's most important resource, this reading of the Beinecke Map (essentially private and functional) also has implications at the nation-building level: wool figured as a major source

---

[46] Threlfall, *Ancestry*, #7604 (ERO D/A BW 35/67). On the practice of ignoring such material in the last testament, see Parker, *Commonplace Book*, 6, and Emmison, *Essex Wills*, p. xix.

[47] Long, *Technology*, 19 & ff. Several Essex towns were important to the wool trade, but 'there is little evidence to show that clothmaking was ever the main industry at Harlow'; see L. H. Bateman, *History of Harlow* (Harlow, 1969), 91; also *The Victoria History of the County of Essex*, viii: *Chafford and Harlow Hundreds*, ed. W. R. Powell (Oxford, 1983), 142.

[48] Hindle, 'Roads and Tracks', 197; see also Stenton, 'Roads of Gough', 16, among others.

of taxation and a prime target of wartime purveyance, not to mention as the realm's staple export.[49]

In any case, whether Beinecke MS 558 fell among the scientific paraphernalia earmarked for John, or instead passed to Thomas along with the family shop and its accoutrements, the *post*-Tudor history of this manuscript remains difficult to trace. In 1970, Thomas Butler's commonplace book passed into the collection of New Haven's Beinecke Rare Book and Manuscript Library, arriving as Item #3 in a set of 410 books, maps, and manuscripts acquired between 1938 and 1970 by Henry C. Taylor: 'man of business, sportsman, war-time officer in the US Navy'. Henry Taylor took his inspiration and direction as a collector from a list of books recommended in *A Seaman's Grammar*, by Captain John Smith (1579–1632), as 'important furnishings of the master's cabin in a well-found ship'.[50] The Taylor Collection, consequently, has two major branches: technical material on navigation, and books by or about 'the men who discovered and explored America'. Despite its inclusion of a chart registering 'what [moon] maketh full sea at many portes', Thomas Butler's manuscript by no means constitutes one of 'the fundamental books of the sea' such as formed the core of Taylor's library, nor will it ever have experienced 'the rough [handling]' of 'practical use by seamen' as did a number of particularly treasured items.[51] Still, what is interesting about this book's presence in the Henry C. Taylor Collection is the way it accrues new interpretive resonance, the way its operative 'social meanings' become altered, by virtue of its new bibliographical associations. For not just surrounding the manuscript physically, but now also framing it conceptually, is the tidy captain's library of Henry Taylor's nautical imagination.

Thomas Butler's manuscript had for four centuries been accruing social meanings (as well as losing them); but effective from the moment of its acquisition by Taylor, the book's basic character became subject to revision. It underwent a change in profile based on the company it would come to keep during the middle years of the twentieth century. Specifically it would appear that, presumably for the first time in its history, the

---

[49] Bowden, *Wool Trade*, pp. xv–xvi; Long, *Technology*, 19.

[50] Lawrence C. Wroth, 'Foreword' to *The Henry C. Taylor Collection*, ed. J. S. Kebabian (New Haven, 1971), p. vii; Kebabian, *Taylor Collection*, 1.

[51] Kebabian, *Taylor Collection*, p. ix; Wroth, 'Foreword', p. vii; Kebabian p. xxi. Included in the collection are three (printed) books by Leonard Digges, #153, 200, 201.

manuscript's single image of note—'The Map off Ynglonnd' near the centre of the volume—takes on an iconic role with regard to the material around it. Through a process of codicological synecdoche, the map appears to have become the manuscript's definitive item, its identity-imparting representative. The Beinecke map image provides not only an epistemological bridge to the rest of the Taylor collection, with its nautical and exploratory focus, but also comes to function as the compendium's organizational locus, a thematic touchstone with reference to which the 'internal' meanings of the rest of the book's items would come to be reconfigured.

In elevating the Beinecke Map to the status of manuscript icon (through activation of a link to other early cartographic material), the Taylor Collection revises the effective meaning, also, of the rest of the material in what was once Thomas Butler's manuscript—in particular the codex's astrological treatises. Nautical varieties of the very scientific instruments Butler owned—the quadrant, the astrolabe—had developed parallel to (but along different timelines from) the standard, terrestrial forms of these devices. The Mariner's Astrolabe, for example, had been in shipboard navigational use since classical times, but the standard astrolabe was not adapted for use in land surveying until late in the sixteenth century.[52] Improved techniques for nautical navigation during the seventeenth and eighteenth centuries, as an informed collector like Henry Taylor surely knew, developed indirectly out of the astronomical computation that earlier periods had put to astrological use. However, any such retrospective understanding of the latent relationship between early modern astrology and the shipboard navigational practice of subsequent years—precisely the vertical historical insight which drove Taylor to acquire this item—must be recognized as by no means an epistemological given, a historically stable 'fact' (however ingenious and well informed) 'about' this manuscript and its material.

For in fact, its chart on the 'floud' and 'ebbe' of domestic harbor tides aside, the Beinecke manuscript (much like the map itself) does not demonstrate any particular concern for nautical matters.[53] Rather, the eventual navigational 'implications' of Butler's astrological practice, this material's indirect contribution to the discourse of seagoing exploration that Henry Taylor took as his collecting focus, are meanings produced

---

[52] *Dictionary of the Middle Ages*, i. 602–3; Long, *Technology*, 47; and Evelyn Edson and Emilie Savage-Smith, 'An Astrologer's Map: A Relic of Late Antiquity', *Imago Mundi*, 52 (2000), 20.

[53] See Birkholz, 'Gough Revisited'; also discussion below.

essentially in retrospect. To look back upon Tudor astrology armed with a knowledge of what future technological innovation it would enable is to invoke an explanation at best inactive in the mid-sixteenth century. In his admiration for the scientific practice of 'the men who explored . . . North America' (and thereby laid the grounds for his own naval and entrepreneurial career), Henry Taylor displays a markedly teleological and to some extent nationalist progressivism. He reads Thomas Butler's astrology, in a first sense, through the lens of his manuscript's Map of England, but moreover in light of what he knows to be the later developments in nautical science. In doing so, to borrow a phrase from Michel de Certeau, Taylor 'poaches upon' the textual resources stocked within this manuscript in a manner Thomas Butler would never perhaps envision.[54] So do we each, in turn; the point is that each such act of poaching, of 'readerly appropriation', effectively reconstitutes the work so acted upon. During the so-called 'golden age' of Tudor surveying, of Christopher Saxton and his printed county maps, the Beinecke Map may have appeared mystifying, out of place—best explained away as a commonplace book's antique idiosyncrasy. However, when this manuscript becomes a part of Henry Taylor's travel-oriented collection, suddenly, according to a newly imposed logic, Butler's Map of England loses its sense of being arbitrary, and takes on instead a dominant role in terms of characterizing the compilation it inhabits. From Taylor's nautical historian's perspective, astrology and cartography no longer seem such strange bedfellows. And indeed to reflect upon such a link—the way stars were once held to direct men's affairs, not just used to guide their ships—may have appealed to a specifically post-war version of Anglo-American Manifest Destiny. As one of just a handful of manuscripts in an otherwise printed collection, Thomas Butler's astrological commonplace book imparts a degree of old world charm, a founding virility and authenticity, to a new world merchant-sailor's library.

Following Thomas Butler's and prior to Henry Taylor's, the only imaginative engagement with the Beinecke manuscript whose terms we may realistically hope to reconstruct[55] is that of topographer and antiquary

[54] Michel de Certeau, *The Practice of Everyday Life*, trans. Stephen Rendall (Berkeley, Calif., 1984), 165–76 ('Reading as Poaching'); Chartier, *Forms and Meanings*, 1–4, 83–97; also 'Texts, Printing, Readings', 156–7.

[55] I do not explore the matter here, but Beinecke MS 558 also contains a small amount of post-Tudor annotation, including what appear to be cross-references to the work of seventeenth-century astrological authority William Lilly (e.g. fo. 2ᵛ, 'Lilly pag.331'); a heavily glossed geniture or astrological figure (fo. 3ᵛ); and an original horoscope for July 22, 1612 (fo. 66ᵛ). For Lilly, the

John Brand (1744–1806). Brand's bookplate—an engraving of an
ivy-strewn ruin, carved with inscriptions identifying him as an Anglican
minister, a Fellow of the Society of Antiquaries, and an Oxford
graduate—appears inside the front cover of Beinecke's gilt brown calf
binding (a feature Brand himself probably added).[56] Reverend Brand's
principal scholarly work (which the *DNB* characterizes as 'interesting'
though highly untidy and frequently 'desultory') was his *Observations on
Popular Antiquities* (1813), left unfinished at his death. Insofar as this is
an account 'chiefly illustrating the origin of our Vulgar Customs,
Ceremonies, and Superstitions' (or so his first redactor Henry Ellis subti-
tles it), Brand's *Observations* suggests, in straightforward-enough terms,
just how 'the far-famed Secretary of the Society of Antiquaries' probably
saw Thomas Butler's Tudor manuscript.[57] Nothing if not illustrative of
'Vulgar Customs' and 'Superstitions', the book that would become
Beinecke 558 is already, by the time of John Brand's acquisition of it, fully
overgrown in an epistemological sense, its 'scientific' items as ruined and
ivy-strewn as is the building on the bookplate branded to it.

Especially relevant to reconstructing Beinecke MS 558's post-Butler,
pre-Taylor meanings are the contents of John Brand's massive library. In
April of 1807 London auctioneer William Stewart published, in advance
of a sale that would spread over thirty-seven days that May and June, a
catalogue entitled *Bibliotheca Brandiana*, whose list of 'unique, scarce,
rare, curious and numerous' items extended to 8,611 printed books and
243 manuscripts. The better to entice a book-buying public, Stewart
trumpets Brand's 'unrivalled' reputation 'as a Collector of every Thing
relative to popular decayed Antiquity and Topography'; and in fact the
auction received considerable notice—Thomas Dibdin gives an account
of the choicest items in (appropriately) *The Bibliomania, or, Book Madness* (1809).[58] Brand's library featured works on 'Heraldry, Pedigrees and
Arms' above all, but numerous books comparable to Thomas Butler's are
also enrolled within *Bibliotheca Brandiana*: various miscellanies and com-

'most successful' (but also 'most abused') figure in the 'golden age of English almanacs'
(1640–1700), see Bernard Capp, *English Almanacs 1500–1800: Astrology and the Popular Press*
(London, 1979), esp. 24, 57–9.

[56] See, however, Seymour De Ricci, *English Collectors of Books and Manuscripts 1550–1930*
(Bloomington, Ind., 1930), who asserts that 'according to his contemporaries' Brand 'never had
a book bound or mended', 10. The dossier does not comment on the binding (now in poor repair), but the presence of Brand's bookplate establishes a *terminus ad quem*.

[57] *DNB* vi. 213–14.

[58] Thomas F. Dibdin, *The Bibliomania, or, Book Madness* (London, 1809), 605–11, 452–54.

monplace books, plus a great many works on astrology.[59] I have located no references to Beinecke MS 558 in Brand's multi-volume *Observations*, but what its location within Brand's library suggests ultimately, regarding the manuscript's operative meaning in these years, is that in a primary sense it had come to be identified, simply, as *old*, as a privileged witness to English antiquity ('unique, scarce, rare', pants Stewart). This attribution of meaning is not quite irrespective of content. Any Brand book will throw light on 'origins' but should also distinguish itself in being suitably 'curious'.

The essentially antiquarian characterization of Beinecke 558 that I have attributed to John Brand departs considerably from the technological progressivism of Henry C. Taylor, who finds something worth recovering in Thomas Butler's book, a proto-science to build new worlds upon, rather than something having fallen away, the once 'popular' now 'decayed'. It may be too reductive to assert that the basic difference in approach to Butler's manuscript taken by Brand and by Taylor (by the English eighteenth century and the American twentieth?) amounts to looking backward with a map, versus looking forward through it. Still, Henry Taylor's vision of this book—however blatantly *re*visionist— would seem to fit the more comfortably with Thomas Butler's own scientific and aggressively up-to-date compilatory practice.

The multiple 'social meanings' of the Beinecke Map, I have asserted, remain perennially 'subject to change', as well as inextricably tied up with the larger fates and meanings (also the bibliographical locations) of its host manuscript. The relative arbitrarity of the shifts in epistemological character that Beinecke 558 undergoes, with its entry first into John Brand's antiquarian hoard, and later into Henry Taylor's ship-captain's library, may be underscored by comparison of this book's fortunes with that of Thomas Butler's other, better manuscript. Yale Medical Library 26 travels a very different path from Harlow in Essex to New Haven in Connecticut. Between Thomas Butler and Yale University, only Henry Taylor's and John Brand's ownership of Beinecke 558 may be established with full confidence, but we know more about the 'great written book with a boarded cover that Isaac wrote', a folio treasure that (by design or irony) now rests a quarter of an hour's walk away. A gift of Louis M.

---

[59] There are various miscellanies (e.g. #233, #73) and a few commonplace books (those of Ralph Thoresby and Dr Woodward the Naturalist, #1215–16), plus a great many manuscripts on astrology (#22, 29, 86, 92, 116, etc.) as well as numerous printed books and tracts, including two copies of Digges's *Prognostication* (#175, 201).

Rabinowitz—a major collector of Italian painting—in 1949, Yale Medical 26 now carries two bookplates, both with accompanying inscriptions: 'John [Yarmouth] Ives' (d. 1776) notes that the book was 'Formerly in the collection of Dr. Beevor'; and below this it is added (by 'John Borthwick' in 1830) that the volume had been 'bought in London in 1772 by Wm. Borthwick the Younger of Crookston'.[60] Also of interest is an undated (mid-to-late twentieth-century) handwritten memorandum, addressed to 'Barbara' from 'G.K.', which now forms part of the archive dossier for Beinecke 558. 'G.K.' apologizes that the matter lies 'beyond the chronological limits of my work', but posits an intimate relationship between these two manuscripts: YM 26 has texts and tables 'very like, if not identical to' those in Beinecke 558. G.K. might also have noted that the two books share a hand—Isaac's, presumably—as the folio copyist appears to have contributed material (pre-fabricated booklets) to the heterogeneous mix bound together to form Beinecke.[61]

Some four and a half centuries after Thomas Butler's death in Harlow, his manuscripts have come together again in New Haven—or at least, they threaten to. Shared hand and 'identical' items or not, there is no evidence that G.K., Barbara, or anyone else ever transported one or the other manuscript those fifteen blocks across town, thus composing a minor retrospective of mysterious Isaac's scribal labour, of Thomas Butler's scholarship and compilation. Given the revealing ways in which such issues as a 'desire for the past' and the 'pleasure' of the medieval have been interrogated recently, it might be worth admitting to my craving to see these sibling manuscripts reunited.[62] But perhaps just as productive (and

[60] New Haven, Yale Medical Library, MS 26, fo. i. For a catalogue description see W. H. Bond and C. U. Faye, *Supplement to the Census of Medieval and Renaissance Manuscripts in the United States and Canada* (New York, 1962), 59. For two older (but fuller) descriptions (in which 'Borthwick' appears as 'Bothwick'), see archive dossier. The bookplate of 'John Borthwick of Crookston' also appears—alongside that of 'Hannah D. Rabinowitz'—in New Haven, Yale University Library MS 285; Bond and Faye, 50.

[61] New Haven, Beinecke Library, MS 558, archive dossier, p. iii. Although it is not noted in the material accompanying Beinecke 558 or YM 26, there is now in New Haven yet another English commonplace book 'devoted almost entirely to astrology' and produced in these years: Yale Medical Library MS 45, c.1551. See Bond and Faye, *Supplement*, 62. Yale Medical 45 not only shares items with YM 26 and Beinecke 558, but also appears to share a hand—a point suggesting that pre-copied 'astrological booklets' may well have been available for acquisition through Gemini's shop. Like YM 26, Yale Medical 45 bears the bookplates of both Ives and Borthwick. It was acquired in 1959.

[62] Nicholas Watson, 'Desire for the Past', *Studies in the Age of Chaucer*, 21 (1999), 59–97; and for 'the value of reclaiming the issue of enjoyment *for* social and cultural and historicist projects', Louise Fradenburg, ' "So That We May Speak of Them": Enjoying the Middle Ages', *New Literary History*, 28 (1997), 205–30, esp. 206–7, on the humanities' complicity 'in the construction of

enjoyable) as to indulge such a Dickensian urge, by dwelling upon these books' shared Harlow youths and New Haven retirements, might be to pursue a related pleasure—that of considering what meanings have attached to Yale Medical 26 during the interim. Once, both Thomas Butler's books would have been classed as definitively astrological, but different owners and different taxonomies have laid different claims upon them.

If individual codices have complicated histories, even more complex are the histories of the cultural discourses that aspire to make sense of book-knowledge. Discursive and disciplinary histories interact with particular textual artefacts in direct and indirect ways, as consumers seize upon aspects of a book not only according to the logic of established systems of knowledge, but also in terms of newly emergent (or revitalized) taxonomies. Disciplinary modes of understanding do not just accompany texts already identified as appropriate, then (i.e. help direct the experience of encountering the expected). Rather, alternative frameworks are constantly developing, are always available for readers to choose among; so any textual artefact (however apparently stable in its meanings) is perennially subject to reconfiguration, to re-imagination according to new experience—each differently disciplined and differently located reader potentially transposing the textual score into an alternative key (or at least striking different chords from the last). To judge by the marks of ownership laid upon Thomas Butler's 'great book', not to mention its current archival classification (Yale Medical Library 26), this deluxe manuscript has been 'read' above all as constituting an appropriate prize for a certain class of man—a physician—but indeed a certain *kind* of physician. Less a practical scholarly resource (for centuries now) than a marker of intellectual curiosity and social/economic achievement, Yale Medical 26 describes its physician-owner as liberally educated, scientifically enlightened but tolerant toward (even bemused about) the misapprehensions of the past: a man of professional but also ironic bearing.

The divergent fortunes and epistemological characters of Thomas Butler's two manuscripts over the centuries since their dispersal owe as much to changes in the organization of thought as they do to differences between these books in material terms. Luxuriantly copied and copiously illustrated, Yale Medical 26 includes a calendar 'with twelve charming

oppositions between productivity and pleasure which privilege the former term at the expense of the latter—oppositions many of us would be unlikely to tolerate *in* our work' (emphasis not added).

and quaint colored drawings of the occupations of the months', along
with a 'very fine and large' astrolabe and numerous zodiacal illustrations.[63] However, from as early as the time of 'Dr. Beevor' (the mid-
eighteenth century) this volume would seem to have derived the essence
of its identity from a sequence of four full-page anatomical figures
that appear among its opening folios (Figs. 4–5). The library of 'Suffolk
Herald Extraordinary' John Yarmouth Ives (dispersed in 1777) had a
character comparable to that of his fellow antiquary John Brand. But not
only was *Doctor* Beevor apparently a practising physician; strikingly
enough, eventual donor Louis M. Rabinowitz—who also contributed
to Yale's purchase of the Paneth Codex, 'one of the most noted early medical manuscripts extant in this country'—served himself as director or
trustee for three New York hospitals.[64] Given that one now consults YM
26 in a panelled room at the heart of Yale University's formidable down-
town medical complex (a site accessible only after obtaining a lay-visitor's
pass and having coursed in alongside a tide of aqua scrubs), it seems fair
to say that the path this book has taken has been not only largely determined by the presence of those anatomies, but moreover distinctly
marked by developments in the West which have deposited medical
science at a particularly elevated place in the cultural (also economic)
hierarchy. At the time of Isaac's writing, medicine had just begun its long
march into professionalization, a journey to the top of the social heap
that has carried Thomas Butler's 'great written book with a boarded cover'
along with it.[65] The Rabinowitz Collection, incidentally, included paintings by Titian, El Greco, Rubens, Van Dyck, Hieronymus Bosch, and
Pietro Lorenzetti—elevated company, for a small-time woollen-draper's
book of astrology.[66]

[63] New Haven, Yale Medical Library, MS 26, archive dossier, pp. ii–iii; see Bond and Faye,
Supplement, 59, for contents. The typescript notes that this astrolabe 'may well be one of the earliest English of that type', as it resembles extant astrolabes of *c*.1350; however, Bond and Faye note
that 'the base of the astrolabe is cut from a musical ms., *c*.1500'.
[64] *The National Cyclopedia of American Biography*, xlix (New York, 1966), 199–200; Louis M.
Rabinowitz's *New York Times* obituary appeared on 28 Apr. 1957, 86: 3.
[65] On medical professionalization, see John Henry, 'Doctors and Healers: Popular Culture
and the Medical Profession', in S. Pumfrey, P. L. Rossi, and M. Slawinski (eds.), *Science, Culture
and Popular Belief in Renaissance Europe* (Manchester, 1991), 191–221.
[66] Lionello Venturi, *The Rabinowitz Collection* (New York, 1945). A great majority of the subjects are religious, but included in the Rabinowitz Collection, intriguingly given the cartographic context of our discussion, are two portraits (by Titian and F. Hogenberg) of Gerard
Mercator. In 1956 Mrs Louis M. Rabinowitz presented to New York's Pierpont Morgan Library
a Map of Palestine (now MS M.877) apparently made by Pietro Vesconte (Venice, *c*.1300); see
Bond and Faye, *Supplement*, 368.

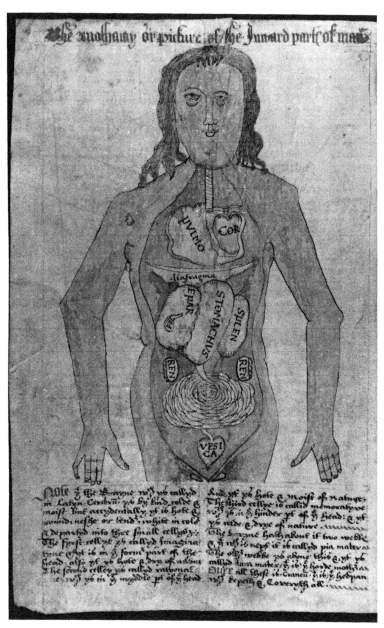

FIG. 4. 'The Anothamy or picture of the Inward parts of man'.

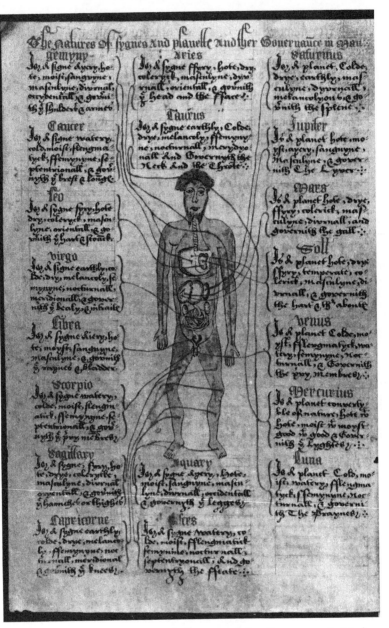

FIG. 5. 'The Natures of sygnes and planettes and ther Governaunce in Man'.

For its part, Thomas Butler's commonplace book is now stored within the Beinecke Library's General Collection of Early Books and Manuscripts. Efficiently catalogued and housed in architectural splendour, the General Collection boasts (according to last year's brochure) a particular strength in English literature and history, as well as 'substantial holdings' in 'New World exploration'.[67] Except within the pages of a 1971 catalogue edited by J. S. Kebabian, Beinecke 558 no longer figures as a part of anything that might be called a 'Taylor Collection'—Taylor's seven manuscripts having been folded into the General Collection, for conservation and security purposes.[68] Given that its current archival call-number ('Beinecke MS 558') fully suppresses the previous link to Taylor, it could be argued that the manuscript's once-definitive nautical association has now dissolved. Henry C. Taylor's revisionist interpretation of this manuscript, as a piece relevant to his collection, has effectively been undone; his appropriation of the map, his 'poaching' upon Tudor astrology, figures now as marker of an (expired) historical moment itself.

On the other hand, though its link to Taylor may have atrophied, Beinecke 558 does now form part of the holdings of an institution celebrated for its strengths in early cartography—there is even a specific fellowship to support such research. Henry C. Taylor has ceased to be relevant, except as benefactor and footnote, but the meaning of Thomas Butler's map today is impacted by its proximity to New Haven's substantial cartographic resources overall. These resources are to be found a few buildings over from the Beinecke, in the Map Room of Sterling Memorial Library; a few blocks across campus, at the Yale Center for British Art (where 'all the important British cartographers are represented'); and taking a more expansive view, in the rich sequence of cartographic archives to be found along the New England coast—for example at the John Carter Brown Library (Providence, RI), at the Houghton Map Library (Cambridge, Mass.), and at the Osher Map Library (Portland, Me.).[69] What this concentration of resources means, for the Beinecke Map, is that future encounters with it may well occur in the context of an artificially heightened cartographic consciousness. That is, researchers will not happen upon this image in the context of surveying, say, Merchant-Drapers' Guild accounts or documents relating to the 1555

[67] *Visiting Fellowships 2001–2002*, Beinecke Rare Book & Manuscript Library, Yale University.
[68] Kebabian, *Taylor Collection*, pp. ix–xxi.
[69] 'The Alexander O. Vietor Fellowship in Cartography and Related Fields or in American History', Department of Rare Books and Archives, *The Yale Center for British Art Fact Sheet* (n.d.).

Highways Act at the Public Record Office, or while browsing Tudor commonplace books at the British Library. In this sense, to encounter the Beinecke Map in twenty-first-century New England will amount to something very different from how the experience might have been fifty years ago in London—or for that matter, at the Essex Record Office in Chelmsford, where copies of various Butler family wills are to be found.

Thomas Butler clearly prized his great book of 'medico-astrological' material, but found his commonplace book, of scientific notes beside business accounts, of horoscopes but also maths problems, unworthy of direct mention in his will. Nonetheless, Beinecke 558's history of splendid neighbours, at Yale as in Brand's and Taylor's collections, helps underscore this comparatively modest artefact's full embeddedness in the processes of political and cultural translation that lie at the heart of the historical—and especially the *medieval*—enterprise in America. Not only in major strokes but in minor ones, it might be observed, do the processes of *translatio imperii* and *translatio studii* continue.

The transfer of Thomas Butler's second-best manuscript to America, of course, represents nothing like the coup (for nation, and for industrialist philanthropy) realized in Henry Huntington's early-century acquisition of the Ellesmere Chaucer.[70] Nor for that matter does the capture of this modest manuscript's modest map—Butler's England—fall quite within the usual purview of American cartographic collecting: individuals and institutions alike have tended to focus on North America (and/or its regions), for reasons practical and ideological. But what precisely will a map of 'Ynglonnd'—of old England—have meant in *New* England in these years? What might it mean, in particular, to an ambitious private library desperate to establish its cultural relevance and thereby contribute to the demonstrable wealth and glory of a burgeoning nation, an emergent empire? To ask what a manuscript map of England means to mid-century US collectors (and Ivy League fundraising circuits) raises a fundamental question about the foundational and legitimizing cultural role played by all things English—antiquities in general, but particularly maps and literary manuscripts—in these years of America's attempt to get out from under British cultural hegemony. Earlier I asked whether the Beinecke Map is even visible nowadays, outside of the filters imposed by

[70] For an enthusiastic appraisal of the importance of this acquisition, see Martin Stevens and Daniel Woodward (eds.), *The Ellesmere Chaucer: Essays in Interpretation* (San Marino, Calf., 1995), 1–13, 15–28; also ibid., Alfred David, 'The Ownership and Use of the Ellesmere Manuscript', 302–26.

a cartographic historiography that celebrates Christopher Saxton, that dwells on technological 'developments' like surveying and printing (i.e. that functions above all teleologically). Now I ask: to what extent can we expect to understand the Beinecke Map (let alone come to terms with its various fugitive meanings), if we do not draw explicit attention to the system of US cultural imperialism that has enabled me to examine this artefact in the first place? In short, can I write cartographically inflected cultural history, in any meaningful sense, without re-engaging the categories of 'culture' and 'history' from my specifically cartographic, indeed my specifically American literary medievalist standpoint?

The layers of historical meaning described above, bits of social grit I now regard as encrusted onto the Beinecke Map, were by no means discernible to me as I stared in rapture at my 'New Haven Gough Map' on the day I first encountered it. Yet had not Thomas Butler's cast-off manuscript been transported like some indentured immigrant to America—a process that raised its relative critical value markedly, due to the scarcity of early manuscripts this side of the Atlantic—it is unlikely that I would have ever encountered it.[71] My meeting with the Beinecke Map should be seen as no chance or even flatteringly fortuitous discovery. Rather, this textual encounter—as well as the credentializing scholarship now emanating from it—must be regarded as fully orchestrated, an ultimately unsurprising by-product of the twentieth-century American academic experience: a meeting of cultural anxiety and social imperialism, of historical desire and economic hegemony.

To forward such points smacks alternately of piousness and disingenuousness. I forward them anyway, despite the risk involved, because it seems to me that 'our best resource' as scholars interested in challenging the discursive formations we have inherited—I follow David Lawton in this—'may be a version of the hermeneutic circle in which we consciously bring our modernity into dialogue with our understanding of the medieval'. Lawton's recent observations on the American medievalist 'enterprise' make it very clear that, if we are to unpack the scholarly implications of 'our modernity', one category crucial to investigate is nationalism.[72] In a complementary spirit, Rita Copeland has emphasized

[71] In an American archive, the keen young medievalist may well proceed by calling up every manuscript, in turn, which answers to any two of a given three markers: say—medieval, England, geography. But who (except a resident scholar or on-site archivist) would be so foolhardy at the British Library, the Bodleian, or the PRO?

[72] David Lawton, 'Analytical Survey I: Literary History and Cultural Study', *NML*, 1 (1997), 240, 246.

our collective need 'to interrogate the traditional allegiances of literary histories to teleological constructions of national identity'. According to Copeland, 'this is a task for which medieval studies can present peculiarly privileged credentials, as the Middle Ages is the traditional battleground on which literary histories vie to stake their claims for national origin'.[73]

Our 'understanding of the medieval' needs to be put into dialogue with 'our modernity', but if recent work in this vein has demonstrated anything, it is that such diachronic conversations do not take place in quiet corners all their own—as the ardent medievalist might prefer. Rather, conversations between the medieval and the modern typically depend upon an early modern interpreter. The acts of mediation and translation performed by the first caretakers of the medieval have long been a source of irritation to medievalists, yet if the conversations Lawton and Copeland prescribe are to come off at all, it is inevitable that the voice of the go-between (however cloying) will itself leave significant, even determinant trace. The work of Tudor medievalists such as Leland and Bale produced 'powerful discursive frames for the writing of English literary history', Simpson has said.[74] The substance as well as 'professed motive' of Leland's research was 'largely bibliographical'.[75] But as Wallace remarks, 'love of learning and love of place conjoin most intimately' for Leland; in fact the bibliographical comes ultimately to be subsumed within the rubric of the topographical. Leland's goal was not simply to compile an ad hoc register of manuscripts and landscapes, an uneven gazetteer of antiquities, but to produce finally 'a vast body of writing that would image forth Henry's kingdom'.[76]

The absurd degree of Leland's corporational ambition in this project—his desire to 'image forth' the Tudor political body comprehensively, to insert himself at the point where topography meets history meets government—anticipates the conceit of a story by the Argentine poet and medievalist Jorge Luis Borges (1899–1986). In this tale 'the cartographers of the Empire', swollen with ambition, produce a sequence of larger and larger-scale maps until finally they 'draw up a map so detailed that it ends up exactly covering the territory'. This model is found preferable to the messy landscape it comes, in fulfilled bureaucratic fantasy, to replace—that is, until 'the decline of the Empire sees this map become frayed and

[73] Rita Copeland, 'Introduction: Gender, Space, Reading Histories', *NML*, 2 (1998), 4.
[74] Simpson, 'Ageism', 217.
[75] J. D. Mackie, *The Earlier Tudors 1485–1558* (Oxford, 1952), 32.
[76] Wallace, 'Dante in Somerset', 35, 34 n.

finally ruined, a few threads still discernible in the deserts . . . [a] ruined abstraction . . . rotting like a carcass'. According to Jean Baudrillard, Borges's 'fable' has become outmoded of late as a viable 'allegory of simulation', offering us now 'nothing but [a] discrete charm'. In the hegemonic postmodern moment imagined by Baudrillard, 'the territory no longer precedes the map, nor survives it. Henceforth it is the map that precedes the territory . . . it is the map that engenders the territory.'[77] John Leland's eventual decline into mental illness, recent commentators imply, may be attributed to the pressures created by his inordinately vast, his un*reason*ably ambitious scholarly project: we might say, his attempt to engender England, to birth a nation.[78] Still, the importance to the discipline of contemporary medieval studies of such bold, epoch-making and ground-shaking projects as Leland's—not to say Baudrillard's—continues to rise. John Bowers observed recently that to dismantle 'the artificial barrier that stubbornly persists between the Middle Ages and the Renaissance' amounts to 'one of the primary jobs of a medievalist of the twenty-first century', but an even more critical task may be to challenge that imaginative rampart currently being erected between a dynamic postmodern present (invested, as usual, with a self-evident discursive priority) and all incarnations of a less fit, purportedly rigid past.[79]

Because Tudor caretakers of the medieval tend to privilege bibliography and topography in their acts of husbandry, so, justifiably, have recent essays by medievalists investigating the 'project of the present' frequently dwelt on precisely these categories, seizing upon spots where paradigms of the spatial and of the textual collide.[80] Such gestures contribute to what has been characterized as a turn toward space in English medieval studies—that is, an intensification of our engagement, collectively speaking, with propositions developed by cultural geography and architecture (next may be ecology). Certainly much has been gained (especially by those

[77] See Edward Soja, *Thirdspace: Journeys to Los Angeles and Other Real-and-Imagined Places* (Oxford, 1996), 241–4. The dictum that 'the map is not the territory'—perennially cited—goes back to Korzybski (1948); see J. B. Harley, 'Deconstructing the Map', in Trevor J. Barnes and James S. Duncan (eds.), *Writing Worlds: Discourse, Text and Metaphor in the Representation of Landscape* (London, 1992), 233.

[78] On Leland having been 'driven mad beneath the accumulated weight of his empirical data', see Marchitello, 'Political Maps', 24; also Wallace, 'Dante in Somerset', 34 n., 37; Lawton, 'Surveying Subject', 35–6; and Simpson, 'Ageism', 214, 221–2.

[79] John M. Bowers, review of Peggy Knapp, *Time-Bound Words: Semantic and Social Encounters from Chaucer's England to Shakespeare's* (London, 2000), *Speculum*, 73 (2002), 941.

[80] See e.g. Wendy Scase, ' "Strange and Wonderful Bills": Bill-Casting and Political Discourse in Late Medieval England', *NML*, 2 (1998), 225–48; also n. 12, above.

who study maps) in this new climate of widespread interest in the spatial. Beyond a flurry of nods toward landscape and its metaphors, we are now treated to flexible and sustained analysis of how space is constructed in various medieval contexts, of how geography, as more than 'simply a stable site for historicization', works actively to determine social relations.[81]

At times forgotten, however, during today's medieval space-programme, is the cultural form commonly regarded as the ultimate repository of ideas about geography: the map itself. It can be instructive to tally just how rare leaps across the chasm from the *metaphorically* cartographic to the *actually* cartographic really are, even in interdisciplinary medieval studies. Scholars posit that text and image, like time and space, are less binaries than collaborative channels of experience,[82] yet it remains the case—certainly in discussion of premodern state-making and epoch-building—that the 'claims [to] national origin' of *literary* histories receive the bulk of attention. This seems a missed opportunity, if for no other reason than that those engaged in writing the realm into existence were also those most interested in figuring it graphically. If we remain unmoved by the attention contemporary critics lavish on maps (as devices specially suited to paradigmatic thinking), we might take a cue from Leland, whose opus incorporates both cartographic sketches and architectural views, and look to divert our discipline's turn toward space into an explicit turn toward *maps*.

III. What Butler Sayth

Later I will press the question of cartography's special relationship to paradigms of cultural history and to narratives of English nationalism, especially literary ones. First however, in order best to utilize the unique critical space opened up—however provisionally—by this Tudor medieval map, we need to weave the Beinecke manuscript back into the sixteenth century. This is not the venue for a full-scale biographical sketch of

---

[81] For medieval studies and the 'project of the present', see Copeland, 'Gender, Space', 1. Regarding the 'spatial turn' see Copeland, 6–7, and Lawton, 'Surveying Subject', 9–10; also Lawton, 'Literary History', 250, regarding 'the burgeoning reference to cultural geography' in medievalist work. For a text important in the recent turn toward space across the academy (a refrain: 'it is now space more than time that hides things from us': 1, 6, 61), see Edward Soja, *Postmodern Geographies: The Reassertion of Space in Critical Social Theory* (London, 1989). For geography as more than a 'stable site for historicization' (*per* David Harvey), see Soja, 65.

[82] Suzanne Lewis, *Reading Images: Narrative Discourse and Reception in the Thirteenth-Century Illuminated Apocalypse* (New York, 1995), 2.

Thomas Butler, or for reconstruction of a Harlow merchant-draper's place in the local and national markets and communities of his day.[83] Nonetheless, what is important to note is that Butler constitutes quite an anomaly, with respect to the well-born coterie of gentleman scholars (scientists, antiquarians) and London entrepreneurs (printers, instrument-makers) who comprised Tudor England's cartographic community. Earlier I said I would examine that particular 'act of cartographic redeployment' our compiler performs when he reproduces Gough's image and highway data within the pages of his commonplace book. No matter how Butler procured his material, merely the existence of an *opportunity* to copy a given exemplar does not explain the impulse of reproduction, let alone the implications of that copying. To understand these, we need to consider the dynamics of textual reception, or what Chartier describes as 'the process of *construction of meaning* by which readers diversely appropriate the object of their reading' (emphasis mine).[84]

What exactly is a map—and not of the universe or Harlowbury manor, but of England—doing in a book otherwise devoted to astrology and (secondarily) business and household notes? How does an antique image of the realm fit or not fit with the rest of Beinecke's contents, and potentially with a Tudor businessman's 'self-fashioning' concerns?[85] Following Chartier, we may judge that such copying constitutes a case of 'readerly appropriation'. But if so, to what end—other than the very partial explanation of practicality, a householder's need to get around? In short what 'construction of meaning' is argued by the copying of *this* map, into precisely *this* textual venue?

The formulation of such questions reveals my indebtedness to trends in historicist scholarship, for recent years have seen a 'renewed interest in the actuality of manuscript' as well as in the artefacts and dynamics of print culture.[86] Energized by contributions from a variety of disciplines, periods, and national traditions, 'The History of the Book' is a field

---

[83] See Birkholz, 'Gough Revisited'.   [84] Chartier, 'Print Culture', 4.

[85] See Stephen Greenblatt, *Renaissance Self-Fashioning: From More to Shakespeare* (Chicago, 1980), for the classic formulation; subsequent scholars have adapted the paradigm for use in non-literary contexts. For a production roughly analogous to Beinecke 558—a medieval astrological compendium which includes a late-antique map (perplexingly, as 'the map does not seem to be particularly relevant' to the rest of the material)—see Edson and Savage-Smith, 'An Astrologer's Map', esp. 15, 18, 20, 21. Edson and Savage-Smith's map is a 'zonal' *mappamundi* (the type usually appearing with astrological material), as opposed to a regnal map, yet their conclusion that its function was 'to orient users to their place in the world, both geographically and cosmographically' accords well with my findings regarding Beinecke.

[86] Kay, 'New Philology', 317.

48   Daniel Birkholz

currently in the ascendant. Still, careful attention to what Stephen
Nichols calls 'the manuscript matrix' has long informed the critical approach of medievalists—whether Old Philologists, New Philologists, or
Just Barely Passable Philologists.[87] To approach the Beinecke Map by way
of its host manuscript, then—which is to say, in terms of the unique epistemological and materialist perspectives Beinecke 558 provides—is hardly
a methodological innovation. Instead, to proceed in such a manner is to
continue examining this Tudor document from a stubbornly medieval
perspective.

Earlier I argued that from the standpoint of paradigms ruling the history of cartography, the Beinecke Map of England 'becomes medieval'
sometime in the second half of the sixteenth century. Scholars interested
in map-printing and surveying have studied these years closely. But as P.
D. A. Harvey relates, a third theme 'constantly recurs' in accounts of
Tudor map-making: 'that of the involvement of antiquarians and historians'.[88] Humphrey Lloyd, whose meteorological judgements appear in
both Butler's manuscripts, provides a good example. Lloyd is well known
for his historical and geographical writings; most famously he takes on
Polydore Vergil, in defence of traditional British historiography and its
founding myth of Brutus the Trojan—an account likewise crucial to English literary history, not incidentally. Historians of cartography remember
Humphrey Lloyd best for his having sent to Dutch atlas-maker Abraham
Ortelius, upon his deathbed in 1568, new maps of England and Wales.
Lloyd's links (via Beinecke 558) to our own obscure Thomas Butler on one
hand, and on the other to major figures such as his friend Ortelius, his
publisher Thomas Gemini, and his brother-in-law the great antiquarian
John Lumley, make him a striking example of the interconnectedness of
cartographic, scientific, and historical discourses in Tudor Britain.[89] As
May McKisack has observed, 'the taste for history was widespread' in
these years.[90] But so too was a taste for cartography. As we have seen, it was
antiquaries such as Leland and Lloyd who stood at the forefront of the

[87] Stephen Nichols, 'Introduction: Philology in a Manuscript Culture', *Speculum*, 65 (1990),
4, 8, 9. *Speculum*'s special issue on 'The New Philology' (ed. R. Howard Bloch and Stephen
Nichols) continues to elicit impassioned response, although not often from those falling into my
third category.
[88] Harvey, *Maps in Tudor England*, 25.
[89] McKisack, *Medieval History*, notes the application to Lloyd of the epithet 'Geographis-
toricus' and to his ranking in reputation beside Leland and Bale: 56–8.
[90] Ibid. 71.

original push to develop a new, multi-functional map of the realm—that is, a definitive replacement for Gough and its outmoded derivatives. Much historical writing from this period concerns itself implicitly with the maintenance (if not construction) of aristocratic privilege: particularly notorious in this respect are heraldry and genealogy. But if there existed a thorough interweave (as Richard Helgerson, Howard Marchitello, and Lesley Cormack have observed) between the scholarly modes of cartography and 'chorography' (i.e. the kind of thick 'local historical-geographical description' those such as Lloyd and Leland produced), it is also true that enthusiasm for matters antiquarian was 'shared by nobility, gentry and at least some members of almost every profession'.[91] Chorography served as a means of establishing claims to social status, through association with antiquities architectural and bibliographic—but the genre's largely transparent social function in no way limited interest in chorographical writing to just the higher classes. An emergent merchant-gentry, acquiring property in the open market resulting from the Dissolution, had as much to gain as a weakening landed aristocracy did to lose.[92]

Scholars have long posited a link between the rise of a merchant middle class in late medieval London and the emergence of a new literary/bibliographic genre: the Tudor commonplace book.[93] One hallmark of such books, as David R. Parker has stressed, is their idiosyncrasy: each collection is 'discernibly personal'. Parker finds 'no absolute unity of taste' within the commonplace books of Tudor London, despite their compilers' shared class orientation, but certain 'trends [do] emerge'.[94] Most significant to this argument is that each of the books highlighted by Parker contains a strong antiquarian element. Especially noteworthy—not least as it is 'perhaps the richest example of the English commonplace book'— is Oxford, Balliol College MS 354, compiled during the first third of the

[91] On chorography and its intimate (but ideologically at odds) relationship to cartography, see Marchitello, 'Political Maps', 14, 21–7, 30 (22–4 for Leland); Cormack, 'Good Fences', 655–61, and Helgerson, 'The Land Speaks', 71–5, 52–8, 81–2. See also McKisack, *Medieval History*, 71.

[92] On merchant class 'fluidity' and 'movement from the merchant class into the landed gentry' see Sylvia L. Thrupp, *The Merchant Class of Medieval London* (Ann Arbor, 1962), 191–287, esp. 279–87. On the link between an open land market and surveying, see Eden, 'Elizabethan Surveyors', 76.

[93] Parker, *Commonplace Book*, 4–6, 38–9, 16. On literacy, 'the conduct of life', and books generally see Thrupp, *Merchant Class*, 155–63, 248–9.

[94] Parker, *Commonplace Book*, 2–3, 159–60; 162.

sixteenth century by London merchant Richard Hill. Although Parker allows that Balliol 354's narrow, ledger-book format 'could be characterized as innovative', he repeatedly categorizes Richard Hill's book 'as a "medieval" manuscript'. Parker regards Hill, quite unequivocally, as 'a reader who was primarily interested in looking backwards much more often than forwards'.[95]

Hill was hardly alone among Tudor commonplace-book keepers in his conservative literary tastes, and in his adherence to what Parker calls 'a fundamentally "medieval" view of the world'.[96] On reductive class grounds, Thomas Butler might appear likely to share much with the compiler of Balliol 354, but Beinecke 558 is manifestly *not* Richard Hill's sort of book: even its few 'historical' items demonstrate more interest in the present than in the past. Fo. 48ᵛ's 'Kronykel of Ynglonnd made short' is framed after the manner of a universal history (it begins by computing the number of years from the Creation to the founding of Britain) but picks up in earnest only during Butler's lifetime, and shows itself particularly interested in 'looking forward' by leaving several years blank.[97]

A handful of this manuscript's texts fit within the (generous) parameters Parker lays out for the genre, but overall Beinecke 558 differs notably, in what it contains and what it does not, from other Tudor commonplace books. The scarcity of antiquarian material is just part of this. Entirely absent are lyrics, romances, political items, the literature of social-climbing, and—one marginal comment aside—even devotional material.[98] In place of such fare is Beinecke's astrology and meteorology, plus its later folios' household and mercantile data—all of which textual groups can help calibrate our judgements concerning the precise nature of cartographic appropriation here on display. Given that Beinecke 558 presents (so to speak) multiple identities as a compilation, our earlier question still stands, if anything sharpened by this book's departure from the conventions (flexible as they are) of the Tudor commonplace book: what is a map of England *doing* in a such a compendium?

The Beinecke manuscript's 'Map off Ynglonnd' both derives from a medieval exemplar, and (I have argued) gets reconstituted as such (i.e. 'becomes medieval' again) some years after its mid-century production.

[95] Parker, *Commonplace Book*, 83–4.   [96] Ibid. 84.
[97] See Fig. 9; fo. 85's calendar (which doubles as an accounts register) similarly highlights the immediate past, but extends even further into a foreseeable future: it is completed only through 1547, but has been prepared for 1540–70.
[98] Parker, *Commonplace Book*, 159–62.

But judging by all that can be ascertained concerning this man, his interests, and his community, Thomas Butler's copying of the Gough Map was not the act of a Tudor medievalist. Unlike Richard Hill's, the impulse was not antiquarian, and not—despite the adjacent chronicle and chart of reigns—in any usual sense 'historical'. Technically this cartographic text was as contemporary, in terms of effective use-value *circa* 1547–54, as the book's other items, some of which (if not composed on the spot) were procured with remarkable timeliness. Digges's *A Prognostication of Right Good Effect*, for instance, extracts from which are scattered throughout, must have been encountered by Butler right around the time of its first printing (by Gemini in 1553) if not beforehand. Richard Hill's commonplace book may have looked backwards, but Thomas Butler's is marked less by any antiquarian sensibility than by a remarkable currency.

Above we touched on Beinecke 558's service as a 'shop-book' in the years following Butler's commission of Yale Medical Library 26 (with its duplication of items and lavish layout). However, second only to Beinecke's prevailing astrological orientation—though directly related to it—is this compendium's *domestic* orientation. The commonplace book's explicitly dual focus—on matters of the heavens and matters of the household—is a characteristic reinforced by Beinecke's connection to Yale Medical 26. Beinecke 558 also contains medical items, but Yale Medical's preponderance of such material, together with its elaborate (and perhaps personalized) anatomical 'portrait'-diagrams, suggests a marked intensification, late in life, of its owner's interest in medicine.[99]

One text copied into both manuscripts details 'What tyme It ys good to take or receyve Medycynes' (YM 26, fo. 5ʳ; Beinecke 558, fo. 83ʳ). The piece is straightforward: it sets out the proper time to ingest a given herbal remedy, or to undertake a particular domestic action, according to astrological parameters. What it demonstrates is how mutually dependent were the discourses of medicine and astrology in this period. We must

---

[99] Two of the four anatomies are copied from Hieronymous Braunschweig's *The Noble Aperyance of Surgeri* (London, 1525); archive dossier pp. i–ii. For reproductions from this work see Nancy G. Siraisi, *Medieval and Early Renaissance Medicine: An Introduction to Knowledge and Practice* (Chicago, 1990), figs. 38, 40, 42–3. I have located no evidence to support my notion that Beinecke's anatomies may be personalized by way of documentary 'portrait' heads (see Figs. 4 & 5—are these Thomas Butler and Isaac, respectively?), but such a practice (of drawing a patron or copyist's face onto a generic body-diagram) seems to me feasible, if impossible to corroborate. The *DNB*, incidentally, notes that Gemini authored 'a compendium of anatomy [a pirated abridgement of Vesalius, 1543], with copper-plate engravings by himself', xxi. 118–19. Digges's 1555 *Prognostication* includes an engraving of the 'zodiac man' (or 'viscera man'); see R. T. Gunther, *Early Science in Oxford*, vol. iii (Oxford, 1925), 17.

avoid reading Thomas Butler as provincial and unsophisticated, somehow 'charming and quaint' himself (as the illustrations in YM 26 have
been described), on grounds of his ownership of books like this. Knowledge of astrology, it may be noted, constituted (along with geometry) an
important prerequisite to the formal study of medicine. And not only did
astrology amount to a '[standard] element in the skills of the learned practitioner', it conferred a competitive advantage in the early 'medical market place'.[100] If 'What tyme It ys good to take . . .' links medicine to
astrology straightforwardly, more surprising is that included alongside its
sets of ailments, herbal remedies, and stages of the moon are instructions
regarding proper times to undertake quotidian tasks: when to take one's
bath, when to get one's hair cut, and so on. The medical mode operative
here, or so historian of popular healing John Henry would observe, is
hardly the post-Enlightenment world's detached scientific and professional one.[101]
    Beinecke 558 has virtually no texts of a social-climbing nature, no cour-
tesy literature. Thus while the interest in medicine latent here (but developed in YM 26) arguably may be read as evidence of class ambition, it
makes better sense to see Thomas Butler's curiosity about medicine as a
subset of his concern for matters astrological—and matters domestic. A
desire for more precise anatomical and medicinal knowledge may have
been spurred on by deteriorating health, but rather than being ultimately
status oriented (much less proto-professional), the medical texts in these
manuscripts have (for Thomas Butler and his family, if not for later collectors like John Brand or Louis M. Rabinowitz) demonstrably practical
ends. An intimate knowledge of the human body—its organs, their
shapes and positions, their elemental composition—served to sharpen an
astrologer's sense of the planets' material effects.
    Instead of dismissing astrology as a 'pseudo-science', with the usual
condescension of the present toward the past, it is important to insist
upon the discipline's full legitimacy as a realm of scientific inquiry in these
years. Between 1300 and 1700, astrological practice 'was neither obscure
nor implausible', reaching high points in influence and popularity
around 1660. A deep investment in matters astrological was 'present
throughout society', but a common scholarly gambit in arguing for astrology's historical relevance has been to stress the discipline's 'traditional

---

[100] Henry, 'Doctors and Healers', 207.
[101] Ibid. 199, 209, 217; for 'literate and technical medicine', see Siraisi, *Medieval/Renaissance Medicine*, p. ix.

association with kings and court'.[102] However, rather than justify astrology through its association with medicine, its attractiveness to those in power, or even its deployment in mercantile self-fashioning, a better tactic is to approach the question of cultural significance by way of the discipline's own internal distinctions.

Astrological inquiry divides into two realms: the 'natural' and the 'judicial'. Natural astrology concerns weather, agriculture, and human events of a mass nature—disasters, epidemics, wars, famines, revolts, and so forth. Judicial astrology, by contrast, concerns human affairs on a level that is comparatively precise; typically it generates 'judgements' (predictions or advice) regarding specific individuals and/or enterprises ('inceptions'). Results in judicial astrology are determined through the casting of 'nativities' and 'horaries': the nativity is a diagram which records the positions of the planets at the precise moment of a person's birth (Fig. 6); while the horary produces a like diagram for the moment at which a given question is asked ('moved') or received. Whether nativity or horary, such a diagram of the planets' positions is called a 'figure'—although much better known is a later term, the 'horoscope'. The figure, as Patrick Curry has stressed, is judicial astrology's fundamental conceptual unit.[103]

The danger with a complex technology like astrology is that we may become lost in the details, caught up in examination of the system for its own sake. More important is that we examine what Curry calls 'the matter of interpretation'. For the skill of the early modern astrological practitioner lay above all not in computation, but in 'translating [astrology's] symbolic system . . . into the vernacular, in a meaningful way'. Contrary to modern-day belief, within this discipline there prevailed a considerable degree of uniformity regarding interpretation—'real internal constraints'—such that any given figure, once cast, would meet with general consensus (among experienced practitioners) as to the major features of its meaning. As Curry notes, however, 'these constraints were never completely determining, so the horoscope was never interpretively closed'. It can be difficult—here in the remote present, on the far side of 1660—to

---

[102] Patrick Curry (ed.), 'Introduction' to *Astrology, Science and Society: Historical Essays* (Woodbridge, Suffolk, 1987), 1; Hilary M. Carey, 'Astrology at the English Court in the later Middle Ages', in Curry, *Astrology, Science and Society*, 41. On the discipline's changing fortunes, see Curry, *Prophecy and Power: Astrology in Early Modern England* (Princeton, 1989), 2, 7, 19, 31.

[103] Curry, *Prophecy and Power*, 7–12; see also Anthony Grafton, *Cardono's Cosmos: The Worlds and Works of a Renaissance Astrologer* (Cambridge, Mass., 1999), 24–5. Regarding astrological practice in the fourteenth century, see Laura A. Smoller, *History, Prophecy and the Stars: The Christian Astrology of Pierre D'Ailly, 1350–1420* (Princeton, 1994), 3–24.

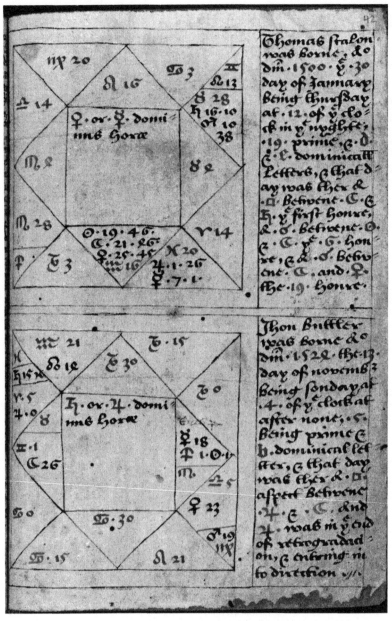

FIG. 6. Horoscopes of 'Thomas Stalon' alias Butler, born 1500, and his eldest son 'Jhon Buttler', born 1524.

eliminate condescension, and to credit a discredited discipline for its remarkable influence, vigour, and cross-cultural coherence. What most needs recognizing about this now-fossilized hermeneutic system is the tremendous 'richness and elegance of astronomical symbolism in the hands of the skilled practitioner'.[104]

Aesthetic qualities—astrology's conceptual 'elegance'—may have attracted some, but another attraction was surely the sense of control the discipline offered. As detailed in Anthony Grafton's recent study *Cardano's Cosmos*, leading astrologers lived a life marked by publication anxiety, professional rivalry, and celebrity commissions (Grafton's protagonist spent a month at Windsor, doing a horoscope of Edward VI).[105] However, as Beinecke 558 helps us see, Thomas Butler of Harlow's astrological practice is tenaciously domestic: his primary concern is not for royal houses or the affairs of state, but for the state of his own house, and for the affairs of the family woollen-shop. Butler's will makes this clear enough, but the point is underlined on fo. 63ᵛ of his commonplace book, where family nativities and other genealogical notes are recorded. Similarly relevant in terms of Beinecke's household astrological orientation are procedures for determining 'how to find a thing lost in house or field', 'what a messenger bringith', and 'whether a child to come be male or female', among others in this vein (fos. 9–14ᵛ). Thomas Butler's domestic astrology culminates in four half-page horoscopes (Fig. 6): in addition to his own, he produces charts for eldest son 'Jhon Buttler', second son Thomas, and daughter Alice (fos. 42ʳ⁻ᵛ).

Arguably a majority of the items in Beinecke MS 558 concern the domestic realm directly or indirectly, or display an ultimate orientation towards the institution of the household—this as opposed to the more nebulous commitment to study of natural phenomena that marks the work of scholars like Digges or Lloyd, or the high-stakes debates about celebrity horoscopes (Nero, Martin Luther) which occupied professional astrologers like Grafton's Cardano. My characterization of Beinecke 558 as effectively a household manual coincides with the findings of F. G. Emmison, who has observed (based on a study of Essex wills) that far and away the overriding social allegiance displayed by sixteenth-century artisans and merchants was toward 'their family units [and] households'.[106]

---

[104] Curry, *Prophecy and Power*, 13–15; Grafton makes many of the same points: 85, 82, 121.

[105] On treatment of 'the horoscope as a literary form, and one of remarkable flexibility'—the model was 'hermeneutical, not geometrical'—see Grafton, *Cardano's Cosmos*, 82, 121.

[106] Emmison, *Essex Wills*, pp. xiv–xvi.

In this light Thomas Butler's construction of astrological authority, his 'readerly appropriation' of a scientific (and implicitly religious) *auctoritas*, may be understood as analogous to his need to construct a viable paternal and professional identity. That is, what we will see to be his anxiety to establish his own authority as an astrologer—one who knows in an inscrutable world, one who can trace and measure the impact of the heavens upon earthly affairs—connects directly to the demands of masculine, mercantile self-fashioning. The Tudor middle-class head of household needs to display his competence in protecting family and business assets, needs to demonstrate his effective management of both working and domestic space.

In digesting a wide range of material on meteorology, astronomy, and prognostication into his book's opening section (fos. 1–22), the compiler of Beinecke 558 takes pains to cite his sources. *Incipits* and *explicits* are conspicuously large and done in red ink even for very brief items (e.g. 'thus endth the judgments of affixionimy taken out of haly abenragell'; fo. 14'). Also, local attributions are ubiquitous—even minor claims are justified with 'Thus saieth humfrey Loyde' (fo. 6') or 'as sayth Leonard Digges' (fo. 4'). This pattern of hyper-citation establishes Butler's keen consciousness of scientific authority, of a kind of market in astrological expertise—a point conveyed best by notes he copies for divining 'how thou shalt spede in thy journey': 'Dyvers auctors have dyvers opynyons', the Arab philosopher Almansor (d. 891) allows, 'but I saye thou must note the ascendent' (fo. 2').

Despite its consensus regarding methodology, early modern astrology amounts to a contested field—as the careful tone here illustrates—in which the 'diverse opinions' of 'diverse auctors', past and present, serve as landmarks by which the novice astrologer may navigate. Despite his obvious reliance on the pronouncements of others, especially in the realm of natural astrology, Butler the compiler nonetheless does hazard to add one comment of his own, on the subject of earthly phenomena and their significance. After having provided on fo.4' his mark and signature— 'Thomas Butler of Harlow in Essex' (Fig. 7)—at the bottom of the verso there appears another marginal addition, the reminder that 'often ought I to remember Jhesu my redeemer'; then in continuation across the gutter: 'and yet all shall be done that god will have done I sayth butler' (fos. 4'–5').

In its first sixteen folios Beinecke 558 activates no fewer than eight astrological *auctors*—ten, if we include 'god' and 'butler'. Yet the tone struck here is neither contentious nor unduly deferential. This

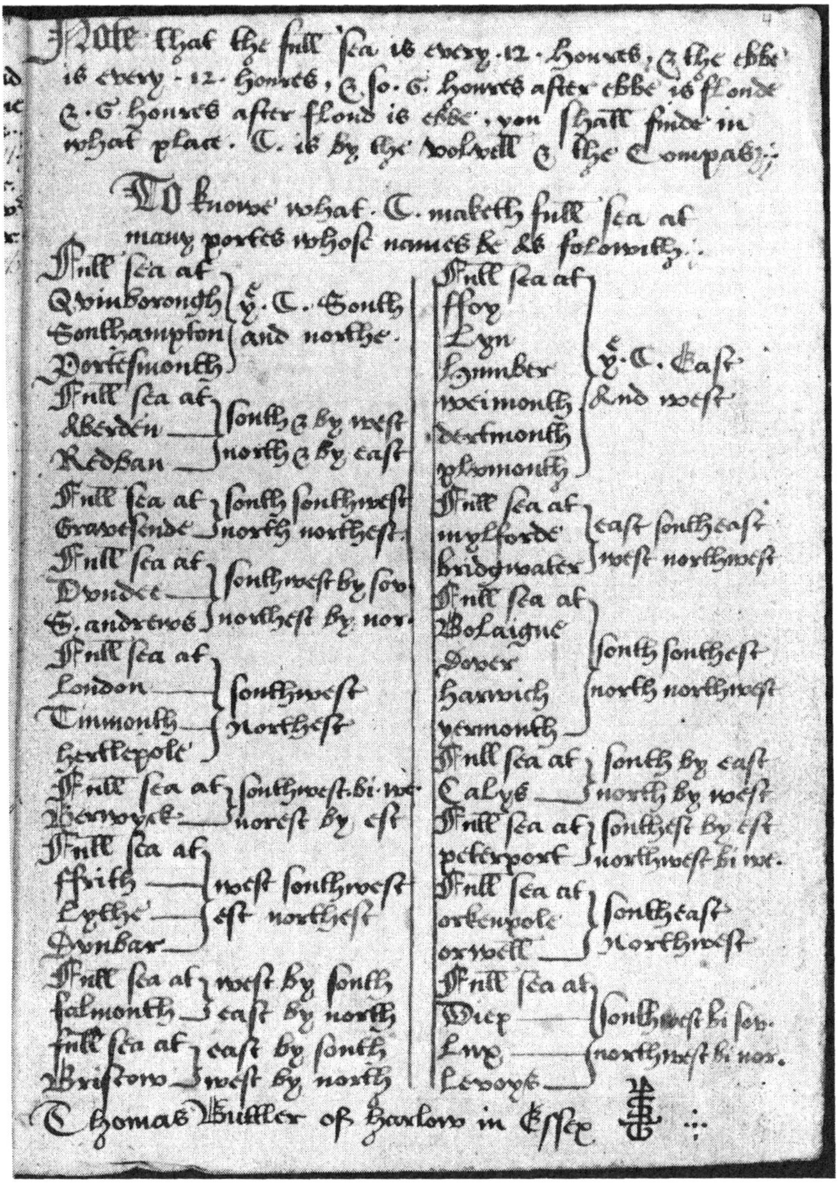

Note that the full sea is every .12. houres, & the ebbe
is every .12. houres, & so .6. houres after ebbe is flonde
& .6 houres after flood is ebbe, you shall finde in
what place .C. is by the roolvell & the compas.

To knowe what .C. maketh full sea at
many portes whose names be as foloweth.

Full sea at Qwinborongh / Sonthampton / Portesmonth } y .C. South and northe.	Full sea at ffoy / Lyn / Hymber / weimonth / dertmonth / plomonth } y .C. East and west
Full sea at Aberden } south & by west / Redban } north & by east	
Full sea at Gravesende } south southwest / north northest	Full sea at mylforde } east southeast / bridgwater } west northwest
Full sea at Dondee } southwest by sou / S. andrews } northest by nor	Full sea at Bolaigne / Dover / Harwich / yermonth } south southest / north northwest
Full sea at London } southwest / Tinmonth } northest / Hertlepole	
Full sea at Barnocke } southwest bi we / norest by est	Full sea at Calys } south by east / north by west
Full sea at ffrith / Lythe / Donbar } west southwest / est northest	Full sea at peterport } southest by est / northwest bi we.
Full sea at falmonth } west by south / east by north	Full sea at orkenpole } southeast / oxwell } northwest
Full sea at Bristow } east by south / west by north	Full sea at Diep } southwest bi sou. / Luy } northwest bi nor. / Lesoys

Thomas Buttler of Harlow in Essex

Fig. 7. 'what [moon] maketh full sea at many portes' (copied from Digges), with
signature by 'Thomas Buttler of Harlow in Essex'.

astrological digest offers technical help—it sharpens the reader/practitioner's procedure—but rather than staging public theoretical disputation (all texts are in English), it directs astrological inquiry toward discrete domestic ends. In this respect, the vernacular mode and voice assumed by the Beinecke manuscript anticipates the (more fully developed) rhetorical persona which marks that later household compendium of meteorological data and proverbial wisdom, the Almanac, a genre whose popularity soars (not coincidentally) at about the time astrology's influence begins to wane.[107]

Thomas Butler's bit of devotional marginalia—'all will be done as god will have done'—does not so much challenge as *contextualize* the claims to astrological expertise activated above it. In so doing, Butler does not diminish the authority of his discipline, but he does importantly reinforce his own authority. Ultimately, a compiler is an arbiter: and so also, presumably, around 'my own hous in town' (fo. 63ᵛ) and in the woollen shop at 'Bromleys', what 'sayth Butler' matters most of all (or *ought* to anyway, according to the logic of masculine desire). The particular means of Thomas Butler's performance of patriarchal authority—his deference to the will of God—may be as remarkable in the context of the rest of the Beinecke manuscript (wholly non-devotional) as it is conventional otherwise. In any case it serves to bring this Essex merchant-draper's astrological practice, as well as his role as household head (caster of family horoscopes, registrar of commodity prices, rentals and cloth-cutting techniques) within the overarching sanction of religious observance. Astrological practice may seem, by modern-day standards, to activate a heterodox spirituality, a kind of 'black magic' inherently at odds with ecclesiastical structure; but worth attending to is Thomas Butler's final bequest providing for 'the amending of the highway' between the parish churches of Harlow and Latton, as well as for 'the maintenance of the song books and other necessaries' there. Just as God, the weather, and the farmer/father/reader sit comfortably together in the early Anglo-American Almanac (that is: patriarchy, meteorology, and agrarian Protestantism are mutually reinforcing), so might we argue that Thomas

[107] See Capp, *English Almanacs*, esp. 23–66. Delano-Smith and Kane, *English Maps*, chart the appearance in almanacs (beginning late sixteenth century) of lists of fairs, diagrams of instruments, and eventually regnal and county maps, 'plus lists of towns and their distances from London'; 243, 288, 148; also Capp, 29–31. Given the Latinate milieu of Grafton's Cardano, it is noteworthy that Butler's manuscript is entirely in English, with one exception: the rubric ('*nomina pro amore et vita*') to an alphabetical table of names. This item is bound near the back of the book (fos. 73ᵛ–74) and copied in another hand; YM 26 has a similar table (fo. 37ᵛ).

Butler's marginal appeal to an authority even more secure than his astro-logical ones contributes to the stability of his position as community pillar and household head. Such a book helps construct its owner as the (self-evident) locus of domestic power: the source of knowledge, status, and capital alike.

IV. Astrology and Geography

If Thomas Butler's casting of horoscopes for his children displays how an astrologer's practice could benefit his household unit—these diagrams measure the impact of heavenly bodies upon the bodies and lives of Alice, Thomas the Younger, and John—nevertheless we should note that nativities are not Beinecke 558's only astrological figures. Arranged neatly over sixteen folio pages of Yale Medical Library 26, but crammed into half that area here, are a year's worth of solar sightings, each diagram giving a single day's measurements for the sun.[108] We are profoundly conditioned nowadays, in our world of sacralized nation-states, by the ubiquity of territorial maps: at present the outlines of political bodies (their purported physical shapes) rank second only to flags as signs of collective identity. In such a climate it can be difficult to make the cognitive leap this argument requires. For what must be recognized is that a map of England's inclusion in a manuscript like Beinecke 558 is a great deal stranger, more eccentric, and mystifying as a compilatory act, than is the presence of those hundreds of astrological diagrams (to most of us, inscrutable) on whose heels it appears. I have suggested that astrology answers a directly domestic need, that its practice lends authority to a Tudor household head like Thomas Butler; and indeed as the later genre of the Almanac makes clear, a map of the realm would *in time* come to fit perfectly well (as would a highway chart) within the complex of texts appropriate to a working household compendium. Yet these are post-Tudor developments, tied to social conditions not yet operative: Beinecke 558 prefigures and so helps explain the Almanac, but the reverse isn't quite true. We remain at a loss as to what 'readerly appropriation' or 'construction of meaning' may be implied, in Butler's incorporation into his book of this 'Map off Ynglonnd'.

The question needn't have been so vexing as it is. Unfortunately

---

[108] The diagrams cover fewer pages in Yale Medical 26 (fos. 27ᵛ–35ʳ) than in Beinecke 558 (fos. 22ᵛ–41) but the pages measure 307 × 205 mm vs. 205 × 150.

Beinecke's prototype, the Gough Map, is unlike most medieval maps in that it contains no astrological, cosmographical, or meteorological content whatsoever. Portolan charts are structured by wind-roses (i.e. rhumb-lines) and dependent on latitude, and most *mappaemundi* at least represent the winds (as cardinal directions) if they do not indeed include climactic zones, zodiacal symbolism, even astronomical data. Given that some 90 per cent of extant medieval maps classify as *mappaemundi* or portolan charts, it may be argued that a cosmographical/meteorological presence effectively underlies (and hence inflects the meaning of) virtually any work of medieval cartography.[109] A generation after the time of the Beinecke Map's copying, what is more, the astrolabe itself acquired an innovative use. In addition to being used for charting the heavens, these instruments came to be employed in land surveying—that is, in the making of terrestrial maps, not just astrological ones.[110]

That the astrolabe's purpose as an instrument was to take sightings, to fix the location of bodies in a field (whether sky or landscape), begins to suggest what a map of the realm might be doing in an astrological manuscript. Though the discipline's discursive context is astronomical—its grammar planetary, not terrestrial—astrology as a practised craft has elements that are in a crucial sense geographical. Earlier I suppressed Patrick Curry's quite particular phrasing regarding the 'figure' or horoscope diagram, astrology's fundamental structural unit, but Curry's words are worth unveiling here. Literally, every astrological figure amounts to 'a *map* of the planets' positions'—with the crucial distinction that any such configuration is relevant only 'for the moment concerned, as seen from *the place* concerned' (emphasis mine). In other words, what matters in the casting of a figure is not simply an intersection between time (the precise moment of nativity or inception) and the relative positions of bodies in the heavens (planetary, solar, lunar). Also crucial, and in need of diagrammatic registration by the astrological practitioner, are the relative spatial positions of *human* bodies (both individual and, as we shall see, social/political). Put simply, 'the locus of the horoscope was a place on earth'.[111]

Beinecke 558 demonstrates this manner in which astrology is grounded, shows how the celestial cannot be read as separate from the geographical, on almost every page. In item after item the positions of heav-

---

[109] See David Woodward, 'Medieval *Mappaemundi*', in Harley and Woodward, *The History of Cartography*, 286–358, esp. 292.

[110] See n. 52, above.   [111] Curry, *Prophecy and Power*, 12.

enly bodies are tied to the elements (the material essences of earthly bodies: mineral, human, topographical) and so rule their operations and movements. A few items in the compilation stand out for their explicit geo-astrological nature, for the way they make unmistakably clear how the variable of 'place on earth' comprises one of the discipline's 'real internal constraints' governing interpretation. One text concerned with place—and in neither a cosmographical nor yet an abstract scientific mode; rather, it is geographical in an English *regnal* context—is the table of harbor-tides mentioned above (Fig. 7). On one hand the data recorded by this page has innate practical appeal: for a man who trades in wool, salmon, and herring (fo. 64^r), and whose book includes a set of arithmetical story-problems on mercantile themes (e.g. 'ther was in a ship 30 marchants—15 cristians & 15 sarasins . . .'; fo. 43^v), domestic harbour details (because relevant to shipping) might well prove useful. Yet in the context of this manuscript's ominous pronouncements regarding the revolutionary implications of thunder, comets, and eclipses (fos. 4^v–5), the observation (after all, incontrovertible) that the sea rises and falls in accordance with phases of the moon surely speaks to something beyond commercial logistics. The phenomenon of tides, we might imagine, has been demystified only for those of us in the triumphant present, a post-superstitious age that puts its faith in scientific method. However, to interpret tides as evidence of the direct relationship between heavenly motions and earthly ones is itself a proof that resolves an ecological conundrum definitively. For 'Thomas Butler of Harlow in Essex' to insert his signature and stylized mark precisely where he does, on a page enrolling three-dozen insular place-names, may be as much as to locate himself, together with his town and his county, in the context of the larger realm of a mercantile England. Moreover, such placement of self and community also operates with respect to the realm of the skies: its eclipses and thunderclaps, its comets and planetary migrations, in sum all those heavenly events which frame and rule human activity. For Butler to incorporate himself here (with a mark probably matching the one he would ratify his will with a few years later) is to assert his own definitive place on earth *with conscious regard to* the heavens.[112] It is to register precisely what

---

[112] Because no original wills are extant for Essex before 1602, the documents in Emmison, *Essex Wills* vol. i, are abstracted from probate registers, where signatures and other personal authenticating marks are obviously not reproduced; p. xxiii. See pp. xxvii–xxviii regarding editorial method. Beinecke's list of ports, incidentally, appears to have been copied from Digges's *Prognostication*.

geographical locus the figure (or map-diagram) of his unique planetary configuration (i.e. his chart/nativity) may be grounded by.

Two brief geo-astrological texts found in Yale Medical Library 26 (they lie opposite the book's astrolabe, between 'The Declaratyon off the zodyack' and 'The natures of the twelve houses' on fo. 35ᵛ) similarly serve to pin us down, both book and reader, onto the geographical matter and social substance of an Essex merchant-draper's world. The first item lists 'the Dystaunce off Realmes from the pole in Latytude' (included are Scotland, England, Ireland, etc.), while the second records latitudes for fourteen 'townes in Englond' (nearby Colchester, St Albans, and London among them). Even more basic to Butler's bibliographic project is another minor text, a key (found near the front of Beinecke, fo. 3ᵛ) to the system of astrological shorthand both manuscripts employ throughout. Here zodiacal signs and planets are not written out in brown letters, but denoted by red symbols. This key identifies each, explains the sign's general interpretive significance, and notes finally what terrestrial matter (or element) falls under its sway: for example, '[Mars] is of wrath, strife, detthe and war, and governith yron'. Such direct causal links between heavenly sign and earthly element—analogous to the moon's influence over tides— have domestically useful implications. As Zahell's *Judgment of Theft* instructs, 'if thou findeth that the thief be in the house, and thou wouldest know the place that [the stolen item] is in', cast your fortune in the matter and 'if it be [Mars] it signifieth to be in a kitchen or in a place of ffyer [fire]' (fo. 16ᵛ).

The principle that astronomical positioning rules terrestrial motion receives its most radical extension in the early modern astrological sub-field we now call medicine. Planetary influence by no means stops at the boundary demarcated by the individual human corpus—a unitary body—but in fact continues its subdivision much further. The ultimate physical 'locus of the horoscope', we might say, is a 'place on earth' in the sense that the human body is the site at which all the world's elements, the unspecialized substances of creation, come perfectly together. The map of the heavens that is the astrological figure, in this sense, has an analogy in the map of the body that is the anatomical figure—a model whose members, extremities, and inward organs are (appropriately) subject to discrete astrological influence themselves. Yale Medical 26's full-length drawing of a 'viscera man' (Fig. 5), in which individual bodily organs are linked to different astrological signs (bold connecting lines are drawn, no less), makes this case quite decisively. In short, as for the individual human being, so for the particular body part; but indeed (to anticipate our next move) so also for that unique social/political collectivity, the authorized legal-sacral entity that is at once royal body and community of the realm, at once territorial expanse and literary/historical construct.

If we take Patrick Curry's spatial metaphor seriously—that the horoscope or astrological figure constitutes a *map* of a special kind—we should conclude that Thomas Butler's commonplace book contains not one but hundreds of cartographical texts, making it a kind of astrological atlas. This proposition cannot help but throw attention onto the instrument responsible for having produced (in Grafton's phrasing) so many 'two-dimensional schematic renderings of three-dimensional configurations'—that is, Butler's astrolabe itself.[113] The key components of any astrolabe are its movable parts. These enable the astronomical computation that lies at the heart of astrological inquiry. Insofar as Thomas Butler's will makes much of a 'great astrolabe that was wont to hang over the sphere in the hall', it should come as no surprise that Beinecke 558's leather and vellum astrolabe is decorative as well as functional. The elegance of this instrument (Fig. 8) is enhanced by serpentine flourishes affixed to its cross-pieces, as well as by stylized animal heads that serve as tabs for its rotating hoops; similar carvings appear on extant wooden astrolabes.[114] At the centre of the Beinecke astrolabe, moreover, there sits a vellum disc whose role (in a computational sense) is wholly superfluous and whose communicative mode is essentially pictorial or symbolic— this as opposed to the mechanical, mathematical functionality of the device overall. As indicated by twin bars marked 'HORIZON' that extend outward from this disc (diagonal in my photograph), standing unmistakably present here at the centre of the Beinecke astrolabe, and providing symbolic grounding for its computational apparatus, is the earth. Not just metaphorically but indeed technically speaking, this tiny disc constitutes a view, a landscape, a map—in short an image whose definitive mode of representation is cartographic. Just discernible here (moving clockwise from left) are a hilltop tree; a seagoing ship; a freestanding homestead or shop; a rolling, furrowed field—and looming astride all this, an oversized well-to-do man, stylish in hose and hat.

However extraneous it may appear, this tiny map at the heart of the Beinecke astrolabe serves as the pivot upon which turns Thomas Butler's entire enterprise in this manuscript. As this disc rotates (or more to the

---

[113] Grafton, *Cardano's Cosmos*, 24.

[114] See R. T. Gunther, *Early Science in Oxford*, vol. v (Oxford, 1929) and *Astrolabes of the World*, vol. ii (Oxford, 1932); *Dictionary of the Middle Ages*, i. 602–3.

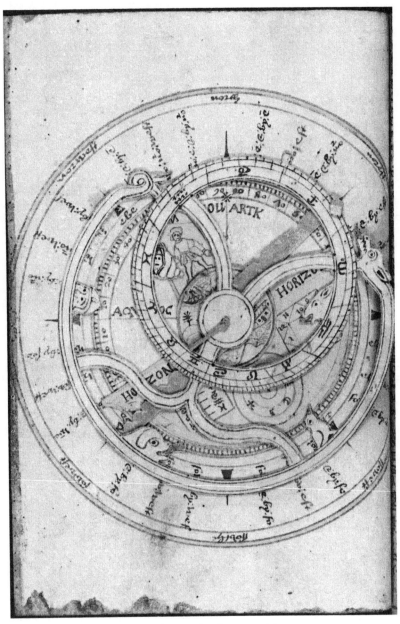

FIG. 8. Paper and Vellum Astrolabe.

point as the computational wheels around it are manoeuvred into place) so proceed the affairs of Thomas Butler, his family, even his community. This much is asserted on every page of Beinecke 558, where a belief in the influence of the stars is everywhere implicit. By such means, through the graphic expression made possible by this instrument, are a set of interlocked Essex lives rendered two-dimensional, their salient features (of character, environment, and event) transposed onto diagrams able to render human experience coherent. Virtually all orders of experience are accessible to astrological inquiry—from recovery of a lost item to discovery of pregnancy; from determination of personal traits to prediction of career prospects; from the care of one's physical health to the cares (famine, war, pestilence, revolt) threatening the health of one's town, region, and realm. In other words there exists an astrological continuum, not just the single binary of 'planetary' and 'bodily' but rather a full spectrum of communities and ecologies along which any practitioner's inquiry or subject's experience continually travels. Individual agents may not be isolated from the larger groupings and systems under whose influence they operate, and to whose balanced functioning they contribute—after all, astrology's conceptual poles of 'natural' and 'judicial' may remain distinct theoretically, but they bleed together in practice.[115] The operative point here is that between celestial constellations and human individuals there intervene any number of identifiable bodies, natural theatres, and (especially) human corporations—religious, professional, political—which not only mediate experience but indeed possess astrological character themselves, qualities distinct and measurable. In short, just as can 'Thomas Butler', 'Ynglonnd' can have its fortune cast.

The kingdom of England's fortunes and characteristics as an astrological 'subject' in its own right do not, it is true, enjoy overriding consideration in either Thomas Butler's manuscripts or his social imagination—preoccupied as both are with matters closest to home. Still, Butler's rehearsal of the meteorological judgement (copied from Digges) that comets serve not only as 'Signes of earthquakes' and other natural trauma, but also as reliable indicators 'of warres, changing of kingdoms, & contreys' (fo. 4ᵛ), should establish the principle of astrology's full applicability at the regnal level. In accord with this is Yale Medical 26's memorandum on 'What Lands planetts do Governe': the moon or 'Luna' rules 'over Inglond & Flanders', for example (fo. 35ᵛ).

Above we witnessed our compiler's insertion of self and town onto a

[115] Curry, *Prophecy and Power*, 10.

chart of domestic ports, and to this we linked his interest in the locations (by latitude) of English towns; but even more relevant, to what increasingly seems a project of establishing the realm's material and civic dimensions, is Butler's meticulous chart of town-sequences and distances, a network of the realm's roads that helps articulate an overall bodily structure for England. In this context, other 'miscellaneous' texts collected into Butler's books—e.g. Yale Medical 26's 'Compas off Inglond' (fo. 25^r), which details the island's geographical breadth and names its first inhabitants—begin to seem less and less idiosyncratic, and more and more akin to an astrologer's technical interest in his subject's vital statistics, especially the operative factors of 'location on earth' and time of 'birth' or 'inception'. As noted above, on a spare page in Beinecke 558 Butler duly records nativity information for his household ('I was born [the] 31st day of January on Thursday at 12 at nytt; it was in 1500'; fo. 63^v), which when combined with the variable of 'place on earth' ('Harlow in Essex') amounts to a database for the casting of family fortunes, raw material from which to generate astrological charts. We might regard Butler's various notes concerning the realm of England's measurable location, in time and across space, in much this same vein. The proposition works particularly well for certain texts, such as Beinecke's abbreviated chronicle, with its computation of years elapsed between the Creation and the arrival of Brutus (fo. 48^v). But to interpret Thomas Butler's Map of England as itself ultimately a species of astrological diagram—at the very least a graphic text that shares key features and interpretive resonances with the horoscope—can help to resolve the question of what an image of 'Ynglonnd' is doing in the midst of a sequence of meteorological treatises and prognosticatory tables. To thus characterize Thomas Butler's surprising foray into cartography as *astrological* not only squares this act with his practice as a compiler overall; such an interpretation also begins to acknowledge just how thoroughly the disciplines of early modern astrology and cartography are entwined in one another, both conceptually and practically. They share a discursive mode, in that both 'map' a given field; they employ the same instrument, the astrolabe; and they express themselves via the same structural unit, the 'figure' that doubles as map and horoscope.[116]

[116] For an early use of the rhetorical term 'figure' (lat. *scema*) in a cartographic sense (indeed, in a regnal mapping context), see Matthew Paris's commonplace book 'Figure of Britain' (or *Scema Britannie*), reproduced in Crone, *Early Maps*, plate 4. For discussion see Birkholz, *The King's Two Maps*, ch. 2: 'Figuring Britain: Regnal Mapping and Matthew Paris'.

It does not, of course, make sense to read the Beinecke Map of England as an *actual* astrological figure itself. Regnal maps and horoscope diagrams perform analogous functions, but do so, after all, on an entirely different scale (one charts the locations of towns, another the positions of planets). Yet certainly the relationship between these disciplines goes well beyond the arbitrary, amounts to more than just a function of chance manuscript proximity. Instead, I would suggest that the early English map of the realm's implicit links to astrological practice are crucial to its social interpretation—and what is more, that this association holds consequences not simply for the history of cartography and/or the history of science, but moreover for English literary nationalism and cultural history.

The Map off Ynglonnd's nearest neighbours in Beinecke MS 558—the highway table on fo. 47^r, plus the chronicle and chart of reigns on fos. 48^v–49^r—may appear where they do (probably appear in the first place) because they are textually related to the map on fos. 47^v–48^r. Groups of texts (in both manuscript and print culture) typically travel together, meaning something resembling this constellation (tellingly buffered by blank pages on fos. 46^v and 50^r) probably appeared in, or on, Butler's exemplar—a proposition supported by at least one later commonplace-book map of England, which similarly includes charts of kings' reigns.[117] These texts immediately flanking the Beinecke Map, like those further afield, reinforce its astrological orientation, but more than the others they raise issues relevant for literary/cultural history. Early English chronicles are virtually obsessed with territory (especially its penetration), just as early maps (historians of cartography now concur) 'encompass concepts of time as well as space'.[118] Accordingly, in fo. 49^r's 'Reigns off aull the Kyngs sene the Conquest' (Fig. 9) we see more than just an attempt to compute England's age, i.e. to ground the matter of insular history securely in the temporal dimension. Additionally, insofar as this chart records each monarch's place of burial as well as period of rule, we witness a pronounced mingling of the political and the geographical, an interment of the royal body (repeated every generation) within the material

---

[117] Ann Arbor, University of Michigan Library, Rare Book Room MS 4 (D11.C73): a commonplace book 'written in England, after 1584'; one of 26 MSS presented by Colonel Thomas M. Spaulding for the Stephen Spaulding Collection; purchased 1946. See Bond and Faye, *Supplement*, 291. Like highway charts and maps of the realm, charts of kings' reigns would become a standard feature of the almanac; see Capp, *English Almanacs*, 29–30.

[118] Evelyn Edson, *Mapping Time and Space: How Medieval Mapmakers Viewed their World* (London, 1997), p. viii.

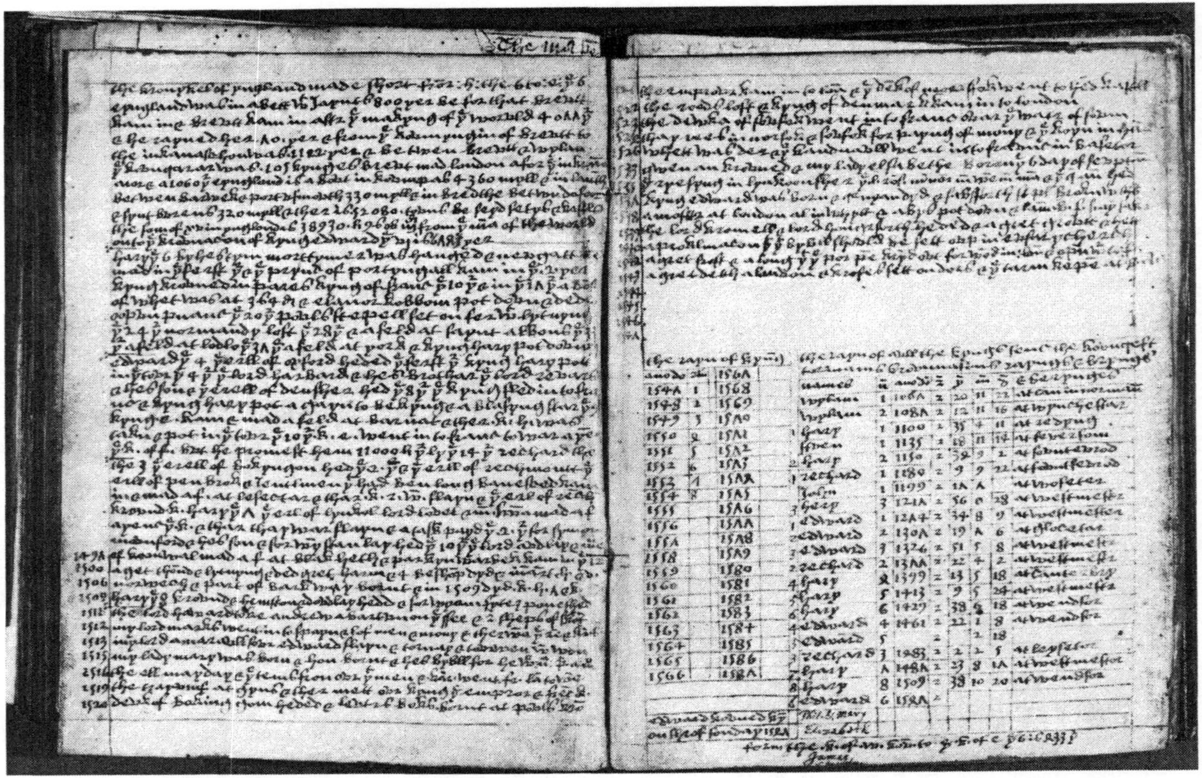

Fig. 9. 'The kronykel of Ynglonnd made short' and 'the rayn of aull the kings senc the kounqest'.

substance of the realm. The ceremony has obvious ecclesiastical underpinnings but its secular political dimensions—the alignment it effects between body politic, body royal, and body territorial—are directly and
intimately related to the central ideological claims of early regnal cartography.[119] Increasingly during the Tudor era and with special intensity
under Elizabeth, the 'figure of England' or map of the realm comes
to function as an accepted, even primary vehicle for the expression of
English national identity. Whether superimposed or placed one upon the
other, the icons of monarch's body and map of the island together function as a potent shorthand for the corporate entity England. Images like
the famous Ditchley Portrait (in which Elizabeth 'towers over an England
drawn after the Saxton model') provide convenient evidence of this ideological conjunction (between body of the queen and body of the realm),
but as Richard Helgerson has shown it is as a literary/historical (or 'chorographical') construct that this cultural fiction has its most elaborated
expression.[120]

Seen in such a context, Beinecke 558's chronicle and chart of reigns
serve more as companion pieces to the map of England they travel
with, than merely as repositories for the realm's temporal statistics,
graphic record of its place in time. In what amounts to an inversion of
the role played by pendant-maps that accompany medieval universal
histories (and so provide a stage for what happens), Beinecke's abbreviated account of the Tudor years—and in particular the irregular annals
into which it devolves—may be said to work as a ledger of outcomes, in
other words an enrolment of the sequence of astrological judgements
(or historical events) England's chart has generated.[121] Significantly, the
particular shards of historical data chosen for inclusion here possess an astrological quality or tone themselves, in the sense that what gets written
down for a given year (battles, plagues, weather, beheadings, comets,
births, etc.) tends to sound like results predicted in the casting of a
horoscope: in 1506, 'Norwech & part of Barkway burnt'; in 1512, 'my

[119] See Birkholz, *The King's Two Maps*.
[120] Helgerson, 'The Land Speaks', 54–5, 81–2. Helgerson argues that the Ditchley Portrait's
unambiguously royalist 'ideological effect' is opposite of 'what most people bought an atlas to
see—a representation of the land itself'; the 'cartographic representation of England', in this
view, 'showed royal authority . . . to be a merely ornamental adjunct to that country', 56.
[121] See Suzanne Lewis, *The Art of Matthew Paris in the Chronica Majora* (London, 1987),
who argues that Paris's 'cartographic enterprises' amount to 'direct extensions of his work as historian', meant 'to serve as an elaborate pictorial illustration' or 'visualization' of his text: 322, 325,
364.

lord Marquesse Dorset went into Spaine & lost men & money'; in 1526, 'whett was dear'; in 1537, 'kyng Edward was born'; in 1539, 'the lord Hungerford was beheadid & ther was a great drought & hete'; in 1542, 'a gret frost & a long & open warre in Fraunce'; in 1543, 'a gret detthe in London & kropes [failed]'. Regnal astrology on this evidence may be regarded as a hybrid of the judicial and the natural, concerned with individual lives (Hungerford's, King Edward's) and inceptions (Dorset in Spain) but principally in the context of their impact on the stability of a larger collective, a national community as beset by 'frost', 'drought', and pestilence as by political intrigue and 'open warre'. Most annals tend toward the laconic and the paratactic, yet the coalescing here of the voice of history and the voice of astrology, equally severe and ominous, seems especially pronounced.

Beneath Beinecke's annals there are four lines left open, labelled '1544', '1545', '1546', '1547'. Half-charted yet empty, this controlled white space underlines strongly the notion of this text as a literary/historical work-in-progress, an account of 'England the nation' (and its corporate fortunes) that is universally grounded, stretching back from Edward VI through Brutus to the Creation, yet ultimately open ended.[122] The compositional process here implied may well appear less *pre*modern than *post*modern—a quality surely appropriate, if not inevitable, given Lawton's exhortation that we 'consciously bring our [post]modernity into dialogue with our understanding of the medieval'. In this view the astrolabe amounts to a kind of narrative-machine, generating initially a literature of prognostication, then ratifying this draft with the revised text of witness, the stamp of historical outcome. Produced all told is a story-diagram of lives (and of English national life) that is always already charted, calculable in its 'major features' and general contours, yet continually unfolding in terms of its discrete effects. Butler's symbiotic map and chronicle figure as the ground upon which astrology works to reveal its universal mysteries, the logic of destinies made manifest. But whether the charts he composes and the destinies he writes are private/familial or public/communal (his manuscripts devote space to both), what may be most significant is that Thomas Butler's text-making—in collective—is first and last a *vernacular* enterprise.

---

[122] For development of a proto-nationalist consciousness, see Thorlac Turville-Petre, *England the Nation: Language, Literature and National Identity 1290–1340* (Oxford, 1996). On 'Astrology and the Narration of History', and the apparent conflict between Christian and astrological views of time, see Smoller, *History, Prophecy and the Stars*, 61–84.

V. The Vernacular Map

What, finally, are the implications for literary study of the discussions staged above, on early regnal cartography, a woollen-draper's commonplace book, and premodern astrological practice? If the astrological treatises addressed by this essay had been *not Thomas Butler's* but, say, fellow amateur enthusiast Geoffrey Chaucer's, such a question would probably be moot—so powerfully authenticating is the word 'Chaucer' that anything it touches becomes literary by association, as well as irreproachably English. Invocation of the name of the master (Our Father of English Literature) was always inevitable, once my title proposed that early maps might prove capable of 're-charting' (astrological and cartographic puns intended) English literary history. In part, this is because Anglo-American literary medievalism remains definitively 'tilted toward Chaucer'.[123] At the crux of the matter is Chaucer's traditional deployment as the foundational voice of English culture. According to the mainline account, his works (the *Canterbury Tales* especially) constitute a turning point in the development of a quintessentially English—which is to say, vernacular as opposed to Latinate and/or European—national identity.[124] Above we noted the general alignment between literary histories and nationalism, but as Linda Georgianna argues, particular attention should be paid to the (especially influential) 'Whig interpretation of history' which 'although capable of much variation . . . stresses above all the continuity of the English past'. Lying at the heart of this vision is 'the ideology of a transhistorical "Englishness"', a quality 'dependent upon an almost mystical link between ethnicity, language and nationality'.[125] Notable peaks come in Alfred's Anglo-Saxon and with Shakespeare, but valorized above all in such a historical narrative is 'Chaucer's England', site of a (later imperial) nation's decisive early vernacular revolution, where undone in the stroke of a generation are the twin yokes of Latinate clerisy and Norman captivity.

One consequence of a nationalist historiography that privileges vernacular expression in English (at the expense of Anglo-Norman and

---

[123] Lawton, 'Literary History', 246.

[124] Among many possible citations, see the (old) *Cambridge History of English Literature* (Cambridge, 1907–27), ii. 374; J. J. Jusserand, *A Literary History of the English People*, i (London, 1895), 267; and Andrew Sanders, *Short Oxford History of English Literature* (Oxford, 1996), 47. Such paradigms no longer hold sway, as the new *Cambridge History* demonstrates; n. 128, below.

[125] Linda Georgianna, 'Coming to Terms with the Norman Conquest: Nationalism and English Literary History', *Yearbook of Research in English and American Literature*, 14 (1998), 35–7, 43.

72   Daniel Birkholz

Insular Latin) is that 'a very large number of works, the study of which
could alter drastically our understanding of English literary culture . . .
have been routinely ignored as not really "English" at all'. Georgianna
chronicles the damage done by sub-periodization within the medieval era
(e.g. the 'chronological trick that simply erases the twelfth century'), but
the aspect of Whig historiography I wish to highlight concerns territori-
ality—the fact that in this particular incarnation of the medievalist project, 'history, scholarship, and fiction alike worked to produce the
national romance of a *separate*, free and ancient *English nation*' (emphasis
mine).[126] To understand how maps potentially re-chart English cultural
history requires that we acknowledge the fundamental role played (both
formally and ideologically) by regnal cartography—that is, by the specific
technology of the insular map as a comprehensive, unitary, graphic image
of 'the realm'—in early programmes of state consolidation and colonial
expansion. The importance of literary expression (e.g. the genres of
chronicle and romance) to the process of articulating a 'separate . . . English nation' should by no means be downplayed; but cartography allows
for the imagination of the realm as realm (a coherent geographical and social body) in a manner and with an immediacy and grasp that remains unmatched, then as now, by other cultural media. To study the collected
works of Thomas Butler will never enjoy self-evident legitimacy. But perhaps a virtue can be made of the fact that future approaches to hybrid
texts like Gough and Beinecke (and to the territorial communities they
engender) will doubtless prove just as subject to disciplinary patrolling,
and just as bound by shifting critical fashions, as ever. History's frames
never disappear without replacement. Still, my final gesture in this essay
must remain—as is appropriate to any exercise in historiography—not
only provisional, but self-consciously so.[127]

Garnering much interest recently has been the theoretical category
(and specific historical workings) of medieval 'vernacularity'—a phenomenon still usually located to the fourteenth century, but no longer restricted to narrow 'literary' settings; instead, a more flexible and inclusive
notion of 'medieval writing' now prevails.[128] Writers on vernacularity
have emphasized the underlying role played (in the development of late

[126] Georgianna, 47, 45, 40.
[127] As Georgianna remarks, 'literary history is necessary even if impossible', 'undoubtedly a
fiction but useful nonetheless so long as it recognizes its own provisionality'; ibid. 34, 42.
[128] See David Wallace (ed.), 'General Preface' to *The Cambridge History of Medieval English
Literature* (Cambridge, 1999), p. xvi. One goal of the project is 'to help ease the bottleneck that
has formed, in literary criticism and curricular design, around late fourteenth-century England':
p. xii.

medieval writing in English) by various forms of lay 'literacy': verbal, visual, documentary, performative. Such quasi-textual modes of cultural expression develop in devotional, bureaucratic/administrative, and to some extent trade and craft-guild contexts.[129] Katherine O'Brien O'Keeffe has shown (based on differences in manuscript conventions) 'that literacy in Latin and [in] literary Old English were distinct phenomena', but one conclusion shared by scholars of Middle English (the point can be confirmed for contemporary cartographic practice) is that 'literacy in Latin'—literacy in this context meaning conversance with the texts, images, materials, and practices of international ecclesiastical culture—does more than vaguely crouch behind late medieval vernacular literary production.[130] Consistently decisive in the interpretation of medieval maps (of all genres) are what might be called the building blocks of visual and textual literacy, such that to read a cartographic text in these years (c.1360, say: the date of our extant copy of Gough) was to activate a set of graphic and verbal, intellectual and codicological conventions which had their original home, by and large, securely in clerical Latin culture. Regnal maps cannot be regarded otherwise than as vernacular productions, in a basic sense, yet it must be stressed that virtually all medieval cartographic literacy consists of borrowed elements. In this condition of hermeneutic dependence, early English cartography runs a course parallel to that taken by vernacular literary production. What takes place may be described in both cases as a process of epistemological transfusion: co-optation of those modes of thinking and knowing (established strategies for making cultural meaning) that are conceptually potent and moreover readily available. Such processes of cultural translation, of course, unfold fitfully (and only rarely may be said to occupy any stable location along a spectrum of intercultural gradients), but it is not too much to say that in both these disciplines the long-term trajectory leads from a universal, Latin, ecclesiastical realm (Christendom) over into an insular, vernacular, secular one (the nation-state).

The qualifications this assertion requires are potentially overwhelming. Yet here we reach a decisive moment for the concept (or more

[129] See especially Wendy Scase, 'Writing and the Plowman: Langland and Literacy', *Yearbook of Langland Studies*, 9 (1995), 121–31, with responses by L. Clopper and G. Morgan, 132–9; Michael Clanchy, *From Memory to Written Record: England 1066–1272*, 2nd edn. (Oxford, 1993); and Nicholas Watson, 'Conceptions of the Word: The Mother Tongue and the Incarnation of God', *NML*, 1 (1997), 85–124.
[130] Katherine O'Brien O'Keeffe, *Visible Song: Transitional Literacy in Old English Verse* (Cambridge, 1990), 190, 22, 12; Rita Copeland, *Rhetoric, Hermeneutics and Translation in the Middle Ages: Academic Traditions and Vernacular Texts* (Cambridge, 1991), esp. 7, 180–2.

accurately, my heuristic figure) of a 'vernacular map'. Concerning the interface between literacy and vernacularity in medieval England, 'the really significant point', as Michael Clanchy emphasizes, 'is that the dynamic of literacy was religious'.[131] Raymond Williams has argued that 'religion rather than literature' may be 'the most inclusive mode for apprehending culture'—and certainly I am sympathetic to the notion of questioning literature's claim to hegemony among cultural forms. Still, as Lawton implies (in glossing Williams on 'culture'), to award *any* single discourse priority in the multidimensional matter of 'apprehending culture' would be unwise.[132] Nonetheless, in the intertwined projects of articulating national identity and engendering the territorial state, it seems to me that cartography possesses especially strong credentials, as a 'mode for apprehending culture'—at least, *at the national level.* In any case the really significant point to be made about medieval English vernacularity, I would submit, is that its dynamic is implicitly *geographical.* For in this period English vernacularity is inherently insular, as opposed not only to the universalism of prevailing ecclesiastical discourses, but also to the linguistic colonialism of later eras.[133]

Suggestive parallels exist between the England of the late thirteenth century (the era of Gough's prototype) and that of the early to mid-sixteenth (the years of Beinecke's copying). In particular, 'the expansion of secular power into sacred spaces', a trend cited as 'the most evident feature' of Henry VIII's later reign, has analogy in initiatives pursued under Edward I—for example, removal of the icons of Welsh and Scottish sovereignty (the Crown of Arthur and the Stone of Scone) to Westminster Abbey, where they were incorporated into the shrine of the royal saint Edward the Confessor.[134] Following the lead of his father Henry III (d. 1272), Edward I adopted heraldic designs emphasizing his descent from

---

[131] Clanchy, *From Memory to Written Record*, 13.   [132] Lawton, 'Literary History', 239.

[133] On the imperial and eschatological imperatives of 'Orosian' geographical texts including *Mandeville's Travels* and the Hereford Cathedral *mappamundi*—and with implications for the bibliographical and topographical compilation work of John Leland—see Lawton, 'Surveying Subject', esp. 19–26. As Lawton argues, 'the sort of map Leland thinks he is making is the *national version* of a *mappamundi*, a text in which space and time are synchronous' (emphasis mine)—although for its part the Hereford Map (unlike Beinecke or Gough) 'does not show any great interest in the nation as the myth on which modern readers are still more or less unfortunately fixated' (36, 11).

[134] See Colin Burrow, 'The Experience of Exclusion: Literature and Politics in the Reigns of Henry VII and Henry VIII', in Wallace, *Cambridge History*, 819, 793, 806; R. R. Davies, *Domination and Conquest: The Experience of Ireland, Scotland and Wales 1100–1300* (Cambridge, 1990), 125–6; and Paul Binski, *Westminster Abbey and the Plantagenets: Kingship and the Representation of Power* (New Haven, 1995), 105, 135, 138.

St Edward; for his part Henry VIII had the Earl of Surrey executed, purportedly for having quartered the arms of royal St Edward with those of
his own family. The reigns of the mid-sixteenth century reprise those of
the thirteenth century further through their investment in the concept of
monarchy as essentially 'sacral'; both periods saw vigorous promotion of
'the cult of royalty'.[135] And insofar as Henry VIII commits himself to a
'theory of "imperial" monarchy', he also recalls Edward I. In neither reign
was there yet a 'definite association with the subjugation of provinces or
colonies', but as John Guy comments, nonetheless 'Henry VIII, like
Edward I, initiated a policy of territorial centralization within the British
Isles. He subsumed Wales administratively within the realm of England
and asserted feudal suzerainty over Scotland.'[136] With regard to Henry
VIII's territorial ambitions, Simon Adams judges similarly that the operative 'parallel to be drawn' is to Edward I—a point most true 'from a
British perspective', or in other words, precisely the perspective that in-
forms the imperial-insular genre of the early English regnal map.[137]

That both Henrys (III and VIII) outfit their successors with the same
politically loaded, ancient and sacral English name may help communi-
cate the sense of nostalgia operative during the reign of Edward VI, for the
political stability, administrative innovation, and military success that
were (and still are) synonymous with the name of Edward I: 'English
Justinian', 'Flower of Chivalry', 'Hammer of the Scots'.[138] Much might be
made of the deployment of the bodies (natural and political) of these
three kings, all Edwards, in the long premodern project of 'bodifying'
England as a realm—especially insofar as Edward the Confessor, Edward
I, and Edward VI reside at (or dwell near) those definitive scenes in the national romance, respectively, of Conquest, Crusade, and Reformation. At
any rate, each of these reigns, while obviously distinctive in political and
territorial conditions, is notably invested in the project of articulating
(however incrementally) a 'separate . . . English nation'.

[135] For the devotion of Henry III and Edward I to St Edward, see Binski, *Westminster Abbey*,
esp. 52–89. On Tudor pageantry, imagery, and politics, see Sydney Anglo, *Spectacle, Pageantry,
and Early Tudor Policy*, 2nd edn. (Oxford, 1997), and *Images of Tudor Kingship* (London, 1992).

[136] John Guy, 'Monarchy and Counsel: Models of the State', in Collinson, *Sixteenth Century*,
117, 118. Henry's attempts to justify his 'royal supremacy' recall the conflict between the Papacy
and the Holy Roman Empire that dominated the thirteenth century (and resulted in eventual
articulation of the western secular state).

[137] Guy, 'Monarchy and Counsel', 117–22; Adams, 'Britain, Europe and the World', 188–215;
191.

[138] For Edward I, see Maurice Powicke, *The Thirteenth Century: 1216–1307* (Oxford, 1952),
227–30.

English literary histories tend to find their medieval crisis point in the late fourteenth century; but before the writers of this generation could imagine a vernacular England, a handful of innovative regnal cartographers already had. It is not my object to argue causality, but the vernacular literary explosion of the late fourteenth century might well be regarded as having been 'figured' (indeed conceptually enabled) by the ambitious vernacular *mapping* initiatives undertaken over the course of the century preceding—a programme of surveying the realm, and then committing it to graphic representation, that culminated in the remarkably comprehensive Gough Map but generated also a set of affiliated documents.[139] Familiarity with the avant-garde technology of the regnal map—a persuasive new way of seeing, a 'mode for apprehending' the island of Britain as a coherent geographical and political entity—will have marked the experience of many from the reign of Edward I onwards. This applies particularly to those in royal service: king's clerks and couriers; itinerant commissioners, purveyors, and justices. But the point also applies to private individuals involved in commodity exchange at the regional or national level—those such as Thomas Butler of Harlow, who trades in wool but also wheat and other foodstuffs (Beinecke 558, fo. 64ʳ), and indeed headlines his annal-entry for 1526 with the observation that 'whett was dear' (fo. 49ʳ). I find it intriguing in this regard—here at the crossroads of commodity, crown, map, war, and realm—that in 1325 a royal clerk named Robert of Nottingham, out requisitioning wheat for the king's wars in the vicinity of the River Trent, records distances between stations on his itinerary using the same mileage figures that the Gough Map later registers.[140]

The temptation is to press here—that is, seek to enforce a thesis of medieval cartography's special influence, specifically its claims to having figured 'national origin' ahead of other candidates (e.g. literature, religion). However, even to articulate such a proposition threatens to reduce our discussion to merely one more entry in the sweepstakes of academic priority: whose text, period, or sub-field did what first. Such a move would not only violate the critical spirit of what has gone before; worse, it would

[139] On grounds that the Gough Map displays local knowledge in places (Lincolnshire, South-East Yorkshire), and that there are regional differences among later maps indebted to it (recall the Beinecke highway table's expertise in the vicinity of Essex), it has been posited that multiple versions of the Gough Map may have existed simultaneously, 'kept at London and other centers with local details added'; see Parsons, *Map of Britain*, 15, and Hindle, 'Roads and Tracks', 196.

[140] See Hindle, 'Roads and Tracks', who notes that Robert 'appears to have had an early [c.1325] edition of the [c.1360] Gough Map with him', 198; Exchequer Accounts, Miscellaneous, 309/29.

amount to just another reinscription of teleological nationalism, only this time with cartography instead of literature playing the coveted lead.

It may be too much to assert that in reproducing an antique map of the realm (by transforming 'Gough' into 'Beinecke') Thomas Butler brings his own Tudor modernity consciously 'into dialogue with [his] understanding of the medieval'.[141] Whatever may be made of Butler's historicism, in now engaging with this document it becomes our obligation to consider not just a single hermeneutic looping between Butler's world and ours, between the premodern and the modern. The figure of a circle has undeniable elegance, but the interpretive geometry required in the case of the Beinecke Map is complex and tangled—meaningful inflection has come at every stage in its journey from past (from its many pasts) into present. We cannot afford, in other words, to bypass Brand and Taylor, to dismiss the interventions of Louis M. Rabinowitz or the Beinecke curatorial staff, any more than we can dismiss the early history of the regnal map form—or ignore, for that matter, our current climb forward toward whatever next textual upheaval or quiet displacement awaits Beinecke MS 558. If we make it our business to watch for them, we will see that compelling new historicisms—synchronic and diachronic, each bearing claims that should not be disinherited—explode from this text at every turn in its fortunes.

The attraction of the premodern astrological figure lay in its 'potential richness and elegance', as well as its promise of control. So too early cartography—although the greater point may be that in each system the technology of the figure is 'never interpretively closed'. Whether the future within which the Beinecke Map is encountered—fifty, 100, 500 years from now—resembles more closely a globalized corporate village, polarized camps of armament and terror, or some less demoralizing, as yet unimagined configuration, we can be certain that the genre of the regnal map, quintessential model of the nation-state, will require and reward re-engagement. For purposes of resistance, cooptation, conglomeration, nostalgia: who can say? Our only certainty is that the process of cartographic redeployment will continue. Butler's pen-drawing remains (for now), but what is made of it keeps changing.

University of Texas at Austin

---

[141]   John M. Ganim, 'The Experience of Modernity in Late Medieval Literature: Urbanism, Experience and Rhetoric in Some Early Descriptions of London', in J. J. Paxson, L. M. Clopper, and S. Tomasch (eds.), *The Performance of Middle English Culture* (London, 1998), 77–96.

Refiguring the Veil: The Transvaluation of Human History in Marie de France's Yonec

Suzanne M. Verderber

I. Salvation History as Romance

Yonec, the seventh lay in the collection by Marie de France, recounts the story of a lady, imprisoned by her husband, who prays for a lover to come and rescue her.[1] One does, in the form of a huge goshawk that is miraculously transformed into a handsome knight. This essay is ultimately concerned with interpreting the implications of a single yet strange detail of this scene, the fact that before the lady sees the majestic bird, she first lays eyes upon its shadow: 'Quant ele ot fait sa pleinte issi, | L'umbre d'un grant oisel choisi | Par mi une estreite fenestre' (ll. 105–7) ('Having lamented thus, she noticed the shadow of a large bird through a narrow window . . .' (87)). This is one of several moments in which the lay recapitulates and transfigures salvation history: the birth, death, and resurrection of Christ, and the Last Judgement. The shadow, in the context of the unexpected arrival of a winged creature in the closed chamber of a lady, recalls the Annunciation.[2] In Luke, Mary asks Gabriel how she

[1] The seventh lay following the order proposed by Rychner, which he bases upon British Museum, Harley 978. All citations from the lays are quoted from his edition: *Les Lais de Marie de France*, ed. Jean Rychner (Paris, 1973). English translations are from *The Lais of Marie de France*, trans. Glyn S. Burgess and Keith Busby (London, 1986).

[2] Several critics have examined the Annunciation iconography in *Yonec*: M. B. Ogle, 'Some Theories of Irish Literary Influence and the Lay of *Yonec*', *Romanic Review*, 10 (1919), 123–48; Stephen G. Nichols, 'Deflections of the Body in the Old French Lay', *Stanford French Review* (Spring-Fall 1990), 27–50; Susan M. Johnson, 'Christian Allusion and Divine Justice in *Yonec*', in Chantal A. Maréchal (ed.), *In Quest of Marie de France, A Twelfth-Century Poet* (Lewiston, NY, 1992), 161–73; and Jacques Ribard, 'Le Lai d' *Yonec* est-il une allégorie chrétienne?', in P. B. Grout, R. A. Lodge, C. E. Pickford, and E. K. C. Varty (eds.), *The Legend of Arthur in the Middle Ages* (Cambridge, 1983), 160–9. Denise L. Despres studies the relationship between *Yonec* and mysticism in 'Redeeming the Flesh: Spiritual Transformation in Marie de France's *Yonec*', *Studia Mystica*, 10 (1987), 26–39. Victor I. Stoichita demonstrates the complexity of the issue of the shadow in medieval paintings of the Annunciation in *Brève Histoire de l'ombre* (Geneva, 2000), 68–85.

could possibly conceive, since she has never been with a man. Gabriel explains enigmatically that 'Spiritus Sanctus superveniet in te et virtus Altissimi obumbrabit tibi ideoque et quod nascetur sanctum vocabitur Filius Dei' ('the Holy Ghost shall come upon thee, and the power of the most High shall overshadow thee. And therefore also the Holy which shall be born of thee shall be called the Son of God') (Luke 1: 35).[3] In *Yonec*, the knight will father the lady's child, Yonec, who will ultimately slay her husband, representative of an oppressive social system. Both texts thus associate a shadow with the conception of a saviour.

Beyond functioning as a key signifier linking *Yonec* and Scripture, the lay's disruption of a series of hierarchies—allegorical and literal levels, spirit and matter, sacred and secular, man and woman, human and animal—will be shown to turn ultimately upon the rich, problematic figure of the hawk and its shadow. Is the shadow cast by a physical body or not? The first section will propose that *Yonec* aims to transfer the frame of salvation history to the representation of secular history, in the process adding reciprocal desire and sexuality—the physical body—to the tale. The following section interrogates this intertextual relationship at a theoretical level, arguing that in order to refute hermeneutic conventions which would have dictated reading the literal level of *Yonec* as an integumentum, a deceitful 'veil', the lay poses as a simulacrum (a shadow) of the literal level of Scripture. Following Gilles Deleuze's explication of the powers of the simulacrum, such a strategy indicates an attempted appropriation by the romance of the status of the scriptural literal level, the only text in the twelfth century understood to have a literal level that is *true*. At the thematic level, the simulacrum destabilizes traditional hierarchies of truth and falsity, appearance and essence, the ultimate point being to 'unfound' (to use Deleuze's term) an oppressive social order that presents itself as legitimate.

The essay concludes by drawing upon Lacanian psychoanalysis, the branch of theory most capable of addressing issues of symbolic legitimacy and signification, to explore how a transfer of 'truth' from the allegorical to the literal/historical levels of meaning, and from an oppressive social system to a new one, is enacted in the lay. The Lacanian proposition that the subject can occupy different positions in relation to the phallus—masculine, feminine, or perverse—is used to interrogate conventional hermeneutic approaches to the literal level, to show how a feminine,

---

[3] Latin citations are from the *Biblia Sacra, Iuxta Vulgatam Versionem* (Stuttgart, 1983); English translations are from *The Holy Bible: Douay Rheims Version* (Rockford, Ill., 2000).

perverse reading values and preserves that level—the material signifier—rather than discarding it to reach the Christian signified. This is important because the literal level is the textual site where the events of human history are recorded, and thus the preservation of this level is crucial to a narrative strategy that aims to fit the events of human history into the framework of salvation, in order to sanctify the transformational events that are recorded therein.

This transfer of the frame of salvation history to secular events is evident in the lay's transformation of the scriptural figure of the shadow. While the conception of Christ in Luke's account is accomplished by *only* a shadow, one that is not cast by a sensible body (permitting of course no intermingling of lovers' bodies), the shadow in *Yonec* transfigures the scriptural shadow in such a way that it immediately indicates the presence of an earthly body, that of the hawk. God's corporeal form will not be made visible to humankind until after the divine conception, through His incarnation in Christ. Conception in *Yonec* re-presents the Annunciation scene to inscribe corporeality and sexuality, absent in the Gospel account, by attaching a body to the shadow, a hawk that will be transformed into the lady's lover. Indeed, the scene is a repetition of the Incarnation, with the difference that a hawk, a popular hunting bird, becomes man, rather than God becoming man through the logic of the Trinity. The flesh and blood corporeality of the hawk lover will not only be made present, but will be insisted upon within the lay through the numerous metamorphoses he undergoes. *Yonec*'s re-embodiment of the scriptural signifier is symptomatic of an attitude that adds earthly materiality and human desire to the scriptural account of the conception and birth of Christ.

The lady calls for rescue in order to escape her oppressive circumstances. The foundation of the socio-symbolic order, its kinship system, and her constrained position within it, is clearly staked out from the start: 'Pur ceo k'il ot bon heritage, | Femme prist pur enfanz aveir, | Ki aprés lui fuissent si heir' (ll. 18–20) ('because his inheritance would be large, he took a wife in order to have children, who would be his heirs' (86)). This section contains a bitter complaint against not only her husband, but also against the social structures that sanctioned her placement in such a miserable situation, linking, in effect, the personal to the political. Her imprisonment prevents participation in religious ritual: 'Jeo ne puis al mustier venir | Ne le servise Deu oïr' (ll. 75–6) ('I can neither go to church nor hear God's service' (87)), and she condemns her family and the larger social body as the driving force behind this marriage, this trafficking of her person, in the first place: 'Maleeit seient mi parent | E li autre communalment | Ki a cest gelus me donerent | E de sun cors me marïerent!' (ll. 81–4) ('Cursed be my parents and all those who gave me to this jealous man and married me to his person!' (87)).

Her only recourse is fantasy, the calling for a magical lover, which she does, importantly, in the name of God. We are told that the month of April has arrived, the time of new love in medieval lyric and romance, and the lady, finding herself alone in her chamber, prays for precisely that. In both *Yonec* and Luke, the lady is interrupted by the winged intruder while reading or glossing. Louis Réau, comparing Byzantine and Western representations of the scene observes that 'au moment où elle est surprise par le message de l'Ange, elle n'est pas occupée à des travaux manuels . . . elle médite sur la Bible ou plus précisément, selon les Pères de l'Église, sur la prédiction d'Isaïe: Ecce Virgo concipiet qui la prépare à ce qu'elle va entendre'.[4] Mary is engaged in the exegetical practice of reading the Old Testament as a prefiguration of a New Testament event; she reads Isaiah not for its historical content, but rather to discover her own fate.

Although the lady in *Yonec* does not hold a book in her hand when the hawk enters, she can still be said to be performing a type of reading. She orally glosses romances that she has retained in her memory, comparing their plots to her own miserable situation, seeking in them a fantastic resolution to her problems:

> Mut ai sovent oï cunter
> Que l'em suleit jadis trover
> Aventures en cest païs
> Ki rehaitouent les pensis.
> Chevalier trovoent puceles
> A lur talent, gentes e beles,
> E dames truvoent amanz
> Beaus e curteis, pruz e vaillanz,
> Si que blasmees n'en esteient
> Ne nul fors eles nes veeient.
> Si ceo peot estrë e ceo fu,
> Si unc a nul est avenu,
> Deus, ki de tut ad poësté,
> Il en face ma volonté!
>
> (ll. 91–104)

---

[4] Louis Réau, *Iconographie de l'art chrétien: iconographie de la Bible II, Nouveau Testament*, 3 vols. (Paris, 1957), ii. 180.

I have often heard tell that in this country one used to encounter adventures which relieved those afflicted by care: knights discovered maidens to their liking, noble and fair, and ladies found handsome and courtly lovers, worthy and valiant men. There was no fear of reproach and they alone could see them. If this can be and ever was, if it ever did happen to anyone, may almighty God grant my wish! (87)

She could be speaking either of Guigemar, who tastes love for the first time with a noble lady whom he met through fantastic circumstances, or Lanval, who, exiled from Arthur's court, finds love with a magical lady for a time visible only to him. For the lady, it is the romance genre that opens the possibility of imagining alternatives to the socio-symbolic order already in place. Both the Virgin and Yonec's lady 'read' prophecies of their own fates; in the place of the codex or roll of twelfth-century depictions of the Annunciation, the *malmariée* glosses romance plots she retains in memory, tales that she has heard rather than read. Orally transmitted romance replaces the Old Testament in this adaptation of biblical iconography, and is depicted not only as worthy of exegesis, but as a vehicle of liberating truths.[5] This affirmation of secular, vernacular orality alongside sacred, Latin textuality parallels the transvaluation at work in the Prologue, where Marie asserts the value of the casting of oral lays into written verse rather than translating Latin texts into *romaunz*. Both secular and sacred texts, now, are given the authority to prefigure future realities. The replacement of the Old Testament by orally trans- mitted romances again, as in the case of the shadow as a sign, indicates a transfiguration of a scriptural sign to give it a secular meaning that affirms human desire.[6]

---

[5] Dafydd Evans observes that the *chansons de malmariée* are often 'in direct conflict with the established social and religious codes. Adultery on the part of the *malmariée* is not merely con- doned . . . but triumphantly proclaimed as just revenge on a vicious system.' 'Marie de France, Chrétien de Troyes, and the *malmariée*', in Peter S. Noble and Linda M. Paterson (eds.), *Chrétien de Troyes and the Troubadours: Essays in Memory of the late Leslie Topsfield* (Cambridge, 1984), 159–71: 162. A parallel can be drawn between the lady's 'use' of romance in *Yonec*, and Janice Radway's argument that women read modern romance novels to manage anxiety produced by patriarchy, asserting that the fantasy resolutions of these novels provide nurturance and reassurance often absent in their readers' everyday lives. See Janice A. Radway, *Reading the Romance: Women, Patriarchy, and Popular Literature* (Chapel Hill, NC, 1984).

[6] Slavoj Žižek's reading of the Annunciation, as depicted by Rossetti, also points out this atmosphere of suppressed sexuality: 'How does Mary react to this astonishing message, to this original "Hail Mary"? The painting shows her frightened, with a bad conscience, withdrawing from the archangel into a corner, as if asking herself "Why was I selected for this stupid mission? Why me? What does this repulsive ghost really want of me?" The exhausted, pale face and the dark eyeteeth are telltale enough: we have before us a woman with a turbulent sex life, a licen- tious sinner—in short, an Eve-like figure . . .' *The Sublime Object of Ideology* (London, 1999), 113–14.

Both women react to the intrusion of the winged creature with terror. In Luke, Gabriel reassures Mary: 'quae cum vidisset turbata est in sermone eius et cogitabat qualis esset ista salutatio et ait angelus ei ne timeas Maria invenisti enim gratiam apud Deum' ('Who, having heard, was troubled at his saying, and thought with herself what manner of salutation this should be. And the angel said to her: Fear not, Mary, for thou hast found grace with God') (Luke 1: 29–30). *Yonec*'s lady mimics Mary's posture; she trembles, covers her head, and the now-transfomed knight tries to calm her with soothing words:

> La dame a merveille le tint;
> Li sens li remut e fremi,
> Grant poür ot, sun chief covri.
> Mut fu curteis li chevaliers,
> Il la areisunat primiers:
> 'Dame, fet il, n'eiez poür:
> Gentil oisel ad en ostur!
> Si li segrei vus sont oscur,
> Gardez ke seiez a seür,
> Si fetes de mei vostre ami! . . .'
>
> (ll. 116–125)

The lady was astounded by this. Her face became flushed, and she trembled and covered her head, being very afraid. The knight was extremely courtly and spoke to her first: 'Lady, do not be afraid! The hawk is a noble bird. Even if its secrets remain a mystery to you, be assured that you are safe, and make me your beloved!' (87)

Here the hawk, a representative of secular nobility, replaces Gabriel, messenger of God.[7] The genealogical legitimacy of the hawk is inscribed in the words it uses to soothe the frightened lady, 'Gentil oisel ad en ostur!' (122). The adjective 'gentil' betrays Marie's knowledge of the Latin name for 'austour', *accipiter gentilis*. While the signifier 'gentil' is linked to the hawk in both the bird's Latin name and in Marie's verses, it has two slightly different denotations in each language: in Latin, it is either an adjective signifying 'family', 'hereditary', or 'tribal', or a noun signifying 'clansman' or 'kinsman'; in Old French it is an adjective signifying 'nobility'. Marie fragments and preserves the Latin name for goshawk while

---

[7] Susan M. Johnson makes precisely this point: '[The hawk's] ability to change form can only be accounted for by magic and yet his first words to the lady, "N'eiez pour" (v. 121), "Be not afraid", echo the phrase used so often in the Bible when angels appear to mortal men.' Johnson, 'Christian Allusion', 165.

drawing attention to its meaning in Old French, a move that on the one hand emphasizes the materiality of the signifier through its fragmentation, translation, and infusion with new meaning, and on the other that emphasizes the bird's association with noble lineage. Just as the hawk's shadow signifies, in addition to its textual associations, sexual desire and the body, and the life of the human being on earth, the hawk itself symbolizes secular nobility, heredity, and genealogy.

Other events in *Yonec* reinforce its close adherence to Scripture. In a scene recalling the Passion and Crucifixion, the husband sets a trap for the hawk in the form of iron spikes planted in the window. The hawk arrives and is pierced through his body as he tries to pass through. Becoming a martyr, echoing Christ's mission, he tells the lady that he is dying for her love ('Pur vostre amur perc jeo la vie' (l. 320)) ('for love of you I am losing my life' (90)), and that she should be comforted by a second prophecy: that she will give birth to a son named Yonec who will avenge them by slaying their enemy. This prophecy of a miraculous birth is thus the completion of the lay's adaptation of the Annunciation, instantiated with the initial arrival of the hawk. Against Muldumarec's wishes, the lady follows him back to his kingdom, a spectacular, enclosed city, seemingly composed of silver, recalling the New Jerusalem, composed of gold, as described in Apocalypse 21: 18.[8] He comforts her by giving her a ring which will efface the husband's memory of the past, and a sword which she is to give to Yonec to avenge his murder. Here he makes another prophecy: she, her husband, and Yonec will find his tomb and hear of his death; at this moment, she shall give Yonec the sword, and he will slay his father's murderer. A period of waiting ensues. Yonec is born and in due time is dubbed a knight. That same year, the family sets out for a religious feast, becomes lost, and ends up at a castle populated by holy people. In the chapter house, they come to a tomb covered with rich fabric, surrounded by candles, and the tearful inhabitants tell them Muldumarec's story, how he died for a lady of Caerwent, whom he loved, and how they are awaiting the arrival of his son to avenge his death. Hearing this, the lady realizes the period of waiting has ended, and explains to her son that the tomb belongs to his father, wrongfully murdered by her husband. She gives him the sword, and falls dead upon the tomb. Yonec beheads the husband and becomes the ruler of the city. The

---

[8] '. . . et erat structure muri eius ex lapide iaspide ipsa vero civitas auro mundo simile vitro mundo . . .' ('And the building of the wall thereof was of jasper stone: but the city itself pure gold, like to clear glass').

question remains: for what purpose does *Yonec* pose as a secular double or shadow of salvation history?

II. *The New Testament and its Doubles*

Yonec has been created through a 'folding' of salvation history, resulting in the projection of a double, a shadow, a theatrical re-presentation of the story performed by secular actors. Given the complexity of twelfth-century thought on both sacred and secular hermeneutics, and Marie's own insistence on exegesis in the Prologue, it is worthwhile to explore the intertextual relation at a theoretical level.[9] As a secular romance, the literal level of *Yonec* would traditionally be seen as an integumentum, a potentially deceptive veil, possibly concealing a deeper Christian, philosophical, moral truth. But could the lay's adherence to the literal level of Scripture possibly cause it to 'absorb' some of that sacred text's properties? This transmission of properties would specifically entail a change in the status of the lay's literal level, from integumentum or veil to image of the scriptural literal level, viewed as *historically true*. While thus far the figure of the shadow has been read to signify a corporeal desire absent in Scripture, it is also of extreme importance in the scriptural exegetical tradition, both as a figure for figural language itself, and as a figure for the Old Testament in relationship to the New. The shadow figures the relationship between texts and between levels of meaning, and thus is crucial for understanding *Yonec*'s relation to Scripture. In the *Didascalicon* Hugh of Saint Victor uses the shadow to figure the relationship between literal and allegorical levels of Scripture: '. . . per umbram venitur as corpus. Figuram disce, et invenies veritatem' ('Following the shadow, one comes to the body: learn the figure, and you will come to the truth).'[10] The shadow is also used to figure the relationship between the Old and New Testaments. Henri de Lubac indicates many locations where the figure is used in this way: 'De telles précisions, à vrai dire, n'étaient pas du tout nécessaires

---

[9] The prologue situates the lays as texts to be glossed following the method of the grammarian Priscian. Spitzer notes that 'Marie de France, thinking "medievally" . . . sees her own book as only another "text", which will be "glossed", after the manner of the Old Testament commented on by Tertullian, Augustine, Jerome, etc.—after the model of Virgil and Ovid "moralized".' Leo Spitzer, 'The Prologue to the *Lais* of Marie de France and Medieval Poetics', *Romanische Literaturstudien 1936–1956* (Tübingen, 1959), 3–14: 10.

[10] *Patrologia Latina*, 176, col. 0801C. English translation from Jerome Taylor (trans.), *The Didascalicon of Hugh of St. Victor* (New York, 1991), 138.

pour un chrétien de l'ére patristique ou médiévale, tant il était habitué, à la suite de saint Paul et de l'Épître aux Hébreux, à opposer les réalités les plus certaines de l'Ancien Testament à celles du Nouveau comme la "figure", l' "image" ou l' "ombre" à la "substance", à la "chose même", au "corps" et à la "vérité" . . . et, dans un sens identique, Origène: "Voyons d'abord l'ombre de l'Écriture, pour en chercher ensuite la vérité".[11] In all of these uses, a chiaroscurist poetics figures textual hierarchies in which the allegorical level is privileged over the literal, and the New Testament over the Old; but crucially both also grant the 'shadow' texts a truth value as well, viewing the events they recount as historically true, if not yet completed by their allegorical New Testament complements.

The status of the literal or historical level of Scripture came under tremendous scrutiny in the twelfth century. At one extreme, Hugh of Saint Victor argued for the utter importance of study of the literal level of Scripture to the understanding of its deeper levels of signification, while at the other Peter Lombard disregarded the literal level almost entirely in his gloss of the Psalter.[12] Although command of the literal level of Scripture remained in the service of an allegorical interpretation, Hugh emphasized the fundamental importance of the letter, placing this level at the very foundation of the scriptural edifice. The scriptural signifier was thereby seen as true and indispensable, if potentially contradictory. Lubac summarizes this view of the literal or historical level of the Bible as true:

Elle raconte une série d'événements, qui se sont réellement passés, et dont il est essentiel qu'ils se soient réellement passés. Elle n'est ni un exposé de doctrine ab-straite, ni un recueil de mythes, ni un manuel d'intériorité. Elle n'a rien d'intem-porel . . . La révélation divine n'a pas seulement eu lieu dans le temps, au cours de l'histoire: elle a elle-même forme historique . . . Aussi ne sera-t-il jamais possible d'oublier l'histoire, ni de la remettre en question, ni de s'en affranchir ou de la mépriser.[13]

Where the literal level of Holy Scripture was seen as the foundation, or *fundamentum*, of the spiritual meaning, a term Lubac locates in Alcuin, Gregory, Bede, Jerome, Alain de Lille, and Hugh of Saint Victor, the literal level of the secular text is conceptualized as an integumentum.[14]

The most common interpretive practice associated with secular or pagan texts entailed decipherment of the text's surface or literal level, or

[11] Henri de Lubac, *Exégèse médiévale: les quatre sens de l'Écriture*, 2 vols. (Paris, 1993), i. 443.

[12] A. J. Minnis, *Medieval Theory of Authorship: Scholastic Literary Attitudes in the Later Middle Ages* (Philadelphia, 1988), 47.

[13] Lubac, *Exégèse Médiévale*, i. 429–30.   [14] Ibid. 436–9.

integumentum, to bring to light the truths hidden within them. Macrobius (c.400) set the terms the debate would follow for centuries, arguing
that a specific type of fable could in fact contain deeper truths, but simultaneously positioning their literal levels as deceitful. Those belonging to
this group, *narratio fabulosa*, may contain holy knowledge beneath a veil:
'aut sacrarum rerum notio sub pio figmentorum uelamine honestis et
tecta rebus et uestita nominibus enuntiatur. Et hoc est solum figmenti
genus quod cautio de diuinis rebus philosophantis admittit' (7) ('a decent
and dignified conception of holy truths, with respectable events and characters is presented beneath a modest veil of allegory. This is the only type
of fiction approved by the philosopher who is prudent in handling sacred
matters').[15] The uncovering of a fable's truth is evoked as a sort of striptease;
letters compose a veil that permits the truth to hide behind a mask. In
William of Conches's twelfth-century extension of Macrobius, a broader
definition of fable is promoted, 'embracing every kind of imaginary narrative . . . but in particular, imaginary narrative that has a significance
beyond the simple narrative meaning'.[16] Despite the fact that he argued
that a broader range of fables were capable of serving as vehicles for truth
than Macrobius, accepting even sordid and adulterous tales, he followed
Macrobius in his attitude towards the integumentum: when used in the
sense of a 'veil' or 'covering'—in his commentary the term could also
refer to the deeper meaning[17]—the integumentum was to be discarded
to reveal the deeper truth beneath.

In sum, despite the fact that secular hermeneutics and the Arts began
to exert a significant impact on scriptural exegesis in the twelfth century,
the literal level of the two types of texts still assumed a distinct value: the
literal level of the Bible was held to be true in itself while simultaneously
indicating a deeper, spiritual meaning, while the literal level of pagan and
secular texts was viewed as a veil that required decipherment in order for
the deeper truth of the text to be revealed. *Yonec* poses interpretive problems that cut across both categories. On the one hand, it is a romance; its
value thus hinged on the debate concerning the interpretation of *narratio
fabulosa*. On the other hand, through its copying of scriptural signifiers,

[15] Macrobius, *Commentaire au Songe de Scipion, Livre I*, ed. Mireille Armisen-Marchetti
(Paris, 2001), 7. English translation is from Macrobius, *Commentary on the Dream of Scipio*,
trans. William Harris Stahl (New York, 1952), 85.
[16] Peter Dronke, *Fabula: Explorations into the Uses of Myth in Medieval Platonism* (Leiden,
1974), 16–17.
[17] Ibid. 25.

Yonec weaves biblical motifs into its literal level, and thus invites a reading that takes into consideration exegetical principles pertaining specifically to this sacred text.

Jacques Ribard reads the literal level of *Yonec* as an integumentum, proceeding as a twelfth-century exegete, extracting the Christian *sens* through a careful decipherment of the *littera*:

Le personage-pivot du lai serait la dame, figure de l'âme humaine, aspirant à vivre un amour spirituel fécondant, épanouissant, auquel font obstacle le viellard jaloux et sa soeur, la "vieille", représentants d'une conception archaïque, scélerosée et étouffante de la religion—la Synagogue. Muldumarec serait la figure du Messie, un Christ souffrant, crucifié, dont le sacrifice permettrait à l'âme d'atteindre enfin à cet amour mystique, absolu, qu'elle appelait de tous ses voeux ... Sous un habillage romanesque, la poétesse développerait ainsi une large fresque allant de l'Ancien Testament, temps de l'attente et de l'espoir, au règne de l'Esprit Saint, en passant par la venue et le sacrifice du Christ.[18]

While Ribard emphasizes the dependence of the lay upon salvation history, a connection with which I agree, he discards the literal level in order to bring to light the Christian allegorical meaning. The text's signifiers, and along with them any sense of its historical specificity, are cast aside. Discarding the integumentum results in the disappearance of the lady's body (she becomes the sign of a non-gendered human soul), and the image of the repressive social structure more generally, a dubious result in the lays, which are so finely attuned to the expression of female experience.

Yonec may *invite* such a typical Christian gloss to account for its scriptural allusions, but I propose that this invitation is a lure. *Yonec* poses not as a 'veil' for salvation history, but rather as its double, its image, and in this doubling the result is a romance with serious intentions: the interrogation of Platonic hierarchies between truth and falsity, flesh and spirit, heaven and earth, men and women, and humans and animals. If the Old Testament was viewed as an adumbration of the New, perhaps it would be accurate to figure the relationship between *Yonec* and Scripture along these lines as well. *Yonec* is positioned similarly to the Old Testament in the textual economy of salvation; like the Old Testament, it recounts an earthly narrative that is true in a *historical* sense and that will find its match and fulfilment in the New Testament. If the Old Testament is the

---

[18] Ribard, 'Le Lai d' *Yonec*', 165.

double, the 'true shadow' of the New, perhaps *Yonec* represents an attempt to produce yet another double, another copy, which is both critical of the actual social order, and which proposes a new one to put in its place.

Yonec's attempted appropriation of the truthful status of the scriptural literal level can be formulated more precisely through the application of the Platonic opposition between copy and simulacrum as explicated by Gilles Deleuze. Deleuze proposes that the real motive underlying the theory of Ideas is not the reduction of members of a genus into a species, but, 'in very general terms, the motive of the theory of Ideas must be sought in the will to select and to choose . . . the original from the copy, the model from the simulacrum'.[19] The issue at stake is the perceived distance of images from an *original* model, a hierarchy established according to the degree to which the image participates in the truth of the model, which Deleuze also terms the 'foundation': 'The foundation is that which possesses something in a primary way; it relinquishes it to be participated in.'[20] A 'copy' possesses a *resemblance* to the original, a resemblance resulting not from the sharing of any mere superficial, external trait, but rather from an 'internal and spiritual' link.[21] By contrast, the simulacrum is that image which is furthest removed from the original in the descending hierarchy of images; the simulacrum is devoid of truth and, further, possesses a demonic power in that it is potentially subversive of the hierarchy itself: 'That to which they [the simulacra] pretend (the object, the quality, etc.), they pretend to underhandedly, under cover of an aggression, an insinuation, a subversion, "against the father", and without passing through the Idea.'[22]

The Platonic categorization of true and false images, of copies and simulacra, is applicable to the twelfth-century distinction between the literal levels of sacred and secular texts. These terms provide a precise language for explaining the perceived truth of Scripture, which was treated as a copy, its literal level seemingly infused with the inspiration of the Holy Spirit itself. Secular texts were not seen as participating in the divine substance; they were exiled from the textual economy of truth. The simulacrum has the effect of throwing the truthful status of all copies into question, a consequence exuberantly expressed by Deleuze: 'By rising to the surface, the simulacrum makes the Same and the Similar, the model and the copy, fall under the power of the false (phantasm). It renders the

[19] Gilles Deleuze, *The Logic of Sense*, ed. Constantin V. Boundas, trans. Mark Lester (New York, 1990), 253.
[20] Ibid. 255.   [21] Ibid. 257.   [22] Ibid. 257.

order of participation, the fixity of distribution, the determination of hierarchy impossible . . . Far from being a new foundation, it assures a universal breakdown (*effondrement*), but as a joyful and positive event, as an un-founding (*effondement*).'[23] As a simulacrum of salvation history, *Yonec* destabilizes the hierarchy of the literal levels of sacred and secular texts in terms of their proximity to the truth, calling into question the designation of integumenta of secular texts as deceitful. In light of the lay's worshipful attitude toward Christian faith and ritual, it would be incorrect to conclude that *Yonec* aims to 'unfound' the foundation, God and Scripture; rather, the aim is to demonstrate the potential falsity of those phenomena claiming to be true, and the truth of those which superficially appear to be false. The prime motive for this copying of salvation history is to demonstrate the illegitimacy of the old society, embodied in the jealous husband, and the legitimacy of the new one, embodied in Muldumarec and Yonec, and to give the new one symbolic—divine—authority.

The importance of distinguishing copies from simulacra at the thematic level of the lay is obvious when the ambiguous ontological status of the hawk is considered. The inscription of the hawk's shadow in the lay suggests that the bird is a sign to be deciphered, a body that is also a text, demanding an attention to the symbolic resonance of natural things that Marie betrays in other lays as well, particularly *Fresne*, *Bisclavret*, *Laüstic*, and *Milun*, and that was characteristic of the twelfth-century attitude toward nature more generally.[24] Indeed, the hawk lover identifies himself as an integumentum through his declaration to the lady of his own mysteriousness, the fact that he embodies secrets the lady may not discover: ' "Dame, fet il, n'eiez pour: Gentil oisel ad en ostur! Si li segrei vus sont oscur. . . ." ' (ll. 121–3) (' "Lady, do not be afraid! The hawk is a noble bird. Even if its secrets remain a mystery to you. . . ." ' (87)). The rhyming of 'ostur' and 'oscur' emphasizes the close relationship between the two words; the use of the word 'oscur' is particularly significant, as it is used also in the collection's Prologue to designate ancient texts that await glossing: 'Es livres ke jadis feseient, | Assez oscurement diseient. . . .' (ll. 11–12) ['in the books which they wrote . . . to express themselves very obscurely. . . .' (41)).

The hawk is a privileged type of sign, a 'countersign', a term Stephen Nichols introduces in his reading of *Guigemar* to account for

---

[23] Ibid. 263.
[24] M.-D. Chenu, *Nature, Man and Society in the Twelfth Century*, ed. and trans. Jerome Taylor and Lester K. Little (Toronto, 1997), 115–19.

Socratis were juxtaposed in an original collection of these seven works together, and that the division of that original collection into two parts which our two manuscript groups represent simply made the separation between the *Florida* and the *De Deo Socratis* at the wrong point, a few pages before rather than at the end of the *Florida*. By this means the final part of the *Florida* was isolated from the rest of its work and became attached to the beginning of the *De Deo Socratis*. For convenience, and in the belief that they were originally the final part of the *Florida*, the five sections of the 'false preface' will be analysed at the end of this chapter.

The meaning of the title *Florida* is closely bound up with the issue of the nature of the collection. The evidence of its transmission and original book-divisions already discussed makes it certain that our *Florida* derives by a later act of excerption from an original work of the same title in four books attributed to Apuleius. The absence of any preface or conclusion (though these could theoretically have been lost in transmission) suggests this, as does the unevenness of selection: a self-respecting sophistic writer seems to me unlikely to have composed an anthology from his own works in the form we have, in which extracts of six or seven pages (*Flor.* 16 and 18) were set next to extracts of six or seven lines (*Flor.* 5). The nature of the original four-book work may be guessed at from its title as well as from the content of the extant collection. *Florida* means literally either 'flowery parts', which might indicate choice selections culled from a longer original without stylistic reference, or pieces with 'flowery' style; these are the alternative explanations of the title offered since the Renaissance.[9] The adjective *floridus* can certainly be applied to style (cf. *TLL* 6. 1. 925. 72 ff.). Quintilian uses it of a middle style of writing which is full of pleasing ornament and digression, the verbal equivalent of a *locus amoenus* (12. 10. 60):

medius hic modus et translationibus crebrior et figuris erit iucundior, egressionibus amoenus, compositione aptus, sententiis dulcis, lenior tamen ut amnis lucidus quidem sed virentibus utrimque silvis inumbratus.

This is not inappropriate for the ornamental language of the most epideictic parts of the *Florida*, as some have argued.[10] However, it is not clear

[9] Already found together in Scioppius (1594), 84: *sunt enim hi Floridorum libri nihil nisi mera fragmenta, ab aliquo Apulei studioso ex diversis eius libris in unum comportata, tamquam ἐκλόγαι et floridiore dicendi genere expressa.*

[10] On the Quintilian passage see the useful discussion of Austin (1948), 199, especially his reference to Cicero *Orat.* 96, where an *insigne et florens orationis pictum et expolitum genus* is associated with the epideictic style of the fifth-century sophists. For a summary of views on the meaning of *floridus* for the *Florida* see Hijmans (1994), 1719–23.

that flowery style is the criterion for selection for the *Florida*: our collection includes extracts which have little stylistic colour of this kind and which seem to be chosen for their function or subject matter (e.g. *Flor.* 5 and 11). Moreover, the weight of the linguistic evidence for *floridus* and its cognates *flos*, *flosculus*, and *florens* suggests that the title *Florida* should indicate primarily an anthology on any principle; though style will naturally play an important role in selection, the selection will not be limited to the stylistically 'flowery'.[11]

Three passages in particular point this way. The first occurs in the preface to Justin's epitome of the *Historia Philippica* of Pompeius Trogus, an epitome possibly contemporary with Apuleius[12] (Justin *praef.* 4):

horum igitur quattuor et quadraginta voluminum . . . cognitione quaeque dignissima excerpsi et . . . breve velut florum corpusculum feci.

Here *flores* is applied to the excerpts made by Justin, excerpts analogous to those of the *Florida*, particularly in the matter of retaining the books of the original, reduced in Justin to a few paragraphs each. The second passage is in the preface to Aulus Gellius' *Noctes Atticae*, itself a collection of varied selections and excerpts from Apuleius' period (Gellius *NA praef.* 6):

namque alii Musarum inscripserunt, alii Silvarum, ille Πέπλον, hic Ἀμαλθείας κέρας, alius Κηρία, partim Λειμῶνα, quidam Lectionis Suae, alius Antiquarum Lectionum atque alius Ἀνθηρῶν et item alius Ἐρωτημάτων.

Here Gellius, in listing titles of other (lost) works of miscellaneous compilation like his own, mentions ἀνθηρά, of which *Florida* is a translation (cf. Quintilian 12. 10. 58 *floridum (nam id ἀνθηρὸν appellant)* . . .): the term clearly refers to an anthology, and there is no necessary link with style given the other titles mentioned.[13]

The final passage is from a letter of Claudianus Mamertus, presbyter of Vienne in the fifth century AD (Claud. Mam. *Ep.* p. 205. 14 ff. Engelbrecht):

e summis auctoribus . . . doctiora quaeque velut thyma fraglantia et fecundiora veluti quaedam florida praecerpens.

This is the only other occasion in classical Latin apart from Apuleius' title

---

[11] *TLL* 6. 1. 925. 72 ff. (*floridus*), 936. 45 ff. (*flos*), 938. 15 ff. (*flosculus*), 923. 24 ff. (*florens*).
[12] On the date of Justin see above, Ch. 1 n. 97.
[13] For discussions of the Gellius passage cf. Holford-Strevens (1988), 20–2, and Vardi (1993).

Florida that the neuter plural adjective *florida* is used substantivally. Again it describes excerpting activity, this time applied to the teaching activities of the writer's correspondent, the rhetor Sapaudus, who selects the best passages of the classics in instructing his pupils, on the grounds of learning (*doctiora*) and intellectual richness (*fecundiora*) rather than flowery style. Claudianus Mamertus may well be influenced by Apuleius' title *Florida* here; he knew Apuleius' works well, and another of his correspondents was Sidonius Apollinaris who similarly had access to the works of Apuleius.[14] In any case, the use of *florida* and similar terms to describe choice passages culled from larger works seems beyond dispute, and these passages indicate that the title *Florida* suggests 'choice blooms' collected in an anthology. Our *Florida* is thus a collection of excerpts itself excerpted from a choice collection; further definition of the principle of excerption must await a full analysis of the extant *Florida*, together with the excerpts falsely attributed to the preface of the *De Deo Socratis* (see Section 4 below).

3. ANALYSIS OF THE *FLORIDA*

Florida 1

In these fifteen lines Apuleius, in an elaborate simile, compares stopping at a city to give a speech with stopping at a shrine while travelling: this is clearly meant as a compliment to the city concerned, which is not named. Carthage has been suggested as a possibility,[15] and this could be so if *Flor.* 1 predated Apuleius' residence at Carthage in the 160s; it is unlikely that Apuleius would talk in this way about his home city, since the passage clearly concerns a visit to a city en route to somewhere else (2 *ita mihi ingresso sanctissimam istam civitatem, quamquam oppido festinem . . .*). Here Apuleius is shown as the professional travelling speaker in true sophistic manner, just as in *Flor.* 21 (below) and in the *Apologia*, where he mentions a speech given at Oea where he stopped on the way to Alexan-

---

[14] Claudianus Mamertus *Anim.* 2. 9, p. 137. 1 Englebrecht *cernas hic alium situ fetutinarum turpium ex olenticetis suis ac tenebris . . . oris inhalare sentinam:* the noun *olenticetum* is otherwise found only at Apuleius *Apol.* 8, which also joins it with the otherwise very rare noun *fetutina: nocens lingua mendaciorum et amaritudinum praeministra semper in fetutinis et olenticetis iaceat.* For Mamertus' substantial knowledge of Apuleius see Alimonti (1975).

[15] So Scotti (1988), 126 n. 2 (her brief article is the nearest thing to a commentary on *Flor.* 1 and is very useful); other North African cities with major cults (e.g. Lepcis Magna or Alexandria) are possible.

dria (55). Allusions to travelling and compliments to the city where the speaker has arrived are naturally common topics in the opening of sophists' speeches,[16] and there is every indication that this passage constitutes the beginning of a speech. Aelius Aristides, in a recognizably cognate conceit, begins a speech to a Roman audience by claiming that he had vowed that very speech as an offering to the gods for safe passage on his journey (*Or.* 26. 1 K), and a similar extended simile is used by Lucian to open the first book of the *Verae Historiae:* Lucian compares readers/audiences and athletes, Apuleius speakers and travellers, and the two similes are articulated in a closely similar way.[17] These similarities suggest that this type of structure is a typical kind of sophistic opening, though the style is very much Apuleius' own: in the opening sentence, the characteristic jingle of *aliqui lucus aut aliqui locus* and the rhyming asyndetic isocola of *votum postulare, pomum adponere, paulisper adsidere* are typically Apuleian.[18] Strongly Apuleian too are the two similarly rhythmical and carefully balanced sets of four isocola in the second sentence which list with careful learning and colourful language the various types of sacred site a traveller might encounter (*aut ara floribus redimita | aut spelunca frondibus inumbrata | aut quercus cornibus onerata | aut fagus pellibus coronata, | vel enim colliculus saepimine consecratus | vel truncus dolamine effigiatus | vel caespes libamine umigatus | vel lapis unguine delibutus*). This yields not only verbal pyrotechnics but also an impression that the speaker is both learned and pious, matching Apuleius' similar self-projection in the *Apologia*.[19]

---

[16] Allusions to travel: Dio *Or.* 7. 2, 9. 1. Encomium of place arrived at expected: Dio *Or.* 33. 2.

[17] Lucian *VH* 1. 1 'Just as athletes (῞Ωσπερ τοῖς ἀθλητικοῖς) and those who are seriously concerned with the care of the body do not care only for good physical condition or the gymnasia, but also for relaxation at the appropriate time (indeed they suppose it the most important element in their training), so (οὕτω) in my view it is fitting for those concerned with literature (τοῖς περὶ τοὺς λόγους ἐσπουδακόσιν) to relax the mind after extensive reading of more serious works and to prepare it to be readier for subsequent exertions'. The word of comparison begins the work in both cases (*ut*/῞Ωσπερ), followed by a similar long and elaborate *comparans*, and picked up by a correlative *comparandum* (*ita*/οὕτω), both *comparans* and *comparandum* being in the dative case (*religiosis … mihi*/τοῖς ἀθλητικοῖς … τοῖς περὶ τοὺς λόγους ἐσπουδακόσιν).

[18] For these features of Apuleian style see Bernhard (1927).

[19] Learning in *Apologia passim*, piety e.g. *Apol.* 54–6. The detail about sacred objects has a feel of Varronian antiquarianism: the seventh book of Varro's *Res Divinae* was devoted to *loci religiosi*, the twelfth to *sacra privata* (cf. Augustine *Civ.* 6. 3). For Apuleius' knowledge of Varro cf. Ch. 1 n. 93.

Muldumarec, the founder of a new lineage. Treatises dedicated to the use of hawks in hunting indicate that the goshawk embodies gender alterity as well. One of the most well-known treatises, the *De arte venandi cum avibus* of Frederic II, composed in the mid-thirteenth century, is a compendium of scientific knowledge concerning birds used in hunting. Although most likely composed a half-century later than the lays, I introduce it here because it explains in detail the issue of sexual dimorphism in birds of prey, that is, the larger size of the female than the male. The text asserts that 'La femelle est plus grans dou male.'[33] Sexual dimorphism is the subject of a lengthy exposition that attempts to account for, through humoral theory, the larger size of the female than the male, the only known case of such a phenomenon, according to the writer, in the animal kingdom. The inequality is due, he says, to the great heat of both male and female birds of prey, which accounts for their propensity to move more than other animals, as well as for their courage in hunting. Since proper body size is achieved through the intermingling of the correct proportions of heat and humours, the female's larger size is explained by the fact that she has a greater proportion of cold, moist, and thick humours than the male, which serves to moderate the great heat characteristic of both males and females of the species. The male's small size is explained by excessive proportion of heat in his body compared to the proportion of humours. The male, smaller than the female by about one-third, is often called a 'tiercel'.[34]

Marie's goshawk is possibly intended to be female, given its great size: 'L'umbre d'un grant oisel choisi . . .' (l. 106) ('. . . she noticed the shadow of a large bird . . .' (87)).[35] Although it is impossible to know for certain whether Marie was cognizant of sexual dimorphism in hawks, the lady's precise observations of the bird upon its arrival suggest that

[33] Gustaf Holmér (ed.), *Traduction en Vieux Français du De arte venandi cum avibus de l'Empereur Frédéric II de Hohenstaufen, Édition critique du second livre d'après tous les manuscrits* (Lund, 1960), 59–69. The following English translation is available: Frederick II, *The Art of Falconry*, ed. and trans. C. A. Wood and F. M. Fyfe (Stanford, Calif., 1943). An introduction to this field and bibliography of early manuals is to be found in Baudouin Van den Abeele, *La Fauconnerie au Moyen Âge* (Paris, 1994). On falconry and hawkery in literature, see, by the same author, *La Fauconnerie dans les lettres françaises du XIIe au XIVe siècle* (Leuven, 1990).

[34] Holmér, *De arte venandi*, 62.

[35] Van Den Abeele provides an example of a thirteenth-century text in which a goshawk appears and is specifically designated as female. In the *Roman d'Auberon*, Judas Macchabé sees 'un ostur fourmé' perched in a large tree that will plunge and attack its prey, giving the hero the idea to do the same to his enemy. 'Fourmé' refers to the female sex: 'Le *fourmé*—mot dont ce texte fournit la première attestation—désigne la femelle de l'oiseau de proie, plus grande et plus forte que son partenaire.' *La Fauconnerie dans les lettres*, 222–3.

she had some specific knowledge of birds of prey (she notes the 'giez' on its feet and the number of times it has moulted, another signifier of metamorphosis, to be discussed). While earlier French manuals tend to concentrate less on anatomy and more on medical treatments of sick birds, those circulating in the Arab world as early as the eighth century emphasize that the larger bird is female and thereby more prized.[36] These works, particularly those of Moamin and Ghatrif, were widely disseminated in Europe, starting in the eighth and ninth centuries.[37] A consideration of the hawk as potentially female has broad implications, for in these terms, the bird, like the communicant in the Eucharist scene, becomes sexually hybrid, rendering impossible a social system predicated on sexual hierarchies.

A further aspect of hawk symbolism in the *Aviarium,* the act of moulting, underlines the hawk's association with earthly transformation. In the Prologue, Hugh represents himself as a dove, and the text's addressee, Rainier, as a hawk: '. . . et qui rapere consueveras domesticas aves, nunc bonae operationis manu silvestres ad conversionem trahas, id est saeculares' ('. . . and so that you who were accustomed to seizing domestic fowl, now with the hand of good deeds may bring to conversion the wild ones, that is, laymen').[38] The trait accounting for the hawk's placement in the genus *accipiter,* which Isidore of Seville derives from *capere,* 'to take'[39]—is the bird's tendency to seize prey with its talons. As a nobleman who has become a member of the secular clergy, Rainier embodies the possibility of the transformation of a human being's situation on earth. The hawk's seizing of domestic fowl is a figure for Rainier's acts of war, while the seizing of wild fowl represents his conversion of wayward, 'wild' souls to Christianity. The notion of earthly transformation is elaborated through glossing of the hawk's tendency to moult. The lady in *Yonec,* of course, takes note of the number of times the hawk has moulted; the *Aviarium's* metaphorization of conversion as moulting is adapted from Gregory's commentary on Job 39:26 ('Doth the hawk wax feathered by thy wisdom, spreading her wings to the south?'):

---

[36] François Viré, 'Essai de détermination des oiseaux-de-vol mentionnés dans les principaux manuscrits arabes médiévaux sur la fauconnerie', *Arabica,* 24 (1977), 138–49: 139.

[37] See François Viré, 'La Fauconnerie dans l'Islam mediéval (d'après les manuscrits arabes, du VIIIème au XIVème siècle)', in *La Chasse au Moyen Âge: Actes du Colloque de Nice 22–24 juin 1979* (Nice, 1980), 189–97: 190 and Van den Abeele, *La Fauconnerie au Moyen Âge,* 28–9.

[38] Clark, *Aviarium,* 118–19.

[39] Isidore de Séville, *Étymologies, Livre XII: des animaux,* ed. and trans. Jacques André (Paris, 1986), 266–8.

Unde beatus Gregorius, 'Agrestibus accipitribus moris est ut flante austro alas ex-
pandant quatenus eorum membra ad laxandam pennam veterem venti tepore
concalescant. Cum ergo ventus deest, alis contra radium solis expansis atque per-
cussis, tepentem sibi auram faciunt sicque apertis poris, vel veteres exsiliunt vel
novae succrescunt. Quid est ergo accipitrem in austro plumescere nisi quod un-
usquisque sanctorum tactus flatu Sancti Spiritus concalescit, et usum vetustae
conversationis abiciens novi hominis formam sumit? . . . Penna namque veteris
conversationis gravat, et pluma novae immutationis sublevat, ut ad volatum
tanto leviorem quanto noviorem reddat.'

Whence the blessed Gregory states, 'It is the custom of wild hawks when the
south wind blows to spread their wings so that their members grow warm in the
temperate heat of the wind, in order to loosen the old feather. Thus, when there
is no wind, with wings spread and flapping in the sun's ray, they create for themselves a warming breeze, and with their pores opened, either the old feathers fall
out, or new ones grow from beneath. Therefore, what is the hawk's growing of
feathers in the south wind but every one of the saints growing warm, touched by
the breath of the Holy Spirit, and, rejecting the ways of the old society, taking on
the form of a new man? . . . For the feather of the old society oppresses, and the
plumage of the new change lightens, so that it may render [the man] so much the
lighter as the newer for flight.'[40]

In choosing to embody the lover in the hawk, Marie has thus selected a
species associated with a polymorphousness extending far beyond its
transformation into a man or a woman: metamorphosis is endemic to the
symbolic representation of the hawk, and an informed medieval reader
would most likely have grasped this. Here, as in the lay's presentation
of the Eucharist, the conversion of material reality to a spiritual state is
central, in the warrior Rainier's conversion to the secular clergy, in the
conversion of 'wild' souls to Christianity, in the transformation of an old
oppressive society to a new, 'lighter' one. Of the many transformations
that occur in the lay, the most important is precisely the overthrowing an
old society, that embodied by the jealous husband, to be replaced by a
new one, that ruled by Muldumarec, and, subsequently, by Yonec, the
avenger of his father's death.

The sanctity of Muldumarec's polymorphousness is established
through the juxtaposition of his transformations with those that occur to
the bread and wine in the Eucharist itself. Why is transubstantiation not
also, in Boivin's words, 'une remise en cause du pouvoir créateur de Dieu'?
Precisely because, of course, it is God who blesses these transformations.
But then, Marie seems to ask, why can't other physical transformations

also be divine? A debate did persist, even in the twelfth century, over whether Christ's body and blood was truly present in the bread and wine, or whether the latter were mere symbols of the former. Hugh of Saint Victor's mystical interpretation of the ritual accepted the reality of the transformation, but played it down, emphasizing instead its power to establish an *inner* resemblance between Christ and the communicant, as long as it is received in 'faith and love'; he distinguishes between its inner substance—Christ's body and blood—and its outer appearance, bread and wine, which he likens to the outer human appearance of Christ during his life on earth.[41] Hugh's simultaneous acceptance and de-emphasis of the reality of transubstantiation, to the point that the communicant who cannot receive in reality need only feel faith and love to experience union with Christ, reflects a discomfort with the notion of physical transformation. It also follows the logic of the simulacrum; inner resemblance to God takes precedence over external appearance.

In *Yonec*, by contrast, no such discomfort with physical metamorphosis is evident; the spiritual and physical logic of the sacrament is transferred to the substance of the communicant him/herself, to affirm that entities prone to metamorphosis, hawks or bread and wine, can indeed be participants in divine substance. Nichols makes this point in his reading of the scene: 'The mystery of the Mass naturalizes the transgressive nature of the knight's shape shifting. It is not simply a matter of pointing out the commutativity between body and domestic objects like bread and wine in transubstantiation, but more fundamentally to show that the mystery of the Eucharist itself subsumes alterity. Whether the communicant be male or female, the same mystical union with the body of Christ was meant to occur.'[42] The point is that the metamorphosis of species need not be viewed with suspicion, and that the created hierarchy of species can withstand mutability and flux while remaining within God's jurisdiction.

III. The Name (No) of the Father, the Assent of the Mother

Is it possible to extend this logic to the conventional understanding of the literal level of the secular text? If the mutable, potentially deceptive hawk,

---

[41]   Gary Macy summarizes Hugh's opinion succinctly: 'To receive the sacrament worthily one must receive in faith and love. Further, if one cannot receive the outward sign of the Eucharist, faith and love alone are sufficient to gain the spiritual union with Christ.' *The Theologies of the Eucharist in the Early Scholastic Period: A Study of the Salvific Function of the Sacrament according to the Theologians c.1080–c.1220* (Oxford, 1984), 83.

[42]   Nichols, 'Deflections', 38.

symbol of secular nobility, possesses a divine resemblance, cannot the same be said of the lay itself, that regardless of the form its literal level takes, it is still infused with the Holy Spirit, still capable of resembling God? While the concepts of copy and simulacrum are capable of pointing out the conventionality of all hierarchically ordered systems, they are not adequate to express the transfer of legitimacy from one system to another. The transvaluations at work in *Yonec* do not ultimately aim to eradicate notions of divine substance and immanence, but rather to unveil the divine foundation of a new hierarchy, a new social order; in this sense, *Yonec* is a conservative text, ultimately affirmative of the passage of power through men. Lacanian psychoanalysis does provide a useful concept for expressing this transfer—the phallus—a concept that is also useful for re-visiting the problem of the status of the literal level in the lay, not surprising given the fact that Lacan was as fascinated with the operation of the signifier as the medieval exegetes.

From a Lacanian perspective, the most striking feature of the twelfth-century approach to secular and pagan texts is the certainty expressed in the connection between signifier and signified. Each signifier is assigned a stable Christian signified, an interpretive process that causes the material signifier itself to evaporate, to expire, in the process of 'giving birth' to its deeper meaning. A sort of interpreting 'machine' is at work, into which secular narratives are fed, and out of which the same Christian meanings emerge, again and again. The phallus, the signifier of symbolic law, describes not the textual input or the output, but rather the hidden rule which determines the conversion of one into another, in addition to ordering kinship systems, such as that in which *Yonec*'s lady is trapped. The phallus is not an organ or an object; it is a signifier that maintains the illusion that that there is indeed a signified, a meaning, an end to signification: 'For [the phallus] is the signifier intended to designate as a whole the effects of the signified, in that the signifier conditions them by its presence as a signifier.'[43] Lacan's mystical rhetoric underlines the illusoriness of this meaning: '[The phallus] then becomes the bar which, at the hands of this demon [*Scham*, shame] strikes the signified, marking it as the bastard offspring of this signifying concatenation.'[44]

Not all subjects are positioned in the same way with respect to the phallus and castration; the position which structures the logic of conventional medieval hermeneutics represents only one possibility, one with an

[43] Jacques Lacan, *Ecrits, A Selection*, trans. Alan Sheridan (New York, 1977), 285.
[44] Ibid., 288.

investment in sustaining the illusion of the truth of phallic law. Other subjective positions are characterized by mistrust of the phallus, by doubt in the ability of symbolic systems to 'say all', to encompass the totality of truth: the feminine and perverse positions. The position defined by an investment in the truth of phallic law is that associated in Lacanian theory with a specifically masculine *jouissance*. This formulation refers to the trajectory followed by the male in the Oedipus complex: erotically attached to the mother, he perceives her 'castration' and fears that the same punishment awaits him unless he gives up his attachment, his *jouissance*, and takes his place in the social order alongside his father. Lucie Cantin explains this position with reference to Sophocles' play: 'Appelé à porter les conséquences et à devoir assumer seul la responsabilité d'actes qui s'avèrent être des crimes commis à son insu, Oedipe témoigne de la façon dont le masculin est sans équivoque et sans échappée possible, planté dans l'univers créé et régi par le signifiant et le symbole qu'il a pour fonction de soutenir au-delà de son être et de sa personne, au-delà donc des enjeux de satisfaction pulsionnelle et narcissique.'[45] The subject in this position (who *could* be a woman) denies the inevitable excess of non-meaning that results from any act of signification.

Secular hermeneutics is aligned with the masculine position, having the effect of leaving behind everything expressed at the literal level (seen as an integumentum) pertaining to historical, earthly life, producing an enormous field of suppressed meaning. Meanwhile, it is precisely the *feminine* position from which a critique of this procedure could be launched, the feminine subject never ceasing to draw attention to the signifier's failure to convey a totality of meaning. Cantin suggests that this difference is perhaps attributable to the fact that the woman is not subject to castration in the same way as a man, that is, she lacks an organ in the imaginary of her body, which in turn requires that her accession to language be an ethical act, an act of choice:

L'absence de cadrage offert par la culture (sous le mode d'un organe à perdre) pour marquer la primauté du symbolique sur la logique de la satisfaction pulsionnelle est peut-être ce qui donne l'impression que l'assomption de la castration pour une femme suppose toujours à un moment, une position éthique, une 'décision' de s'en tenir au signifiant et au langage en dépit de leur inconsistance. L'absence de nouage dans l'imaginaire de son corps des effets du symbolique sur le réel de la jouissance lui fait très tôt l'expérience que le langage ne dit pas tout le

[45] Lucie Cantin, 'La Masculinité au-delà du phallus, un style et une éthique pour la pulsion de mort', *Savoir: psychanalyse et analyse culturelle*, 5 (2000), 125–57: 126.

réel, que ce n'est pas tout de la jouissance possible qui tombe sous le coup de l'interdit.[46]

While the feminine subject may choose to accept the symbolic order, she may continue to perpetually point out its contingency and insufficiency in its efforts to totalize the Real. A feminine critique of secular hermeneutics would object to the total dissolving of the signifier in the signified, and a feminine reading would 'hystericize' the literal level by pointing out those aspects of the text repressed by conventional interpretive practice, paying heed to the integumentum (the 'skin' of the secular text the location of its symptoms). The narrative of *Yonec* is structured in such a way to prevent the discarding of its literal level; by posing as a simulacrum of Scripture, it problematizes the conventional distinctions between fact and fiction, truth and falsity.

As an image of Scripture, the lay's story of salvation takes place on earth, in historical time, rather than in messianic time. The significance of this shift from a messianic to a historical register is expressed powerfully by Nietzsche whose ongoing attack on Christian idealism involves a demystification of a core component of its doctrine, one with particularly nefarious effects on the 'will to power': the promotion of the belief in a 'better beyond', that misery on earth is to be endured because it will be compensated for after death, in eternal life:

When the center of gravity of life is placed, not in life itself, but in 'the beyond'— in nothingness—then one has taken away its center of gravity altogether. The vast lie of personal immortality destroys all reason, all natural instinct—henceforth, everything in the instincts that is beneficial, that fosters life and that safeguards the future is a cause of suspicion. So to live that life no longer has any meaning: this is now the meaning of life . . .[47]

The belief in eternal life, for Nietzsche, is a 'reactive force' which could be used to justify outrages on earth, keeping an oppressed and exploited population subdued by holding them in the expectant thrall of a messianic ideology, and in a transfixed identification with a weak, decadent god.[48] His linking of the belief in the 'better beyond' to the degradation

[46] Lucie Cantin, 'La Fémininité: D'une complicité à la perversion à une éthique de l'impossible', *Savoir: psychanalyse et analyse culturelle*, 2 (1995), 47–90: 52.

[47] Friedrich Nietzsche, *The Anti-christ*, trans. H. L. Mencken (Tucson, Ariz., 1999), 61.

[48] In Deleuze's reading, reactive forces 'decompose; they separate active force from what it can do; they take away part or almost all of its power . . . In each case this separation rests on a fiction, on a mystification or a falsification.' *Nietzsche and Philosophy*, trans. Hugh Tomlinson (New York, 1983), 57.

of life suggests that dissipation of that belief would serve as a basis for the affirmative transformation of human life. In *Yonec*, I discern a struggle to break through the veil of Christian idealism, manifested in an ever-present framework of salvation history, in order to revalue human history, the representation of human events on earth as significant in and of themselves.

Attention to human history as a subject of representation apart from salvation history was only in its nascent stages in the twelfth century. Chenu points out that this burgeoning interest in human history only emerged within a theological frame: 'History remained clearly marked by its birth among, and in a climate of, religious things; only bit by bit was secular history to emerge, after a flourishing "theology" of history.'[49] Earthly events were interpreted from an eschatological viewpoint, which had the effect of casting a veil over the present moment, the 'here and now': 'In all this one observes a typical feature of Christian thought: an involvement with the very texts of scripture when composing historical narrative, and a close attention, in consequence, to the unfolding of the divine plan; but also the risk, in this very fidelity to the Bible, of getting closed up in past history and being cut off from the present.'[50] This greater emphasis on human history was not unique to *Yonec*, and is indeed evident in other areas of twelfth-century culture. In his discussion of the Apocalyptic thought of Joachim of Fiore, E. Randolph Daniel describes an image of the Apocalypse in which the crucified Christ is surrounded by scenes from daily life, a woman feeding chickens, a goat being milked, and so on, and argues that 'the mosaic conveys the overall impression that Christ has come to renew life on earth as well as to make it possible for Christians to enter heaven.'[51] Joachim's interpretation of the Apocalypse was characterized by a renewed optimism concerning earthly reform and progress: 'Although the ultimate goal of Christians was in eternity beyond history, God's plan for humanity would culminate in a historical Sabbath, which would evolve from the past and the present. In his notion of a third status, the age of the Holy Spirit, Joachim expressed the innovative developments of his era, its emphasis on history as having a meaning of its own and the desire to reform and purify the Church within history.'[52]

---

[49] Chenu, *Nature*, 167.   [50] Ibid. 193.
[51] E. Randolph Daniel, 'Joachim of Fiore: Patterns of History in the Apocalypse', in Richard K. Emmerson and Bernard McGinn (eds.), *The Apocalypse in the Middle Ages* (Ithaca, NY, 1992), 72–88: 72–3.
[52] Daniel, 'Joachim', 77–8.

Allegorizing effaces the historical details of the oppressive social conditions in which the lady is forced to live, and thus is incapable of a critique of a kinship system based upon the traffic in women; for a reading performed from a feminine position, in short, the truth is *in* the integumentum, not below or beyond it. And yet, how can a truth claim be made for the integumentum of a secular romance when the dominant hermeneutic paradigms of the day positioned it as a deceitful covering, as a potentially dangerous lie to be unravelled and discarded? *Yonec* renegotiates its identity as a secular romance—a categorization which leaves it vulnerable to a reading which discards its literal level—by repositioning itself as a simulacrum of the single medieval text whose literal level was almost universally declared to be true: the Bible. If the Bible was the one text where the literal level could not be discarded because it was understood to be truthful in itself, one way for a creator of fabulous fictions like Marie to ensure the survival of the poetic language of her carefully constructed tales, to preserve them from the 'ravages' of an allegorical reading that would in effect discard human history itself, was to attempt to appropriate the authority and status of the literal level of Scripture, thus interrogating the valuation of the secular textual surface as false, deceptive, and disposable. In effect, *Yonec* 'masquerades' as an earthly version of Scripture that, like the Old Testament, is positioned as a *true* narrative of events that will find their complement and completion in the New Testament.

A third position in relation to the phallic signifier is expressed here, in the lawless behaviour of the simulacrum: that of the perverse subject. The perverse subject—the fetishist in particular—is aware of the castration of the mother, but, despite this awareness, disavows it, and thus manages to avoid the threat of castration and the father's law. The fetishist disavows maternal castration, but does not completely forget it, cathecting a proliferation of material objects intended to take the place of the missing maternal phallus.[53] Both the fetish and the simulacrum masquerade as substitutes for the real thing, the phallus, thereby interrogating the viability of the symbolic systems that it organizes. Both perverse and feminine positions are operative in the poetics of *Yonec*, the feminine subject in pointing out the lack in the symbolic order, the perverse subject in proposing an aesthetic replacement for that lack. This linking of perver-

---

[53] Sigmund Freud, 'Fetishism', in *The Standard Edition of the Complete Psychological Works of Sigmund Freud*, trans. James Strachey, 24 vols. (London, 1961), xxi. 152–7.

sion and femininity is developed by Cantin who writes that 'le pervers a en effet ceci de commun avec la position féminine qu'il a, lui aussi, entrevu et fait l'expérience du défaut du signifiant et eu accès à une jouissance qui ne tombe pas sous le coup du phallus.'[54] The proliferation of countersigns in the lays indicates the prevalence of the perverse and/or feminine position in relationship to the phallic signifier, the will to undermine conventional meanings and values through surreptitious means. The countersign is 'feminine' in its indexing of a lack or hole in the symbolic order, and 'perverse' in its short-circuiting or denial of phallic law. The countersign's underhanded attempts at the subversion of phallic law aligns its power with that attributed by Deleuze to the simulacrum, the power to undermine the pretension to truth of any representational system.

As I have insisted throughout this essay, *Yonec* does not stop at critiquing or 'unfounding' the oppressive social order; a new one is proposed and demonstrated to possess divine legitimacy. In addition to calling the symbolic order into question, the feminine subject also has the power to confer legitimacy upon that order, to affirm the symbolic legitimacy of the father. Mikkel Borch-Jacobson points this out in his interpretation of Lacan's version of the Oedipus Complex:

> The child (or, more precisely, the boy) must realize that the father *has* the phallus, not inasmuch as he *is* the phallus of the mother (that is, a 'rival object') but inasmuch as he possesses it legitimately, and that the mother, by the same token, cannot have it in any case . . . This will happen only if the mother, instead of making the child her little phallic double, returns him to the father as to the one who legally possesses the phallus. In short, it is necessary that she play the game of the symbolic pact/exchange, by referring to the word and the law of the father as to her own law, as to a 'given word' that she intends to respect (when this is not the case, we get the whole gamut of neuroses, psychoses, and perversions).[55]

In her *chanson de malmariée*, and in her inability (unwillingness) to produce children for her husband, the lady in *Yonec* points out the insufficiency of the old social order. Through a series of symbolic gestures, she confers symbolic legitimacy upon a new social order, a new family line: in calling to God for rescue and receiving a response (in the form of the arrival of the hawk, recapitulation of the Annunciation scene), in de-

[54] Cantin, 'La Fémininité', 53.
[55] Mikkel Borch-Jacobson, *Lacan, the Absolute Master*, trans. Douglas Brick (Stanford, Calif., 1991), 223.

manding that Muldumarec receive communion, in producing an heir for
him, and finally in handing the sword—a gift from the 'true' father—to
the son, Yonec, to behead her husband in a holy place.

   In *Yonec* an illegitimate socio-symbolic system founded upon the
traffic in women, is 'unfounded', deracinated. Like any social system, this
one presented itself as a manifestation of the true and natural order of
things, as girded in the last resort by phallic law. The lady cries out against
this system, praying to God to create a new one, resembling that of a romance, in which greater human liberties are possible. The evangelist of
this new order, of this earthly 'good news', is the hawk, a creature which
symbolizes earthly transformation and the disorganization of hierarchies,
this latter a potent element when introduced into a rigidly ordered,
Platonic cosmos. Indeed, presented as devoid of light, life, and freedom,
the old society itself seems to be the 'true' simulacrum, the real perversion.
An interpretation which deciphers the lay's literal level in order to reveal
the salvation narrative, following twelfth-century hermeneutic procedure, remains blind to this project of radical social reform *on earth*. Such
a reading sees salvation in the 'better beyond', but leaves earthly transformation behind, along with the text's material signifiers. In masquerading
as Scripture, *Yonec* short-circuits such an approach, attributing to itself
the mark of truth typically reserved for Scripture. Indeed, just as
Muldumarec and his descendants receive the *nom-du-Père*, a strategy is
deployed to grant the same to the text itself, to demonstrate once and for
all that a secular text, a mere romance, can also be a divine and truthful
creation.

   Pratt Institute

Chaucer and the Queering Eunuch

Alastair Minnis

At the beginning of her highly influential 1980 article 'The Pardoner's Homosexuality and How it Matters', Monica McAlpine remarked that 'the possibility that the Pardoner may be a "mare" is often ignored in favor of the belief that he is certainly a "geldyng", or eunuch'; she sought to restore the balance by offering a detailed argument 'in favor of viewing the Pardoner as a possible homosexual'.[1] The situation has now been reversed: recently it is the case for the Pardoner's homosexuality which has been put most vigorously.

The English term 'homosexual' does not appear until 1869, and it has been argued that the notion of homosexual *identity*—as opposed to homosexual *behaviour*—arose long after the Middle Ages (though there is disagreement about exactly *when*). The general procedural problems of historicist inquiry into this matter may be illustrated with reference to Craig A. Williams's book on 'Roman homosexuality'.[2] This study makes it clear that Roman mores were very far from contemporary constructions of homosexuality and indeed of heterosexuality. A different binary operated, between '*men*, the penetrators, as opposed to anyone else, the penetrated. The penetrated *other* included women, boys, and slaves; adult Roman men who displayed a desire to be penetrated were consequently labelled deviants and anomalies.'[3] A major concomitant of these cultural

I am very grateful to David Wallace and Steven F. Kruger for their stimulating comments on previous versions of this essay.

[1] Monica McAlpine, 'The Pardoner's Homosexuality and How it Matters', *Publications of the Modern Language Association of America*, 95 (1980), 8–22: 8. All Chaucer citations are from *The Riverside Chaucer*, general ed. Larry D. Benson (Boston, 1987).

[2] Craig A. Williams, *Roman Homosexuality: Ideologies of Masculinity in Classical Antiquity* (Oxford, 2000).

[3] Ibid. 7. Penetration meant subjugation; masculinity meant domination. 'What was most important for a man's reputation was that he was thought to play the insertive and not the receptive role in penetrative acts. If he played the penetrative role, he might do so with either male or female partners, or both, as he pleased; the sex of his partner had no bearing on his own status as a man' (225). According to Mathew Kuefler, what happened subsequently was that Christianity came to offer Roman men, troubled by the military and political collapse of the Empire, a renewed valorization of their ideals of masculinity (to the detriment of some of the movement's

values was that 'men were not encouraged to make any meaningful distinctions between homosexual and heterosexual practices as such'.[4] And so, the contemporary understanding of 'homosexuality' as denoting an exclusive sexual preference and (far more crucially) a distinctive gay identity is simply not in play here; we are faced with major cultural differences and paradigm-shifts. Williams emphasizes this point in explaining the title of his book: he is, he says, 'reifying' the concept of homosexuality 'only temporarily and for strategic purposes'.[5]

A similar 'reification' is at work in much current criticism of the Pardoner, where it tends to cloud rather than clarify the issues—and this despite the fact that some of the most perceptive writers on the subject have proclaimed their wish not to be reductive, to leave the matter of the Pardoner's sexuality open. Such a move characterizes two of the studies with which the present discussion is in conversation, those by McAlpine and Steven F. Kruger. McAlpine remarks, 'It is neither likely nor desirable that such a reading [i.e. of the Pardoner as homosexual] will replace the view of the Pardoner as a eunuch: rather, it is to be hoped it will shed new light on familiar aspects of Chaucer's rich characterization.'[6] And yet—later she declares that 'the Pardoner's homosexuality is a profound part of his being'[7] and (in the Pardoner's altercation with the Host) sees him as using 'his homosexuality as a weapon'.[8] A similar manoeuvre features in Steven Kruger's paper, a contribution of impressive intellectual and ethical ambition which does not shrink from confronting Chaucer's creation

most radical doctrines, including the putative belief in 'a genderless and sexless ideal', 'no more male or female'). 'Some Christian men might have been encouraged . . . to see themselves as "eunuchs for the sake of the kingdom of Heaven"' (294), but the 'new masculine ideal presented itself to them both as a repudiation of the classical heritage *and as its ultimate fulfilment*': men of the Roman élite 'found it easier to offer their allegiance to a value system that sustained their own sense of themselves', including their sense of masculine identity and superiority, even if that superiority manifested itself 'in the self-sacrifice of martyrdom or asceticism'. A related development was the rejection of certain practices previously considered to have no bearing on their own status as men, such as pederasty. The 'ancient dichotomy' between 'penetrated males who were stigmatized and penetrating males who were not . . . was largely abandoned in late antiquity in favour of a condemnation of both roles as unmanly' (95). Matthew Kuefler, *The Manly Eunuch: Masculinity, Gender Ambiguity, and Christian Ideology in Late Antiquity* (Chicago, 2001), 2, 95, 287–8 (italics mine), 294.

    [4] Williams, *Roman Homosexuality*, 225.   [5] Ibid. 4–5.
    [6] McAlpine, 'The Pardoner's Homosexuality', 8.
    [7] Ibid. 15. However, she goes on to say that 'the church's moral theology tended to focus on acts, not on persons . . . It understood homosexual acts only as the perverse behavior of basically heterosexual persons' (16). If this is true (and I myself believe there is much truth in it; see below, 126–7), surely it is deeply problematic to claim a specifically homosexual identity for the Pardoner?
    [8] McAlpine, 'The Pardoner's Homosexuality', 17.

as 'a self-proclaimed hypocrite and cheat'.[9] Kruger is not 'concerned to "prove" the Pardoner's (indeed unprovable) homosexuality'; merely 'convinced that Chaucer wants us to see, as part of the Pardoner's sexual "queerness", the *possibility* of homosexuality'.[10] Nevertheless the enterprise of a bold 'claiming of the past for present ends'[11] is commended, and Kruger proceeds to claim the Pardoner as a gay ancestor and his tale as a site at which we can 'intervene . . . to locate and excavate the operations of medieval homophobia'.[12] The Host's 'revulsion' may be a 'moment of homosexual panic'; Chaucer is said to 'admit in the standoff between Pardoner and Host the possibility that an angry homosexual voice might present real challenges to dominant heterosexual paradigms'.[13] From an unproved and indeed unprovable proposition we have moved to authorial admission of possibility, and there seems to be no doubt that the Host's attack is 'couched in the terms of medieval homophobia'.[14]

All of this is in marked contrast to the strategy of Donald Howard, whose reading is determined *not* to make the Pardoner less unnerving and mysterious than, in Howard's view, he actually is. He finds the Pardoner '*feminoid* in a starkly physical way', and goes on to complain that 'Critics *soften* [my emphasis] this unnerving fact into "feminine" or "effeminate", and so it is widely believed that he is homosexual.' Howard's own reading resists such 'softening', wishing to maintain the status of the Pardoner as 'a mystery, an enigma—sexually anomalous, hermaphroditic, menacing,

---

[9] Steven Kruger, 'Claiming the Pardoner: Toward a Gay Reading of Chaucer's Pardoner's Tale', *Exemplaria*, 6 (1994), 115–39: 121.

[10] Ibid. 125.   [11] Ibid. 120.

[12] Ibid. 139. The appropriateness and relevance of the term 'homophobia' is of course highly problematic in face of the admission that 'homosexuality' is inadequate as a category of historical analysis. Craig Williams has confronted this methodological difficulty by drawing the conclusion that, 'Because I avoid speaking of homosexuality and of homosexuals in antiquity, it follows that I cannot predicate homophobia of ancient Romans' (Williams, *Roman Homosexuality*, 261 n. 18). A similar point could be ventured about fourteenth-century Englishmen.

[13] Kruger, 'Claiming the Pardoner', 137.

[14] Ibid. 135. Similar moves characterize two other relevant studies of the Pardoner, Glenn Burger, 'Kissing the Pardoner', *PMLA*, 107 (1992), 1143–73, and Robert S. Sturges, *Chaucer's Pardoner and Gender Theory: Bodies of Discourse* (New York, 2000). However, Burger's article uniquely posits a challenging connection between two 'open secrets', the Pardoner's supposedly deviant sexuality and the popular demand for quick 'spiritual fixes' as obtained (for example) by highly rewarding pilgrimages to merely local sites and easily gained indulgences of vast power and promise. For my reservations about the imminence of the latter 'open secret' among the Canterbury pilgrims see my article 'Reclaiming the Pardoners', *Journal of Medieval and Early Modern Studies* 33(2003), 311–34, which makes a plea for fresh scholarship on Chaucer's Pardoner *qua* pardoner. I would also quibble with Burger's reductive sexualization of the practice of 'social kissing'.

contradictory'.[15] And that is precisely where I myself want to leave the Pardoner (though I would quibble with the epithet 'menacing'),[16] where I think he *has* to be left, given the paucity of detail Chaucer has given us.

Another way to further the debate is to appeal to some of the core principles of queer theory itself. Within the contemporary academy queer theory now encompasses the study of *diverse* forms of sexual dissidence, each of which calls in question the heterosexual matrix. As Jeffrey Weeks explains, such theory reveals that 'sex, gender and desire are not necessarily reducible to the neat binaries of "heterosexuality" and "homosexuality"'; it functions as a powerful reminder of 'the perpetual inventiveness of a collective sexual politics which stretches towards different ways of being'.[17] However, 'queerness paradoxically remains in danger of keeping firmly in place the very structure it seeks to overthrow', in defining itself 'broadly against a blanket notion of heteronormativity'.[18] Given the large number of tears and tangles in the late medieval 'blanket notion of heteronormativity', such a danger should hold few fears for Chaucerians: to locate the Pardoner on one side or other of the binary divide is blatantly to travesty the complexity and contestation of his constituent discourses. But risks there certainly are. Claiming the Pardoner as a gay man (with the Host being outed as a homophobic ancestor) may imply an essentializing of 'his' sexuality—and such essentializing is precisely what queer theory has set out to challenge and disrupt. Rather, the Pardoner's 'corporeal signification', to borrow a term from Judith Butler,[19] can—and should—be read in irreducibly different ways. And such reading is effectively underpinned by the fluidity of many of the crucial medieval categories.

That fluidity may easily be illustrated. McAlpine sums up the semantic range surrounding 'mare' with admirable economy: ' "Mare" must be a term commonly used in Chaucer's day to designate a male person who, though not necessarily sterile or impotent, exhibits physical traits suggestive of femaleness, visible characteristics that were also associated with

[15] Donald R. Howard, *The Idea of the Canterbury Tales* (Berkeley, Calif., 1976), 344–5.

[16] Rather than 'menacing' I find him ultimately a pathetic figure, who is desperately in search of empowerment. However, this view is some distance away from Lee Patterson's contention that the Pardoner is best taken as a figure of despair; a reading which, in my view, lacks a sufficiency of specific textual evidence. For Patterson's latest version of this reading see his article, 'Chaucer's Pardoner on the Couch: Psyche and Clio in Medieval Literary Studies', *Speculum*, 76 (2001), 638–80.

[17] Jeffrey Weeks, *Invented Moralities: Sexual Values in an Age of Uncertainty* (Cambridge, 1995), 115.

[18] Joseph Bristow, discussing Weeks's views, in *Sexuality* (London, 1997), 221.

[19] Judith Butler, *Gender Trouble* (New York, 1990), 136.

eunuchry in medieval times and that were thought to have broad effects in the psyche and on character.'[20] But then—unfortunately, from my point of view—she continues, 'The gloss that most satisfactorily fulfills these criteria is "a homosexual" '; this despite her remark that 'even if the primary meaning of "mare" was "an effeminate male", a second meaning may have been "a possibly homosexual male" '.[21] Rather than closing down discussion, going for a single totalizing gloss, I believe that we should respect and maintain the fluidity indicated by McAlpine's original statement.[22] She claims that the Pardoner's 'physical description, once it is set in the context of medieval sexual theory', provides 'the strongest evidence of the Pardoner's possible homosexuality';[23] in my own view the evidence proves just how irresolvable the problem is.

Had the Pardoner been forcibly castrated it seems reasonable to assume that Chaucer would have informed us of that defining moment in his life. It has widely been assumed that a different kind of eunuchry is at issue; hence W. C. Curry's landmark discussion of the Pardoner's sexuality compares him to men who had been gelded but identifies the Pardoner himself as a *eunuchus a nativitate* or congenital eunuch.[24] However, it now

---

[20] McAlpine, 'The Pardoner's Homosexuality', 11.   [21] Ibid. 11, cf. 12.

[22] McAlpine acknowledges that 'the lines between [the] various sexual phenomena were fluid in medieval theory'—but from this she infers that 'references to effeminacy, hermaphroditism, and eunuchry could serve as a code for homosexuality' (13). While this (or at least some of this) may well have happened, it was certainly not inevitable.

[23] Ibid. 13.

[24] W. C. Curry, *Chaucer and the Medieval Sciences*, rev. edn. (New York, 1960), 54–70. It must be added that several scholars have accepted (somewhat uncritically) notions of actual castration, physical dismemberment, and/or absence mainly or merely as a basis for symbolic readings of Chaucer's Pardoner. Robert Miller presents him as a *eunuchus non Dei*, a sinner who has cut himself off from virtue and good works: 'Chaucer's Pardoner, The Scriptural Eunuch, and The Pardoner's Tale', *Speculum*, 30 (1955), 180–99. In ch. 6 of her *Chaucer's Sexual Poetics* (Madison, 1989), Carolyn Dinshaw argues that the Pardoner's relics at once indicate his own 'fragmentariness' (both physical and psychological) and function, quite inadequately, as 'substitutes for his own masculine lack'—they 'cannot really produce that desired integrity, and he knows it' (161–4, 167–8). Furthermore, the Pardoner reveals the nature of human language itself as it functions 'in a postlapsarian world, cut off from primary wholeness and unity: he acts according to what I call . . . eunuch hermeneutics' (158–9). Lee Patterson's recent discussion of the Pardoner ('Chaucer's Pardoner on the Couch') concludes that the notions of eunuchry and sodomy which the text adumbrates should be read symbolically, particularly since 'in later medieval England castration as a punishment for any crime is very rare, if not in fact entirely absent' (hence at this time 'the castrate or eunuch' was an altogether uncommon figure), and 'sodomy, as either social practice or ideological construct, was a minor presence in Chaucer's cultural world' (659, 660, 663). In a manner reminiscent of Miller's article, Patterson concludes that the 'direction in which medieval thought points' is 'toward symbolic sterility' (663–4). And so: for eunuchry and sodomy read *simony*, which here takes two forms, the merchandising of indulgences and false preaching. 'As a simoniac who both sells spiritual goods and fails to sow God's seed in the field of holy

seems clear that the notion of congenital eunuchry could accommodate many physical conditions, ranging from people who had been castrated or had a sexually debilitating 'birth defect'—undescended or small testicles,[25] hermaphroditism imagined or actual. My term 'actual' designates people with the distinct anatomical condition which nowadays is sometimes termed 'intersexuality'.[26] The term 'eunuch' could also be applied to men who had been rendered 'effeminate' and hence mare-like by some other medical cause. On one theory, if sperm from the right-side testicle lodged in the left side of the uterus, a womanly male would issue (ideally, such sperm should lodge in the right side of the uterus, producing a manly man); an alternative theory held that foetuses which develop in the middle of the uterus are hermaphroditic, possessing both male and female qualities.[27] Any of these conditions, it would seem, could be responsible for such aspects of the Pardoner's physical appearance as glaring eyes and beardlessness (I(A), 684, 689–90).

Alternatively, the Pardoner's body may be regarded as the product of a particular combination of the humours. Women are naturally cold and

mother church, the Pardoner would have been seen by a contemporary audience as impotent twice over' (668). But if Chaucer had wished to present the Pardoner as a spiritual sodomite *specifically*, why did he not make explicit use of this well-established and easily understood metaphor, rather than adumbrating it with the term 'mare'? Further, why did he make this symbolic connection even harder to follow by including that term within an account of the Pardoner's physical appearance rather than of his moral shortcomings?

[25] Curry himself quotes a description by the tenth-century Arabian physician Rasis of the man who 'castratus non fuit, sed sine testiculis natis vel parvissimos habens eunuchus apparet' (*Chaucer and the Medieval Sciencies*, 59). Cf. Peter of Abano's commentary on the pseudo-Aristotelian *Problemata*, which defines 'eunuchs' as those 'who lack testicles or who have small or weak ones'. *Problemata Aristotelis cum commento* (Florence, 1518), fo. 62ʳ (on *Problemata* iv. 26).

[26] Cf. the useful summary discussion of 'current-day explanations and typing' by Alice Domurat Dreger, *Hermaphrodites and the Medical Invention of Sex* (Cambridge, Mass., 1998), 35–40. Concerning frequency, Dreger offers the following 'rough statistic': 'in the United States, probably about one to three in every two thousand people are born with an anatomical conformation not common to the so-called typical male or female such that their unusual anatomies can result in confusion and disagreement about whether they should be considered female or male or something else' (42). 'Given roughly four billion births per year in the United States', she continues, 'it may be estimated that several thousand medically defined 'intersexuals' are born each year; hence 'there are now living in the United States tens of thousands of people who were born to be labelled "intersexual" ' (43).

[27] Constantine, *De coitu*, 7; in *El tradato de andrología de Constantino el Africano, Estudio y edición crítica*, ed. E. Montero Cartelle (Santiago de Compostela, 1983), 106–8. That Chaucer knew something of this treatise may be inferred from his reference to it in the *Merchant's Tale*, IV(E) 1810–11. Cf. Joan Cadden, *Meanings of Sex Difference in the Middle Ages* (Cambridge, 1993), 62–3, 93, and H. A. Kelly, 'The Pardoner's Voice, Disjunctive Narrative, and Modes of Effemination', in Robert F. Yeager and Charlotte C. Morse (eds.), *Speaking Images: Essays in Honor of V. A. Kolve* (Asheville, NC, 2001), 411–44: 419–20.

humid, whereas men are hot and dry, declares (pseudo-) Aristotle in the *Problemata*.[28] However, as Peter of Abano explains in his commentary on this text, if a man should have a cold and humid complexion, he will be woman-like in nature and behaviour.[29] The problems of such men are explained graphically by 'Aristotle': like girls during puberty, they are 'insatiable' because they are unable to emit enough seed, and so they constantly desire *coitus*.[30] Cold can, it seems, attack normative masculinity in many ways. If a man's testes are naturally cold, says Constantine the African, he tends towards effeminacy and his hair-growth is inhibited.[31] According to 'Aristotle', 'neither eunuchs nor women are hairy, because of their great moisture',[32] whereas a man 'grows hair when he begins to be capable of sexual intercourse'.[33] Indeed, abundant hair-growth is evidence of virility, a point elaborated by Evrart de Conty (*c*.1330–1405), physician to King Charles V of France (and translator into French of the *Problemata* with material from Abano's commentary). In his *Le Livre des Eschez amoureux moralisés* Evrart explains that the beard, *inter alia*, marks the distinction between the sexes and separates men from women more easily;[34] it shows man's great dignity (*grant dignité*) and powerful heat (*chaleur vertueuse*), and makes known his generative power. 'And so wise philosophers say that animals which have more hair, and birds that have

---

[28] *Problemata*, iv. 25, in *Aristotle: Problems*, ed. W. S. Hett (Cambridge, Mass., 1936–7), i. 127.

[29] *Problemata Aristotelis cum commento*, fo. 62ʳ.

[30] *Coitus* in general seems at issue here, with such a congested condition being seen as perfectly consonant with normative heterosexuality. However, both author and commentator touch obliquely on the theory that 'those with whom the semen travels to the fundament desire to be passive' sexually, whereas 'those with whom it [the semen] settles in both places', i.e. the 'normal' place and the fundament, 'desire to be both active and passive' in intercourse (*Problemata*, iv. 26; ed. Hett, i. 129). An excellent account of Peter of Abano's 'inarticulate' and 'evasive' response to this passage has been provided by Joan Cadden, 'Sciences/Silences: The Natures and Languages of "Sodomy" in Peter of Abano's *Problemata* Commentary', in K. Lochrie, P. McCracken, and J. A. Schultz (eds.), *Constructing Medieval Sexuality* (Minneapolis, 1997), 40–57.

[31] *De coitu*, 7; 96–8. Pseudo-Aristotle had even gone so far as to suggest that bare, and hence cold, feet are bad for sexual intercourse: 'the body intending sexual intercourse should be warm and moist within', so that the semen can easily flow: *Problemata*, iv. 5; ed. Hett, i. 113.

[32] *Problemata*, x. 42; ed. Hett, i. 231.   [33] *Problemata*, iv. 4; ed. Hett, i. 111–12.

[34] This function of clear sexual differentiation is, Evrart declares, the 'principal end and the greatest profit' which nature intends by the beard. If women had beards, one couldn't sufficiently tell the difference which exists, and which should exist, between men and women by nature, from which great inconvenience (*grant inconvenient*) would follow. Boys, he continues, don't have beards not because of any lack of natural heat and strength (which, as Avicenna says, they possess in abundance), but because of their excess of moisture. As young men become potent (*poissans*), they begin to grow beards. *Le Livre des Eschez amoureux moralisés*, ed. Françoise Guichard-Tesson and Bruno Roy, Bibliothèque du moyen français, 2 (Montreal, 1993), 343.

more feathers', than others of their kind 'are more potent (*poissans*) than others'.[35] There are aesthetic considerations also: 'The beard looks very good on men and is an honest and beautiful thing'. In contrast, Nature 'ordained no beard at all for women, for it would be repugnant to their complexion, which is cold compared to that of men'. Relating all this to the Pardoner, it is important to note that he did not have to be a *castratus*, or indeed any kind of eunuch at all, to lack the capacity to grow a beard; a cold and humid complexion in general, and cold testicles in particular, would have done the trick. Furthermore, hairy men were horny men, but a *lack* of facial hair could also indicate strong desire, due to the tendency of men with cold and humid complexions to suffer from trapped semen. That having been said, however, if we wish to return to the 'eunuch' (on our inclusive definition), we can do no better than enlist the help of Razi, as translated by Gerard of Cremona, who asserts that 'a man who has not been castrated but was born without testicles or with very small ones' looks 'like a eunuch, that is, he never grows a beard'.[36]

Running in parallel with those medical discourses was a moral one: the excessive love of women made a man effeminate. In his argument for 'The Sexual Normality of Chaucer's Pardoner'[37] Richard Firth Green offers *inter alia* the example of the lustful Assyrian king, Sardanapalus, who, according to Gower's *Confessio amantis*, was so beset with the fiery 'rage of love' that he quite unmanned himself, became a fish out of water:

> . . . he so rioteth,
> And wax so ferforth wommannyssh,
> That ayein kinde, as if a fissh
> Abide wolde upon the lond,
> In wommen such a lust he fond . . .
>
> (VII, 4318–22)

A less drastic moral condition was that of the effeminate man who is sexually capable but unsuccessful, an obvious case being furnished by Absolon in the *Miller's Tale*, with whom the Pardoner has much in common. It is no coincidence that in the fifteenth-century continuation of the *Canterbury Tales* known as the *Canterbury Interlude* (which prefaces

---

[35] On the comparison between hair and feathers see *Problemata*, iv. 31; 133.

[36] *De re medicine*, ii. 57, *signa eunuchi*, in *Scriptores physiognomonici Graeci et Latini*, ed. R. Foerster (Leipzig, 1893), ii. 178.

[37] Richard Firth Green, 'The Sexual Normality of Chaucer's Pardoner', *Mediaevalia*, 8 (1982), 351–8. Green has been supported by C. David Benson, 'Chaucer's Pardoner: His Sexuality and Modern Critics', *Mediaevalia*, 8 (1982), 337–49. See also much of the material in Kelly's extraordinarily learned study, 'The Pardoner's Voice'.

the *Merchant's Tale of Beryn*), the Pardoner's character has been developed with features derived from Chaucer's Absolon.[38] The *Beryn*-poet's Pardoner is sexually *capable* and heterosexually lecherous, but fails miserably in his attempt to seduce Kit the barmaid. Perhaps the later poet found in Chaucer's construct a man whose pride in his sexual prowess far exceeded his actual achievement. This figure, then, is certainly in possession of testicles; rather the point is that, like Absolon, he is unmanly in respect of his failed sexual performance—here is the locus of his inadequacy, and the reason why he is an appropriate target for insults of a type which call his manhood in question.[39] This character is clearly consonant with the one who desires a jolly wench in every town (VI(C), 453) and who asks the Wife of Bath to teach 'us yonge men' some practical philosophy in the art of love (III(D), 186–7). For the purpose of this particular argument, size doesn't matter—though small success in love might be taken as implying small testicles, and a feminoid appearance and manners could, within the economy of the narrative, bode ill for a man's chances in love.

It would seem, then, that the possibilities on offer for historicist interpretation of his sexuality are many and various. To that cornucopia I wish to contribute the argument that the eunuch-figure in medieval thought affords rich prospects for a queering of the Pardoner which moves beyond his recent reification as homosexual or indeed gay. Judith Butler writes:

If the term 'queer' is to be a site of collective contestation, the point of departure for a set of historical considerations, and futural imaginings, it will have to remain that which is, in the present, never fully owned, but always and only redeployed, twisted, queered from a prior usage.[40]

---

[38] *The Canterbury Tales: Fifteenth-Century Continuations and Additions*, ed. John M. Bowers (Kalamazoo, Mich., 1992), 60–79. Of course, the Pardoner of the *Canterbury Interlude* is in many respects a very different figure from Chaucer's; he lacks pardons, preaching, and relics. But the fact that he appears in a *fabliau* or ribald tale may be related to the Canterbury pilgrims' initial expectation of Chaucer's Pardoner: they expect him to tell them of 'ribaudrye' and want to pre-empt that (VI (C), 324–6). A radical reappraisal of the relationship between the *Beryn*-poet's Pardoner and Chaucer's has recently been offered by John Bowers, who believes that the later writer has sought to 'normalize' the original character's sexuality. 'Queering the Summoner: Same-Sex Union in Chaucer's *Canterbury Tales*', in Yeager and Morse (eds.), *Speaking Images*, 301–24: 318.

[39] Here I am thinking particularly of the function of the Pardoner's staff in the *Tale of Beryn*. Perhaps the poet got the idea from the pilgrim's staff wielded by Amant at the end of the *Roman de la Rose*, which features prominently in Jean de Meun's allegory of the impregnation of the virgin Rose. But the pun is obvious enough and no doubt could have been generated without French influence. The Pardoner gives his staff to Kit at the beginning of the tale, and subsequently demands its return, whereupon Kit's lover—clearly the dominant male here—beats him with it. The symbolism of phallic prowess is blatant.

[40] Judith Butler, *Bodies that Matter* (New York, 1993), 228.

The following reading of the Pardoner as a (possible, problematic) 'eunuch'—in part an overhaul of the Curry thesis—may be seen as such a redeployment. One of the main stumbling blocks to this approach has, of course, been the Pardoner's own womanizing claims (VI(C), 453) and his assertion to the Wife of Bath that he plans to wed a wife (III(D), 163–8). Proponents of the 'eunuch' theory—and indeed, advocates of the 'homosexual' theory—have had to read these passages as mere bluster and bravado, designed to mask the Pardoner's actual physical condition or alternatively to get a laugh from the Canterbury pilgrims who have drawn their own conclusions about his sexual impotence (if he is a eunuch) or his sexual preferences (if he is a homosexual). But on at least one body of contemporary opinion, a eunuch—on certain definitions of the condition in question—was deemed capable of marriage, both physically and legally. That is the main thrust of the following argument which, far from attempting to reclaim Chaucer's construct as heterosexually normative, seeks to question the very notion of 'normativity' within critical debate on the Pardoner.

Some preliminary clarifications must be made. There was a general assumption that possession of testicles is essential to maleness. For instance, Arnold of Villanova (who produced a substantial number of medical treatises at Montpellier in the 1290s) quoted 'the ancients' as believing that the testicles were the principal organs inasmuch as they supplied the *virtus* (virility, power) of the whole body.[41] Peter of Spain (who taught medicine at Sienna during the period 1246–50) declares that, while 'sexual desire' (*desiderum in coitu*) comes from the liver, the 'act of love is in the testicles' and the natural 'stimulation to intercourse' is located 'in one member, and this is in the testicles'.[42] Little wonder, then, that castration or genital deficiency was deemed a major threat to male integrity and identity. However, throughout the Middle Ages castration normally meant the removal of the testicles but not the penis, *pace* the assumptions

---

[41] *De coitu* (Basel, 1585), 307–8; cf. Yves Ferroul, 'Abelard's Blissful Castration', in Jeffrey J. Cohen and Bonnie Wheeler (eds.), *Becoming Male in the Middle Ages* (New York, 1997), 129–49: 141.

[42] From the B-version of his commentary on Constantine's *Viaticum*; see Mary Frances Wack, *Lovesickness in the Middle Ages: The 'Viaticum' and its Commentaries* (Philadelphia, 1990), 234–7. According to Aristotle the testicles are not necessary for generation; he thought that 'they play only an external role in the emission of semen, a role that was not essential and could be missing'. Galen, however, saw them as essential, 'as a place in which the already produced semen could be further elaborated and prepared for its generative role'. See Aidan McGrath, *A Controversy Concerning Male Impotence*, Analecta Gregoriana, 247, Series Facultatis Iuris Canonici, sectio B, n. 49 (Rome, 1988), 32.

of some recent discussions of Chaucer's Pardoner.[43] Therefore eunuchs retained feelings of sexual desire—they could have penile erections, and indeed there was a view (here exemplified by the words of St John Chrysostom) that 'far from assuaging the lusts of the flesh', castration 'exacerbates them'.[44] One may also recall here Shakespeare's eunuch Mardian (a *castratus*), who has 'fierce affections' and thinks lasciviously of 'what Venus did with Mars' (*Antony and Cleopatra*, I. v).

There was certainly a widespread assumption that a man who was deprived of his testicles, or who had lacked them at birth, was incapable of fathering a child. But, given that 'eunuchs' generally retained their penises (and once again we must emphasize that 'eunuchry' could include such medical conditions as undescended or abnormal testicles), some authorities actually believed that they *were* capable of semination. Furthermore, given that in 'eunuchs' the capacity for sexual intercourse remained, was that not sufficient to satisfy at least one of the reasons for marriage, irrespective of whether they were capable of begetting children or not? In his *Sentences* Peter Lombard defined two *causae matrimonii*, the procreation of children and (following the Fall from Eden) the provision of a 'remedy' (*remedium*) for concupiscence,[45] the point being that, as St Paul said, it was better to marry than to burn (1 Cor. 7: 9): the institution functioned to control and contain sexual desire. Was it not better, then, for lustful 'eunuchs' to marry? After all, the marriage of old and sterile men had been defended, by St Augustine and many others. Some passages in the *Decretales* of Pope Gregory IX suggest that it is the *potentia coeundi* (the physical capacity for intercourse) which is required of both partners, not the *potentia generandi*.[46] On this argument, if a given 'eunuch' was capable of the former, it might be concluded that there was no impediment in canon law to his marriage.

Considerable controversy came to centre on the issue of whether the ejaculate of 'eunuchs' was 'valid' (*validum semen*, later termed *verum semen*, 'true seed').[47] Predictably, the discussion was plagued by

[43] As e.g. Dinshaw, *Chaucer's Sexual Poetics*, 165–8, and H. Marshall Leicester, *The Disenchanted Self: Representing the Subject in the Canterbury Tales* (Berkeley, Calif., 1990), 411.

[44] Yves Ferroul, 'Abelard's Blissful Castration', 136.

[45] Cf. Chaucer's formulations of the two causes, in the *Wife of Bath's Prologue*, III(D), 126–8, and the *Parson's Tale*, X, 919.

[46] Cf. McGrath, *Controversy*, 57.

[47] Cf. McGrath, *Controversy*. This impressively learned study takes its point of departure from the brief *Cum frequenter* of Pope Sixtus V (27 June 1587). In Spain some eunuchs and spadones who lacked both testicles were getting married and claiming the right to do so; 'they based this claim on their alleged capacity for the act of intercourse which they had discovered

terminological confusion and failure to make clear distinctions between the different kinds of condition which fell under the general definition of 'eunuchry'. But the central issue was clear enough: might the marriage debt be paid by penile emission of a kind which could not result in pregnancy? Opinion was, of course, divided. Guido de Baysio ('Archidiaconus'; d. 1313) rules out marriage for a man lacking both testicles on the grounds that both the *causa prolis* and the *causa vitandae fornicationis* must be satisfied;[48] similar views are expressed by Aegidius Bellamera (d. 1392).[49] Raymond of Peñiafort's treatment is indecisive,[50] while Hostiensis promotes the 'one testicle' theory, i.e. the notion that a man with only one testicle may marry,[51] presumably because this enables him to produce true seed. Dominicus de Soto (1492–1560) took it as an 'infallible and most certain rule' that a man who is incapable of semination is incapable of marriage, but his understanding of 'semination' is not altogether clear, and it has been suggested that he means seed of *any* kind, including seed which lacked the power to impregnate.[52]

Indeed, even among the many voices raised in support of the notion that a man lacking both testicles may contract marriage there was some disagreement as to whether he must have the ability to emit true seed. In his *Summa super Decretum* Hugutio of Pisa (d. 1210) suggests that marriage can be contracted by a man who emits semen even though it may not be suitable for generation.[53] Joannes Teutonicis (d. 1245), glossing Gratian, begins by seeming to deny the possibility of eunuchs marrying, but later states that erection and penetration are important, rather than semination.[54] The same opinion was held by Michael Medina (d. 1578)[55]

during illicit [i.e. extra-marital] relations with women' (19). So the Nuncio had asked the pope's advice. The response was that without the production of true seed a man is impotent and incapable of contracting marriage. McGrath seeks to reconcile this with the Decree of the Sacred Congregation for the Doctrine of the Faith of 13 May, 1977, which holds that 'ejaculation of semen elaborated in the testicles is not required for true marital intercourse' (5).

[48] *Rosarium decretorum*, pars 2, C. 32, qu. 7, c. 25 (Venice, 1481), unfo.

[49] *Remissorius, qui posterior est tomus commentariorum in Gratiani Decreta*, C. 32, qu. 7, 6a pars (Lyon, 1550), fos. 55ᵛ–56ʳ.

[50] *Summa de poenitentia et matrimonii, cum glossis Joannis de Friburgo*, De matrimonio, lib. iv, tit. 16, 3 (Rome, 1603), 560. Cf. the discussion in McGrath, *Controversy*, 70, 85–6.

[51] *Summa aurea*, lib. iv: de frigidis etc. (Lyon, 1568), fo. 315ʳ⁻ᵛ.

[52] *In quartum sententiarum*, lib. 1, dist. 34, qu. 1, art. 2 (Venice, 1575), ii. 246; cf. McGrath, *Controversy*, 94–7.

[53] *Summa super decreto*, quoted from Vatican Library, MS Vat. Lat. 2280, fo. 288ᵛ, by McGrath, *Controversy*, 69, cf. 86.

[54] Cf. McGrath, *Controversy*, 67–8.

[55] *De sacrorum hominum continentia*, lib. V, c. 77 (Venice, 1569), 498.

and Bartholomaeus Ugolinus (d. 1610).[56] A particularly full account is provided in the *Sentences* commentary of Peter of La Palud (d. 1342), who contrasts the *act* and the *effect* of generation (the latter meaning the procreation of children).[57] Thanks to this distinction, Peter can easily support the marriage of old men who lack the capacity to impregnate their partners. As far as castrates and 'spadones' are concerned, if a man is incapable of both the act and the effect, no marriage can take place. Marriage is quite possible, however, for a man who can have an erection (*virga erigitur*) and perform the sexual act even though the seed which he produces is 'invalid'. If a man has an erection but is incapable of emitting seed, then he may be able to deflower a virgin (here Peter quotes Ecclesiasticus 20: 2) but he cannot marry. St Antoninus of Florence (1389–1458) follows La Palud in singling out as the crucial factor the emission of seed, even though it is *invalidum ad generandum*.[58]

Here, one might say, is some good news for the Pardoner: even if he is a 'eunuch' he would be capable of contracting marriage, according to a substantial body of contemporary opinion. Hence there is no reason to dismiss either his lust for a wench in every town or his professed desire to marry as screens for physical and legal impossibilities. Whatever else is doubtful about the Pardoner, we can allow him his penis—and that, in the minds of many, was sufficient to allow such a man to marry, no matter whether he had small testicles, just one (of whatever size), or none at all. Others would have insisted on his ability to produce (some sort of) seed. More good news: many thinkers believed that 'eunuchs' could do just that.

I am *not*, however, suggesting that the definitive answer to the problem of the Pardoner's sexuality is to read him as a 'heterosexual eunuch', however tempting that prospect may be. Much of the above material could, of course, be used in a claiming of the Pardoner as a 'homosexual' or a 'bisexual' eunuch.[59] My purpose has been to present yet another possibility, in support of Howard's view (or at least part of Howard's view) that our Pardoner remains 'an enigma' who resists reduction to a single sexual

[56] *De sacramentis novae legis tabulae perutiles*, De matrimonio, cap. 19, n. 1 (Rimini, 1587), fos. 127ᵛ–128ʳ.
[57] *In quartum sententiarum*, dist. 34, qu. 2, art. 1 (Venice, 1493), fo. 170ᵛ.
[58] *Summae sacrae theologiae, pars tertia*, lib. 1, cap. 12, 2 (Venice, 1571), fo. 12ᵛ.
[59] For a recent discussion of the theorizing of bisexuality, together with a critique of some versions of queer theory, see Jonathan Dollimore, *Sex, Literature, and Censorship* (Cambridge, 2001).

identity or to one set of sexual preferences. As Glenn Burger and Steven Kruger say, 'Historical work itself has written out or over what might have been queer, unstable, nonnormative in medieval sex and culture.'[60] I submit that consideration of the Pardoner's deviant body in view of the range of conditions covered by 'eunuchry' in Chaucer's day can help to restore a sense of such instabilities.

· To summarize the state of play so far: the Pardoner may be seen as a man (1) who has undescended or abnormal testicles, or (2) who was generated on the left side or in the middle of his mother's womb. Either condition, it would seem, was capable of producing a feminoid appearance, involving such features as glaring eyes and beardlessness. Shifting the principles of categorization somewhat, three further possibilities may be added, once again from our previous discussion: (3) a man could become effeminate due to his excessive sexual desire for women, (4) a man who looked like a woman was likely to have his masculinity called in question, and (5) the same was true of the man who lusted after women but was dismally unsuccessful in his pursuit of them. None of these five situations or conditions necessarily involved anything other than heterosexual normativity (but already an elastic definition of 'normativity' is being assumed here). This could be said to apply even in the case of the congenital 'eunuch' who, as I have argued above, was seen as capable of heterosexual desire and legally entitled to marry (though much depended on which canon lawyer or theologian you talked to).

Moving the argument a stage further, it may be noted that *any* of these possibilities could give rise to jokes about the protagonist 'lacking balls', and hence being like a *geldyng or a mare*, the semantic common denominator between the two terms here being exploited.[61] Recent discussions of the dynamics of insult in the Pardoner's portrait have tended to focus on (allegedly) homophobic verbal abuse. But there are other possibilities. The following extracts from a poem by the thirteenth-century *jongleur* Gautier le Leu provide an excellent point of departure for an exploration of some of them.

> Nos avons çaiens un bruhier,
> un durfeüt, un hebohet.
> Ahi! Con Damerdex me het
> qui fui des bons vallés aquius,

---

[60] Glenn Burger and Steven F. Kruger (eds.), *Queering the Middle Ages* (Minneapolis, 2001), p. xvii.

[61] Cf. Patterson, 'Chaucer's Pardoner on the Couch', 661.

et des cortois et des gentius,
si pris cest caitif par nature. . . .
Et cis ribaus me tient plus vil
que le femier de son cortil,
mais je sai bien, par Saint Eloi,
qu'il n'est mie de bone loi,
ains est de çaus del Mont Wimer:
il n'a soing de dames amer.

(398–403, 425–30)[62]

What have we here? An impotent, n'er-do-well, a wretch! Ah me! The Lord God must hate me! That I, who disdained fine young men, who were well born and courteous, should then take up with this congenital weakling! . . . This scoundrel shows me less regard than he does the dungheap in his barnyard. But I know well, by Saint Loy, that his morals are no better than that of those on Mount Wimer. He doesn't care about loving women.[63]

Montwimer was perhaps the oldest Catharist centre in France and certainly the principal one in the country north of the Loire. In May 1239 about 180 heretics were burned there, accusations of homosexuality having figured in the charges against them. But this poem is far from being an actual account of how a man emulates those heretics by preferring sex with men to intercourse with the woman who is railing against him here. The point is rather that the sexual desires of this widow-woman are insatiable; no new partner can please her, no matter how hard he tries—and that particular poor *caitif* has tried long and hard. 'Lady, you have a greedy mouth in you that too often demands to be fed. It has tired my poor old war-horse out. I've just withdrawn him all shrunken and sore. One cannot work so much without getting weary and limp.' As Gautier remarks, though her new lover may 'be lively and quick and can well strike and plunge, he will still be despised in the morning'.[64] In this poem, which elaborates antifeminist clichés about the prodigious sexual appetites of widows, the coded accusation of homosexuality functions as a

[62] Ed. Charles H. Livingston, *Le Jongleur Gautier le Leu: étude sur les fabliaux* (Cambridge, Mass., 1951), 178–9.

[63] McAlpine uses this poem also, but in a (very free and misleading) different translation and to a different end; 'The Pardoner's Homosexuality', 12–13. I am grateful to David Hult for valuable discussion of the poem's difficult opening lines, and here draw on the translation of Robert Hellman and Richard O'Gorman, conveniently reprinted in The *Canterbury Tales: Nine Tales and the General Prologue*, ed. V. A. Kolve and Glending Olson (New York, 1989), 320–6.

[64] *The Canterbury Tales*, ed. Kolve and Olson, 324.

means of insulting the hapless partner's virility, rather than as a matter-of-fact declaration of his impotence, let alone of any actual sexual deviancy. The man (identified as young, and hence at his sexual peak) is unambiguously and actively heterosexual, but not man enough for the ball-breaking *veuve*. 'Goliath gapes too often. I can't satisfy him; I'm likely to die before I do! . . . You have so milked and drained me that I am half dead, and half mad too.'

By the same token, *geldyng* and *mare* are neither literal description nor scientific definition—but meant to be insulting. And in insult there frequently is some crucial distance between the offensive accusation and the actuality (indeed, in many cases the degree of insult seems to be in direct proportion to the distance—the further the better). How best to call a man's virility in question because he is *either* very interested in women but effeminate in appearance (perhaps due to that very interest) *or* because his heterosexual achievements never quite live up to his own high opinion of his womanizing skills? This could be done simply and effectively by characterizing him as a man with no balls—a gelding or a mare, indeed. The idea of castration is obviously evoked there, and if 'mare' should carry the suggestion of homosexuality, so much the better—the insult is all the stronger. But this does not mean, of course, that the individual in question is actually lacking his physical equipment or does not know how to use it properly (according to medieval norms); to suppose that would be to misunderstand what kind of language is in use here, to miss the point of the mockery. The constituent discourses of effeminacy have been enlisted in the service of caricature. A form of caricature which (on this argument) should not be mistaken for the homophobic mockery of one who smells a gay pardoner in the wind.

Furthermore, we must concede the existence of actions which are so horrendous that no insult, however ugly or literally inaccurate, seems too nasty to be hurled at their perpetrators. In particular, there is a long-established tradition of using sexual slurs to strike at deviancies of a kind which have little if anything to do with sexuality. Generations of British schoolchildren have known that

> Hitler
> Has only got one ball,
> Goering
> Has two, but they are small.
> Himmler
> Has something similar,

But Goebbels
Has no balls
At all!

This (anonymous, of course) song, sung to the tune of the 'Colonel Bogey' march, dates from the period 1939/40, when Britain faced invasion and cultural annihilation by Hitler and his henchmen; within that historical context, its acerbic humour is quite understandable. Contemporary parallels are not hard to find. According to the British *News of the World* (4 November 2001), America's public enemy no.1, Osama bin Laden, once lived a 'degenerate' life, being 'forced to pay hookers to satisfy his cravings because he was a sexual inadequate'. His rage against the United States is said to stem from the humiliating reaction of an American woman, who laughed when she saw his 'minuscule sexual organs'. It would seem, then, that he 'Has two, but they are small'. Another newspaper published on the same day, the *Mail on Sunday*, assured its readers that 'Mohammad Atta and at least five' of the other 11 September hijackers 'were secretly gay'.[65] 'Demonization' this may be termed, but that sounds like a weasel word if the people under attack are perceived as genuinely demonic and hence deserving of everything they get hurled at them. Who cares about offending the sensibilities of a Hitler or bin Laden? Interpretive relativism must have its limits, if any kind of moral judgement is to operate; otherwise we are faced with the terrifying and totally unacceptable prospect of a world in which nothing is sacred, nothing is right or wrong, but everything is equally true, and the will to fight evil or an enemy is eviscerated. On the logic of this argument, no insult directed against the Pardoner can be too offensive, no slur too extreme, given his utter lack of moral scruples and disgusting greed for material reward. He is deeply objectionable for reasons which have nothing to do with his sexuality, but reference to that sexuality (however understood) is an effective if crude way of expressing well-founded disapproval.

And yet: such righteous indignation need not destroy the thought that however morale-boosting colourful claims of the kind illustrated above may be, they give a bad name to physical conditions and sexualities which are perceived as non-normative. The very terms of reference which are drawn upon in such publicly sanctioned verbal abuse bring out the

---

[65] Here I follow the report 'A tale of sex and violence' published in the *Guardian* (10 Nov. 2001), *The Editor*, 5.

deep-seated intolerances of that public.[66] They depend on an assumption that out there are groups of supposedly deficient or deviant people who really perform the 'unmanly' or 'unnatural' actions which the rhetoric of insult implicates. But the Pardoner's relationship to one or other of those groups remains problematic. And the matter cannot be resolved through reference to his terminal exchange with Harry Bailly. There are several possible motives apart from homophobia for the Host's verbal assault on the Pardoner. Bailly has just been singled out, in front of all his fellow pilgrims, as the person among them who is most enveloped in sin, and throughout the Pardoner's narrative his profession of innkeeper has been disparaged. Does he, then, reach for homophobic insult to express an anger which has arisen from other causes? That interpretation has some appeal. But there is nothing distinctively or conclusively homophobic about the Host's language. If the Pardoner's claim about his rampant philandering (VI(C), 453) is taken at face value, then this character's 'coillons' would make a prize relic (much sought after as a cure for impotence, if we may pursue this discourse of mock-sainthood a little further!), and the threat of their removal would hit the Pardoner where it really hurts.[67] On this reading his sexual pride is the Host's target—a cruel cut indeed. If on the other hand the Pardoner is to be seen an an Absolon-like heterosexual inadequate—or as 'lacking balls' in any of the other ways outlined above—then the 'relic' in question would be rather a poor specimen, not unlike those small fragments of bone which have survived in their 'seintuaries' to the present day, and their display would reveal just how little physical support the Pardoner's pretensions really have. In short, there is much room for interpretation of the Host's dynamic of insult in heterosexist terms.

The Pardoner's actual 'homosexuality' (or inclination to homosexual acts) remains unproved and is (I believe) unprovable. Moreover, it is not even clear—and here the case of the Pardoner parts company with those of the psychopaths mentioned above—whether Chaucer meant to raise

---

[66] To state the obvious (which nevertheless bears constant statement and acting upon): it is perfectly possible—and ethically preferable—to name the evils which men do without implicating other activities that have no necessary causal relationship with them.

[67] This approach finds much support in the arguments of Benson and Green (cited in n. 37 above). See also Green's later article, 'The Pardoner's Pants (and Why They Matter)', *Studies in the Age of Chaucer*, 15 (1993), 131–45, where it is suggested that the Host's reference to his adversary's dirty breeches (VI(C), 948–9) recalls a popular *fabliau* narrative wherein a friar or some other lecherous clergyman cuckolds a husband who then discovers his discarded trousers; the wife's honour is saved when this garment is taken to be the relic of a saint.

the spectre of homosexuality within his rhetoric of insult. In particular, the sense of *mare*=homosexual has not been established beyond all reasonable doubt in the case of General Prologue I(A) 691, *pace* the *Riverside Chaucer's* staggeringly confident gloss, which does not even add the prudent caveat of a question-mark.[68] The verbal parallels adduced have been few indeed; Walter of Châtillon's complaint about how 'men make women of themselves, and stallions become mares (*se mares effeminant et equa fit equus*)', is the most telling.[69] This is hardly indicative of a well-established and widely understood meaning. *Mare*, in crucial association with *geldyng*, may simply have the implication of 'lacking balls', however metaphorically or literally that may be taken, in line with whichever of the readings outlined above.[70]

Attempts to bolster the interpretation of *mare* as 'homosexual' by interpreting the Pardoner's playful escapade with the Summoner in terms of homoerotic attraction are also, in my view, unconvincing; that passage can be explained by the scenario of 'two wild and crazy guys ready for a little fun', to borrow a phrase from David Benson.[71] Engaged in contrapuntal performance of heteronormativity, they sing their litany of mutual priapic prowess, noisily claiming their positions as dominant males in the *olde daunce* of heterosexual love. Revelling in their fantasy of sexual conceit, the Pardoner and Summoner are probably on the brink of homosocial boasting about who can have the most women or piss the highest. 'Hoot . . . and lecherous as a sparwe' (626), the Summoner seems to be a sexual predator who preys on 'The yonge girles of the diocise' (664).[72] Furthermore, he is described as 'A good felawe to have his concubyn | A twelf month' and then desert her (650–1), the term 'good felawe' (as we know from Sir John Clanvowe's discussion thereof) having currency as a label for a certain kind of urban *bon viveur* who spent a lot of time in

[68] *Riverside Chaucer*, 34 (gloss on l. 691).

[69] *Medieval Latin Poems of Male Love and Friendship*, ed. and trans. Thomas Stehling (New York, 1984), 80–1; the parallel was noted by Jill Mann, *Chaucer and Medieval Estates Satire* (Cambridge, 1973), 146.

[70] Thus I have no problem *in principle* with the hypothesis that part of the force of the *geldyng* or *mare* gibe derived from notions of effeminacy that (*inter alia*) resonated with a category of men who were seen as practising sodomy or even as sodomites. My point is simply that firm evidence for this specific possibility is hard to come by, and there are other possibilities available.

[71] Benson, 'Chaucer's Pardoner', 343.

[72] Though at *Miller's Tale*, I(A), 3769, Chaucer uses 'gerl' to refer to a young woman, the term could designate a child of either sex: see the *Middle English Dictionary*, s.v. *girl(e)*; cf. Morton Bloomfield, 'Chaucer's Summoner and the Girls of the Diocese', *Philological Quarterly*, 28 (1949), 503–7. It is possible that in the context of the description of the Summoner, 'yonge girles' is meant to signal the indiscriminate nature of lust; cf. our following discussion.

taverns and brothels.[73] Clearly, the Pardoner and he have a lot in common—little wonder that Chaucer should describe him as the Summoner's 'freend' and 'compeer' (670). But they seem very far from being 'the first recognizable "gay couple" in English literature', as John Bowers puts it;[74] their sexual predilections may well lie elsewhere.

And yet: Bowers's queering of the Summoner highlights an issue of the first importance for any consideration of medieval sexual preference. 'The sexual axis operative in this culture was defined more precisely as chaste/lecherous rather than straight/gay, and a lecherous man was thought to have no bounds in the expression of his sexual appetites.'[75] The truth of that contention is borne in upon us again and again, by a wide range of medieval sources. 'Remove whores from the world and you will fill it with sodomy', declares the fourth book of the treatise *De regimine principum* which was, at least in part, authored by Thomas Aquinas;[76] here the assumption is that if inordinate sexual desire is denied one outlet it will seek another, irrespective of gender. If no woman is available, a man's desires may be satisfied with another man. In other words, hereterosexual lust is bad, while homosexual lust is very bad—but they are on the same scale, and there is no doubt about which is the lesser of the two evils. Similar reasoning underpins one of the recommendations in the Lollard *Twelve Conclusions*: the clergy, who live in luxurious conditions, should be married, to guard them against falling into homosexual practices.[77] In *Cleanness*, when the Sodomites demand that the beautiful angels (described as 'myry' young men, with flowing silk-like hair and beardless chins, 787–91) should be handed over to them, Lot offers his daughters in their place. Lust, it would seem, is no respecter of persons, or of bodies—as is made abundantly clear by a poem 'Against Intemperate Love [written] in an Assumed Voice (*sub assumta parabola*)' which has survived in a German manuscript of the late twelfth century:

[73] *The Works of Sir John Clanvowe*, ed. V. I. J. Scattergood (Cambridge, 1975), 71–2.
[74] Bowers, 'Queering the Summoner', 305.   [75] Ibid. 302.
[76] *De regimine principum*, iv. 14, in *Opera omnia* (Parma, 1852–72), xvi. 281. This notion has a long history. In Renaissance Venice, the authorities encouraged female prostitutes to offer themselves on designated *ponti delle tette* ('tit bridges'), thus saving young men from same-sex involvements.
[77] English text in Anne Hudson, *Selections from English Wycliffite Writings* (Cambridge, 1978), 25; for a Latin version see *Fasciculi zizaniorum Magistri Johannis Wyclif*, ed. W. W. Shirley (London, 1858), 360–9. According to this account and the Latin treatise which Roger Dymmok wrote in refutation of the *Conclusions*, they were pinned to the doors of Westminster Hall during the session of Parliament in 1395. See further the excellent discussion in Carolyn Dinshaw, *Getting Medieval: Sexualities and Communities, Pre- and Postmodern* (Durham, NC, 1999), 57–99.

Langueo quippe volens, medicinam cogito nolens. . . .
Dilexi multas parvas puer et vir adultas;
dilexi multos parvos puer et vir adultos.

(14, 22–3)

I am truly sick with desire; I know the remedy and don't want it. . . .
As a boy I loved many little girls, and as a man many women;
As a boy I loved many little boys, as a man I have loved men.[78]

All this is very far from any sense of distinctive and defining sexual preference, a substantial distance away from the concept of 'gay identity'.
What we are dealing with here is a *continuum* of erotic possibility.[79] It
would be rash, then, to assert that the Pardoner and the Summoner are
physiologically and/or psychologically and/or morally *in*capable of same-
sex unions, either with each other or with other men, though there is no
clear evidence, I believe, for the view that Chaucer wanted them to be
read as having acted in that way or being interested in doing so. Furthermore, that erotic continuum is paralleled and supported by medieval
medical discourses which seem to accept that Nature is eminently capable of producing a wide range of biological configurations: womanly
women, manly women, hermaphrodites, womanly men, manly men;
men with one, two or no testicles, with large, medium-sized or small
testicles. . . . Terms such as 'normal' and 'abnormal', 'heterosexual' and
'homosexual', thus stand revealed as constitutive of inadequate binaries
which obscure rather than clarify medieval thought about gender.

At the very least we should sustain 'a certain ironic distance' from such
terms, imagining quotation marks around their every occurrence.[80]
Chaucer's Pardoner confounds 'the naturalized appearance of gender in
its heterosexual guise', to borrow a phrase from Joseph Bristow's commentary on Judith Butler.[81] And there are excellent prospects for a type of
queer theory which accepts just how queering the relevant medieval discourses can be—especially when they are freed from the normalizing, bi-
narizing tendencies of other medieval discourses on the one hand, and of
much modern scholarship on the other. Of course, we should not exaggerate or overplay the cultural status of those queering discourses; the
hegemony of heteronormative ideology in Chaucer's day is not to be

---

[78] *Poems of Male Love*, ed. and trans. Stehling, 90–1.
[79] On this topic, in addition to Bowers's discussion see Carol J. Clover, 'Regardless of Sex:
Men, Women and Power in Early Northern Europe', *Speculum*, 67 (1993), 363–87.
[80] To borrow phrases from Williams, *Roman Homosexuality*, 6.
[81] Bristow, *Sexuality*, 215.

denied. But neither should they be written out of history, their purchase in current criticism resisted. At the risk of sounding offensively 'queerer than thou', I would venture the suggestion that some of the 'queer' Pardoners we have been offered are just not queer enough.

Ohio State University

What's the Pope Got to Do with It?: Forgery, Didacticism, and Desire in the Clerk's Tale

Larry Scanlon

I. Unfinished Business: Didacticism and the Crux

The didactic has become historicism's final frontier. With the advent of the New Historicism and related trends, the problem of the didactic, traditionally central to the study of the literary past, has receded into the distance.[1] Where they have addressed didacticism at all, these newer trends have been most comfortable converting the problem to a matter of ideology, glossing a text's didactic aspirations with a particular set of contemporaneous political and ideological interests, or treating them as an alibi for such interests. But the new forms of historicism have largely failed to

---

[1] The term *new historicism* was coined by Stephen Greenblatt in the introduction to a special double issue of *Genre*, 'The Forms of Power and the Power of Forms in the Renaissance', *Genre*, 15/1 and 2 (1982). From the very beginning its status was largely heuristic (Greenblatt describing it 'as no single critical practice', p. 5). The term is most precise when used of Renaissance studies, the field where it originated. Its application to medieval studies is particularly vexed, in part because the trend it describes emerged a few years later than in the Renaissance, at a point when, as Lee Patterson declared, the term was already 'irredeemably vague' ('Introduction: Critical Historicism and Medieval Studies', in Patterson (ed.), *Literary Practice and Social Change in Britain, 1380–1530* (Berkeley, Calif., 1990), 1), and in part because, as many medievalists have complained, the Renaissance New Historicists typically adopted an extremely hackneyed view of the Middle Ages. Nevertheless, Renaissance New Historicism had an enormous influence on medievalists, especially those working on Middle English. Moreover, the rough and ready definition Louis Adrian Montrose offers, a fascination with 'the historicity of texts and the textuality of history' ('Professing the Renaissance: The Poetics and Politics of Culture', in H. Aram Veeser (ed.), *The New Historicism* (New York, 1989), 15; cited approvingly by Greenblatt in *Learning to Curse: Essays in Early Modern Culture* (London, 1990), 3), fits the subsequent trend in medieval studies as well as it does the original one in Renaissance studies. It is that wide variety of work with which I am concerned here, and I employ the more neutral, if even vaguer term 'newer historicism' as a convenient catch-all. For a survey and evaluation of such work in Middle English studies, see David Lawton's excellent 'Literary History and Cultural History', *New Medieval Literatures*, 1 (1997), 237–69.

confront the didactic on its own terms.[2] In their desire to contrast them-selves with older historicisms and to demonstrate their congeniality to textual analysis, they have tended to adopt the vanguardist stance both New Critical formalism and poststructuralist theory have in common. For the older historicism, in the didactic text the past spoke its beliefs plainly and unequivocally. For formalism, moral discourse voided a text's literary specificity; its literariness was thus to be found in precisely those moments when it resisted the didactic, and by extension, its own histori-cal moment. For the newer historicism, under the influence of poststruc-turalism, 'literariness' morphed into 'textuality', yet the resistance to the didactic lingered, reinforced by new historicism's necessary focus on the synchronic relations between a text and its social context. Didactic claims typically present themselves in transcendent terms; a synchronic analysis will almost inevitably be forced to translate them into synchronic terms (i.e. as the expression of a particular ideological or political interest), or to read their relation to the historical as some form of resistance.

New historicism's overriding commitment to the synchronic can be summed up by its characteristic dependence on the anecdote. As Cather-ine Gallagher and Stephen Greenblatt explain in their retrospective ac-count, the anecdote provides 'the touch of the real', that is, it recovers 'a confident conviction of reality, without giving up the power of literature to sidestep or evade the quotidian and without giving up a minimally so-phisticated understanding that any text depends upon the absence of the bodies and voices it represents'.[3] Although the anecdotal method set out

---

[2]   Catherine Brown's recent *Contrary Things: Exegesis, Dialectic and the Poetics of Didacticism* (Stanford, Calif., 1998) is an important exception.

[3]   Catherine Gallagher and Stephen Greenblatt, *Practicing New Historicism* (Chicago, 2000), 31. It is worth noting that the phrase 'a minimally sophisticated understanding that any text de-pends upon the absence of the bodies and voices it represents' tacitly acknowledges the large con-ceptual debt new historicism owes to deconstruction. Absence is one of the key terms in *Of Grammatology* and a number of other works by Derrida (a term Derrida himself appropriated from Lacan). Though accurately regarded as Foucaultian, the newer historicisms are most Fou-caultian in their notions of history. New historicist studies quite typically combine a decon-structive reading of a text's internal dynamics with a Foucaultian analysis of its social context. Greenblatt has elsewhere noted that what he values most in the anecdote is its 'insistence on con-tingency' (*Learning*, 5); in *Practicing*, he and Gallagher argue that the anecdote provides the methodological foundation for New Historicism's commitment to 'counterhistory', to 'delayed and alternative chronologies . . . resistances to change . . . unevenness' and 'the reality of unre-alized possibilities' (47). Even as it enables 'an escape from conventional canonicity' into the re-alities of history, the anecdote also enables the new historicist practitioner to elude the stereotypes of historical metanarratives which deconstruction and poststructuralism were so ruthlessly exposing (31). In their introduction, Gallagher and Greenblatt compare the move be-yond the canonical to the culture as a whole with 'what Ezra Pound in an early essay calls "the

not to 'epitomise epochal truths' but to 'undermine them', its indis-
putable success has all the same had the effect of reinforcing conventional
schemas of periodization.[4] The anecdote is a synchronic structure *par
excellence*, and any critical method reliant on it must always seek the in-
telligibility of a literary object in its immediate historical context. The
problem of the diachronic will necessarily be bracketed. This essay will
venture into the forgotten territory of the didactic, and it will argue that
didactic can be properly understood only as a diachronic problem. My
text is the *Clerk's Tale*, Chaucer's version of the Griselda story, arguably the
most influential and widely disseminated didactic narrative medieval
culture ever produced. Certainly the story has had an extraordinary durability. Appearing first as the final tale in Bocaccio's *Decameron*, it generated hundreds of retellings in half a dozen languages between the
mid-fourteenth century and the mid-eighteenth, retellings which thereafter continued at a slower pace right up to the present. With the obvious
exception of the Arthurian legends, no medieval narrative has had a
broader and more influential posterity than this tale, with its odd combination of piety, male aggression, and feminine submission. Moreover,
what is most remarkable about this posterity is its repeated traversal of
period boundaries. Unlike the Arthurian legends, the Griselda story is
specifically late medieval, and the zenith of its influence extends through
the Middle Ages to the Renaissance, and through the Renaissance to the
Enlightenment. In the case of England the continuity can be traced with
precision, for the story literally connects Chaucer to Richardson, the first
vernacular *auctor* to the founder of domestic fiction.[5]

Contrary to the modernist stereotype which takes all didactic texts to
be fundamentally closed, the *Clerk's Tale* is radically open, rising out of a
welter of historical trends, and aspiring, through its effects on the moral

---

method of Luminous Detail" whereby we attempt to isolate significant or interpreting "detail"
from the mass of traces that have survived in the archive' (15). As the historical anecdote is no less
fictional 'in the sense of things made' than a literary work (52), the deployment of anecdotes puts
the new historicist literary scholar on an equal footing with the historian, demonstrating that
historical materials are as receptive to literary-like close readings as the literary texts.

    [4] Gallagher and Greenblatt, *Practicing*, 51. As Gallagher and Greenblatt themselves acknowl-
edge, when counterhistory successfully displaces 'prevailing modes of historical thought and
methods of research . . . it ceases to be "counter" ' (52).

    [5] For the influence of the Griselda story on Richardson, see Veronica Bassil, 'The Faces of
Griselda: Chaucer, Prior, and Richardson', *Texas Studies in Literature and Language*, 26 (1984),
157–82. For the dispersion of the story between Chaucer and Richardson, see Lee Bliss, 'The Renaissance Griselda: A Woman for All Seasons', *Viator*, 23 (1992), 301–43; and Viviana Comensoli,
'Refashioning the Marriage Code: The *Patient Grissil* of Dekker, Chettle and Haughton', in *Renaissance and Reformation*, 13 (1989), 199–213.

lives of its readers, to participate in the large and extended transformation these trends were effecting. That is, instead of a simple textual ideal confronting a stable historical reality, what we find in the tale is a narrative whose didacticism structures itself as a form of diachronic extension. To help conceptualize this sort of diachrony, I will suggest the didactic text be understood neither as a univocal statement of belief, nor as an ideological alibi, but as a form of desire. And in place of the anecdote, I will suggest didacticism's relation to history can be best approached through the crux. If the frame of reference for the anecdote is synchronic, for the crux it is diachronic. Where the anecdote provides a touch of the real, fleetingly returning the literary object to its own historical moment, the scandal of the crux is its exposure of the expectations of the reader, its equation of the literary object with its futurity. Both anecdote and crux constitute forms of disturbance and surprise. But the anecdote is a disruption, a discontinuity, an absence, while the crux is an excess, an unexpected surplus of signification. The frustration of the crux is not simply that it is unintelligible, but that it is something extra, something left over, something that seems egregious or unnecessary in relation to the rest of the text. My reading will concentrate on three such moments in the tale. The first is the espousal scene, which has proved especially important to recent scholarship. The third is the tale's conclusion, a crux of long standing, where the Clerk's ironic appeal to the Wife of Bath seems to undercut everything that has gone before. In between, I will analyse a seldom remarked but persistent detail, the forged papal letter Walter produces to justify his divorcing Griselda. In no way instrumental to the causal movement of the narrative, this detail invokes the larger institutional context of the late medieval court only to offer a view of that context which, as we shall see, substantially contradicts its historical reality.

Cruxes are usually resolved by referring them back to some neglected aspect of the text's historical moment. This crux makes specific reference to two prominent institutional features of later medieval society, the widespread forgery of official documents, and the papacy's direct regulation of aristocratic and royal marriage. Yet the detail is so counterfactual we cannot read it simply as the depiction of an independent historical reality. Instead, its extreme artificiality renders the historical reference itself diachronic in nature. As a fictional transformation it constitutes an implicit commentary on the historical processes it transforms. For this reason I offer this crux as the limit case of the tale's didactic ambitions, its production and project of its own peculiar form of domestic desire out of historical and ideological particulars. As my reading attempts to take the tale's didactic aspirations on their own terms, it also takes Chaucer seriously as a teacher, who not only offers his readers moral guidance, but also a sustained meditation on the origins and nature of such guidance. And here I draw as much on Chaucer's continuing influence within our own literary culture as I do on the traditions of Chaucer scholarship.

II. Griselda's longue durée: From Canon Law to Top Girls

As particularly striking evidence that Chaucer's shade still walks among us, one could cite the play *Top Girls*, by the contemporary feminist playwright Caryl Churchill, first staged in London in 1982. Griselda appears in the first act. Along with a number of other legendary or actual women from the past she helps the play's protagonist, a Thatcherite executive named Marlene, celebrate her recent promotion at a fashionable restaurant. Churchill's recourse to Griselda is noteworthy because it confounds two of the most basic distinctions structuring the modern understanding of Chaucer and his cultural authority. The first is the epochal distinction between medieval and modern. The second is the conceptual boundary between high culture and low. For Churchill uses Griselda to typify the traditional, self-effacing, stay-at-home housewife. She thus draws this gloss on popular ideologies of the domestic not from the world of nineteenth-century fiction, where most current scholarship locates its source, but from the premodern Father of English poetry himself, and the archetypal canonical text of the British tradition. Moreover, her treatment of Griselda insists on the story's continuing vitality.

Marlene's exchanges with the other historical figures tend to foreground their pastness, as they frequently refer to the differences between their circumstances and hers. But she treats Griselda as a contemporary, particularly in her quasi-psychotherapeutic criticism of Walter. As Griselda tells her story to the others, Marlene announces, 'I can't stand this. I'm going for a pee,' and she exits.[6] The ideology which Griselda bespeaks is not only alive for Marlene, but dangerous. She literally cannot bear to be in the same room with it. The minor breach of etiquette represented by her declaration, 'I'm going for a pee,' underlines the materiality of the confrontation. Faced with a gender ideology she finds unbearably repressive, Marlene responds by asserting the autonomous needs of her own body. The play will go on to reveal the profound dilemma which

---

[6] Caryl Churchill, *Top Girls* (London, 1984), 23.

Marlene's annoyance masks. In the last act we learn that Angie, introduced in Act II as Marlene's niece, is actually her daughter, whom Marlene, as a working-class teenager, left with her sister to raise in order to pursue a career. Like Griselda Marlene must abandon her maternal rights as the price of social mobility. This repressed fact is a defining condition of Marlene's biography, and despite her achievements, it links her more closely to Griselda than to any of the more heroic figures in Act I. Angie, the abandoned child, serves as a synecdoche for the huge self-denial entailed by Marlene's transformation to Thacherite corporate executive.

The heroic foremothers Marlene takes as her soulmates are heroic because they were ahead of their time. Trapped in an ignorant past, they insisted on freedoms only the present has come to recognize as rightful. But in spite of their heroism, these figures are less valuable iconographically to Churchill than Griselda, and that is an irony that haunts the entire play. They hold in place the complacent boundary between past and present which Griselda's symbolic relevance to Marlene unsettles. In order to make sense of Marlene, Churchill must reach back to Chaucer for a domestic ideal that modern feminism has ostensibly left far behind. Her ambivalent portrayal of Marlene paradoxically rehabilitates Griselda. Moreover, this rehabilitation offers a specifically historical argument all the more striking for the fact Churchill takes it for granted. By using Griselda as the archetype for a repressed domestic ideal, Churchill implicitly assigns the cult of domesticity an origin in the later Middle Ages. She treats Chaucer less as a major author, than as the initiator of a discursive practice, to borrow Michel Foucault's somewhat inelegant phrase.[7] Chaucer makes a plausible source for the Griselda story, for it is Chaucer who brings the story to Britain, as part of its explosive dispersion across Europe in the fourteenth and fifteenth centuries. This was an act of cultural foundation of some significance since the story became a crucial antecedent to modern ideals of domesticity. But Churchill's view flatly contradicts a wealth of recent scholarship which treats the emergence of domesticity as an early modern phenomenon. Indeed, making this connection has been a matter of some urgency. Such scholarship, be it Marxist, feminist, or Foucaultian in orientation, has striven to establish its progressive politics precisely by insisting on a synchronic model of culture, by seeking the significance of domestic ideals in their imbrication

---

[7] Michel Foucault, 'What is an Author', in *Language, Counter-Memory, Practice: Selected Essays and Interviews by Michel Foucault*, ed. and introd. Donald F. Bouchard, trans. Bouchard and Sherry Simon (Ithaca, NY, 1977), 131–6.

within the power relations of their own historical moment. To this current consensus, the durability of the Griselda story poses the problem of the diachronic. And it poses this problem not simply as a matter of the continuity of tradition but as a matter precisely of the interrelation between culture and power which the new historicist scholarship has opened up.

Top Girls also offers another, more local, contrast with recent Chaucerian scholarship. In the past two decades the *Clerk's Tale* has achieved a new prominence in the criticism of the Canterbury collection, largely as a response to the same feminist *Zeitgeist*. However, while Churchill's treatment stresses the story's ideological core, the most powerful of recent scholarly treatments of the tale, beginning with Anne Middleton's in 1980, and including those of David Wallace, Carolyn Dinshaw, and more recently, Linda Georgianna, and Sarah Stanbury, stress precisely Chaucer's ironic distance.[8] These readings are all very different from each other and a number of them mention the story's durability, but for the most part they do not explore its ramifications.[9] Concentrating on that durability can help us to integrate the more directly ideological questions raised by *Top Girls* with the issues of rhetorical and textual complexity explored so convincingly by this recent scholarship. Given the privilege over literary form which medieval scholarship has traditionally accorded questions of belief, it would be possible to argue that the tale's ideology contains the complications Chaucer introduces, or even renders our perceptions of them suspect. However, it seems more promising to examine the possibilities of interdependence between these two aspects of the tale. What we need to understand is how Chaucer's complex ironies could

[8] Anne Middleton, 'The Clerk and His Tale: Some Literary Contexts', *Studies in the Age of Chaucer*, 2 (1981), 121–50; Judith Ferster, *Chaucer and Interpretation* (Cambridge, 1984), 94–121; Carolyn Dinshaw, *Chaucer's Sexual Poetics* (Madison, 1989), 132–55; David Wallace, ' "When She Translated Was": A Chaucerian Critique of the Petrarchan Academy', in Patterson (ed.), *Literary Practice and Social Change in Britain*, 156–215, a revised version of which can be found in Wallace, *Chaucerian Polity: Absolutist Lineages and Associational Forms in England and Italy* (Stanford, Calif., 1997), 260–98; Elaine Tuttle Hansen, *Chaucer and the Fictions of Gender* (Berkeley, Calif., 1992), 188–207; Linda Georgianna, 'The Clerk's Tale and the Grammar of Assent', *Speculum*, 70 (1995), 793–821; Carolynn Van Dyke, 'The Clerk's and Franklin's Subjected Subjects', *Studies in the Age of Chaucer*, 17 (1995), 45–68; Sarah Stanbury, 'Regimes of the Visual in Premodern England: Gaze, Body, and Chaucer's Clerk's Tale', *New Literary History*, 28 (1997), 261–89.

[9] Stanbury, 'Regimes of the Visual', constitutes something of an exception, although she is not particularly interested in the durability of the Griselda story *per se*. Instead, she uses the *Clerk's Tale* as the focus of a compelling and wide-ranging meditation on spectacularization and the status of the visual in late medieval culture.

themselves be part of his act of cultural foundation. Paradoxical as it may seem, the critical distance he establishes in relation to the domestic ideology of the Griselda story may itself be a feature of that ideology. Thus, the goal is not to reduce Chaucer's complexity, but to insist on the complexity of the discourse of domesticity he helps initiate.

Traditionalist readings have long taken Chaucer's didactic concerns as prima-facie evidence that the *Clerk's Tale* must be read as a repository of stable medieval values. This view has subsisted in some of the more recent readings to the extent that they assume an antithesis between the tale's didactic moments and its ironic ones. Yet, with this assumption of stability, both of these views reconstruct the tale's didacticism anachronistically; they ignore the tale's manifold novelties. The date of the *Decameron* is 1353. Petrarch does not produce his translation until twenty years later, and it is this translation which enables the story's diffusion northward first to Paris, where four versions of the tale appeared between the early 1380s and 1400, and then to London. Even if Chaucer produced his version in the late 1390s toward the end of the Canterbury period, it would have been new to a majority of his readers. More importantly, the ideology of marriage which the story promotes, or at least explores, was also relatively novel.

With its definition of marriage as an arena of spiritual struggle, the Griselda story corresponds to the later medieval Church's long and gradual sacralization of marriage. Indeed, insofar as its narrative turns on the promise Walter extracts from Griselda, the story depends specifically on the doctrine of marriage formation first propounded in the decretals of the latter half of the twelfth century and dominant by the end of the thirteenth. This doctrine held that the central element defining the validity of a marriage was the consent of the two parties. Even more strikingly, the story's advent in the latter half of the fourteenth century coincides exactly with the period which James Brundage and other historians have identified as the moment when lay authorities began to reclaim the regulation of marriage from the Church.[10] The Church had been interested in marriage from its very beginnings. Indeed, David Herlihy has argued persuasively that the nuclear family, proverbially an artefact of emergence of modern capitalism, actually owes some of its key features to two basic

---

[10] James Brundage, *Law, Sex, and Christian Society in Medieval Europe* (Chicago, 1987), 3–4. As Brundage notes, 'modern states appropriated much medieval canonistic doctrine. A substantial part of legal doctrine about sexual activity and about matrimony in the Western world remains bound by its medieval Christian origins to this day.'

emphases of early Christian penitential regulation, exogamy and monogamy, and can be seen to emerge as early as the eighth century.[11] However, considered as a whole-scale bureaucratic enterprise, the clerical regulation of marriage really began in earnest in the eleventh century with the advent of canon law. Georges Duby has characterized this period as a competition between two models aristocratic and clerical, with the clerical eventually emerging triumphant.[12] Duby is certainly right in conceptual terms; the Church did succeed in re-imagining as primarily sacral and ethical an institution whose previous purpose had been almost exclusively the management of property rights. Nevertheless Duby's 'two models' thesis ignores some other crucial factors. First, Church involvement generally stemmed from lay solicitation. Second, the clerical sacralization largely supplemented the institution's investment in property rights instead of displacing it. Finally, three centuries after the Church took administrative control of the institution away from the laity, the laity began to take it back. For these reasons what Duby views as the triumph of the clerical should be viewed more precisely, as Brundage does, as a process of laicization. And this process, as ideological and philosophical as it was institutional, involved the production of cultural artefacts like the Griselda story. For whatever other cultural functions the sudden dispersion of the story may have served, it was clearly a fictive re-enactment of evolving struggles surrounding the emergence of the consensual theory of marriage.

At the same time, an overly functionalist view of the story imposes a synchronic frame on what is, even in its novelty, a radically diachronic process. The challenge is to capture the historicity of the tale's discourse precisely in its projection of the durative through the particular. The opposition between the fictive or poetic and the historical is a diachronic one, which only manifests itself through time. Moreover, all particulars, both poetic and historical vary in duration themselves. Thus, the

[11] David Herlihy, *Medieval Households* (Cambridge, Mass., 1985). Herlihy begins by noting that in the eighth century, medieval society began to move definitively away from the asymmetric 'household system of antiquity', in which 'different sectors of society possessed fundamentally different domestic units', toward a domestic system 'commensurable and comparable' across 'all levels of the social hierarchy' (v). Although Herlihy identifies a number of factors driving this change, he names chief among them the Church, which 'sought to impose a common rule of marriage upon all the faithful in all social classes. Two of its commands had a powerful impact upon marriages and the formation of households: exogamy and monogamy' (61).
[12] Georges Duby, *Medieval Marriage: Two Models from Twelfth-Century France*, trans. Elborg Foster (Baltimore, 1978). See also Christopher N. L. Brooke, *The Medieval Idea of Marriage* (Oxford, 1989), 119–43.

distinction between poetic tradition and other diachronic historical processes is ultimately a relative one, and it is not only possible but usual for historical forces to register within poetic structures in varying degrees of specificity. As a result of this variation, it is virtually impossible for a poet to respond to a historical trend without also treating it with some critical distance. Chaucer foregrounds the didacticism of the Griselda story by assigning it to the Clerk, that idealized figure who would gladly 'lerne and gladly teche'.[13] In the tale's prologue the Clerk's dialogue with the Host combines an explicit acknowledgement of the story's provenance with a brief exploration of the institutional relations between clerical learning and political community. Taxed by the Host to put aside the 'Heigh style' and rhetorical colours clerks use for the instruction of kings, the Clerk will nevertheless insist on telling a tale he 'Lerned at Padowe of a worthy clerk', though he pointedly declares he will eschew Petrarch's proem and its 'heigh stile' (IV, 16–20, 26–7, 41–55). In response to the Host's jocular rejection of clerical learning, the Clerk both acknowledges the difference between clerical and lay culture, and insists on the utility of learning to the latter. In contrast to the more traditional picture offered by the Host of king instructed by clerks, the Clerk identifies Petrarch as 'the lauriat poete' whose 'rethorike sweete' forges a political community out of the power of poetry, illuminating 'al Ytaille of poetrie' (IV, 31–3). But he supplements this invocation with that of 'Lynyan', Giovanni da Lignano, professor of canon law at Padua, who illuminated Italy with philosophy, law, or 'oother art particuler' (IV, 34–5). This second invocation suggests that the specifically lay communal authority produced by laureate poetry remains dependent not only on clerical learning generally, but canon law specifically, that is, on the power of clerical learning to structure and police its own institutional setting.

It also suggests Chaucer was well aware not only of the influence marriage regulation devised by the Church was already having in lay circles, but also of the way that knowledge was refracted in this story he drew from Petrarch and Petrarch's French translators. Chaucer intensifies the connection by intensifying the refraction. Walter's contract with Griselda is prefigured by his contract with his people, and the negotiations leading up to that contract rather neatly pit the more traditional, 'aristocratic' model against the consensual model developed by the canonists and the

---

[13] Geoffrey Chaucer, *General Prologue* in the *Canterbury Tales*, in *The Riverside Chaucer*, ed. Larry Benson et al. (Boston, 1987), I, 308, p. 28. All subsequent citations are to this edition. Fragment and line numbers will be given in the text.

papacy. Walter's people, seeking the political stability that would come
with an heir, entreat him to get married, offering, in Petrarch's words, to
find him a wife 'descended of such illustrious parentage that you should
hope to have of her the noblest things'.[14] Walter responds by insisting on
his right to choose his own wife, and rejecting the aristocratic association
of virtue with class status. Chaucer reproduces this portion of Petrarch's
text quite faithfully, but earlier on in the adviser's entreaty he adds another
characterization of the marriage contract. The adviser makes this suggestion to Walter:

> Boweth youre nekke under that blisful yok
> Of soverayntee, noght of servyse,
> Which that men clepe spousaille or wedlock . . .

(IV, 113–15)

This deployment of the term *soverayntee* is particularly striking, as it
straddles both models of marriage formation. On the one hand, the adviser is obliquely reminding Walter, his sovereign, that sovereignty depends on the maintenance of the dynastic line, which depends on the
proper arrangement of a state marriage. On the other hand, his opposition of 'soverayntee' to 'servyse' suggests an empowerment for the principals within the marriage contract more applicable to the consensual
model that Walter will demand. Moreover, this use of *soverayntee* recalls
similar uses in the *Wife of Bath's Prologue* and *Tale* (III, 818, 1037–40) and
anticipates the one in the *Franklin's Tale* (V, 751). In three cases the term is
associated with schemes to increase the reciprocity between husband and
wife, and in the *Franklin's Tale*, it is part of a contract between Arveragus
and Dorigen. Thus, with the addition of these lines to his sources in the
Clerk's Tale, Chaucer foregrounds the interdependence between the two
models. The complexity of this narrative frame, which engages the evolution of medieval marriage customs at their broadest, most diachronic
level of generality, will enable him to achieve a similar complexity as his
narrative engages with more historically specific social and institutional
practices. In the espousal scene Chaucer makes another addition to his
sources: the metaphor of translation.

[14] Francesco Petrarca, *Epistolae Seniles*, Book XVII, Letter 3, in J. Burke Severs, *The Literary
Relationships of Chaucer's 'Clerkes Tale'* (New Haven, 1942), 256: 'Querende autem coniugis
studium nobis linque, talem enim tibi procurabimus que te merito digna sit, et tam claris orta
parentibus ut de ea spes optima sit habenda.' Subsequent citations are to this edition. Page numbers will given in the text.

III. *The Griselda Complex: A Problem of Translation*

Christiane Klapisch-Zuber's essay, 'The Griselda Complex: Dowry and Marriage Gifts in the Quattrocento' merits more attention among Chaucerians than it has received. Like Caryl Churchill, Klapisch-Zuber is interested in the ideological continuities of the Griselda story. She gives the name *Griselda Complex* to the symbolic interconnections among various 'nuptial practices of the Quattrocento . . . which assured that women and dowry goods pass, without too much friction, into the houses of the husbands'.[15] She demonstrates that certain customary gifts from the groom and his family to the bride, including a wardrobe or 'countertrousseau', provided a counterbalance to dowering practices that had become increasingly formalized and subject to legal regulation, and notarial confirmation.[16] The importance granted these gifts helps solve the 'conundrum' which dowries pose to 'all economically oriented interpretations of marriage portions', that is, all interpretations which see marriage as a market, or traffic in women. As Klapisch-Zuber formulates it, 'Why . . . would the family into which a woman was about to enter demand supplementary payments—a dowry, a trousseau—when by the marriage of one of its sons it had already acquired rights over the bride, her labor, and her descendants?'[17] The customary gifts to the bride, which previous historians have dismissed as archaisms, constituted 'a clandestine counterdowry'—symbolically preserving the character of reciprocity and exchange, of 'gift and countergift', in a system of marriage relations grown increasingly commercial, patrilineal, and virilocal.[18]

Klapisch-Zuber is a social historian, not a literary scholar, but her analysis necessarily entails a reading of the Griselda story. Like Caryl Churchill she sees the story as affirming patriarchal structures and male authority. She focuses on the moment of Griselda's translation. This moment is also crucial to two of the best—if not the two best—recent readings of the *Clerk's Tale*, Dinshaw's 'Griselda Translated', and Wallace's

---

[15] Christiane Klapisch-Zuber, 'The Griselda Complex: Dowry and Marriage Gifts in the Quattrocento', in *Women, Family and Ritual in Renaissance Italy*, trans. Lydia Cochrane (Chicago, 1985), 246.

[16] This even included the institution in 1430 by the Florentine commune of 'a sort of dowry insurance', which 'guaranteed a "decent" dowry . . . to any girl whose father had thought to make a deposit in the Monte delle Doti when she was a child' (Klapisch-Zuber, 'Griselda Complex', 214).

[17] Ibid. 215.   [18] Ibid. 213–24.

'"When She Translated Was"'. It occurs immediately after Walter and
Griselda's betrothal. They emerge from her father's hut, and Walter commands his ladies-in-waiting to replace Griselda's rags with finery appropriate to her new station:

> Hir heris han they kembd, that lay untressed
> Ful rudely, and hir fyngres smale
> A corone on hire heed they han ydressed,
> And sette hire ful of nowches grete and smale,
> Of hire array what sholde I make a tale?
> Unnethe the peple hir knew for hire fairnesse
> Whan she translated was in swich richesse.

(IV, 379–85)

It in no way diminishes the achievement of either Dinshaw or Wallace to
observe that in a certain respect Klapisch-Zuber's reading of this scene is
more literal than theirs. They both exploit the rich associations of the
word 'translated' in this context in order to gloss Chaucer's wider textual
and rhetorical strategies. By contrast, Klapisch-Zuber—admittedly using
Boccaccio rather than Chaucer as the basis of her reflections—takes this
scene to be literally about the exchange of clothing. That is, she takes it as
a fictionalization of the Florentine countertrousseau:

In Griselda—taken virgin, poor, and naked . . . richly adorned for the wedding
ceremonies in the presence of her baron husband's vassals, then sent back by him
en chemise to the hut in which she was born—Boccaccio's contemporaries would
have recognized acts and behaviors rooted in the nuptial practices of their times.
Toward the middle of the fourteenth century, the husband's dressing of his bride
still possessed the quality of compelling ritual action, and the compulsion would
have been immediately been perceptible to the readers or hearers of the tale.[19]

If Klapisch-Zuber is right about the contemporary ideological importance of the countertrousseau—and she makes a pretty convincing
case—what impact does that have on the more rhetorical readings of Dinshaw and Wallace? For their readings this scene is the linchpin securing
Chaucer's ironic distance from the ideological matter of the tale. It might
be possible to dismiss the discrepancy as arising from the simple difference between Boccaccio's text and Chaucer's, except that Klapisch-Zuber
intends the correspondence she identifies to account not only for Boccaccio's version of the story, but its subsequent 'immense popularity', and

[19] Ibid. 228–9.

both Dinshaw and Wallace associate Chaucer's critical distance with Boccaccio's.[20]

Tellingly, for both Dinshaw and Wallace, Chaucer's distance from the tale's ideology is also a distance from Petrarch. For Dinshaw, the Clerk's self-conscious fascination with *translatio* is a fascination with the trope's inevitable exclusions. On the basis of this scene she observes that 'In the *Clerk's Tale translatio* is represented as an act performed on the female body, but women's experience does not enter the conceptualization.'[21] The Clerk counteracts this 'turning away from the female', and 'restores to our attention what has been translated out by Petrarch'.[22] Yet this restoration is deconstructive rather than straightforward; it consists largely of self-conscious interpretive manoeuvres Dinshaw identifies in this chapter and elsewhere in her book as reading 'like a woman'.[23] Wallace's approach to translation is less deconstructive, but it still focuses on language and its particular politics. Griselda's translation 'from village to court attire' is imperfect: 'the dress and ornaments that represent this translation cannot fit Griselde exactly'. Chaucer's 'actively critical' re-translation of Petrarch 'restores the narrative to the vernacular . . . the commons to the narrative', and 'the female body to itself'. In the tale's 'manifold' failure 'to enforce its own closure' we realize 'these terminating contradictions and incoherencies . . . issue from similar qualities within the tale itself and, by extension, from within its acknowledged Petrarchan source'.[24] For both Dinshaw and Wallace, Chaucer's rhetorical sophistication enables him to break with the very authority from which he derives the matter of his text.

There is an impasse here, one which corresponds, at least in part, to disciplinary incongruences between history and literary studies. The social historian's first concern is necessarily social structure; the literary scholar's, just as necessarily, the structure of literary form. The same narrative moment has been subjected to both of these disciplinary imperatives, and the result is divergent, if not contradictory, readings, with the

---

[20] This even included the institution in 1430 by the Florentine commune of 'a sort of dowry insurance', 228. In Dinshaw, the association is fleeting and indirect; she argues, partially following Middleton, that Petrarch's translation of Boccaccio into Latin removes the tale from a female readership; and that his allegorization means the tale is no longer for women 'in particular'. The Clerk's retranslation and his complications of the tale's moral counterbalances these tendencies in Petrarch (*Chaucer's Sexual Poetics*, 150–3). Wallace is more direct. Chaucer's retranslation of the tale returns it to its original spirit, whether Chaucer actually knew the *Decameron* or not (*Chaucerian Polity*, 277–86).

[21] Dinshaw, *Chaucer's Sexual Poetics*, 147.   [22] Ibid. 147, 152.

[23] Ibid. 154. See also 3–27, 52–64.   [24] Wallace, *Chaucerian Polity*, 287–93.

historian on one side and the two literary scholars on the other. I find the divergence all the more striking given the large amount of common intellectual ground these three scholars share. A commitment to feminism drives all three projects; Dinshaw and Wallace are profoundly sympathetic to history, especially social history; while Klapisch-Zuber shows herself equally respectful of textual complexity. It might be possible to argue that the historical correspondence she has identified ought to outweigh the complications demonstrated by Dinshaw and Wallace. Such an argument would follow the imperative of traditional literary history that all interpretive arguments must be checked against historical fact, and those which do not conform discarded. Whatever the continuing validity of that imperative, in this case it will not work for a couple of reasons. First, Klapisch-Zuber's correspondence is not a fact in any simple sense. That is to say, one could certainly legitimately describe the Florentine and dotal practices she describes as fact or a set of facts; likewise the persistence of the ostensibly archaic customary gifts to the bride. Yet neither of these facts forms the crux of her argument or the basis of the correspondence. What does is the symbolic interconnection between the two—that is between dotal practices and customary gifts—and that interconnection is nothing other than Klapisch-Zuber's interpretation. It is not directly supported by the wealth of archival and narrative evidence she brings forward, but depends instead on the internal coherence of the arguments with which she links this evidence. Chaucer's text is no less a historical fact than late medieval marriage practices. Why should we privilege interpretation of the one over the other, especially since in both cases what we are dealing with are symbolic structures? This brings me to the second problem. In order to link the Griselda story to the symbolism of *quattrocento* marriage ritual, Klapisch-Zuber actually overstates its continuity, momentarily obliterating the textual specificity literary studies can never evade. She introduces the parallel just after noting that the 'nuptial "gifts" could be borrowed and . . . later had to be given back'.

The Griselda immortalized by Boccaccio in the last story of the *Decameron* stands as emblematic of just such a cruelly restricted husbandly generosity. Behind the edifying story, some have deciphered the plot lines of a popular tale.[25]

But it is Petrarch, not Boccaccio who makes the story edifying. As Wallace demonstrates in detail, Boccaccio concerns himself primarily with the story's moral lapses. The tale's narrator in the *Decameron* is the

---

[25] Klapisch-Zuber, 'Griselda Complex', 228.

smart-aleck Dioneo, who throughout the work 'exploits his privilege of speaking last to ironize, subvert, or disperse the theme that has supposedly unified the day's storytelling'.[26] Fed up with a day's worth of tales of virtuous rulers, Dioneo offers instead 'marquis, whose actions . . . were remarkable not so much for their munificence as for their senseless brutality. Nor do I advise anyone to follow his example . . .'[27] The main stake in Petrarch's implicit rivalry with Boccaccio is precisely Petrarch's discovery of a moral in the story which Boccaccio's narrator had so emphatically declared to have none. It is more than understandable that Klapisch-Zuber would read Petrarch's didactic ambition back onto Boccaccio's original version. For it is Petrarch's version that is most directly responsible for the story's subsequent dissemination. It is Petrarch's version the French translators translate, and it is Petrarch's version to which Chaucer returns. Paradoxically, by translating the story into Latin, Petrarch made it more accessible to other vernacular traditions; by reconfiguring its moral status, he gives it the didactic impulse that dominates most of the subsequent vernacular retellings, especially in England. Still, it is Chaucer who brings the story to England, and it is precisely his relation to this didacticism in question here.

As a possible way past this impasse, I would now like to appeal to the notion of desire. I can illustrate its centrality in the first instance by returning once more to the language of the specific stanza we have been considering. The stanza's first four lines concern the borrowed clothing, the primary concern of the ideological reading. The fourth, 'Of hire array what sholde I make a tale?' is an ostentatiously self-conscious interposition of the narratorial voice of the sort for which Chaucer is justly celebrated. It prepares for the translation metaphor in the final line so key to the ironic reading. But the sixth line raises the problem of desire in a way that neither reading fully comprehends: 'Unnethe the peple hir knew for hire fairnesse'. This sudden revelation of Griselda's fairness is radically paradoxical. Precipitated by her borrowed finery, it differs so sharply from her previous aspect that onlookers scarcely recognize her as herself. Yet can there be any doubt that this fairness is Griselda's and Griselda's alone? The moment of revelation simply gives public form to an inner virtue that has been there all along. This is a revelation which is not one. In its paradox, it expresses an equally paradoxical desire. It is a desire both double and single; a desire for both outward finery and inner virtue, yet—in

[26] Wallace, *Chaucerian Polity*, 278–9.
[27] Giovanni Boccaccio, *The Decameron*, trans. G. H. McWilliam (Harmondsworth, 1972), 813.

its insistence on translation—a desire that the two become the same even in their difference. Griselda's fairness is the sign of this union, the inner virtue which redeems the very finery to which it is opposed. This curious desire is the ground where ideology and irony meet. For if the ritual significances of bridal exchange provide the stanza's ideological context, then what that ideology does in this stanza is precisely to seek a transcendent ground beyond itself, namely Griselda's fairness. Similarly, if the translation metaphor, and the narratorial interposition provide the stanza with its ironic distance from this ideology, they do so appealing to the same ground by what Dinshaw calls the Clerk's 'identification' with Griselda. The stanza's narratorial irony, whether the Clerk's, or Chaucer's, exposes the credulousness of an ideology that would equate a bride's finery with her inner worth, but it does so in the interest of a more authentic convergence with Griselda's point of view. Thus, both the stanza's ideology and its irony participate in the same complicated economy of desire.

This point can be generalized as follows: desire has a structure more thoroughly diachronic than either ideology or irony. Ideology arises from the synchronic conjunction of a particular subject position with a particular social formation. (On this point, there is no difference between classical Marxist notions of 'false consciousness', or the more modulated formulae introduced by Althusser, ideology as representing 'the imaginary relationship of individuals to their real conditions of existence'.[28] Both are equally synchronic.) Irony is a slightly more diachronic notion than ideology, but as Paul de Man explains in his classic discussion, its diachrony is the diachrony of rupture: 'Irony divides the flow of temporal experience into a past that is pure mystification and a future that remains harassed forever by a relapse within the inauthentic. It can know this inauthenticity but it can overcome it.'[29] Irony is structured by the present's instantaneous disenchantment with the past, a disenchantment that cuts it off from any prospect of a future. By contrast, desire is retroactive, as Slavoj Žižek argues.[30] It seeks to recover from the future a replacement for what it has lost in the past. Although Žižek is concerned specifically with the desire as it is understood by Lacanian psychoanalysis, his description fits a variety of other contexts, including, strikingly enough, the Christian

[28] Louis Althusser, 'Ideology and Ideological State Apparatuses (Notes towards an Investigation)', in *Lenin and Philosophy and Other Essays*, trans. Ben Brewster (New York, 1971), 162.

[29] Paul de Man, 'The Rhetoric of Temporality', in *Blindness and Insight: Essays in the Rhetoric of Contemporary Criticism*, 2nd rev. edn. (Minneapolis, 1983), 222.

[30] Slavoj Žižek, 'Che Vuoi?', in *The Sublime Object of Ideology* (London, 1989), 100–5.

piety dramatized by this tale. For it is the very essence of Christian piety to seek in the future what it has lost in the past, to strive for the transcendent state lost in the Fall. If we view the long dissemination of the Griselda story as the extended enactment of a particular form of cultural desire, we can view its didactic motives as ideological and ironic at once, whether we are treating particular instances, or the process as a whole. In the case of Chaucer, it seems entirely plausible that he would mark his introduction of this form of desire to an English reading public with the ambivalences that Dinshaw, Wallace, and other recent critics have noted.

IV. Walter's Papal Letter: Institutional Fakery and Moral Transcendence

Reading didacticism as a form of desire helps explain the Griselda story's formal and rhetorical dependence on the specificity of the institutional structures it invokes. As Petrarch shifts the story's moral focus from Walter's wickedness to Griselda's virtue, he also makes the theme of good governance more prominent.[31] The double revision makes Griselda's moral transcendence curiously dependent on the political particularities within which it is enacted, a condition which Petrarch's conclusion at once conceals and exposes.

The aim in now reworking this story in another style is not so much that married women of our time might imitate the patience of this wife, which seems to me scarcely imitable, than that I might stir readers at least to imitate the constancy of this woman, that as she submitted to her husband, they might dare submit to God.

Hanc historiam stilo nunc alio retexere visum fuit, non tam ideo, ut matronas nostri temporis ad imitandam huius uxoris pacienciam, que michi vix imitabilis videtur, quam ut legentes ad imitandam saltem femine constanciam excitarem, ut quod hec viro suo prestitit, hoc prestare Deo nostro audeant . . . (288)

Older criticism usually construed this moral as allegorical, a misconception that persists in some more recent ironic readings.[32] As Charlotte Morse points out, the Griselda story is an exemplum, not an allegory, and

---

[31] Michaela Paasche Grudin, 'Chaucer's *Clerk's Tale* as Political Paradox', *Studies in the Age of Chaucer*, 11 (1989), 71–8.

[32] The oddest instance is Giuseppe Mazzotta, *The World at Play in Boccaccio's 'Decameron'* (Princeton, 1983), who reads Boccaccio's version as a prospective parody of what he takes as Petrarch's allegory.

this passage certainly displays an exemplary logic.[33] It does not require its readers to interpret Griselda; it hopes they will imitate her. Indeed, what older criticism took as this moral's denial of the tale's literal surface, its assertion of Griselda's inimitability, is in fact part of its construction of her as a figure of nearly unattainable desire. That desire depends on the very same narrative particulars the moral seeks to deny. Griselda's virtue is *Constantia feminae*, 'a woman's constancy'. It is not fully imaginable outside the unique domestic sphere within which it emerges, the household of a sovereign. Without Walter's tests Griselda could not display her exemplary piety, and the tests would not have been possible without Walter's dominant position within their marriage. But Walter can be that dominant only because he is no ordinary husband.

It is true that Petrarch's moral normalizes Walter's status, concealing his public power. Yet to characterize that concealment as a repression, whether allegorical or ideological, is to miss the point. For it is actually an extension of the drive toward transcendence animating the entire passage. The transcendence which the moral assigns to Griselda's suffering necessarily depends on the literal meaning it denies. But this paradox is precisely the point. Griselda's suffering is meaningful because it is excessive from the very beginning. Griselda treats as sacred imperatives the unreasonable demands of a wicked husband, who misuses his political authority to carry them out. By treating them as sacred, Griselda makes them sacred and thereby consecrates the domestic space which the demands construct. Petrarch's moral simply re-enacts this consecration. He generalizes her constancy as feminine as a necessary intermediate step to setting it before all readers. In this way, the public peculiarities of Griselda's status as marchioness are indispensable, yet never fully expressible.

The authority of this moral is similarly indirect. It expresses its ideal almost entirely in the third person. The first person of the narratorial voice appears only once, and then only in the dative of a subordinate clause, *que michi . . . videtur*, 'which seemed to me'. Petrarch's indirection no doubt encouraged the construction of Griselda as a domestic ideal directed specifically at women, but it also meant that that ideal, for all of its subsequent dominance, was constructed out of a more generalized desire. The most explicit of the fourteenth-century Parisian redactors on this point

---

[33] Charlotte Morse, 'Exemplary Griselda', *Studies in the Age of Chaucer*, 7 (1985), 51–86. More recently, Lynn Staley, in David Aers and Lynn Staley, *The Powers of the Holy: Religion, Politics and Gender in Late Medieval English Culture* (University Park, Pa., 1996), has argued for allegorical reading focusing on 'those very points where the allegory falters' (236).

was the anonymous author of *Le Menagier de Paris*, probably unknown to Chaucer.[34] This work was a conduct book addressed to the author's wife. He includes the tale as an illustration of her duty to be humble and obedient. The 1619 chapbook, *The Ancient True and Admirable History of Patient Grisel*, was the most widely disseminated version of the tale in seventeenth-century England. It bears the engaging subtitle *How Maides, by her Example, in their Good Behaviour, May Marrie Rich Husbands, and Likewise Wives by their Patience and Obedience May Gain Much Glorie*. Yet this chapbook is also notable for its restoration of many of the narrative particulars that had fallen away in previous early modern versions such as John Phillips's interlude, *The Comodye of Pacient and Meeke Grissill*, and *The Pleasant Comodie of Patient Grissell*, by Thomas Dekker, Henry Chettle, and William Haughton. As Lee Bliss explains, these included

the marquis's stated preference for liberty of the constraints of marriage; his refusal of the nobles' offer to pick him a suitable wife; the parallel contracts of obedience with his subjects and with Grisel; the new wife's display of admired political as well as domestic virtues; the absence of human motivation beyond the marquis's own willfulness; Grisel's request, as each child is taken from her, that its body be given burial to protect it from wild beasts and birds; the twelve more years spent together as man and wife before Grisel is sent back to her father; the feigned papal dispensation allowing the marquis to remarry.[35]

The restoration of these elements strongly suggests not only a diachronic, but indeed historicist dimension to the figure of Griselda as domestic ideal. Nearly all of the elements relate specifically to her status as marchioness; none of them would seem especially relevant to the domestic experience of the seventeenth-century bourgeois reader to whom the chapbook was presumably directed. The persistence of the last detail is particularly curious. As it assumes knowledge of the medieval papacy's direct jurisdiction over the marriages of the higher nobility, it is the most institutionally specific, yet it is also most extraneous as regards the causal necessities of the plot. Although largely unremarked by modern criticism of the *Clerk's Tale*, the detail has persisted long beyond the seventeenth century. Churchill's Griselda recounts it in her otherwise compressed rehearsal of her story.[36]

---

[34] The early French versions of the Griselda story show the same tensions and complexities as Chaucer's. See Kevin Brownlee, 'Commentary and Rhetoric of Exemplarity: Griseldis in Petrarch, Philippe de Mézières, and the *Estoire*', *South Atlantic Quarterly*, 91 (1992), 865–90.

[35] Bliss, 'Renaissance Griselda', 319.

[36] Churchill, *Top Girls*, 24. Cited in the text on pp. 133–5 below.

The forgery is part of the story from the very beginning. Boccaccio links it to Gualteri's final test:

Many years after the birth of his daughter, Gualteri decided that the time had come to put Griselda's patience to the final test. So he told a number of his men that in no circumstances could he put up with Griselda as his wife any longer, having now come to realize that his marriage was an aberration of his youth. He would therefore do everything in his power to obtain a dispensation from the Pope, enabling him to divorce Griselda and marry someone else . . .

Shortly thereafter Gualteri arranged for some counterfeit letters of his to arrive from Rome, and led his subjects to believe that in these, the Pope had granted him permission to abandon Griselda and remarry.[37]

Petrarch retains the detail but compresses it, excising the initial motivation—Gualteri's rationalization to his advisers—and placing additional emphasis on the forgery's public function, consistent with the monarchical cast he imposes elsewhere on the narrative.

. . . when twelve years from the birth of his daughter had passed, he sent messengers to Rome, who brought back from there counterfeit papal letters, through which it was made public among the general populace that for his own peace and that of his people he had had license given to him by the Roman pontiff to reject his first marriage and take another wife.[38]

Le livre Griseldis, Chaucer's main French source, also retains the detail, translating Petrarch almost word for word.[39] By contrast, Chaucer expands the detail, spending more time on it even then Boccaccio. I give his rendition in full:

---

[37] Boccaccio, *Decameron*, 819; Boccaccio, *Decameron*, vol. iv of *Tutte le opere di Giovanni Bocccacio*, ed. Vittore Branca (Milan, 1976), 949: 'Ma essendo più anni passati dopo la natività della fanciulla, pavendo tempo a Gualteri di fare l'ultima pruova della sofferanza di costei, con molti de' suoi disse che per niuna guisa più sofferir poteva d'aver per moglie Griselda a che egli conosceva che male e giovenilmente aveva fatto quando l'aveva presa, e per ciò a suo voleva procacciar col papa che con lui dispensasse che un'altra donna prender potesse e lasciar Griselda . . . Non dopo molto tempo Gualteri fece venire sue lettere contrafatte da Roma, e fece veduto a' suoi subditi, il Papa per quelle aver seco dispensato di poter torre altra moglie e lasciar Griselda . . .'

[38] Petrarch, in Severs, *Literary Relationships*: '. . . cum iam ab ortu filie duodecimus annus elapsus esset, nuncios Romam misit, qui simulatas inde litteras apostolicus referrent, quibus in populo vulgaretur datam sibi licensiam a Romano pontifice, ut pro sua et suarum gencium quiete, primo matrimonio reiecto, aliam ducere posset uxorem . . .' (276)

[39] *Le Livre Griseldis*, in Severs, *Literary Relationships*, 277: '. . . comme depuis la nativité de sa fille eust xii ans, il envoia a Romme ses messages qui lui apporterent lettres faintes, par lesquelles il donnoit a entendre au peuple que le pape pour la paix de lui et de ses gens lui donné congié et dispensacion de soy de partir de sa femme et prandre une autre.'

> Whan that his doghter twelve yeer was of age,
> He to the court of Rome, in subtil wyse
> Enformed of his wyl, sente his message,
> Comaundynge hem swiche bulles to devyse
> As to his crueel purpos may suffysen
> How that the pope, as for his peples reste,
> Bad hym to wedde another, if hym leste.
>
> I seye, he bad they sholde countrefete
> The popes bulles makynge mencion
> That he hath leve his firste wyf to lete
> As by the popes dispensacion,
> To stynte rancour and dissencion,
> Bitweye his peple and hym; thus seyde the bulle,
> The which they han publiced atte fulle.
>
> The rude peple, as it no wonder is,
> Wenden ful wel that it hadde be right so . . .
>
> (IV, 736–51)

Some lines later the Clerk reports Walter's explanation to Griselda:

> I may nat doon as every plowman may.
> My peple me constreyneth for to take
> Another wyf, and crien day by day;
> And eek the pope, rancour for to slake,
> Consenteth it . . .
>
> (IV, 799–803)

Chaucer's expansion maintains Petrarch's emphasis on the forgery's public function and adds two new features. First, he actually describes Walter's dealings with the papal *curia*, rather than leaving them implicit. He thereby elevates Walter's status relative to the *curia*, and implies their collusion. Walter informs them of 'his wyl' in 'subtil wyse', and by command dictates what sort of bull they produce. Second, Chaucer makes the forgery an explicit part of Walter's continuing delusion of Griselda. He thereby explicitly marks Walter's illicit transposition of his public authority into the domestic. (It is worth noting that Caryl Churchill retains this motivation for her Griselda: 'He sent me away. He said the people wanted him to marry someone else who'd give him an heir and he'd got special permission from the Pope. So I said I'd go home to my father.')[40] The net effect of these two revisions is to increase Walter's power in both public

---

[40] Churchill, *Top Girls*, 24.

terms and domestic ones. Given the ironic logic which founds Griselda's exemplarity, this increase in Walter's power is also an increase in her virtue, but the revisions have another effect as well. They intensify the detail's extraneity, rendering much more problematic its causal relation to the rest of the plot. The initial rationale provided by Boccaccio has now been definitively lost, and that was the one which was most plausible. In the *Clerk's Tale*, Walter's motive in seeking the forged letters is no longer to placate sophisticated courtiers; it is to convince Griselda and the populace. Yet that motive fits uneasily with revisions Chaucer makes elsewhere.

Throughout the tale, Chaucer emphasizes the extraordinary malleability of Walter's people. In one of his additions, the 'sadde folk' among them decry the people's utter inconstancy (IV, 995–1002). Why is divorce the one point where Walter's management of them requires outside help? The same question can be asked about Griselda. Why is this the one point where her oath of absolute obedience might falter? Why would she object to an illegal divorce when she has already acquiesced twice without hesitation to what she believes is infanticide? Chaucer seems no less fascinated by the potential power of this forged document than the rude people. These lines are extraordinarily repetitious, drawing out Walter's machinations, imagining once that the pope has allowed him to divorce Griselda for political expediency, and then imagining the same thing again. It is almost as if the repetitions constitute an attempt to get this fascinating possibility under control, an attempt whose failure they make all the more evident. At the one point papal authority enters the narrative it does so in the distanced form of a forgery. It is true these lines have a superficial plausibility, which may explain why they have hitherto gone unremarked. Dispensations came in letters and a sovereign lord like Walter would have appealed directly to the pope to get one. Past that fact, however, the plausibility breaks down. Dispensations were usually given to overcome some impediment and legitimate a marriage, not dissolve it.[41] While lay monarchs often wanted divorce for pragmatic political

---

[41] Historians have frequently noted the papacy's strong predisposition for legitimating existing marriages, in spite of most impediments. A particularly illustrative example of this predisposition can be found in the 1391 register of Pope Boniface IX: a letter instructing the Bishop of Lichfield to absolve a knight who married a woman to whom he was related in the fourth degree, 'expecting more easily to obtain [absolution] once married then before contracted'. In this case, the knight counted on the predisposition when he ignored the impediment, and, just as he expected, he got the absolution anyway. (*Calendar of Entries in the Papal Registers Relating to Great Britain and Ireland: Papal Letters*, vol. iv: *A.D. 1362–1404*, ed. W. H. Bliss and J. A. Twemlow (London, 1902), 412–13.

purposes, usually the lack of an heir, they almost never alleged those reasons, but contrived instead to find an impediment like consanguinity. It would have been entirely counter to papal practice to grant a dispensation like this, even if the pretext Walter concocts were actual.

V. Forgery and Marriage Regulation: Authentication and Desire

Why does Chaucer exaggerate this detail and increase its discontinuity? One obvious reason is his long-standing fascination with the social instrumentality of the textual. Throughout the *Canterbury Tales*, he frequently dramatizes this fascination by focusing on forged or otherwise misappropriated documents, especially in anti-clerical contexts. The Pardoner's suspicious collection of bulls from popes, cardinals, patriarchs, and bishops provides one such instance (VI, 342–3); the summoner's frequent recourse to 'a feyned mandement' in the *Friar's Tale* another (III, 1360). The interest undoubtedly stems from Chaucer's career as a royal bureaucrat, and not only from his post as Keeper of the King's Custom, but also from his diplomatic work. In all probability he would have worked with canonists, who were indispensable on diplomatic missions precisely because of their systematic knowledge of the proper procedures for legal documentation.[42] This detail from the Griselda story may have particularly appealed to Chaucer for it draws the question of the written legal instrument into the central issue of lay sovereignty, and illustrates the role canon law played in the constitution of lay political power. If Chaucer's revisions of the detail increase papal complicity, they foreground even more a profound lay desire for clerical authentication. Counterfeit though it is, the appeal to papal authority projects the narrative definitively beyond the orbit of Walter's own power. In this way it is unlike all the other inscriptions of institutionalized power relations which circulate through the narrative: Walter's initial face-off with his advisers; his translation of Griselda to the status of marchioness; his continual invocations of the potential threat her social mobility poses; and the elaborate staging of the sham marriage to his daughter. All of these details are more easily depoliticized because they are so clearly direct extensions of Walter's own power. They can thus be folded back into a naturalized narrative of marital relations, a simple story of cruel husband and patient

---

[42] Dorothy M. Owen, *The Medieval Canon Law: Teaching, Literature, and Transmission* (Cambridge, 1990), 2.

wife. By contrast, the invocation of the bureaucratic machinery of the papal court implies these marital relations are themselves institutionally constructed and regulated. Moreover, invoking this machinery through the figure of forgery suggests not only that such regulation is arbitrary and contingent, but productive in its very contingency.

Both of these aspects—both the productiveness and the contingency —would have been evident to Chaucer and his audience. Indeed, if anything they would have been more evident to Chaucer and his audience than they are to postmodern scholarship. For the institutional relations to which this fiction of the forged papal letter refers were themselves in the midst of a long struggle to be born. That is to say, they were not yet fully routinized. In order to appreciate why, we will have to examine further both the royal marriage dispensation and problem of forgery, the two phenomena this passage brings together. The examination will take us momentarily away from the language of Chaucer's text. At the same time, as my discussion will show, there is a discursive convergence between these two institutional phenomena which corresponds to the symbolic condensation this passage effects.

If extant records are any indication, papal dispensations were an important feature of royal marriage negotiations in the later Middle Ages, especially in England. The Public Record Office contains a substantial collection of papal bulls relating to royal marriages. Many of these are dispensations to marry in the third and fourth degrees of consanguinity. Edward I, Edward II, and Edward III all requested blanket dispensations for all of their sons and daughters. Edward I and Edward II both received them. These two letters are particularly remarkable in that they seem to be form-letters. Although composed thirty-one years apart, signed by different popes, and the first coming out of Rome and the second out of Avignon, they are completely identical except for the change in the name of the pope.[43] Edward III was refused, perhaps because his request must have come shortly after Innocent VI granted absolution to his son the Black Prince and Joan of Kent.[44] Although related in the third degree of consanguinity and the second degree of spiritual affinity (the Black Prince

---

[43] The dispensation to Edward I, PRO SC7/18/16, is from Honorius IV, and is dated 27 May 1286. The dispensation to Edward II, PRO SC7/24/9, is from John XXII and is dated 1 Apr. 1317.

[44] PRO SC7/34/1. This refusal is dated 18 Dec. 1364. The dispensation, PRO/SC7/22/15 (printed in Thomas Rymer (ed.), *Foedera, conventiones, litterae, et cuiuscunque generis acta publica inter reges Angliae et alios quosvis imperatores, reges, pontifices, principes, vel communitates* (London, 1708), addressed to the Archbishop of Canterbury, the Bishop of London, and the Abbot of Cluny, is dated 7 Sept. 1361.

was godfather of Joan's son from a previous marriage), they married secretly, without obtaining a dispensation. Richard II apparently made no such requests—not surprisingly since both of his marriages were childless. However, he received a dispensation before his own marriage to Isabella, to whom he was related in the third and fourth degrees, and a papal letter of congratulation before his first marriage to Anne of Bohemia.[45] Marriage dispensations were available to lesser nobles as well. In such cases, forgery was a more likely possibility. One of the registers for Urban VI contains a mandate to the Archbishop of Canterbury issued in 1394 reporting that a corrupt papal official named Stephen de Cusantia had forged 'dispensations for marriage and illegitimacy, indulgences for churches, unions of benefices and other graces . . . under the pope's name and bull' and that 'persons ecclesiastical and secular' have carried them back to England.[46]

Such forgeries were a threat precisely because of the Church's strong predisposition to validate existing marriages and make future ones possible. The dispensation or absolution for impediments of consanguinity enabled the Church to maintain its sacramental ideology of marriage and its regulatory role without simply thwarting the lay interests at stake. To this extent, such dispensations and absolutions constitute a tacit acknowledgement that the clerical model of marriage never fully transformed the lay model it partially displaced. At the same time, it would be a mistake to view these exceptions as simply a safety valve or sign of ideological incompletion. For they also bespeak a notion of institutional regulation different from the modern bureaucratic ideal of a fully prescribed and invariant routine. Instead, this notion openly proclaims the necessity that modern bureaucracy represses everywhere as scandalous: that all rules, no matter how fundamental or internally consistent, must be interpreted anew every time they are applied. Rules are not simply privative restraints to be enforced, they are also ideals toward which one continually struggles, and many failures must be forgiven or otherwise accommodated in order that the struggle continue. One could do worse than call this conception of regulation penitential, except that in marriage cases, the Church was as concerned with the equilibrium of the political community as it was with the spiritual condition of the contracting principals. Thus, while Innocent VI, in the text of his absolution of Joan of Kent and the Black Prince, certainly concerns himself with the matter of their

---

[45]   PRO SC7/64/21, PRO SC7/34/17.   [46]   *Calendar of Entries*, 257.

penance, is just as concerned to insist on his interest in the avoidance of scandal and the 'benefit of peace and quiet'.[47]

Such a conflation becomes cynical or hypocritical only if one ignores the spiritual desire driving its institutional logic. Paradoxically, scholarly discussion of medieval forgery has tended to ignore this dimension. For the most part it has concentrated, perhaps appropriately, on the problems forgery poses for modern uses of medieval sources. In one of the few general treatments of the problem, Giles Constable has argued medievalists need to develop a more flexible and culturally specific notion of truth: 'Forgeries and plagiarisms . . . follow rather than create fashion and can without paradox be considered among the most authentic products of their time.'[48] The point is a salutory one, but it still begs an important question. These 'authentic products' are products of a time which is marked precisely by the emergence of textual authentication as an institutional ideal, and as a mode of administrative power. The systematic expansion of its written records was one of the ways the papacy increased its power during the period of reform. Indeed, if it is true, as some have argued, that the twelfth century was the heyday of medieval forgery, then its 'authenticity' would be especially predictable. The 'fashion' that these forgers were following was precisely a new ideal of written authentication; that is, a new intolerance for forgery. Elizabeth A. R. Brown is thus right to object in response to Constable that medieval philosophical 'principles do not suggest that the medieval conception of truth and falsity was radically different from our own'.[49]

At the same time there is a fairly stark distinction to be drawn between medieval and modern notions of institutional authority to which the ideal of textual authentication is applied. Papal authority was transcendent yet derivative. By contrast, modern bureaucracies lay claim to a panoptical neutrality which is no less idealized, but which understands itself as primary rather than derivative. This institutional distinction may help explain how medieval culture could have both the flexible attitude toward forgery that Constable suggests and philosophically absolutist standard of truth on which Brown insists. Michael Clanchy provides perhaps the most comprehensive treatment of the problem in *From Memory*

[47] Rymer, *Foedera*, vol. iii, part 2, 626.

[48] Giles Constable, 'Forgery and Plagiarism in the Middle Ages', *Archiv für Diplomatik Shrifigeschichte Siegel-und Wappenkinde*, 29 (1983), 2.

[49] Elizabeth A. R. Brown, '*Falsitas pia sive reprehensibilis*: Medieval Forgers and Their Intentions', in Wolfram Seitz (ed.), *Fälschungen im Mittelalter: Internationaler Kongress der Monumenta Germaniae Historica, München, 16–19. September 1986* (Hanover, 1988), i. 112.

to Written Record, looking for middle ground between absolutist and relativist positions by viewing medieval notions of authentication as governed by the retention of oral ideals within literate practices.[50] Citing a case where even the great reformer Innocent III, who ran his chancery personally, failed to detect a forged papal bull despite applying 'elementary physical tests', he suggests that the scholastic training of Innocent and his cardinals 'had been predominantly oral in character' causing them to 'prefer touch, speech, and hearing' to the 'intensive study' necessary for 'scientific historical criticism'. Expecting Innocent to observe 'the canons of careful textual criticism' would be 'anachronistic'.[51] Yet even as Clanchy cautions us against one sort of anachronism, he commits another. His opposition between the oral and literate leads him to define the problem of textual authentication as an entirely technological one. Innocent's authentication practices are driven as much by his sheer ignorance of 'the canons of careful textual criticism' (and apparent aversion to 'intensive study') as they are by his positive preference for 'touch, speech, and hearing'.

But ideals of authentication can never be purely technical. As a semiotic process, a mode of differentiation always embedded in very particular institutional structures, authentication is an activity, a way of producing truth, rather than a neutral registration of a truth already fully existent. An authentic document is authentic because it is not forged; as a practical matter, the principle of authenticity is logically dependent on the possibility of forgery. Indeed, the practices of authenticating documents consist largely of ensuring they cannot be forged. Authentication thus depends on formulaic, ritualized bureaucratic procedures. When we confront the problem in its medieval context, what we confront is not simply the institution of such procedures, but also the very ideal of written authentication toward which such procedures refer. It is not enough to note that this ideal coincided with the shift from orality to literacy; we must also recognize the extent to which this ideal drove that shift. As an element of papal reform, the regularization of written records was part of an unprecedented assertion of clerical privilege—an assertion, moreover, that was itself partially founded on a forgery, the Donation of Constantine—in Clanchy's phrase, 'the pope's own title-deed'.[52]

The Donation was the most far-reaching of all medieval forgeries. It

<hr/>

[50] M. T. Clanchy, *From Memory to Written Record: England 1066–1307*, 2nd edn. (Oxford, 1993), esp. 318–26.
[51] Ibid. 325.   [52] Ibid.

'was drawn up before the mid-eighth century, when the papacy was anxious to use and control the Frankish leaders'.[53] The document asserted that Constantine had offered the Church all the *temporalia* of the Empire as a sign of gratitude for his conversion, and it served as one of the papacy's primary supports in its long battle for ideological supremacy over lay rulers. For this reason, despite the paradox, we must view the papal chancery's procedural innovations for the elimination of forgery on the small scale, and the papacy's promulgation of the forged Donation on the large scale as part of the same broad historical trend. I am not suggesting that later popes consciously recognized the Donation as forged, or would not have cared if somehow that fact had been revealed to them. What I am suggesting is that their failure to recognize it as forged cannot be construed merely as technical naivety. They did not question the Donation because the desire it expressed—that Christian spirituality have an insitutionalized social presence whose authority is verifiable—was the same desire driving the conversion of oral custom to verifiable written record.

Nor was this paradoxical connection between institutionalization and forgery restricted to ecclesiology. There was another forgery similar in scope and influence to the Donation. That was the Pseudo-Isidorean Decretals, a widely circulated collection consisting 'largely of forged papal letters and spurious conciliar canons'.[54] Composed somewhere in northern France in the mid-ninth century, it was falsely presented as the work of Isidore of Seville. It was used throughout the Middle Ages, and was an important source for Gratian and subsequent canonists, particulary in regard to marriage. As H. A. Kelly notes, Gratian begins his treatment of the crucial question of clandestine marriage with one of the forged decretals from this collection.[55] While it is true that many of the collection's other canons relating to marriage were actually authentic, that seems less crucial to our purpose than their annexation to a spurious authority. In any case, Gratian and his followers used these canons to construct a theory of marriage formation that was both novel and driven by a logic of authentication. To existing lay notions they brought three innovations: they insisted that marriage be strictly monogamous, indissoluble, and freely contracted. The combination of freedom to contract with the obligation of indissolubility obviously focused marriage more exclusively on the two partners. It also intensified marriage's ideological status.

[53] Jane Sayers, *Innocent III: Leader of Europe 1198–1216* (London, 1994), 12.
[54] Brundage, *Law, Sex, and Christian Society*, 171.
[55] H. A. Kelly, *Love and Marriage in the Age of Chaucer* (Ithaca, NY, 1975), 164.

What had been little more than a frankly political arrangement for the distribution and transmission of property rights became a mode of soliciting and authenticating individual desire. Desire was called forth in the freedom to contract and authenticated, made proper and lasting, by the obligation of indissolubility. The importance of these two factors was such that they increasingly prevailed over competing claims, sometimes over the desires of families, and often over the Church's own prohibitions against consanguinity and affinity. With this change canon law created an ideal of authentication that resembled the conversion from oral custom to written record. A man and a woman created a marriage by the act of contracting it, even in secret. The canonists provided a textual framework whereby such oral performatives were given lasting value.[56]

To sum up: the interrelations among marriage, clerical regulation, and written instrument in later medieval culture were complex and profound. It is to these interrelations that Chaucer's fictional forged papal letter speaks, and it is precisely because of the detail's literal implausibility that it can reveal the deeper interdependence between forgery and authentication and the resultant power of textual structures to shape desire. The detail should itself be seen as an expression of desire—a desire at once highly specific and mediated and diffuse, whose object is the power a written code has to invest gender relations with transcendent value, the power that a forgery dramatizes even more effectively than an authentic instrument would. And this highly specific desire opens into the tale's larger desires: those clustering around the ethical and political ideals Griselda embodies. Griselda's exemplarity begins with the excessiveness of her promise to Walter. She swears to meet his every desire and never to disobey him. The tale stages this promise in a way that matches closely the priority the canonists put on the freedom to contract. To be sure, Walter speaks to Griselda's father first and receives his consent. But despite that,

[56] I want to make it clear I am focusing my discussion mainly on ideals and beliefs. The innovations of the canonists did not displace the more economic relations of marriage in any substantial or wholesale sense. Nor did the Church encourage disobedience to parental wishes in the matter of marriage choices. At the same time, there is no denying that the canonical innovations had a broad influence on the ideology of marriage, and a discernible influence on practice. See Charles Donahue, Jr., 'The Canon Law on the Formation of Marriage and Social Practice in the Later Middle Ages', *Journal of Family History*, 8 (1983), 145–58. For a dissenting view see A. J. Finch, 'Parental Authority and the Problem of Clandestine Marriage in the Later Middle Ages', *Law and History Review*, 8 (1990), 189–204; also, Donahue's response ' "Clandestine" Marriage in the Later Middle Ages: A Reply', *Law and History Review*, 10 (1992), 315–22. On the dissemination of the canon law doctrine among the laity see Kelly, *Love and Marriage*, 163–201; and Frederik Pedersen, 'Did the Medieval Laity Know the Canon Law Rules on Marriage? Some Evidence from Fourteenth-Century York Cause Papers', *Mediaeval Studies*, 56 (1994), 111–52.

and despite his vast class superiority, all depends on her consent. Her freedom to contract literally makes her patience and constancy possible, enabling the excess that structures her suffering and gives it meaning. For, paradoxically, it is the excessiveness of Griselda's freedom that produces a gendered deformation in the obligation of indissolubility. In canonistic doctrine, this obligation is theoretically unmarked, and it was this studied neutrality that occasioned lay resistance. As the Griselda tale laicizes the canonistic model, it defuses the tension by producing a gendered asymmetry. Griselda promises never to disobey. Walter makes no reciprocal promise. When he stages a dissolution of the marriage, the tale necessarily enacts the asymmetry, and a phantom papal blessing hovers over it all, at once enabling it and declaring it impossible.

Griselda's peculiar moral heroism requires not just that she suffer, but that she suffer in response to repeated testing, that her suffering be authenticated and verified. Such suffering consecrates the domestic as a specifically lay space of spiritual virtue. Walter's outrageous tests, in their very outrageousness, express a desire not only that such a space be produced, but that its authenticity be proved again and again and again. This desire for authenticity is not dissimilar to the authenticity which Petrarch himself identified with the tale's moral authority. In one of the letters to Boccaccio concerning the tale, he describes the reactions of two readers to his new version. The first is overcome by tears and cannot finish it. The second reads it without difficulty, but reports he too would have cried, if he could have believed it were true. For the story struck him as inherently unlikely:

> For if it were true, what woman, whether of Rome or any other people, might be compared with this Griselda? Where might I find such conjugal love, where such faith, such signal patience, and constancy?

> nam si vera essent, quae usquam mulier vel Romana vel cuiuslibet gentis hanc Griseldim aequatura sit, ubi quaeso tantus amor coniugalis, ubi par fides, ubi tam insignis patientia atque constantia?

Petrarch listens politely to his friend, but explains to Boccaccio that such extraordinary virtue is possible, citing a series of ancient examples.[57] For Petrarch it is precisely Griselda's excessiveness which ensures her authenticity. The tears of the first reader recapitulate the tears Walter must suppress when he sees how patiently she bears her expulsion—tears which the crowd following her back to her father's hut allow to flow copiously

---

[57] Francesco Petrarca, *Operum* (Basel, 1554), i. 606–7.

(IV, 892–7). This reader's inability to finish the story seems at once an acknowledgement of the impossibility of the desire Griselda fulfils and an insistence that it be fulfilled nonetheless. At the very moment Petrarch offers Griselda as an ideal of domestic sanctity, of *constantia feminae*, he locates her authenticity in her impossibility. Chaucer inherits this paradoxical ideal from Petrarch, and at nearly every opportunity heightens its logical tensions. He too concludes his version of the tale with a meditation on its moral efficacy, modulating Petrarch's suggestions of impossibility into a brief burlesque. Yet even here, where his irony is most explicit, Chaucer never lets go of his didactic ambitions.

VI. The Clerk, the Poet, the Wife and Her Tale: Irony and the Envoy

We come now to a crux of another sort. For most modern readers the *Clerk's Tale* ends in what Carolynn Van Dyke memorably describes as 'a semiotic deadlock'.[58] The Clerk concludes his tale gradually, his amplification of Petrarch's moral giving way to an appeal to 'stynte of ernestful matere' (IV, 1175), and to the parodic *Lenvoy de Chaucer*, a shift in discursive register from the transcendent seriousness of Christian didacticism to the low comedy of the antifeminist tradition. I have no interest in minimizing the generic opposition between the Petrarchan moral and the envoy. Nevertheless, it should be noted that to construe this opposition as a deadlock is to posit a semiotic model that is essentially synchronic. If I have been right to argue that didactic narrative must be read diachronically, even at the level of its formal structures, then other interpretations are possible, and the problem with ironic readings of the tale's conclusion is that they are never ironic enough. That is to say, its most far-reaching irony is not the difference between the didactic and the comedic but their ultimate similarity. The comedy is premissed on the radical impossibility of Griselda's virtue. Yet, as we have already seen, so is Petrarch's moral. As the Clerk explains,

> This storie is seyd nat for that wyves sholde
> Folwen Griselde as in humylitee.
> For it were inportable . . .

(IV, 1142–4)

[58] Van Dyke, 'Subjected Subjects', 60. For a comprehensive discussion of the critical history of the tale's conclusion and of the many interpretive difficulties it poses, see Howell Chickering, 'Form and Interpretation in the *Envoy* to the *Clerk's Tale*', *Chaucer Review*, 29 (1995), 353–72.

Chaucer uses this impossibility to constitute the thematic unity of his conclusion, and the unity it enforces is actually fairly tight, in spite of the generic opposition. In two different ways, Chaucer will suggest that this impossibility must be read diachronically. The first is the formal movement of his language, which is gradual rather than abrupt and makes the shift in genre difficult to pinpoint. The second is the striking appeal to the 'Wyves love of Bathe' (IV, 1170), which returns us to the collection's frame-tale, and uses its slightly broader formal diachrony to highlight the relative novelty of the Griselda story and its domestic ideal.

The Clerk substantially amplifies Petrarch's moral, using nearly four stanzas to translate and expound what was a single paragraph in the original. The first three stanzas constitute a leisurely restatement of the moral itself. The fourth begins in a similar register, with a warning to husbands that could be considered implicit in Petrarch, namely, if we are to take Griselda's exemplarity seriously, not only must men aspire to it as well as women, they must also not take spousal forbearance for granted:

> But o word, lordynges, herkneth er I go:
> It were ful hard to fynde now-a-dayes
> In al a toun Griseldis thre or two . . .
>
> (IV, 1163–5)

In fact this stanza will look in both directions. What begins as a warning to husbands becomes a burlesque on wives, albeit delivered in milder terms than what will follow:

> The gold of hem hath now so badde alayes
> With bras, that thogh the coyne be fair at ye,
> It wolde rather breste a-two than plye
>
> (IV, 1166–8)

The stanza's opening lines anticipate the shift by adopting a slightly more colloquial tone than those preceding: 'But o word, lordynges, herkneth er I go'. Nevertheless, the stanza as a whole could reasonably stand either with the moralizing that precedes or the parody that will follow. The next stanza contains the Clerk's call to 'stynte of ernestful matere' (IV, 1175). Yet that call comes at the end of the stanza, which begins with the apostrophe to the Wife of Bath. Thus, by the time the Clerk announces the shift in genre, it has already occurred.

With this formal sleight of hand, Chaucer locates the didactic in the same indeterminate discursive space as the ironic—not surprisingly, since the impossible, transcendent exemplarity it celebrates must similarly be enacted entirely within the fallen, indeterminate structures of human marital relations. He mitigates the abrupt break with the immediate past that irony characteristically uses a formal support. Instead, the irony of the envoy never fully escapes from the shadow of Griselda's exemplarity, and its quintessentially diachronic form of meaning. As a narrative structure, Griselda's exemplarity must continually retain both the impossibility of its past (Walter's egregious wickedness) and the imperative of its future (the requirement that her impossible achievement be imitated). Thus, the parodic shift from earnest to game, turning precisely on Griselda's impossibility paradoxically reinforces her example's already ironic premiss. The envoy redefines married life as an unending series of petty squabbles, urging noble wives to let no humility nail their tongue, to follow Echo in never holding silent, and to pierce their husbands' breasts with arrows of crabbed eloquence (IV, 1183–1206). But this very degradation implicitly magnifies Griselda's achievement by lengthening the odds against which it was accomplished. The final parody is just another degradation for Griselda to rise above, its irony an after-effect of the more profound impossibilities that constitute the narrative's core.

Chaucer anticipates the preponderance of his modern readership to the extent that he associates Griselda's impossible virtue with a past long lost. The envoy begins: 'Griselde is deed, and eek hire pacience, | And both atones buryed in Ytaille' (IV, 1177–8). Yet even here the envoy's irony turns against itself. For the Clerk introduces the envoy by dedicating it to the Wife of Bath. And indeed, it is the Wife of Bath who is the antique in this comparision. She is antecedent to Griselda, both in the chronology of the tale-telling contest, and in the wider European tradition. Her rhetorical lineage is not only much older than Griselda's, but more clerical. While Griselda is a product of the Italian *quattrocento*, the Wife of Bath is conventionally traced all the way back to fourth-century monasticism and Jerome's *Adversus Jovinianum*. Even in her laicized versions she looks back to La Vieille and *Le Roman de la Rose*. For Chaucer and his contemporary audience, it was the Wife of Bath who spoke for tradition and Griselda who represented innovation. With this closing appeal to the Wife of Bath, Chaucer offers Griselda's exemplary sacralization of marriage as another response to the Wife's dilemmas. Griselda fulfils the desire for transcendence animating the *Wife of Bath's Tale*, albeit in a radically transposed form.

A peasant girl who comes to exercise seigneurial power in her husband's stead, Griselda achieves a share of the sovereignty the Wife of Bath tells us women most want. It is certainly true that this share is momentary, and is quickly overshadowed by Griselda's subsequent submission. Nevertheless, this sovereignty is the public sort the term literally designates. If Griselda only achieves it by completely abandoning any of the household power the Wife's more metaphorical use actually intends, then her literal fulfilment of Alison's metaphorical desire still exposes the idealism implicit everywhere in the *Wife of Bath's Tale*—an idealism no less tenacious for its latency. It is not just that, as Elaine Hansen has observed, the hag gives up all her power for a happy ending and 'a more suitable alignment of the sexes' (*Chaucer and the Fictions of Gender*, 33). It is that from the beginning the hag defines her power in entirely domestic terms. She yields up the secret of her gender for the sole purpose of securing a husband, then restricts her desire for sovereignty to mastery over him, as if the institutional structure of marriage were entirely bounded by the relations between husband and wife. As we have already seen, in relation to this particular idealization, the *Clerk's Tale* is completely disenchanted. From the opening negotiations between Walter and his people to the actual succession of his son the tale has the social functions of marriage constantly in view: the production of heirs, the responsibility of the ruler to the ruled, and the regulatory role of the Church. Moreover, Chaucer has already signalled the absence of this more material view within the *Wife of Bath's Tale* itself, and done so repeatedly. He makes a variety of additions to the narrative: the rape (III, 882–98), the initial characterization of Arthurian Britain as dominated by 'The elf-queene with her joly compaignye', the appeal to the antifraternal stereotype of the *penetrans domos* immediately thereafter (III, 857–81), and the long digression on *gentilesse* and poverty that precedes the narrative denouement (III, 1109–206).

This digression is perhaps the most striking anticipation of the *Clerk's Tale*. It is worth examining briefly for its trajectory extends beyond the *Clerk's Tale* to the *Tale of Melibee*, to the tale, that is, where Chaucer's didactic interests are most clearly and directly on display. In his landmark study, *Chaucerian Polity*, David Wallace links the *Melibee* to the *Wife of Bath's Tale*: as the rape which begins *Melibee* recalls the beginning of the *Wife of Bath's Tale*, so the lady's turn as counsellor prefigures the role of Prudence.[59] But her counsel also prefigures the *Clerk's Tale*. In response to her husband's complaint that she is not only old and ugly, but also low-born, the lady argues that true *gentilesse* is not inborn or passed down from one generation to the next, but 'cometh fro God allone' (III, 1162).

---

[59] Wallace, *Chaucerian Polity*, 221–46. I should note that in his brief treatment of the end of the *Clerk's Tale* (292–3), Wallace prefers the more standard reading.

This argument is essentially the same one Walter uses when his court offers to find him a bride. He reminds his advisers that 'children often been
| Unlyk hir worthy eldres hem bifore | Bountee comth al of God, nat of
the streen | Of which they been engendred and ybore' (IV, 155–8), and this
claim underwrites his subsequent demand that they obey and honour
whomever he chooses to marry, whatever her social position. This argument not only opens up the domestic sphere where Griselda achieves her
peculiar spiritual triumph but it also connects that spiritual achievement
with her social mobility. It is true that both the triumph and the social
mobility come at an exorbitant cost. Nevertheless, by connecting the two,
the tale generates enormous rhetorical and ideological power, making
such social mobility a specifically feminine form of spiritual achievement,
and refiguring the domestic as a zone of specifically feminine spiritual
privilege.

Chaucerians have long recognized that the Loathly Lady draws her argument largely from the fourth book of Dante's *Convivio*. But they have
been less interested in its longer pedigree. In fact, the argument first appears in Aristotle's *Politics*, and is then expanded by Aquinas in his commentary on that work. But the more relevant and proximate source is the
De regimine principum of Giles of Rome, the most widely disseminated
Fürstenspiegel of the later Middle Ages.[60] Like Giles, Dante introduces the
argument that nobility is not inborn as a critique of popularly received
opinion; unlike Giles he stresses the importance of class mobility in the
formation of the noble class. The Lady takes the argument even further.
She characterizes her husband's received belief as not only mistaken but as
arrogance not worth a hen (III, 1112). And drawing from the Romance of
the Rose the claim *gentilesse* comes from God, she is able to push Dante's
interest in social mobility to an extreme that seems to call class hierarchy
itself into question. Moroever, in the very act of deploying this authoritative philosophical argument she momentarily exercises a public role. She
literally domesticates the voice of princely adviser, just as Dante had de-
mocratized it, presenting the *Convivio* as philosophical advice to those
caught up in familial and civic responsibilities (*cura familiare o civile*).[61]

---

[60] Giles's discussion occurs in I. iv. 5. For a citation and brief discussion, see Larry Scanlon,
Narrative, Authority and Power: The Medieval Exemplum and the Chaucerian Tradition
(Cambridge, 1994), 111–14. The *De regimine* was a work of central importance to later medieval
culture, which modern scholarship has almost entirely ignored. Charles F. Briggs, *Giles of
Rome's 'De regimine principum': Reading and Writing Politics at Court and University, c.1275–c.1525*
(Cambridge, 1999) is an admirable first step toward remedying this neglect.
[61] Dante Alighieri, *Il convivio*, ed. Maria Simonelli (Bologna, 1966), I. i. 13, p. 3.

There is no doubt the Lady abandons this ambition in her subsequent accommodation to her husband's desire. Yet like the unresolved issue of the initial rape, the conceptual range of her digression on *gentilesse* so exceeds the grasp of the accommodation that it remains in force as an ironic comment on the tale's ostensible closure. It looks forward to Walter's recapitulation, and its threat to collapse class and gender distinction provides Griselda's exemplary virtue with an even sharper and more radical horizon.

Indeed, with its recycling of stereotypes, *Lenvoy de Chaucer* returns not to this aspect of the Wife of Bath and her tale, but to an earlier moment, to the middle portions of her prologue, and to the anti-feminist tradition, which, by the time she begins her tale, the Wife has largely disabled. To take the envoy as undercutting either the Petrarchan moral, or the *Clerk's Tale* as a whole, means ignoring this complexity, along with all the others Chaucer characteristically builds into this magisterial ending. It means ignoring the larger didactic trajectory that moves through the *Clerk's Tale* to *Melibee*, and the rhetorical sophistication Chaucer brings to his didactic aspirations generally. One can find these aspirations almost everywhere one looks in his work. Thankfully, the older historicist ploy of using them to avoid the challenges of Chaucer's manifold ironies has now been largely discredited. The formalist ploy of reading Chaucerian irony as a defence against didacticism has little more to recommend it. The real challenge is to understand how Chaucer's irony and his didacticism work off of each other. It has been a truism since before Kittredge that Chaucer was fascinated by the institution of marriage. A sophisticated appreciation of his didacticism reveals this fascination as a profound intellectual engagement with one of the central sites of institutional and ideological change in his time, and as a desire not only to understand this change, but to participate in it.

Rutgers University

A Political Pamphleteer in Late Medieval England: Thomas Fovent, Geoffrey Chaucer, Thomas Usk, and the Merciless Parliament of 1388

Clementine Oliver

In the autumn of 1387, reacting to the increasing influence of certain courtiers on King Richard II, a coalition of magnates known as the Appellants formally accused five of Richard's favourites of treason.[1] Finding himself deprived of the support of much of his constituency, Richard acceded to a parliamentary hearing against the accused, and on 3 February 1388, parliament convened in the White Hall at Westminster to decide the fate of several of Richard II's most prominent supporters. One remarkably impassioned account of these treason trials captured the emotionally charged nature of the proceedings:

> There was a mass of people filling the hall even to the corners. . . . Geoffrey Martin, clerk of the crown, stood in the midst of the parliament and for two hours rapidly read out the aforesaid articles. The hearts of some were struck with sadness because of the terrible things contained in the said articles; and the faces of many were swollen with the tears on their cheeks.[2]

I presented an earlier draft of this article at the California Medieval History Seminar at the Huntington Library and would like to thank the participants for their comments. I owe a great debt to Steven Justice and Jason Glenn for providing a close reading of my work, particularly as their observations and suggestions were invaluable.

[1] These magnates were the king's uncle, Thomas Woodstock, Duke of Gloucester; Richard Arundel, Earl of Arundel and Surrey; Richard Beauchamp, Earl of Warwick; Thomas Mowbray, Earl of Nottingham; and John of Gaunt's son Henry Bolingbroke, Earl of Derby. The five principal people accused by the Appellants were Robert de Vere, Duke of Ireland; Michael de la Pole, Earl of Suffolk, chancellor of England 1383–6; Alexander Neville, Archbishop of York; Nicholas Brembre, mayor of London 1377–8 and 1384–6; and Robert Tresilian, chief justice of the king's bench.

[2] 'Una vero hominum congluuies inibi fuerat aule usque in angulos. . . . Galfridus vero Martyn, clericus corone, in medio parliamenti lapsu duarum horarum predictos articulos festinanter lectitando antestetit. Quorundam vero corda concussa sunt mesticia propter inhorribilia in dictis articulis contenta. Et plures vultus turgidos dederunt cum lacrimis in maxillis.' Thomas Favent, *Historia Mirabilis Parliamenti*, ed. May McKisack, in *Camden Miscellany*, 14 (1926), 15.

These are not the tears of an audience caught up in some melodrama. These are the tears of victims who will seek retribution against the accused. We know of these tears shed in parliament on this day because this scene is recorded in the *Historia siue narracio de modo et forma mirabilis parliamenti apud Westmonasterium anno Domini millesimo CCCLXXXVJ, regni vero regis Ricardi Secundi post conquestum anno decimo,* a pamphlet composed shortly after the close of the Merciless Parliament. This pamphlet begins with an account of the activities of the Ricardian faction from late 1386 to late 1387, drawn from the parliamentary articles of appeal against the accused. Next follows a dramatic narrative of the parliamentary trials of the Ricardians in 1388, culminating with the execution of those condemned, and these trials and executions are the focal point of the pamphlet. This narrative of the proceedings against the Ricardians is both precise and detailed, suggesting that the author himself was witness to this parliament. Furthermore, the author's tone is both didactic and ruthless, leaving little room for doubt that he approved wholeheartedly of the condemnation of the accused. The pamphlet ends with the dissolution of parliament on 3 June 1388.

Who wrote this late fourteenth-century polemical tract commonly known as the *Historia mirabilis parliamenti?* In its standardized form, the author's name is recorded in modern bibliographies as Thomas Favent, but we find him in the administrative records of the late fourteenth century as Thomas Fovent.[3] But who was Thomas Fovent? The purpose of this essay is to answer this particular question, and at the same time, to explore the historiographical issues related to the way that historians have traditionally read political writing in late medieval England. However, this essay is not an examination of the *Historia* itself, and therefore I discuss the contents of the pamphlet only briefly and in passing here.[4] Of course, any biography of Fovent is merely a framework for his text, a way of situating the politics of his pamphlet. Who he was, whom he knew, and where he worked are auxiliary to the text itself. Nevertheless, answering the question of who Fovent was requires us to reassess not only his politics, but the very nature of politics in Ricardian England, thereby encour-

[3] From here on in this essay, I have elected to refer to the author of the *Historia* by his name as it is typically found written in the administrative records of the late fourteenth century, that is as 'Fovent'. However, he remains 'Favent' in the citations to the *Historia,* for this reflects the standard bibliographic listing.

[4] The present essay is based on a larger study of the *Historia* itself. See Clementine Oliver, 'A Political Pamphleteer in Late Medieval England: Thomas Favent and the Merciless Parliament of 1388', (Ph.D. thesis, University of California, Berkeley, 2000).

aging us to reconsider the political matrix in which writers such as Chaucer, Usk, and Gower might be located.

Fovent's *Historia*, the only text we can ascribe to his authorship, was brought to the general attention of medieval scholars by May McKisack's 1926 edition of the manuscript.[5] In her introduction to her edition of the *Historia*, McKisack gives us what biographical information she can about Fovent:

> Of the writer little is known. He is probably to be identified with the Thomas Favent, who was clerk of the diocese of Salisbury, who in 1394 received a papal indult to choose his own confessor,[6] and in 1400 received a ratification of his estate in the church of Dinton.[7] Now Dinton was within two miles of Fovant, Wiltshire, and the immediate tenant of the manor was Cicely Fovent, abbess of Shaftesbury, who was certainly kinswoman of Thomas. We might safely write his name as Fovent, and recognize his connection with a Hampshire territorial family of some note.[8]

McKisack also distinguishes Fovent's narrative from all other accounts of the Merciless Parliament, for as she explains, 'the contents of the *Historia* are more in the nature of a political pamphlet than of a chronicle.'[9]

Prior to completing this edition of the *Historia*, McKisack showed the manuscript to T. F. Tout, who included a brief summary of Fovent in his 1926 article, 'Parliament and Public Opinion'. Tout reprised much of the

---

[5] McKisack's edition of the *Historia* was completed for volume xiv of the Camden Miscellany. Andrew Galloway's new translation of the *Historia* has been recently published in the appendix to Emily Steiner and Candace Barrington (eds.), *The Letter of the Law: Legal Practice and Literary Production in Medieval England* (Ithaca, NY, 2002). Galloway's translation undoubtedly will draw greater attention to the *Historia* and thereby encourage further consideration of the *Historia's* relationship to the politics of the period. See also Galloway's article in the same volume, 'The Literature of 1388 and the Politics of Pity in Gower's *Confessio amantis*', for a discussion of Fovent's text as it compares to other records of the treason trial.

[6] *Calendar of Papal Registers, Papal Letters*, vol. iv, ed. W. H. Bliss and J. A. Twemlow (London, 1902), 495. Citation is McKisack's.

[7] *Calendar of Patent Rolls, 1399–1401* (London, 1895–1909), 138. This reads 30 Mar. 1400, Westminster. 'Thomas Fouent, parson of the church of Donyngton [Dinton], in the diocese of Salisbury. By p.s.'

[8] McKisack, in Favent, *Historia*, vi.

[9] McKisack goes on to describe the only existing manuscript of the *Historia*, 'It consists of five parchment membranes stitched together to form a roll. The writing, which is clear and embellished with illuminated capitals, covers four membranes, each measuring $32''9 \times 11\frac{1}{8}''$, except the last, which measures $12'' \times 11\frac{1}{8}''$. The manuscript is complete and in a good state of preservation. It is evident that the Bodleian manuscript is not the author's original draft. The illuminations and the absence of any corrections or insertions in the text, when considered in conjunction with the many lapses from grammar and errors in dates, suggest that this manuscript was the work of a copyist with little knowledge of Latin. The handwriting seems to be of the late fourteenth or early fifteenth century.' McKisack, in Favent, *Historia*, v–vi.

bibliographic information McKisack would include in her introduction to the *Historia*, but he overlaid this information with an interpretive stratum that established Fovent's place within the inherited political blueprint of Richard's reign. Tout says of Fovent:

I suspect him to be a clerk attached to the household of one of the lords appellant, but the few particulars one can glean of his personal history throw no light upon his personal position or political activities. . . . A kinswoman, Cicely Fovant, perhaps a sister, became abbess of the great nunnery of Shaftesbury and founded in 1406 a chantry in memory of her father Robert and mother Edith, who may well have also been the parents of Thomas. Thomas himself obtained in 1393 an indult from Boniface VIII [*sic*] to choose his own confessor and in 1400 received a 'ratification of his estate' in the church of Dinton, a couple of miles north of Fovant, and a village held by the abbess of Shaftesbury of the Crown. This last grant suggests a disturbance of Thomas in the quiet holding of his benefice, such as would naturally result in the later years of Richard II's reign in the case of a violent Lancastrian partisan.[10]

A violent Lancastrian partisan. This is who Tout believed to be the author of the *Historia*. McKisack also thought Fovent a partisan, for she characterizes the *Historia* as possessed of a lively 'partisan spirit', describing its author as a 'political propagandist'.[11] McKisack and Tout's characterization of Fovent as an Appellant propagandist has remained until quite recently the final word on him, echoed again and again in essays describing the sources for the period and in biographies of Richard II.[12] But

---

[10] T. F. Tout, 'The English Parliament and Public Opinion, 1376–88', in E. B. Fryde and Edward Miller (eds.), *Historical Studies of the English Parliament* (Cambridge, 1970), 311–12. Fovent's indult must have come from Boniface IX (1389–1404), not Boniface VIII (1294–1303).

[11] McKisack, in Favent, *Historia*, vi.

[12] John Taylor, *English Historical Literature in the Fourteenth Century* (Oxford, 1987), 207. Taylor says of Fovent: 'Of Thomas Favent himself little is known. He may have been the Thomas Favent who was a clerk of the diocese of Salisbury. This Thomas Favent was connected with the church of Dinton, two miles from Fovent in Wiltshire. . . . Thomas Favent himself received a ratification of estates in 1400, and this may have been due to the troubles which as a Lancastrian partisan he experienced in the final years of Richard II's reign. . . . Favent wrote his account, which is one of the earliest parliamentary pamphlets we possess, from the viewpoint of one who was a strong supporter of the Appellants, the leaders of the baronial opposition in 1388.' Taylor cites McKisack and Tout as his sources. See also Antonia Gransden, *Historical Writing in England II* (Ithaca, NY, 1974), 185. Gransden says of Fovent: 'Some chronicles were deliberate attempts at propaganda. An early example is almost certainly Thomas Favent's tract on the Merciless Parliament of 1388. . . . The strength of its bias in favour of the Appellants indicates that it was composed to justify their harsh acts.' See also Nigel Saul, *Richard II* (New Haven, 1997), 125. Saul refers to Fovent as 'the pro-Appellant propagandist, who in the late 1380s wrote a tract on those lords' behalf'. See also Anthony Steel, *Richard II* (Cambridge, 1941), 145–6. Steel likewise takes his cue from both McKisack and Tout: 'Thomas Favent was probably a clerk in the diocese of

the overtly political and vitriolic tone of the *Historia* itself is not the central issue in this reading of Fovent. Tout's assessment of him as a partisan
is based on a tangle of issues that includes, but is by no means limited to,
the political extremism of Richard II's reign, the function of public opinion in shaping the political landscape of late fourteenth-century England,
the relationship between narrative and propaganda, and finally, this little
matter of the ratification of Fovent's benefice by the crown in 1400. It is
precisely this array of issues, each so radically different in size and scope,
that is concealed within Tout's tidy epithet, 'violent Lancastrian partisan'.

But Fovent was no Lancastrian partisan. Nor is the *Historia* a partisan
document. In order to demonstrate this I will begin with the simplest
issue first, the problem of the ratification of Fovent's benefice. This is the
one fact of his biography that confirmed for Tout that our pamphleteer
was indeed a Lancastrian sympathizer. Tout read Fovent's *Historia* as a
pro-Appellant document, and so Tout posited a 'disturbance of Thomas
in the quiet holding of his benefice' that reflected the inevitable fate of an
Appellant booster, an anti-royalist propagandist whose sentiments had
been brought to the attention of Richard II. As a political agitator, Tout
assumes, Fovent would necessarily have been penalized by Richard's administration at some point for rousing public sentiment against the king's
court. Tout does not elaborate on the details, but he evidently inferred
that Fovent's benefice must have been revoked around 1397 or so, when
Richard II began exacting his revenge against the opposition of 1388.
Richard's campaign to purge the opposition from his kingdom was
neither successful, nor long lived, for by September 1399 Henry IV
had usurped the throne from his uncle, putting an end to Richard's
'tyranny'—Richard's attempt to regain control of his administration by
desperate measures and reckless tactics that ran roughshod over the common rights of his subjects. By late March 1400, the date of the entry of
Fovent's ratification in the Patent Rolls, Henry was safely ensconced on

Salisbury, or perhaps a member of the household of an appellant magnate, it is not known which.
Miss McKisack in the introduction to her edition has made out a good case for the theory that
his pamphlet was written almost immediately after the rising of the merciless parliament, whose
proceedings it exalts and justifies, insisting on their legality and "fullness."' Steel goes on to explain that Fovent's pamphlet 'is of interest for, as Tout has shown, it betrays a consciousness of
what might now be called a "public opinion", which is something new in England, together with
a developed sense of the kind of propaganda necessary to foster and control it.' Only Andrew
Galloway departs from this well-worn path in his recent assessment of Fovent's pamphlet.
Galloway breathes new life into the *Historia* by characterizing it as 'satirical narrative', suggesting that Fovent's work is indicative of 'the intense satirical energy that the challenge of legal and
political authority unleashed'. Galloway, 'The Politics of Pity in Gower's *Confessio amantis*', 84.

the throne. Tout simply assumed that Henry's new administration considered it an appropriate move at this juncture to reward 'Lancastrian partisans' who had helped to stir up opposition to Richard's administration. At this point, Fovent's benefice was duly restored to him, a reward for his long-suffering allegiance to the Appellants and their cause of undermining Richard's supporters. Tout believed of Fovent that his life followed the course of any political partisan's life—his fortune would rise and fall with the political tides.

But this was not the case. Fovent never suffered any recriminations for writing the *Historia*, for the ratification of his estate in Dinton in 1400 had nothing to do with his political activity in 1388. An examination of the records of Fovent's ecclesiastical holdings between 1390 and 1404, the year of his death, reveals only a steady climb up the parish ladder. I will begin with an account of his holdings in Salisbury diocese.

As recorded in the register of John Waltham, Bishop of Salisbury from 1388 to 1395, Fovent was granted his first benefice in 1390, at the church of Berwick St Leonard, in the deanery of Chalke, located in the county of Wiltshire.[13] In 1393, as McKisack states, he received an indult to choose his own confessor.[14] In 1394, Bishop Waltham conducted a visitation of the parishes, and at this time Fovent was still at Berwick St Leonard, now clearly identified as rector of the church.[15] The benefice of Berwick St Leonard, like that of Dinton, was supported by the patronage of the Abbess of Shaftesbury. In 1398, Cicely Fovent, most likely Thomas's sister, was elected Abbess of Shaftesbury.[16] And in 1399, after Cicely's election as

[13] *The Register of John Waltham, Bishop of Salisbury 1388–1395*, ed. T. C. B. Timmins, The Canterbury and York Society (Suffolk, 1994), 76. Entry 552: 'Institution of M. Thomas Fovent, clerk, to ch. of Berwick St. Leonard (*Berewyck sancti Leonardi*), vac. by death of M. John Gyldon; patrons, abbess and conv. Shaftesbury. Salisbury, 29 Dec. 1390.' (Berwick St Leonard is about five miles, as the crow flies, from the town of Fovant, Wiltshire, presumably from where the family took its name.) Though I would have liked to have discovered Fovent's name in an earlier bishop's register, the obstacles proved too great. According to David M. Smith's *Guide to Bishop's Registers of England and Wales* (London, 1981), 190, the register for Robert Wyvil (1330–75) is 'very confused in arrangement'. It is unpublished, but place indexes have been compiled and are available in the Wiltshire County Record Office.

[14] *Calendar of Papal Registers, Letters*, iv. 495. Entry for Nov. 1393 reads: '[Indults to the underwritten persons to choose their confessors, who shall hear their confessions and give them absolution, enjoining a salutary penance.] Thomas Fovent, clerk, of the diocese of Salisbury.' This is McKisack's source.

[15] *Register of John Waltham*, 133. Visitation of Chalke Deanery, 11 Apr. 1394. Entry 973 l: 'Berwick St Leonard (Berewyk Leonardi): Thomas Fovent, R.; William the chapl.; John Dawe, Walter Burstak, Ralph Dawe, and John Dawe, [*sic*] parishioners.'

[16] *Victoria History of the County of Dorset*, ed. William Page and R. B. Pugh (London, 1908), 79. The Fovent family history compiled by L. S. Woodger for *The House of Commons: 1386–1421* also suggests that, given the dates of their respective careers, Cicely Fovent was very likely sister to Thomas. Cf. n. 66 below.

abbess, by her patronage Fovent is instituted at the church of Donhead St Andrew.[17] Fovent remains here only briefly—later the same year, by the process of exchange with the parson of another parish, he is promoted to the Dinton church.[18] The move to Dinton was clearly Cicely Fovent's handiwork, for the Dinton church was also under the patronage of the Abbess of Shaftesbury, and it was quite likely that the church carried with it a generous annuity.[19]

In 1400, Fovent's holdings at Dinton were indeed ratified by the crown, but this was not, as Tout believed, the result of a break in his benefice caused by political activities that transpired some twelve years prior.[20] Instead it was a simple confirmation of the transaction that had taken place a few months before, the crown acknowledging that he now held a minor estate in Dinton. It was the means of his institution at Dinton—the exchange of benefices with John Hereford—that necessitated the ratification to take place. Contrary to what Tout thought, there never transpired a 'disturbance' in Fovent's holdings, for he had never incurred any penalties for his *Historia*. Fovent's ecclesiastical career reflected only the routine promotion from benefice to benefice, helped along by the patronage of his kinswoman, Dame Cicely, Abbess of Shaftesbury. He retained the generous benefice at Dinton until his death in 1404.[21]

---

[17] This institution is found in a nineteenth-century index of Wiltshire institutions compiled by Sir Thomas Phillipps, *Institutiones clericorum in comitatu Wiltoniae, ab anno 1297* (Middle Hill, 1825), 85. The institutions are arranged chronologically, with the name of the benefice, patron, and incumbent, and the reason for the vacancy if it was noted. The entry for 1399 reads, 'Institution of Thomas Fovent to the church of Dunhed St. Andraae by the patronage of Abb. Shaston [Shaftesbury].'

[18] Ibid. 85. The entry for 1400 reads, 'Institution of Thomas Fovent permut. Cum Johannes Hereford to the church of Donyngton by patronage of Abb. Shaston.' John Hereford was instituted to Dinton by patronage of Abb. Shaftesbury in 1399, just prior to Fovent's institution. Ibid. 85.

[19] *Nonarum inquisitiones in curia Scaccarii, 1341* (London, 1807), 170. In 1341, the estate in Dinton is valued at about £22, whereas Donhead St Andrew is valued at about £16.

[20] *Calendar of Patent Rolls, 1399–1401*, 138. The entry for 30 Mar. 1400, Westminster, reads: 'Thomas Fouent, parson of the church of Donyngton, in the diocese of Salisbury. By p.s.' This is McKisack's source. Though Fovent is listed as parson, this is the same position as rector.

[21] Phillipps, *Institutiones clericorum in comitatu Wiltoniae*, 90. As of 1403, Fovent is still at Dinton, for the entry for 1403 reads: 'Institution of Johnannes Neweman, p.m. Roberti Arkylby to the vicarage of Donyngton by the patronage of Thomas Fovent, Rector.' (Arkylby was instituted to Dinton in 1393 by the patronage of Thomas Banastre de Eltisle. See ibid. 78.) By 1404, however, Fovent is deceased: 'Institution of Johnnes Elys, p.m. Thomas Fovent to the church of Donyngton by patronage of Abb. Shafton.' ibid. 91. See also *Calendar of Fine Rolls*, vol. xii (London, 1911–61), 222–3. Entry for 18 July 1404, Westminster: '[Order to the escheator . . . to take into the king's hand and keep safely until further orders all the lands in . . . who held of the king in chief, was seised in his demense as of fee on the day of his death; and to make inquisition

In light of this new information, there are two questions that should be addressed concerning Fovent's supposed Appellant partisanship. The first is why Tout believed that Fovent's *Historia* would inevitably mark him an antagonist to Richard's court and make him a target for retribution. The second question is how Fovent avoided getting into trouble for disseminating an anti-royalist tract. Though these two questions seem to contradict each other, taken in tandem they begin to unravel the issues behind Tout's characterization of Fovent as a 'violent Lancastrian partisan'. The first question hinges on the perceived political extremism of Richard II's reign, as well as the historiographical tradition surrounding Ricardian politics, for Tout believed the factional nature of politics in this period made unmediated participation in politics a perilous enterprise. The second question hinges on our understanding of the role of public opinion in shaping the political landscape of late fourteenth-century England, and asks us, in particular, to reconsider the relationship between propaganda and public opinion in this period. These questions lead us to re-examine not only our understanding of the political world of late medieval England, but also the historiography of political writing for this period.

To begin, Tout's estimation of Fovent as a partisan was no more than an attempt to reconcile the polemical tone of his work with the scant records of his life. The *Historia* invites this sort of reading precisely because its purpose is not entirely clear. As an independent political tract, not part of a chronicle or corpus, it leaves us without a context for interpreting Fovent's writing. Fovent is not Walsingham, not Knighton, not Gower, not Langland—he writes neither as a monastic historian nor as a public poet.[22] The *Historia* is a curiosity in that it is an independent account of a specific political event. In this respect, the *Historia* is nearly unique among late fourteenth-century texts, but its uniqueness is not commented on by those scholars who have discussed Fovent's work—they seem to shy away from making too much of the *Historia's* distinct form. In lieu of directly engaging the *Historia's* fervour or analysing its struc-

---

touching his lands an heir. The like orders touching the lands of the following persons, directed to the escheators in the counties named.] Thomas Fovent, clerk; Essex.' Unfortunately, I have been unable to discover the precise nature of his holdings in Essex.

[22] Galloway however, while characterizing Fovent's satirical style as 'ironic Christian allusion', demonstrates that Fovent's writing shares a particular thematic quality with both Knighton and Gower, something Galloway describes as a broad preoccupation with 'the menacing and unreliable nature of pity as a political and legal instrument'. See Galloway, 'The Politics of Pity in Gower's *Confessio amantis*', 68.

ture, scholars succumb to the temptation of confusing the *Historia* with the event it describes. By this I mean that scholars grant the *Historia* a dual charge—it is at once a source of facts about the Merciless Parliament and at the same time an archetype of the sort of political partisanship that defined the Merciless Parliament.[23] In essence, when scholars read the *Historia*, they read it within the context of the received history of the Merciless Parliament, never outside it.

The received history of 1388 includes two sets of key players, the nobles or Appellants on the one hand, and Richard II and his supporters—be they called favourites or courtiers or royalists—on the other. Tout and McKisack regarded the *Historia* as Appellant propaganda because they saw the Merciless Parliament as a contest between two factions, Richard's court party and the lords Appellant. As McKisack noted, Fovent's *Historia* is thoroughly preoccupied with the proceedings of the Merciless Parliament. The *Historia* is also sharply critical of Richard II's administration. But this does not necessarily mean that Fovent wrote the *Historia* in the service of the Appellants. This alone is not enough to affix to the *Historia* the label of Appellant propaganda.

In the months preceding the Merciless Parliament, as the Appellant case against Richard's supporters gained momentum, the conflict between the Ricardian faction and the Appellants grew in scope and size, embroiling countless secondary political players in the drama, attracting the attention of all those who were connected to the government in one way or another, introducing a multitude of convictions, concerns, and agendas into the event known as the Merciless Parliament. If Fovent's *Historia* is read outside the confines of the two-party Ricardian/Lancastrian framework, a framework which this crisis had outgrown by 1388 in any case, then his criticisms of Richard II's court, as well as his fascination with parliamentary proceedings, become not so much pro-Appellant propaganda as the makings of an independent political position.

Indeed, Fovent wastes few words of praise on the Appellants themselves, concentrating his efforts instead on promoting parliament as the institution most capable of reforming England's government.[24] Thus the

---

[23] Furthermore, it is an archetype of the typically ambivalent relationship between the historian and narrative, particularly political narrative. Both McKisack and Tout say again and again of the *Historia* that it is both an accurate and detailed source that provides information about the proceedings of the Merciless Parliament not available in any other sources from the period. Nevertheless, they caution us that the *Historia* is riddled with bias.

[24] Over the course of the *Historia*, Fovent mentions the Appellants by name rather infrequently, and though Gloucester and Arundel are named far more than the other three

real drawback of labelling the *Historia* propaganda is that it absolves us from addressing the difficult question of his purpose—of whom he imagined to be his audience, of what his own political interests were. If Fovent is considered a propagandist, then he is no more than an industrious partisan, a commonplace character in the political landscape of his day. But his agenda was considerably more complex than this.

As I have explained, Tout unquestionably regarded the *Historia* as political propaganda. At the same time Tout expounded upon precisely what Fovent's real purpose was in writing the *Historia*, the dissemination of political discourse across the public sphere. But can the *Historia* be both Appellant propaganda and an impassioned appeal to public opinion? To ask the same question in slightly different terms, we might wonder whether Fovent really wrote his *Historia* in the service of the Appellant party, or whether he wrote the *Historia* for readers like himself, politically minded Englishmen who were curious about parliamentary politics. Here I ask that we draw a distinction between propaganda and the work of a political pamphleteer. Tout however sees no distinction between the two, primarily because he has formulated the relationship between the rise of public opinion and parliament to underscore partisanship as the dominant political discourse of the period. But perhaps partisanship was not the only political mode available to Fovent.

This assertion calls for a re-evaluation of the meaning of public opinion in late fourteenth-century England. Here I think it is particularly helpful to consider the definition of public opinion offered by Jürgen Habermas as the critical-rational debate between private individuals about the nature of political governance. Habermas links the development of public opinion to the emergence of the public sphere, which he defines as 'the sphere of private people come together as a public'.[25] Because it consists of private people, the public sphere is distinct from the public authorities of the state, represented by the crown. It is, however, necessarily connected to the literary public sphere—the world of letters—a world where private individuals engage in critical-rational public debate, most significantly through the press. Habermas maintains that once the news itself became a commodity, private individuals transformed the public sphere into an arena of debate over political gover-

---

Appellants, Fovent gives few details about them, directly praising their actions only twice. Such treatment is consistent with Fovent's view of the Merciless Parliament as a parliamentary victory, not as an Appellant coup.

[25] Jürgen Habermas, *The Structural Transformation of the Public Sphere: An Inquiry into a Category of Bourgeois Society* (Cambridge, Mass., 1989), 27.

nance, moving politics out of the realm of public figures such as the king and into the realm of private individuals. This is the political public sphere. As Habermas explains, 'The medium of this political confrontation was peculiar and without historical precedent: people's public use of their reason.'[26] This medium is public opinion.

Habermas's public opinion is thus not the collective opinion of the people. As Habermas himself makes clear, public opinion is not concomitant with an 'outraged' or 'informed public'.[27] Instead, it is the opinion of private individuals expressed publicly. This debate over the nature of political governance is conducted by private individuals in public, typically through the printing press, specifically through newspapers.[28] And without such a debate, there would exist no political public sphere, for politics would remain in the hands of those public figures who represent the state, such as the king. Thus we can say of Fovent's pamphlet that it belonged to the category of public opinion, not that it simply informed or responded to public opinion.

However I would not want to accuse Fovent of voicing a reasoned opinion. In many respects, he has much more in common with those Grub Street hacks who, according to Robert Darnton, published the many *libelles* that began to erode the power of the Old Regime in late eighteenth-century France. There is no question that Fovent's *Historia* is overtly critical of certain political figures. But the *Historia* is best described as a passionate and vitriolic political tract, and so perhaps like Darnton's Grub Street pamphleteers, Fovent's authorial voice was born of 'visceral hatred'.[29] This too is a type of public opinion, and it is an important one because it mirrors the often tempestuous and passionate nature of politics.

Both Habermas and Darnton write about specific historical moments, Habermas about the seventeenth and eighteenth centuries, and Darnton about the eve of the French Revolution. The Merciless Parliament of 1388, the subject of Fovent's *Historia*, occurred almost ninety years before the

---

[26] Ibid. 27.   [27] Ibid. 2.

[28] In explaining the relationship of newspapers to public opinion, Habermas cites Karl Bücher: 'Newspapers changed from mere institutions for the publication of news into bearers and leaders of public opinion—weapons of party politics. This transformed the newspaper business. A new element emerged between the gathering and the publication of news: the editorial staff. But for the newspaper publisher it meant that he changed from a vendor of recent news to a dealer in public opinion.' In Habermas, 'The Public Sphere: An Encyclopedia Article (1964),' *New German Critique*, 1/3 (Fall 1974), 53.

[29] Robert Darnton, 'The High Enlightenment and the Low-Life of Literature', in *The Literary Underground of the Old Regime* (Cambridge, Mass., 1982), 40.

introduction of printing to England. Late fourteenth-century England must then surely be another world. Or was it? Both Steven Justice and Wendy Scase have demonstrated that late medieval England was a world rich in political writing, some of it cryptic, some of it incendiary, much of it anonymous, but all of it meant to circulate.[30] The existence of this kind of political writing points to the question too long ignored by scholars of the period regarding the precise nature of public opinion in the pre-print world. Tout goes a long way towards answering this question by singling out Fovent's *Historia* as one of the most important tracts written about parliament from this period, remarking, 'parliament was beginning to interest the man in the street. It was becoming the focus of public opinion.'[31] Here Tout approaches Habermas's definition of public opinion, for the growing interest in parliament in late fourteenth-century England is not terribly far from the critical-rational debate between private individuals about the nature of political governance as described by Habermas. At the same time however, Tout regarded the *Historia* as 'a deliberate effort to educate public opinion to take up the baronial cause'.[32] Accordingly, Tout believed public opinion was merely a force to which the baronial faction appealed for support in order to lend strength to their case against the crown in parliament. In other words, opinion was something to be won, not something to be informed.

All things considered, I think Tout is right to place Fovent's *Historia* at the centre of the developing relationship between parliament and public opinion, but I would characterize it as a looser, if not more nuanced, construct. A non-partisan reading of Fovent demands that we understand the process of engaging the public as a viable and important political activity in its own right, one with ramifications that extend far beyond the programme of the baronial ranks. There is a significant difference between

[30] See Steven Justice, *Writing and Rebellion: England in 1381* (Berkeley, Calif., 1994). See also Wendy Scase, ' "Strange and Wonderful Bills": Bill-Casting and Political Discourse in Late Medieval England', in Rita Copeland, David Lawton, and Wendy Scase (eds.), *New Medieval Literatures*, 2 (Oxford, 1998).

[31] For a slightly different interpretation of the origins of public opinion in fourteenth-century England, see J. R. Maddicott, 'The County Community and the Making of Public Opinion in Fourteenth-Century England', *Transactions of the Royal Historical Society*, 5th ser., 28 (1977), 42. Maddicott observes of Tout's article, 'The novel importance of public opinion in the fourteenth century has often been recognized, but for too long we have looked to parliament alone for its expression. The work of the Commons in parliament was only the last stage in the long process by which opinion was shaped, transmitted and given voice. In that process the county court had a central place.' Significantly, Maddicott concludes that 'the political consciousness thus created was not confined to a provincial elite'.

[32] Tout, 'The English Parliament and Public Opinion', 310.

the dissemination of Appellant propaganda—as Tout regards Fovent's *Historia*—and engaging the public sphere—the process of appealing to the imagined 'public'—but Tout does not draw this distinction. Instead, Tout regards those who courted public opinion, all those who wrote about parliament, as participating in partisan politics.

As a discrete political text, the *Historia* seems all the more vitriolic, all the more charged, for standing alone. Tout and McKisack regard the craft of a pamphleteer as necessarily clandestine because a pamphleteer operates outside a defined textual practice—the *Historia's* textual isolation makes it seem all the more partisan in that Fovent's authorial voice is not grounded in the chronicle tradition. And because the political landscape of late fourteenth-century England is understood to be fragmented by factional affiliation, both scholars have assumed that there existed no indeterminate space in which to receive and read the *Historia*. Thus Tout and McKisack see Fovent's *Historia* as existing only within the network of factional affiliations that defined the Merciless Parliament. The *Historia* has never been examined as a textual position in its own right, for subsequent scholars remained content to lump it in with the Appellant cause.

Of course the real obstacle to making a case for the existence of non-partisan political discourse in late fourteenth-century England is that scholars have always understood Ricardian politics to be perilous by nature, particularly in 1388. Though Tout discusses the importance of public opinion to the parliamentary victories of 1377 and 1386, known as the Good and Wonderful Parliaments respectively, by 1388 the stakes of the political contest had been raised—being on the losing side this time cost participants their lives. By the close of the Merciless Parliament, five men had been convicted of treason, condemned for the crime of accroaching to themselves royal power, and several other lesser offenders—four members of the king's household, two prominent officials, and five judges—were impeached.[33] Some of those convicted escaped, some were spared their lives, many were granted the luxury of having their estates preserved for their heirs, but in all eight were executed.[34] Indeed Fovent himself took careful note of those who lost their careers, their property, and their

---

[33] Those impeached from the king's household were Simon Burley, John Beauchamp, John Salisbury, and James Berners. Their fate was shared by Thomas Usk and John Blake, functionaries both, and the judges Robert Belknap, John Holt, Roger Fulthorp, William Burgh, and John Cary, along with John Lokton, sergeant-at-law.

[34] Those executed were Brembre, Tresilian, Burley, Beauchamp, Salisbury, Berners, Usk, and Blake.

lives during the parliamentary proceedings.[35] Given the Merciless Parliament's outcome, one is certainly justified in wondering whether a political system so fragmented by factionalism could actually sustain a readership of politically minded individuals.

In the treacherous months that surrounded the Merciless Parliament, it seems quite likely that any polemical writer, and thus any readership, would be drawn into the fray, compelled to side with one faction or another. And this is precisely the *Historia's* true significance, for whether or not it was a partisan text, the fact that the *Historia* was intended for circulation lends Fovent's pamphlet a seditious quality. The advent of the *Historia* signifies absolutely that parliament had become the focus of public opinion. It also signifies that an unquantifiable, unknowable, and ulti-

---

[35]   For example, consider Fovent's account of the dismissal of several prominent officers from the royal household: 'Et quia opportune ad spinas, cardones et sizannia defalcanda et extirpanda tunc temporis instetit messis, ratihabicione regis mutuo consensu dictorum commissariorum omnium et appellatorum a domicilio regis plures officiarios expulerunt, videlicet, in locum Johannis Beauchamp, senescalli, Johannes Deuerose, miles, unus de commissariis subrogatur. Et Petrus de Courteney, miles, in camerarium regis, loco dicti ducis Hibernie ordinatur. Predictus vero Johannes Beauchamp, Simon de Bureley, sub-camerarius regis, Johannes Saresbury, hostiarius camere, Thomas Triuet, Jacobus Barens, Willelmus Elmham et Nicholaus Daggeworth, milites, et ceteri clerici officiarii, videlicet, Ricardus Metteford, secretarius, Johannes Slake, decanus capelle, Johannes Lincoln, camerarius scaccarii, et Johannes Clifford, clericus capelle, quia predictorum criminum tanquam participes, pro eo quod ea scientes et non contradicentes et quia quidam ea fieri volentes, diuersis Anglie carceribus usque in parliamentum ad imponenda responsuri sub aresto intrudi mandantur. . . . Et sic squalorosus nidus fixus in arbore quadam quantocius conquassatur, cuius saucissimi sorde volucres dispersim vacillando euolarunt.' Favent, *Historia*, 13–14.

'And because the time of the harvest was now at hand, right for cutting back thorns and uprooting weeds and thistles, by the king's approval, with the mutual consent of all the aforesaid commissioners and appellants, they expelled many officers from the king's household, for example, in the place of John Beauchamp, steward of the household, was substituted John Devereux, knight, one of the commissioners. And Peter Courtney, knight, was appointed chamberlain in place of Robert duke of Ireland. And the aforesaid John de Beauchamp, Simon de Burley, vice-chamberlain, John Salisbury, chamber knight, Thomas Trivet, James Berners, William Elmham, and Nicholas Dagworth, knights, and the rest of the clerical officers, namely, Richard Medford, secretary, John Slake, dean of the chapel, John Lincoln, chamberlain of the exchequer, and John Clifford, clerk of the chapel, because they were considered to have been partners in the aforesaid crimes (because they had known about these things and had not spoken against them and because some of them wished them to happen), they were put under arrest and held in various prisons in England to be handed over to answer for their actions in parliament. . . . And thus this squalid nest fixed in its tree was thoroughly shaken, its birds, wounded by their own filth, flying off hither and yon.'

Fovent is consistently well informed regarding the names and ranks of all those minor players caught up in the political contest between the Ricardians and the Appellants. Furthermore, there is no question that Fovent considered these people important, and this is because Fovent believed their jobs were important, for these men formed the core of Richard's personal administrative staff.

mately uncontrollable readership was being enticed by political discourse to partake in the scrutiny of Richard II's court. Thus Tout assumes that Fovent incurred political disfavour not just for his anti-Ricardian views, but for the very act of pamphleteering, because regardless of his political orientation, disseminating any sort of political writing in 1388 was a fundamentally clandestine proposition. In the end, perhaps the problem for Tout was not so much what Fovent said, but how he said it.

I would suggest that we have been too quick to assume that it was problematic for someone like Fovent to write about politics in 1388, and for this I am sure that Geoffrey Chaucer is to blame. Scholars have long portrayed Chaucer as a consummate political moderate, a genius of self-preservation, artfully advancing his career without risking his neck—a model public poet. As Tout characterizes Chaucer's conduct during 1388, 'the permanent official generally went on his way without much regard to politics. Chaucer was too prudent to be a politician and perhaps prided himself on his aloofness.'[36] Chaucer's prudence, along with his poetry, have each contributed to Thomas Fovent's reputation as a political partisan, and this is because it is impossible to reflect on the implications of public writing and reading during Richard II's reign without reference to Chaucer.

Who was Geoffrey Chaucer? To begin with, Chaucer was an accomplished civil servant. In 1374, Edward III appointed him controller of the wool customs and subsidy at the port of London, a position he held for the next twelve years. In 1386, Chaucer was elected to parliament as knight of the shire for Kent, and so he sat in parliament during the impeachment of England's chancellor, an early parliamentary victory against Richard II's administration known as the Wonderful Parliament. He also served as justice of the peace for Kent from 1385 to 1389, one of a sixteen-member commission that conducted inquests into a wide variety of felonies. And from 1389 to 1391, he was appointed Clerk of the King's Works, a post that, as Martin M. Crow describes it, was 'no sinecure', for it required a great deal of hard work.[37] In this capacity, Chaucer was responsible for the construction and maintenance of such properties as the Tower of London and Westminster Palace, and his duties ranged from record-keeping to the acquisition of materials and supplies.[38] Though the

[36] Tout, 'The English Parliament and Public Opinion', 313.
[37] *Chaucer Life-Records*, ed. M. M. Crow and C. C. Olson (Oxford, 1966), 473.
[38] As Crow describes Chaucer's duties as clerk of the works, 'It was an administrative post with considerable responsibilities and well defined duties, especially with respect to accounting. . . . As the records show, the clerk of the works arranged for the procurement, transportation,

position was not exactly glamorous, the Clerk of the Works was important, and Chaucer would not have been rewarded with the clerkship unless he had shown himself over the years to be a skilled and able administrator.

But despite the demands of these various positions, he still found the time to write the *Canterbury Tales*, a project that he began around 1388. Anne Middleton makes the case that Chaucer's Franklin, along with much of the poetry of Gower and Langland, signified a new literary sensibility that was distinct from the courtly style, a sensibility Middleton terms 'public poetry'. Middleton defines public poetry as 'a coherent set of ethical attitudes towards the world—experientially based, vernacular, simple, pious but practical, active. . . . Its most characteristic concern is the turning of worldly time, that essential middle-class commodity, to "common profit."' Middleton points out that Chaucer, Gower, and Langland were all 'commoners to a man', and their own circumstances inevitably influenced their decision as poets to reject the ideals of chivalric literature in favour of common experience as their terrain. At its best, Middleton believes that public poetry epitomized a 'middle way', 'serving its highest function as peacemaker, and as an interpreter of the common world'.[39] Leaving aside the question of how Chaucer's Canterbury pilgrims succeed in effecting this mediating sensibility, I want to examine how we have determined and distributed the possible options for participating in the public sphere in the late fourteenth century. In other words, I would argue that the 'middle way' was not the only way of appealing to the public in 1388.

Paul Strohm contends that Chaucer took the 'middle way' in his life as well as in his poetry. Strohm has argued that Chaucer was not only a public poet, but he was a public figure as well, a civil servant whose livelihood depended on the goodwill of the crown, but who well understood that his future as a poet might be jeopardized by the factional politics that dominated the system of patronage upon which poets like himself and Gower depended. Both Middleton and Strohm regard Chaucer as espousing the sensibilities of a moderate—Middleton sees this political sensibility as manifesting itself in the mediating functions of Chaucer's poetry, while Strohm believes Chaucer showed himself to be a political

and care of a great store of many kinds of building materials, tools, implements, containers, machines, &c., needed for construction and repair. . . . Also, he had to supervise the sale of branches and bark from the trees purveyed for the king's works.' Ibid. 473.

[39] Anne Middleton, 'The Idea of Public Poetry in the Reign of Richard II', *Speculum*, 53 (1978), 112.

moderate in his civil service career as well as in his craft, for Chaucer carefully balanced his political allegiances so as not to leave himself too dependent on the patronage of the crown.[40] But what exactly does Strohm mean when he describes Chaucer as a moderate? In late fourteenth-century England, unlike early twenty-first-century Britain or America, moderation does not translate into a clearly defined centrist political platform. During Richard II's reign, moderation was at best a programme for negotiating the many political pitfalls of the Ricardian world—in essence, Strohm regards Chaucer as necessarily, admirably, and successfully, cautious both in words and deeds, for he never promoted himself at the expense of manoeuvrability. The implication of Chaucer's moderation is that where he succeeded in negotiating the dangers of factional alliances, others failed.

And perhaps the greatest failure of all in the 1380s was Thomas Usk. Strohm shows Usk as falling headlong into the factionalist traps of London politics, grabbing hold of the hard-earned opportunity to join a side instead of following Chaucer's cautious example of tempering his political ties.[41] Chaucer was certainly the more successful writer of the two, for Usk's only significant work was the *Testament of Love*, a vernacular text composed sometime in the mid-1380s. Strohm sees Chaucer's success, and so Usk's failure, as inexorably linked to the way each writer negotiated the networks of factional affiliation that dominated London in the 1380s. In essence, Strohm asks whether it was possible for any writer in late fourteenth-century England, and more specifically in late fourteenth-century London, to write outside the politics of factionalism. The answer, of course, is no—no public life, no public voice, no public writing was untainted by factional affinity—but Strohm insists that Chaucer managed successfully to negotiate the factionalism that delineated both London's political landscape and the politics of writing in this period, whereas Usk's personal affiliations would in the end cost this writer his life.

---

[40] Strohm maintains that Chaucer was too smart to put all his eggs in one basket: 'Part of Chaucer's success may have been based on an ability to mobilize in his political choices those qualities that readers have found in his literary choices, including even-handedness and receptivity to opposed points of view. . . . Chaucer was true not only to his own characteristic moderation but to the presupposition of bastard feudalism when he tempered his loyalty to the king with a second, Lancastrian tie. . . .' Paul Strohm, *Social Chaucer* (Cambridge, Mass., 1989), 40–1.
[41] Strohm portrays Usk as desperate to belong: 'Londoners like Thomas Usk and Geoffrey Chaucer were confronted constantly with the possibilities and perils of factional affiliations. . . . Although each was a factionalist, each ultimately dealt with matters of affiliation in his own way. Usk embraced the politics of faction completely, while Chaucer sought ways of containing and moderating the impact of its all-or-nothing approach.' Ibid. 84.

Thomas Usk was a contemporary social climber with whom Fovent was quite familiar, for Fovent's *Historia* provides us with information about Usk not found in any other narrative source from this period, referring to him as Sergeant-at-Arms of the king.[42] But if Fovent also knew Usk as the author of the *Testament of Love*, the *Historia* betrays no sign of such familiarity. Fovent quite likely regarded Usk as no more than an infamous Londoner of shifty allegiance, a political opportunist if ever there was one. Usk had spent the early 1380s working for John Northampton's party—Northampton was mayor of London from 1381 to 1383, and he ran on a radical platform that advocated dismantling the monopoly of fishmongers in London.

Usk was initially hired by Northampton's party as a scrivener, a secretary employed to draft bills, but he was soon engaged in tasks more integral to the party cause, such as canvassing various guilds for Northampton's re-election campaign. Northampton's challenger for the mayor's office was Nicholas Brembre, leader of the merchant capitalist party in London and an ardent royalist. Brembre defeated the incumbent Northampton in the election of 1383, and there followed several months of civil disturbance in London instigated by Northampton and his followers. In the summer of 1384, Usk was arrested by Brembre for his part in the agitation, and soon after, hoping to save his own neck, Usk switched allegiance from Northampton's faction to Brembre's, selling his old boss out in the process. Usk was the key witness in the trial against Northampton that took place later that summer, giving his testimony in the form of a written appeal that detailed the conspiracy by Northampton and his associates against Brembre's government. But any benefits Usk hoped to gain from betraying his former associates and aligning himself with the Brembre faction were relatively short-lived, for Usk was tried, convicted, and hanged for treason in the Merciless Parliament of 1388, his head placed atop Newgate for all to see.[43]

The Appellants had targeted Usk as an ardent and dangerous royalist who used his appointment as under-sheriff of Middlesex to fabricate indictments against the king's enemies. But Strohm implies the Appellants singled out Usk for impeachment in 1388 not because Usk had picked the wrong side, but because he kept picking sides—an inconstant factionalist was unquestionably a factionalist of the most dangerous sort, for Usk's political affiliations were determined by nothing more than a shifting set of circumstances, and partisan politics makes no allowance for inconsis-

[42] Favent, *Historia*, 19: 'Fuit enim Usk serviens regis ad arma . . .'   [43] Ibid. 20.

tency. As Strohm concludes of Usk, 'To poor, erratic, overardent Usk, Chaucer must have remained an elusive and constantly frustrating example, with his calmer and broader-based and ultimately more successful attitude towards both the politics and poetics of faction.'[44]

The repoliticization of Chaucer's career by scholars such as Strohm has informed our general understanding of the relationship between writers, readers, and politics in late fourteenth-century England. Strohm asks, 'Did Chaucer need to be so cautious?'[45] Strohm, pointing to Usk's destruction at the hands of the Appellants as evidence, believes the answer is yes. I believe the answer is no—Chaucer only needed to be so cautious as to avoid being Usk, Brembre, or any of the other more conspicuous Ricardian factionalists. Certainly, Chaucer was a king's man, for he worked at jobs that were granted by the good will of the crown, but he was not specifically Richard's man. Thomas Usk, on the other hand, was not even Richard's man. This label was reserved for those higher up the ladder, men like Brembre—Richard's favourites. Usk was simply a convenient fall guy for the court party, targeted by the Appellants as much for his inconsistent loyalties as for his activities as a Ricardian factionalist, for as Strohm points out, the official records of the Merciless Parliament label Usk as a 'faux & malveise person'.[46] Judged a turncoat to the very end of his days, there can be little dispute that when it came to his personal advancement, Usk displayed an acute lack of shrewdness, typically reacting to circumstances that were not of his own making, as opposed to conducting himself through the network of factionalist associations with some degree of foresight. But I would suggest that Chaucer's prudent conduct was not the only alternative model available to Usk. Instead, we must consider the overt, if not imprudent politicism of Fovent's *Historia*.

Strohm's assessment of the impact of faction on the lives of writers leads us to anticipate, much as Tout did, that when Richard reasserted his authority in 1389, or when in 1397 he sought revenge against the Appellants, the Ricardian faction would have condemned Fovent as a political agitator. But no such condemnation ever took place. There are two possible reasons for this. The first is that, despite Tout and McKisack's assessment of the *Historia* as pro-Appellant propaganda, the *Historia* was not actually politically inflammatory enough to get its author into trouble.

[44] Strohm, 'Politics and Poetics: Usk and Chaucer', in Lee Patterson (ed.), *Literary Practice and Social Change* (Berkeley, Calif., 1990), 112.

[45] Ibid. 94.

[46] *Rotuli parliamentorum: The Rolls of Parliament*, vol. iii (London, 1767–77), 234, in Strohm, 'Politic and Poetics: Usk and Chaucer', 87.

The second possibility is that the *Historia* belonged to another category of writing, a category that operated outside the scope of the factional networks—the category of public opinion. The web of factionalism in which Usk found himself caught was precisely the political structure that the *Historia* hoped to render insignificant, for Fovent intended his pamphlet to reach a readership more public than partisan. And though the *Historia* is every bit concerned with the 'common good', Fovent's public wasn't the public of Middleton's poets, for the *Historia* displays no interest in mediation. Fovent's public had a keen interest in parliamentary proceedings, and was hungry for vitriol. Fovent knew this because he wrote the *Historia* for people like himself. Fovent was a bureaucrat, not a partisan. His life, particularly his political life, was not mercurial, not clandestine, not cautious. It was out in the open.

Given this remark, Fovent's career was more like Chaucer's than we might have suspected. As mentioned above, Chaucer worked as a customs officer in the port of London from 1374 to 1386, serving as controller of the wool custom and wool subsidy. Between the years of 1391 and 1394 Fovent too was a customs officer in the port of London, and the records of his appointment in the Fine and Patent rolls disclose that he was assigned to collect the duties on tunnage and poundage.[47] In this capacity

---

[47]   *Calendar of Fine Rolls*, xi. 3. Entry for 8 Dec. 1391, Westminster: '[The like commissions to the following in the ports and places named] Richard Odiham and Thomas Fovent, clerk, in the port of London and all ports and places from there on either side of the Thames as far as Gravesende, and there, on the Essex side as far as Tillebury, and there. By bill of the treasurer.'

Ibid., xi. 104. Entry for 13 Nov. 1393, Westminster: '[Commission during pleasure to . . . and to deliver the moneys forthcoming therefrom at the receipt of the Exchequer. The like to the following . . .] Richard Odiham and Thomas Fovent, in the port of London and all ports and places thence on either side of the Thames as far as Gravesende, and there, and on the Essex side as far as Tillebury, and there.'

Calendar of Patent Rolls, 1391–96, 448. Entry for 11 July 1394, Westminster: 'Appointment, during pleasure, of William Waddesworth as controller of Richard Odiham and Thomas Fovent, clerk, collectors in the port of London and all places thence on the Thames as far as Gravesend and Tillebury, inclusive, of the subsidy of 3*s.* on each tun of wine, and 12*d.* on every pound of other merchandise, except wools, hindes, and wool-sells. By bill of treasurer.' Olive Coleman outlines the arrangement of customs officers in the port of London as follows: 'In London the volume of business (and possibly the demands of patronage) meant that separate appointments usually had to be made in three sectors, the cloth and petty customs, the tunnage and poundage and the wool customs and subsidy. Under Richard twelve persons were appointed to the first, fifteen to the second, and fifteen to the last, the same man occasionally serving in more than one sector.' Olive Coleman, 'Collectors of Customs in London', in A. E. J. Hollaender and William Kellaway (eds.), *Studies in London History* (London, 1969), 183. Coleman's article provides an excellent overview of the importance of customs to the realm during Richard II's reign. See also W. M. Ormrod, 'Finance and Trade under Richard II', in Anthony Goodman and James Gillespie (eds.), *Richard II: The Art of Kingship* (Oxford, 1999). For a list of those appointed as collectors of customs in London under Richard II, see Coleman's Appendix, 194. Crow also provides a table of officials at the London customs from 1374 to 1387. See *Chaucer Life-Records*, 153–6.

Fovent was responsible for collecting the duty levied by parliament on all goods that entered the country through the port of London except for wool, wool-fells, and leather, these items being subject to the wool or 'ancient' custom. The proceeds from the duty on tunnage and poundage collected at the port of London averaged £3,000, not an insignificant sum, but nowhere near the amount garnered by means of the wool customs and subsidy, which averaged £18,000 per annum during Richard's reign.[48] This more modest source of revenue from the tunnage and poundage however was typically earmarked by parliament to finance a particular enterprise such as the war with France, and so the post required an individual who was at once loyal to the crown, deferential towards parliament, and most of all accountable to the public interest.[49]

Whereas Fovent's job at the port of London fell outside the party patronage system, those appointed to collect the wool customs and subsidy received their positions in reward for personal and financial service to Richard II. This was because throughout the 1380s, the crown typically used the revenue from the wool customs as security against which to raise cash, and loans made to the crown by both the city of London and by individuals were thus repaid out of customs receipts.[50] Thus the crown typically granted the appointment to members of London's political and mercantile elite, and it was not unusual for the post to be occupied by an individual who might, at one time or another, also occupy the office of mayor.[51] Indeed, Nicholas Brembre, collector of the wool custom and

---

[48] As Coleman explains, 'The proceeds of the wine tunnage and the alien petty customs could be measured in hundreds of pounds rather than thousands and the general poundage produced something in the region of £3,000.' Coleman, 'Collectors of Customs in London', 184.

[49] *Chaucer Life-Records*, 150. Though Crow refers to this as the petty subsidy, it is nevertheless the same office that Coleman refers to as tunnage and poundage. As Ormrod explains: 'the subsidies were extraordinary levies validated only by some form of consent. There were two subsidies known in England at the beginning of Richard II's reign: the levy on alien and denizen imports of wine and imports and exports of general merchandise, known as tonnage and poundage, which was still very much in its infancy; and the wool subsidy, often known to historians by the pejorative nickname the "maltolt" which it earned when first imposed in 1294–7.' Ormrod, 'Finance and Trade under Richard II', 157–8. As stated in the *Calendar of Patent Rolls*, entry cited above for 11 July 1394, the subsidy for this year was fixed at 3s. on each tun of wine, and 12d. on every pound of other merchandise.

[50] Coleman characterizes the relationship between the crown and the London customs as a 'quid pro quo about which the crown had little choice for as long as it made a habit of borrowing from London and Londoners'. Coleman, 'Collectors of Customs in London', 183.

[51] As Coleman observes, 'Of the fifteen collectors during the reign seven passed the mayoral chair [Adam Bamme, Nicholas Brembre, Nicholas Exton, John Hadley, John Philipot, William Venour, John Warde], three were mayors of the staple at Westminster [Brembre, Exton and Hadley], two were mayors of the staple at Calais [Hadley and Philipot], nine represented the City in parliament [Bamme, Brembre, Exton, Handley, Andrew Neuport, Richard Northbury,

subsidy at the port of London through most of the 1370s and 1380s, was just such an individual. Brembre was one of Richard II's most loyal henchmen, mayor of London in 1377–8, and again from October 1383 to 1386, a prominent merchant capitalist who worked tirelessly to oppose John of Northampton's reformist efforts in London. And while the wool collectors were of a different league from someone like Fovent, nevertheless Fovent would have rubbed shoulders with such folks, men who were part of Richard's personal entourage like Brembre, as he would with men like Chaucer, a king's man in the abstract, rewarded for his loyalty to the crown with the job of controller.

The politics of customs appointments had shifted over the course of Richard's reign, and operations at the port of London had undergone some reform by the time of Fovent's appointment. In the mid-1380s, the Commons in parliament had become increasingly aware of the abuses encouraged by the patronage system, and the attempt to clean up the government's operations was felt not only at the top, with the impeachment of Chancellor Suffolk in 1386, but by those nearer to the bottom, the controllers of customs. As Olive Coleman remarks, 'No one would pretend that the English customs system was without its due share of corruption.'[52] Thus in the Wonderful Parliament of 1386, the Commons presented a petition in parliament requesting 'that all controllers in the ports of the realm who held their offices for life should have their appointments repealed and annulled because they were oppressing the people with extortions and that henceforth no controller should be appointed for life.'[53]

Chaucer was, of course, controller of the wool custom and subsidy at precisely this point. He also sat in this very parliament as knight of the shire for Kent, a situation that must have made the Commons' petition seem all the more inopportune. But little action was taken as a result of this petition, for Richard replied to the Commons' petition that 'these controllers would be examined by his council, and that those found to be good should remain in their office, and that the others would be re-

---

John Organ, Philipot, Venour], at least ten were aldermen. . . . The wool collectors were thus close to the purse strings of the government and of the City whilst many of them were also wealthy businessmen.' Ibid. 184.

[52] Ibid. 183.

[53] 'Item priont les Communes, que toutz les Contrerollours es Portes du Roiaume, que ont lour Offices a terme de vie du Grant le Roi, a cause q'ils sont grauntz oppressions & extorcions a people en lour Offices, soient repellez & adnullez; & que nulle tiel Office soit graunte a terme de vie en temps a venir.' Rotuli parliamentorum, iii. 223. Mentioned in Chaucer Life-Records, 269.

moved'.[54] As Crow observes, there is no evidence that anyone was re-moved from the office of controller as a result of this petition, for there were many of Richard's men still to be found in customs after 1386.[55] Nevertheless, Chaucer tendered his resignation of the controllership in December of 1386, a move that Strohm regards as politically savvy because it was intended to distance him from the Ricardian faction.[56] And per-haps Chaucer's decision was prescient, for at least one of Richard's most prominent supporters who remained in his post at the port of London after 1386, the often noted Nicholas Brembre, did slip into the quicksand of factional affiliation, and was executed for treason in the Merciless Par-liament. The Commons' petition of 1386 reveals that the customs offices were both hot spots for graft and other corrupt practices, and hotbeds of precisely the sort of factional activity that had come to dominate both the city of London and Richard's government in the 1380s. The Commons in parliament knew this, Chaucer knew this, and Fovent himself undoubt-edly knew this.

Fovent's appointment to customs did not overlap with Chaucer's, but they may well have been acquainted with one another—during Fovent's tenure at the port of London, Chaucer served as Clerk of King's Works, and in 1391 oversaw extensive repairs to the wool quay where he had worked for twelve years, and where Fovent then worked. The wool quay was the centre of operations for customs at the port of London, located on one of the many wharves on the north bank of the Thames between the Tower of London and London Bridge. Customs was run out of several buildings along the quay, one housing the wool custom, one the cloth custom and alien petty custom, another for the tunnage and poundage offices that doubled as a storage area for goods, and a house to accommo-date those merchants who did regular business at the port.[57] Though Fovent was responsible for collecting the duty on tunnage and poundage, his job at the port of London would have put him in close proximity with a wide range of notorious figures—the wool quay was certainly the geo-graphical nadir of London's merchant culture. The sort of transactions that took place around the customs houses, the point of entry into

[54] 'Le Roi voet que les persones soient examinez devant son Conseill, & que ceux qi serront trovez bons demoergent avant en lour Offices, & que les autres soient remoevez.' Rotuli parlia-mentorum, iii. 223. Mentioned in Chaucer Life-Records, 269.
[55] Chaucer Life-Records, 269.   [56] Strohm, 'Politics and Poetics: Usk and Chaucer', 93.
[57] See Crow's description of the port of London, Chaucer Life-Records, 171. Crow refers to the cloth custom and alien petty custom as simply the petty custom. He likewise refers to the tunnage and poundage as the petty subsidy.

England for great quantities of merchandise, undoubtedly included many backroom deals, as merchants would try to move their commodities through the port while paying as little in tariffs as they could possibly arrange. But the port of London was also a political nadir, for while the appointments to customs were, in essence, a reward for loyal service to the crown, men like Nicholas Brembre probably regarded their offices as an opportunity to exercise some leverage over the London merchant community.

The port was certainly a juncture of local and national politics, but at the same time the men who worked there, though appointed by the crown, operated more within the matrix of the London political landscape—the crown, a priori, gave them their legitimacy, but it was their relationship to the city of London that gave them their power, and they probably arrogated the authority of their appointments for their own benefit. Along with Nicholas Brembre, several other sometime mayors of London, including John Philipot, William Walworth, and Nicholas Exton, held the position of collector of the wool custom and subsidy. Exton was mayor of London in 1387, and so was directly confronted with the struggle between Richard and the Appellants that preceded the Merciless Parliament, as the two parties vied with one another for the city's support. Philipot and Walworth, like Brembre, were prominent merchant capitalists who opposed the Northampton party in London. And like Brembre, both Philipot and Walworth had stood with Richard II at Smithfield against Wat Tyler during the Peasants' Revolt of 1381. All three had been knighted by the king for their service.

In the late 1380s and early 1390s, the port of London was a veritable bastion of royalist boosters. This clique drifted in and out of the port of London, in and out of London's political offices, in and out of national politics, and in and out of the *Historia*. These men, such as Brembre, formed the political matrix of Fovent's world. He never worked with Brembre at the port of London, for Brembre was executed in 1388, three years before Fovent's appointment to customs. Nor do I think that Fovent was sympathetic to Brembre's politics, nor that he even liked Brembre. Nevertheless, Brembre, Chaucer, and Fovent all occupied the same milieu at one time or another, though it would be something of a stretch to say they ran in the same circles. And this milieu had much more to do with London, with the interplay of London politics and national politics, and with the civil servants whose jobs brought them in close contact with both the crown and this city, than with the Appellant faction. For men such as these, politics was their daily bread.

Specifically we know that Fovent held his post as collector of the petty subsidy with Richard Odiham, a middling player in London politics throughout the 1380s. Odiham was City Chamberlain for most of this period, and he was every bit a Brembre supporter, as is made clear by his run-in with John Northampton after Northampton's electoral defeat by Brembre for the mayor's office in October 1383. As mentioned above, Northampton was tried and convicted for encouraging seditious uprisings in London against Brembre and his supporters shortly after Brembre's election. According to a deposition taken at Northampton's trial in August of 1384, 'The day after the election he [Northampton] ill-treated Richard Odiham, the City Chamberlain, so that he stood in danger of his life on account of his support of Brembre.'[58] Thus Fovent's fellow appointee at customs had been closely tied to the royalist camp in the 1380s.

At the very least, Fovent's appointment makes it clear that he knew some people who knew some people. And even though, from the records of his appointment to customs, the earliest I can place him in London is 1391, I suspect he was around the city in the 1380s, for the *Historia* includes too many references to London politics for him to have been elsewhere.[59] His appointment as collector of the duty on tunnage and poundage however was part of yet another reformist wave, a post-1388 attempt to clean up customs, to rid it of corruption, if this were possible. Coleman specifically cites Fovent's appointment as indication of a change from local burgesses to civil servants in the London customs, a clear shift away from the patronage appointments that were routinely made during the first half of Richard II's reign.[60] W. M. Ormrod too observes the reform of customs in this period, the administration of customs now falling under the jurisdiction of the centralized government and thus no longer remaining solely in the hands of London merchants.[61]

---

[58] Ruth Bird, *Turbulent London of Richard II* (London, 1949), 82. This deposition against Northampton is from the same trial at which Thomas Usk turned state's evidence against his old boss, Northampton, a move that transformed Usk into a card-carrying member of the Ricardian faction. See also Appendix IV ibid., 'Transcript of part of Coram Rege Rolls 507–being one of the inquisitions taken at the trial of John de Northampton', 135: 'Et quia Ricardus Odiham camerarius londonie eis in hoc contrarexit percussus erat in dicto crastino ibidem et male tractatus et stetit in periculo vite sue et omnia hec videns dictus Iohannes Norhampton. . . .'

[59] I offer a detailed discussion of the *Historia*'s relationship to the London landscape in 'A Political Pamphleteer in Late Medieval England' ch. 4.

[60] Coleman, 'Collectors of Customs in London', 193.

[61] As Ormrod states: 'There are strong indications that the period after 1388 was one of interesting and sometimes useful experimentation in royal government, and the reform of the customs administration in the early 1390s has a natural place in that larger story . . . the principal significance of the reform lies in the greater degree of central control that was implied by

But whether Fovent's appointment to customs was part of a wave of
government reformers sweeping into customs or not, there is evidence
enough to suggest that he, like Usk, was well acquainted with the 'political demimonde', as Strohm has characterized Usk's experience of London
politics.[62] And this is something to consider—that Fovent watched the
Merciless Parliament as a Londoner, often viewing the participants in this
national contest from a local perspective.

It is by way of the scene describing Brembre's hanging that Fovent reveals his own political interests, demonstrating his disdain for London's
merchant oligarchy and his support for Northampton, previously
Brembre's chief political opponent in the city. As Fovent tells it, right
before Brembre's execution, the rope around his neck, someone in the
crowd speaks up:

And just as he was about to be hanged, he was asked by the son of Northampton
whether he had in fact done justice to his father or not? For Northampton was
formerly the mayor of the city of London, among all those who lived in that city
outstandingly rich and powerful, and was greatly harassed by nefarious conspira-
cies and alliances devised by certain intimates of his, injurious men intent on his
death (including Brembre, Tresilian, and others), and was condemned to death,
despoiled of his goods, and just barely escaped with his life. And Brembre confessed to having committed these things wretchedly, through his arrogance, for
not only was he unjust in his treatment of Northampton, but he had done these
things for the sake of destroying Northampton. And begging pardon and forgiveness, he was hanged until dead and his throat was cut. Behold how good and
delightful it is to aspire to honours![63]

This is, without question, the single most important passage in this sense
in the *Historia*, for this is the moment when Fovent's own politics become

associating officials of the Westminster administration with the local merchants who normally
acted as collectors of customs in the head ports.' Ormrod, 'Finance and Trade under Richard II',
167–8.

[62] Strohm, 'Politics and Poetics: Usk and Chaucer', 84.

[63] 'Et cum illaquearetur ut penderet, interogauit eum filius Norhampton si predicta suo patri
alias per ipsum illata fueruntne iuritice facta. Fuit enim Norhampton quondam maior ciuitatis
Londonie, dicior et potencior ciuis inter omnes qui fuerunt in ciuitate illa, et per quosdam
familiares pestes mortiferos, Brembre scilicet Tresilian et alios, super quibusdam nephariis
conspiracionibus et confederacionibus enormiter vexatus, deinde morti dampnatus, spoli-
atisque bonis, vix euasit superstes. Et de hiis confitebatur Brembre non pie nec iuste sed violenti
animo destruendi causa Northamptoni (sic) per arroganciam infeliciter ista commisisse. Veni-
amque petens et laqueo pendens occubuit guttere scisso. Ecce quam bonum et iocundum est
sublimari ad honores!' Favent, Historia, 18. In regards to Northampton's status and wealth, Ruth
Bird remarks, 'Northampton himself was a man of position and of considerable, though not
great wealth. His supporters were insignificant in both respects.' Bird, *Turbulent London of
Richard II*, 69–70. For a review of Northampton's personal assets, see ibid 7–13.

clear. The incident is mentioned in no other account of the Merciless Parliament, and his inclusion of it in the *Historia* unequivocally demonstrates that his political sympathies lay with Northampton and his followers. Northampton's cause had been to clean up London, and he worked to curb the political influence of the victualers and merchant capitalists who so dominated the city.[64] This was the lens through which Fovent observed the events of 1388.

Fovent's *Historia* is not as politically naive a document as those scholars who regard it as Appellant propaganda would have us believe. And this is because Fovent himself was not a politically naive man. No bureaucrat in the 1380s and 1390s could afford to be so naive as to unequivocally declare support for one faction or another. And this is precisely Strohm's point about Usk—such affiliations would inevitably cost one his career, if not his life. Those who were factionalists in the extreme, men like Usk and Brembre, were factionalists first and foremost in the matrix of London politics, and in 1388 these men found themselves condemned not just for their connection to the crown, but for their urban affiliations. Fovent was no Appellant propagandist. If he were, he would never have been appointed to London customs by the crown. At the same time, his literary career was hardly as circumspect as Chaucer's. He was a civil servant, and as such he worked alongside other civil servants and other politicians, and somewhere along the way developed a keen interest in parliamentary politics. It seems very likely that he was not atypical, that other civil servants and bureaucrats would have shared his interest in national politics, that they would regard parliament as the centre of their political world because this was the institution that gave the Commons of the realm a voice in creating the policy that governed their jobs and their lives. This was his milieu, his audience for the *Historia*. And though his appointment to the port of London put him in close proximity with one-time Ricardian factionalists, this does not mean that he understood politics only in terms of faction. Rather, he regarded the Merciless Parliament as an opportunity to voice his opinion, and as such the *Historia* transcends the politics and poetics of faction. Unlike public poetry, public opinion need not mediate—conflict was its *raison d'être*.

Though Cicely Fovent had secured Thomas Fovent's advance to the benefice in Dinton, he seems to have remained in London throughout

---

[64] Paul Strohm describes Northampton's political programme as consisting of four points: 'that aldermen should be limited to one year terms, that the Common Council should be elected from the crafts rather than the wards, that no victualer should hold judicial office, and that victualers from outside London could sell freely within the city.' Paul Strohm, 'Politics and Poetics: Usk and Chaucer', 85.

much of the 1390s, as is revealed by records of a protracted lawsuit against one William Wolaston.[65] How he occupied himself during these years, and what else, if anything, he wrote while in London remains a mystery. But there is another piece to this biographical puzzle that should be taken into account. While it is difficult to know how much Fovent's family influenced his political orientation, it is nevertheless worth noting that his father, Robert Osegood, alias Fovent, had represented Shaftesbury in parliament in 1355, and was mayor of Shaftesbury in the same year. It seems parliament was something of a legacy for this family, for his older brother Robert also represented Shaftesbury in parliament in 1390.[66] Robert

[65] *Calendar of Close Rolls, 1396–99* (London, 1911–62), 235. Entry for 13 Dec. 1397, Westminster: 'To the sheriffs of London. Order by mainprise of Robert Richard Kays [*sic*] and Henry Asshburne of Derbyshire and John Rate of Lincolnshire to set free William Wolaston of London, imprisoned at suit of Thomas Fovent for that he and Henry "Williamservant Wolaston" at the parish of St. Sepulchre without "Westsmythefeld" bar London conspired together and indicted the said Thomas for taking the said William at Westminster by force of arms, imprisoning and evil entreating him, keeping him in prison there four days, and delivering him without warrant to the warden of the Flete prison contrary to law and custom of the realm, and falsely and maliciously procured that the said Thomas was taken and imprisoned in the marshalsea prison until he was acquitted before the king in his court.'
   Ibid. 289. Entry for 18 Apr. 1398, Westminster: 'Memorandum of a like mainprise, (under a pain of 100 marks), mutatis mutandis, made by Robert Sapirton and Henry Assheburne of Derbyshire, Walter Coke and Robert Bernes of London for William Wolaston in regard to Thomas Fovent clerk.'
   Calendar of Close Rolls, 1399–1402, 514. Entry for 6 Apr. 1402, Westminster: 'To Thomas de Rempston knight constable of the Tower of London, or to his lieutenant. Order by mainprise of John Neuporte of Kent, John Kighele of Lancashire, John Preston and John Brenchesle, both of Southwerke, to set free William Wollaston, the king's former writ to have him in chancery notwithstanding; as they have mainperned in chancery that he shall do or procure no hurt or harm to Thomas Fovent clerk. This mainprise was taken by the chancellor.' Though I am unable to say much about the precise significance of this lawsuit, or about the identity of William Wolaston, I have discovered two mentions of Wolaston in the *Calendar of Close Rolls*. The first is from *CCR, 1396–99*, 207. Entry for 25 July 1397, Westminster: 'To the sheriffs of London. Writ of supersedeas, and order by mainprise of John Halle of Sussex, William Reyners of Yorkshire and John Pakwode of Warwickshire to set free John Narrauke, if taken by virtue of a writ under the exchequer seal at suit of William Wolaston for debt.' The second is from *CCR, 1399–1402*. Entry for 16 June 1401, Westminster: 'To the same. [William Gascoigne and his fellows, justices appointed to hold pleas before the king.] Like order [by writ of nisi prius] to cause an inquisition whereupon William Wolaston rector of "Bokenamferie" has put himself to be taken before the said justices or one of them, before one of the justices of the Common Bench, John Cokayn chief baron of the exchequer or the justices of assize in Norffolk.'
[66] *The House of Commons: 1386–1421*, ed. J. S. Roskell (Stroud, 1992), 113–14. Tout believed that this Robert was Thomas's father: 'A kinswoman, Cicely Fovant, perhaps a sister, became abbess of the great nunnery of Shaftesbury and founded in 1406 a chantry in memory of her father Robert and mother Edith, who may well have also been the parents of Thomas.' In Tout, 'The English Parliament and Public Opinion', 311. But it seems that Tout was misled, for the note to the entry for Fovent on p. 312 of *The House of Commons* makes it clear that Robert was in fact brother to Thomas and Cicely: 'In the *Cat. Addns. to mss in BM*, 1391–5, p. 325, relating to

Fovent sat in parliament for only one term, but interestingly enough this was the parliament that saw the reintroduction of legislation prohibiting livery and maintenance. Such issues, issues of corruption and reform, were woven into the lives of this family.

If I were to conclude anything definitive about Fovent's politics at this point, I would say that he, much like Tout and McKisack, was enamoured of parliamentary victories. He did not write the *Historia* as Appellant propaganda because he knew that he did not have to, for despite the political dominance of the Ricardian and Appellant factions in 1388, there was some leeway to operate within the bureaucratic milieu as an independent political voice. His sympathies were unquestionably with the Appellants, for he believed they represented the possibility of bringing about the reform of the government. But he also understood that the real mechanism for achieving reform was parliament, and that the relationship between parliament and the public had come to constitute a real political force. Unlike Usk, Fovent never presented himself as a factionalist. Nor did he style himself a propagandist. He was simply a parliamentary pamphleteer intent on disseminating this victory against the crown to a circle of politically minded readers eager for reform—most likely his fellow civil servants. And no matter how fragmented by factionalism the political landscape might have appeared in 1388, nevertheless late medieval politics did make allowances for public opinion, probably because it had no other choice. Factionalism was a participatory politics of one sort, public opinion another. Once politics became accessible to social climbers such as Usk, it was accessible to all, to partisans and reformers alike. Some would choose to align themselves with one party or the other, and some would choose to voice their dissent and look to parliament to protect their interests. Public opinion was an inevitable by-product of the sort of politics that was at the centre of the contest between the Appellants and the Ricardians. Thomas Fovent saw his opportunity and took it. It was very much his for the taking—once the factionalists had opened the door to the public sphere, they were powerless to close it.

In this essay I have revised much of what has been said about Fovent by the only two historians who have written about the *Historia* at length, McKisack and Tout, offering new biographical information that

Egerton 3135, Robert and his wife Edith are said to have been the parents of Cecily [*sic*] Fovent, abbess of the Benedictine abbey of Shaftesbury from 1398 to 1423. But in none of the deeds enrolled in the cartulary is their relationship made explicit, and in view of the time-scale involved it is more probable that Cecily was Robert's sister.' Indeed, the chantry mentioned by Tout was established in 1406, but Robert himself lived until at least 1426.

identifies him as a civil servant with a political sensibility quite distinct from that of the Appellants. Accordingly, I have argued against reading Fovent as a pro-Appellant propagandist, primarily because 'propaganda' is not a useful descriptive, for it oversimplifies the rich and complex nature of the political consciousness of late fourteenth-century England. By maintaining its use we do ourselves an injustice, for not only does it obscure the myriad of political opinions that circulated throughout England in this period, but also it obscures the emergence of the political public sphere. While I have amended much of what McKisack and Tout wrote about Fovent, I have nevertheless elected to keep their characterization of his *Historia* as a pamphlet. Admittedly, conceiving of the *Historia* as a pamphlet is problematic if for no other reason than it is hard to reconcile pamphleteering with the technological limitations of the late fourteenth-century publishing trade. But then Fovent's readership may well have been familiar with the term, for when Usk wrote the *Testament of Love* (1385–7), he thought to describe his poem as a 'leud pamflet', though here Usk elected to swathe his politics in a thin veil of 'florid art-prose'.[67]

Usk's *Testament* aside, elsewhere in this essay I have referred to Fovent's work as a tract or an opinion piece, and I have likened it to the broadsides and bills that were not uncommon in this period. While I believe that

[67] For Usk's use of 'leud pamflet', see *The Testament of Love*, in *The Complete Works of Geoffrey Chaucer*, vol. vii, ed. W. W. Skeat (Oxford, 1897), bk. 3, ch. 9, l. 54, as cited as the second entry in *Oxford English Dictionary*, 2nd edn., s.v. 'pamphlet'. Strohm's description of the *Testament of Love* as 'florid art-prose' is in 'Politics and Poetics: Usk and Chaucer', 98. Of Usk's motivation for writing the *Testament*, Strohm says, 'Finally, pardoned but underemployed in 1385–86, he [Usk] composed his *Testament of Love* in order to persuade the members of the royal faction that he was in full control of his actions and choices and ready for significant service.' Strohm, 'Politics and Poetics: Usk and Chaucer', 97. For a more complete view of Usk's politics as a writer, see 'The Textual Vicissitudes of Usk's "Appeal"' in Strohm, *Hochon's Arrow: The Social Imagination of Late Fourteenth-Century Texts* (Princeton, NJ, 1992), 145–60. For a slightly different view of Usk's intended audience, see Anne Middleton, ' "Perdurable Letters": The *Testament of Love* from Script to Print', *Studies in Bibliography*, 51 (1998), 68–9. Middleton says, 'I dispute the purported *ulteriority* of the work's motives, and of the terms of its intentional artfulness. These are, I shall show, in plain view, and plainly, pervasively, and wittily legible in this remarkably intricate text and book—above all to Usk's fellow "clerics": textworkers and bibliophiles who blend without distinction into the several other occupations covered by this capacious and fluid term in the later fourteenth century. The *Testament*, I suggest, speaks in the first instance to such men, and in their craft-languages—that is, to those who serve, not to the king, lords, or knights as prospective "patrons". It speaks, in short, to others of Usk's kind, to those for whom documentary and bibliographic high literacy is a means and medium of service, whose self-image and skills, and terms of art and connoisseurship, are acquired "on the job" (whatever the job may be).' Perhaps this is also an apt description of Fovent's own relationship to his readership.

these are all fair descriptions of Fovent's text, none of them convey the political force of the designation of 'pamphlet'. A 'pamphlet' perhaps more effectively communicates the idea of a political and public discourse because it implies circulation—it implies that the author's opinion was intended to circulate across a readership that had no direct connection to the author other than the pamphlet itself. This political discourse is important because it both mirrored and shaped the political consciousness of late fourteenth-century England.

But more to the point, though it seems that with the exception of McKisack and Tout, the *Historia* has been overlooked as an important source of information not only about the Merciless Parliament, but also about the political opinions, ideas, and attitudes that surrounded this crisis, this was not always the case. The *Historia* came into vogue, briefly, in 1641. There are at least two known editions of the *Historia*, translated into English, which were printed in that year.[68] Whoever decided to resurrect Fovent's *Historia* realized that all they had to do was churn out a rough

---

[68] Both translations are catalogued under Thomas Fannant. The first is entitled 'An historical narration of the manner and forme of that memorable Parliament which wrought wonders. Begun at Westminster 1386 in the tenth year of the reigne of King Richard the Second. Related and published by Thomas Fannant.' London, 1641. The second is entitled, 'A true relation of that memorable Parliament, which wrought wonders. Begun at Westminster, in the tenth yeare of the reigne of K. Richard the Second. Together with a character of the said amiable, but unhappy King, and a briefe story of his life and lamentable death.' London, 1641. There is also an edition from 1643 entitled, 'A true declaration of that memorable Parliament which wrought wonders. Begun at Westminster, in the tenth year of the reign of K. Richard the Second. With a briefe relation of his life and lamentable death.' London, 1643. McKisack says of the seventeenth-century pamphlet, 'A comparison of this pamphlet with the manuscript shows the former to consist of a rough English translation of the narrative here printed; but the seventeenth-century pamphleteer gave no hint that he was making use of a fourteenth century authority. His preface, indeed, seems designed to prevent his readers from guessing this fact.' Favent, *Historia*, v. While it is true that the seventeenth-century translation does not mention the fourteenth-century source, I however find no reason to interpret this as an attempt by the pamphleteer to hide his source from his reader. I believe that the translation reads more like some reincarnation of a prophetic voice. The translation begins, 'I will therefore speake of that which hath laine hid in the darksome shade of forgetfullnesse, concerning men who have been led away by the deceitfull path of Couvetousnesse, and have come to a most shamefull and ignominious death: a famous example, to deter all men from practising those of the like courses.' Fannant, 'An Historical Narration of that Memorable Parliament', 1–2. But Steel seems to agree with McKisack: 'Favent has long been known in the rough translation of 1641, which however was represented as being an original composition of the time of Charles with application principally to the politics of that day. In this dress it deceived Wallon and other historians of Richard II. The importance of Miss McKisack's discovery of the original Latin text is to show that, though still propaganda, it is at least a contemporary piece of propaganda and that its detail can be trusted more than at one time used to be believed.' Steel, *Richard II*, 146, n. 1.

translation, print it up, distribute it, and they would have a ready-made case against Charles I. This is why McKisack calls the *Historia* a pamphlet in her introduction to her edition of Fovent's text.

There are some noteworthy differences between the seventeenth-century translation and the original, for, as we might expect, the language of the 1641 edition tends to reflect the vocabulary of seventeenth-century politics—words like 'commonwealth', 'public affairs', 'confederates', 'citizens', and 'conspirators' are used repeatedly by the translator. Nevertheless, the translation is very much in line with Fovent's intentions, perhaps the more so because by 1641, parliament was at long last on its way to becoming the political force that Fovent had wanted it to be. The *Historia's* advocacy of parliament as a means of achieving political reform seems to have resonated with the political pamphleteers of the seventeenth century, for they were willing to make use of the inherent political connections between their present and the past instead of emphasizing only the breaks and ruptures. Thus by keeping the designation 'pamphlet', we not only maintain the spirit of Fovent's work, but we acknowledge the inherent connections between the medieval and early modern worlds. To borrow a phrase from David Aers, the *Historia* is 'a whisper in the ear of Early Modernists'. And so by reconsidering Fovent's pamphlet, we too can hear the political world of the late fourteenth century whisper at us.

California Institute of Technology

Commonalty and Literary Form in the 1370s and 1380s

Emily Steiner

[The office of commen doinge] may draw many hearts of noble and
voice of commune into glory.

Thomas Usk, 'Testament of Love'

The 'special force and luminosity' of 'communes' have made that word a
many-focused lens for examining literary production and ideological
conflict in late medieval England.[1] Yet the significance of communes,
both for modern critics and medieval writers, goes well beyond the semantic confines of the Middle English word. It speaks instead to a
broader interest in collectivity, or perhaps more accurately, *commonalty*.[2]
It speaks, that is, to the process by which *collective constructs emerge from
non-noble entities*, the way that a political body, general subject, or
community of the whole takes part in what is socially common. These
collective constructs, whether they are understood to refer to political
institutions, mercantile fellowship, spiritual election, or vernacular translation, share another feature as well: a blurring of the particular to convey
a larger agency, a peculiar tendency to designate and obscure. The word
'communes' itself, for example, might refer in a given passage to food production, labourers, the third estate, the urban populace, a parliamentary

---

[1] Anne Middleton, 'The Idea of Public Poetry in the Reign of Richard II', *Speculum*, 53
(1978), 94–114, here 110.

[2] I am using 'commonalty' in its Modern English sense to designate a social or political formation, as distinguished from 'commonality', i.e. something shared. Admittedly, 'comunalte' or
'comunalite', both derived from the Old French 'communaute', have always been slippery and
easily interchangeable terms with meanings in Middle English ranging from common utility to
fellowship to the urban populace (c.1350–1380) to guild membership (c.1420) to the House of
Commons (c.1450) (*Middle English Dictionary, s.v.* 'communes'). Yet despite the range of historical meanings contained within commonalty, it is nevertheless a conceptually useful term because it nearly always refers, not simply to a collectivity or generality, but to a collectivity of
non-noble people, whether that collectivity is considered to be a distinct corporate body (in later
usage) or a common people at large.

200 Emily Steiner

body, or the general public; such ambiguity is unparalleled in Latin and late medieval French, in which the nominal 'commune' more often signifies an incorporated town or communal holding than it does an estate or the 'menu peuple'. A similar point might be made about the surprising number of terms for heterogeneity in Middle English literature, in which 'sondry folk', 'diverse folk', 'alle manere of men, þe meene and þe riche' serve as imagined audiences, subjects, or authorizing bodies for vernacular poetry.[3] It is almost as if, in the absence of a modern discourse of class, collective constructs, such as commonalty or heterogeneity, end up mediating between social status, on the one side, and literary and political representation, on the other. This is not to suggest that what is being represented in late medieval literature is a middle class tremulously called into being by 'exhortative generalities',[4] or historical actors converging out of a sense of shared capital. It is rather to suggest that late medieval English literature is characterized by its attempts to create a new political language, one at once allusive and opaque.

How do we begin, then, to write a literary history of commonalty, a history, that is, of the relationship between collectivity and its social inflection? And further, what might such a history tell us about the relationship between politics and poetics in late medieval England? This essay starts to address these questions by focusing on what medieval writers call 'clamour', 'murmur', 'common voice', or 'noise'. Clamour, of course, is just one of many characteristics with which a dominant group might stigmatize a subordinate one as rebellious, irrational, insensitive, or abject. We might take as examples the braying asses with which John Gower portrays the 1381 rebels in his *Vox clamantis*, or Chaucer's Trojan citizens whose 'noyse' starts up 'as breme as blase of straw' to exchange Criseyde for Antenor.[5] It becomes clear, however, when looking at late

---

[3] On the social import of Lollard bids to heterogeneity and homogeneity, see Fiona Somerset, 'Answering the *Twelve Conclusions*: Dymmok's Halfhearted Gestures towards Publication', in Margaret Aston and Colin Richmond (eds.), *Lollardy and the Gentry in the Later Middle Ages* (New York, 1997), 52–76, and Christina von Nolcken, 'A Certain Sameness and our Response to it in English Wycliffite Texts', in *Literature and Religion in the Later Middle Ages: Philological Studies in Honor of Siegfried Wenzel*, Medieval and Renaissance Texts and Studies (Binghamton, NY, 1995), 191–208.

[4] Janet Coleman develops this thesis in *Medieval Readers and Writers: 1350–1400* (New York, 1981), 79–113. For important recent revisions to Coleman's thesis, see Helen Barr, *Signes and Sothe: Language in the 'Piers Plowman' Tradition* (Cambridge, 1994); Judith Ferster, *Fictions of Advice: The Literature and Politics of Counsel in Late Medieval England* (Philadelphia, 1996), 27–38; and perhaps most useful, Wendy Scase, ' "Strange and Wonderful Bills": Bill-Casting and Political Discourse in Late Medieval England', *New Medieval Literatures*, 2 (1998), 225–47.

[5] *Troilus and Criseyde* 4.183–6, 194–6. *The Riverside Chaucer*, 3rd edn., ed. Larry Benson (Boston, 1987).

medieval depictions of clamour, that neither its relation to social status nor its literary articulations are fixed or uniform. We shouldn't assume, for example, that clamour is merely a fiction of disorder circulated by those in power, any more than we assume that a group is vulgar the moment that it speaks. Rather, if clamour, generally speaking, supposes some sort of relationship between collectivity and social status, in medieval English texts, clamour is the rhetorical means by which such a relationship can be formulated *in the first place.* We take for granted the idea that social status confers certain kinds of political privilege. It follows therefore that collectivity—an angry crowd, the House of Commons, and so forth—arises out of political necessity: it is composed of people of lower social status than those who are empowered to participate singularly in the political process. In the 1370s and 1380s, however, the relationship between political collectivity and social status was being theorized for the first time, and it was clamour that helped to break it down into its constituent parts.

More specifically, I argue, the Good Parliament of 1376 and Thomas Usk's 'Appeal' of Northampton (1384) show how clamour produces a rhetoric about political collectivity at moments when commonalty is under dispute; at moments, that is, when claims to collective representation, consent, and agency are troubled by the social implications of those claims. The parliamentary rolls use clamour to analyse the difficult relationship between collectivity and social status, and consequently to create or challenge commonalty as a political structure. Usk likewise uses clamour to talk about commonalty, especially as it pertains to emergent political structures. He presumes that civic politics are founded on subtle distinctions between collectivity and social status, and he capitalizes on these distinctions to obtain specific political ends. As we shall see, moreover, debates about commonalty in the political realm resonate as clamour in the *Piers Plowman* B Prologue (*c.*1376–9); at stake for Langland, as for Usk and the parliamentary delegates, is the project of trying to figure out exactly what collectivity has to do, if anything, with social status. More important than the relationship it posits between commonalty and clamour, however, are the ways that *Piers Plowman* interprets legal-political constructs as vernacular allegory. In doing so, it makes commonalty a distinctive feature of poetic practice, at the same time that it uses poetry to excavate the foundations of commonalty. To put this idea a different way, clamour shows how a vernacular poet writing in the 1370s and 1380s might understand topicality not simply as the rehearsal of an event or the appropriation of discourse, but as a set of structural concerns informing politics and poetry alike.

I. Clamour and the Good Parliament

During the course of the reign of Edward III the Commons began to establish themselves as an official commonalty, in part by sponsoring 'common petitions', purportedly dealing with matters of general interest ('pur commune profit'), such as taxation, monopolies, and abuses of maintenance. Previously, the king had claimed to represent the grievances of the realm personally, grievances largely expressed by private petitions or royal initiative. By the mid-fourteenth century, however, statutes might arise from a direct initiative of the Commons, and it is as sponsors of these petitions that the Commons declared themselves to be representative of the community of the whole.[6] Some of these petitions were drafted by communities and even individuals and bore no direct relation to the concerns or persons of the parliamentary Commons. Other petitions record generalized complaints, which probably arose from members' particular debates.[7] What is significant in either case is that the Commons claimed to represent the community of the whole by supporting, and in some respect identifying with, the general complaint of the realm.

The 200 or so delegates to the medieval Commons further defined themselves as an official commonalty by their method of deliberation: they reached consensus not by a poll but by an assessment of the volume of voices shouting for or against a proposition. This method gave the Commons a semblance of unanimity—they all appeared to agree—and a semblance of unity—despite the fact that the representatives to the Commons encompassed a broad social spectrum they nevertheless formally presented themselves as a group defined by a shared political agenda and by a refusal to admit distinction or gradation. The technical term for the vocalized common assent of the Commons was 'clamour', as in the parliamentary records of the accusations against William Latimer, Richard Lyons, and Adam de Bury, each of whom was 'empeschez & accusez par clamour des ditz communes'.[8] By contrast, the thirty to fifty Lords most likely sat according to grade and gave their opinions severally. This system of deliberation defined them as a political group precisely by taking social gradation and individuation into account. In the parliamentary rolls of this period, which are conspicuously sympathetic to the Commons,

---

[6] Ronald Butts, *A History of Parliament: The Middle Ages* (London, 1989), 233.

[7] A. L. Brown, 'Parliament, c.1377–1422', in R. G. Davies and J. H. Denton (eds.), *The English Parliament in the Middle Ages* (Philadelphia, 1981), 127.

[8] *Rotuli parliamentorum*, 6 vols. (London, 1767–77), ii. 324: 'impeached and accused by the clamour of the aforementioned communes'.

'clamour' might also be expressed in terms of degree, as in the proceedings of the 1378 parliament at which the Commons brought up once again a certain Yarmouth petition 'come grant clamour', a phrase suggesting both the unanimity and vehemence of their position (vocalized assent by its very definition implies no opposition—it is a matter of affirmation, not of choice).[9] As will become clearer below, it was this notion of the Commons' clamour that enabled medieval parliamentary delegates to debate the legitimacy of political collectivity and attempt to define its relation to social status.

The Commons, of course, were drawn from the knights of the shire and the wealthiest burgess, whose personal effects depended upon and helped to determine national policy. In that sense, each member effectively represented his own interests, a prerequisite in medieval England for claiming to represent the interests of both the community of the whole and those whom Commons speaker Peter de la Mare once called the 'better people of the shire', that is, those people ideally responsible for electing the delegates.[10] In fact, neither the parliamentary Commons nor the Lords were, technically speaking, a political order defined by social status—the knights of the shire elected to the Commons were scarcely distinguishable from, and were often retainers of, the parliamentary Lords.[11]

With all this in mind, the Commons' clamour would seem to have little socially to do with the generalized public or communities that they claimed to represent through common petitions. Yet it could hardly have escaped anyone's notice that the Commons' clamour, both the practice and its nomenclature, evoked very different and much older ways of forming commonalty, namely those derived from the republican idea of the *vox populi*, or, from the early medieval period, the *vox populi vox dei*, the uniform cry of a social entity temporarily empowered to effect political change. Depending on the context, this *vox* might be associated either with the inaudible complaint of an abject community of the whole (as in

[9] Ibid., iii. 49. Mark Kishlansky makes a similar point about early modern parliamentary practice: 'In early modern parlance, electors gave voices rather than votes and spoke of having voices to give . . . rhetorically, giving voices meant giving assent, agreeing to something rather than choosing . . . As a process it was both anonymous and unanimous' (*Parliamentary Selection: Social and Political Choice in Early Modern England* (Cambridge, 1986), 10–11).

[10] By interest, I mean a stake in the military and financial concerns of the realm, as opposed to lawyers and sheriffs whose 'interests', it was feared, were narrowly professional (Butt, *A History of Parliament*, 254).

[11] The Commons frequently complained that the royal sheriffs were subverting the election proceedings in the shires. See Brown, 'Parliament, c.1377–1422', 119.

the mirror-for-princes tradition), or with the demands of an unruly and spontaneous urban crowd. To take just a few representative examples, in 991 Archbishop Gerbert of Rheims complained that his disgraced predecessor Arnulf had been elected by the clamour of the multitude *(clamoure multitudinis)*, a clamour that had only been taken into account because in Scripture it is said, *vox populi vox dei*. A divinely inspired community of the whole, he was implying, had been confused with a turbulent local mob. To take a very different example, in 1316 Philip V of France sent a letter to eight bailiffs sternly warning them that he knew all about the dangers of travel from the 'grant clamour' of his people. Clamour in this instance bolsters royal authority by appealing to the divinely inspired and politically amorphous community of the whole.[12] Similarly, eleven years later, at the deposition of Edward II, the Archbishop of Canterbury preached a vernacular sermon in which he used the term *vox populi vox dei* to urge the *populus* of London to ratify the proceedings (after the fact!).[13] The point is that the clamour of the parliamentary Commons, although actually signifying the vocalized common assent of prominent individuals, further linked the Commons to the undifferentiated *vox* of a socially inferior or ill-defined *populus,* whether understood as the apolitical generality that the Commons claimed to represent, or the illicit, potentially violent, commonalty that the Commons might be accused of resembling—the urban crowds—and from which they were sometimes accused of drawing support.[14]

[12] These examples are taken from Edward Peters, 'Vox populi, vox dei', in Edward B. King and Susan J. Ridyard (eds.), *Law in Mediaeval Life and Thought* (Sewanee, Tenn., 1990), 91–120. This is exactly the kind of clamour so strategically invoked by Walter in the *Clerk's Tale* as a pretext for his various atrocities: 'the murmur sleeth myn herte and my corage | For to myne eres comth the voys so smerte | That it wel ny destroyed hath myn herte' (628–30). Whereas the people's abject cry creates the possibility of magnanimity, Walter deliberately mis-cites and misinterprets that cry as a power that constrains his will and forces his hand.

[13] This example is taken from Richard Kaeuper, *Chivalry and Violence in Medieval Europe* (Oxford, 1999), 139. As David Aers points out about Gower, Latin makes it possible to transmit uncritically 'a traditional saying which treated the people's voice (*vox populi*) as the voice of God (*vox dei*)'. See 'Vox Populi and the Literature of 1381', in David Wallace (ed.), *The Cambridge History of Medieval English Literature* (Cambridge, 1999), 440. Wendy Scase, writing about the dissemination of broadsides in the fifteenth century, demonstrates that the same phrase (*vox populi vox dei*) 'textualized the political aspirations (purportedly) of a silent populace denied access to public platforms' ('Strange and Wonderful Bills', 244).

[14] Walsingham reports, for example, that when the common people of London ('commune vulgus Londoniensium') heard that one of the officials accused by the Commons had been placed in safe custody, they swore with clamour and threats ('cum clamore et minis') that they would burn down his lodging unless he was produced and tried. When Gaunt and his followers tried to delay the interrogation, the common people raised such a noise and clamour ('tantum strepitum et clamorem') that the duke was forced to comply with their wishes (Henry Thomas Riley (ed.), *Chronicon a monacho sancti albani*, i: *A.D. 1272–1381* (London, 1863), 81–2).

The relationship between commonalty and clamour became a particularly vexed issue in the Good Parliament of 1376. This parliament was famous, among other things, for its newly audacious Commons, which resisted demands for subsidies and indicted several officials associated with the royal party. The royal party and especially the Duke of Lancaster, John of Gaunt, tried to unnerve the Commons by challenging the very mechanisms by which they claimed to speak, both for themselves as a commonalty (as a non-noble, if distinguished, collectivity) and for the community of the whole. The Anonimalle chronicler, for example, tells the following story. When, in 1376, the Commons returned to Parliament after a recess, half of them, at the instigation of Gaunt, were pushed back and shut out of the house, much to the surprise of speaker Peter de la Mare and his companions who had successfully made it inside ('purceo ils ses merveylerent graundement de cest affair'). Gaunt then asked which of those remaining was to present the deliberation and official verdict of the Commons ('la parlaunce et pronunciacion'), and de la Mare indicated himself. When asked to proceed, however, he turned to all the Lords, reminding them that each of the Commons who was there was there by official summons of the king ('par nostre seignur le roy par brief'), as well as by the election of the deputies of various noblemen ('par eleccione des viscountes de diverses countes'). Consequently, concluded de la Mare, it wasn't right for him to speak for the Commons without all of them present: what one says all of them say and assent to ('ceo qe une de nous dist touz diount et assentount'). Gaunt replied that it was sufficient that just two or three of them be there, as was the former custom, but de la Mare stood firm, insisting that he wished neither to speak nor to present the speech of the Commons ('nulle parole vodroit dire ne moustrer') without all of them there. The rest of the Commons were subsequently rounded up and readmitted.[15]

---

[15] V. H. Galbraith (ed.), *The Anonimalle Chronicle* (Manchester, 1970 [1927]), 83–4. 'Et mesme celle four de venderdy les communes ses proferent dentrer en parlement et vendrent al huse de parlement; une partie entrerent et les autres furount rebatez et clos hors et alerent ou ils vodroient. Et quaunt le dit sire Peirs et partie des ses compaignouns furount entrez avaunt les siegnours et virent qe lour compaignouns ne purrount entrer, purceo ils ses merveylerent graundement de cest affair. Den apres le duk de Lancastre, adonqes lieu tenant le roy detener le parlement en sa absence et le prince, a tresgraunt male ease comensa a dire. "Quel de vous avera la parlaunce et pronunciacion de ceo qe vous avez ordine parentre vous?" Et le dit sire Peirs respondist qe par comune assent il avereit les paroles a la iorne, et le duk dist: "Dites ceo qe vous voilliez." "Sire," fist il, "volunters. Seignours, vous savez bien et avez bien conceu qe toutes les comunes qe issy sount venuz sount venuz par nostre seignur le roy par brief et par eleccione des viscountes de diverses countes, et ceo qe une de nous dist touz diount et assentount; par qay al comencement ieo demaunde lenchesone pur qay les unez sount tenuz hors, et pur certayne ieo ne moveray mater avaunt qils soient toutes entrez et presentez." Donqes le dit duk de Loncastre

By shutting out half the Commons, Gaunt clearly wanted to depict them as an illegitimate or subordinate commonalty. To form a commonalty at all, he was suggesting, is immediately to resemble the common crowd or *commune vulgus*: at the moment that a collectivity of non-nobles is politicized it becomes the social counterpart to the community of the whole rather than its legitimate advocate. Similarly, by insisting to Peter de la Mare that his colleagues need not be present, Gaunt was implying that the Commons, rather than each of them speaking for himself, spoke *en masse* and therefore might depend on a charismatic spokesman whether or not they were present, much like Wat Tyler in 1381 speaking for the rebel host at Mile End. Conversely, by insisting upon the old custom of negotiating informally with two or three members of the Commons (called 'intercommuning' in the parliamentary rolls), Gaunt was also proposing that de la Mare, as a knight of the shire ('Sire Piers'), might represent himself alone, as the peerage did. This proposition was as plainly disadvantageous to de la Mare as the first suggestion that the Commons spoke *en masse,* because if he represented himself he would be personally liable for his own opinions. Such singular representation moreover, would place him within the Lords' system of deliberation in which social status determined the weight of the opinion given, an older feudal system of communication in which the common profit was embodied and articulated by individual magnates and addressed by the king himself.[16] As parliamentary historian Ronald Butts explains, the Lords gradually became a separate order in the fourteenth century, not because they were summoned to parliament as a separate order, but because they were summoned individually to parliament, as opposed to the Commons who were officially summoned to parliament, but only after they were locally elected to that position.[17] Consequently, the Lords tended to view themselves as a separate order from the Commons but not, as mentioned earlier, as an exclusive estate. For Gaunt in 1376, however, it was politically expedient to distinguish between order and estate, and he did this precisely by equating the Commons' parliamentary selection with their collective mechanisms of affirmation and report. For Gaunt, that is, the vulnerability of the Commons' position was due not to an essential dif-

---

dist: "Sire Peirs, ceo ne serroit meistre de tauntz de comunes entrer pur doner respouns mes dusz ou tresz purrount soeffire a une foitz, come ad este use avaunt ces hures." Et sire Peirs briefnent respondist qe nulle parole vodroit dire ne moustrer avaunt qils furount toutes assembles.'

[16] J. C. Holt, 'The Prehistory of Parliament', in R. G. Davies and J. H. Denton (eds.), *The English Parliament in the Middle Ages* (Philadelphia, 1981), 25–6.
[17] Butts, *A History of Parliament,* 254–5.

ference in status but rather to the status conferred upon them by their chosen method of representation.

De la Mare, in his turn, carefully defended the Commons' peculiar claims to commonalty by explaining that his was not the undifferentiated voice of a mob, nor did it represent his own opinion (in neither respect was he personally responsible for what he said), but rather the report of the common assent produced by the deliberations of individuals with stakes in the government, individuals summoned by the king, even if previously elected by 'the better people of the shire'. Thus all of the Commons must be present in parliament because they are an assembly of qualified individuals rather than a throng of *commune vulgus;* as such, de la Mare might only report their opinions, not represent them. In short, by making clamour the rhetorical pivot on which commonalty might turn, the 1376 Lords and Commons were forced to hammer out a discourse of collectivity and its fraught relation to social status.

Needless to say, Gaunt did not find these kinds of distinctions congenial to his purposes.[18] As the chronicler Thomas Walsingham reports, he later raged to his followers about the presumption ('tantus tumor et super[bia]') of the Commons, how they were degenerate knights ('degeneres . . . milites') pretending to be lords or princes of the land ('reges sivi principes'). His followers reminded him that the Commons were not common people ('non plebei') parodying their betters, as Gaunt would have it, nor, of course, were they magnates, but rather they were of a different order altogether, if one difficult to pin down: they were armigerous, for example ('armipoten[tes et] strenui, fulciuntur'), and they had gained the favour of both the Lords ('favorem obtinent dominorum') and the London mob ('Londonieses etiam omnes et singuli et commune vulgus') during the reign of Edward III.[19]

The tension in the Good Parliament between clamour and commonalty are further attested to by accounts of the 1378 Gloucester Parliament, in which the royal party attempted to regain the upper hand over the

---

[18] It perhaps comes as no surprise that Peter de la Mare was steward to Edmund, Earl of March, one of John of Gaunt's political enemies (Butts, *A History of Parliament*, 341).

[19] *Chronicon a monacho sancti albani*, i. 74–5. ' "Domine," ait, "Non latet vestram magnificentiam quibus et quantis auxiliis isti milites, non plebei, ut asseruistis, sed armipoten[tes et] strenui, fulciuntur. Namque favorem obtinent dominorum, et in primis domini Edwardi principis, fratris [vestri], qui illis consilium impendit officax et juvamen. Londonienses etiam omnes et singuli et commune vulgus tantum penes eos afficiuntur, quod non permitterent eos vel probis praegravari vel minima injuria molestari. Sed et ipsi milites, accepta contumelia, cogantur contra personam vestram et amicorum vestorum cuncta extrema molieri, quae fors[ita]n alias minime molirentur." '

Commons, especially in regard to subsidies. The chancellor, the Bishop of St Davids, opened parliament, for example, by explaining that it had been called in part to deal with the nasty rumours being spread against certain lords and royal officers. But accusations of sedition, if initially cowing the Commons' speaker into cautious declaimers, did not stop him from expressing astonishment at the Crown's poverty, requesting a copy of the enrolment of the last subsidy, questioning expenses abroad, and, in the end, conceding only a slight increase in the wool tax. Before conceding anything, however, the Commons boldly requested that five or six of the Lords come to negotiate with them in their chapter house. According to the parliamentary rolls, certain Lords refused, on the grounds that that method had only been recently employed, and that the Lords should choose six to ten of their number, and the Commons should do likewise. The delegates should then intercommune ('entrecomuner') or consult informally between themselves as they used to do, in an 'aisee manere' (a genteel and pleasant manner) without 'murmur, crye, & noise'.[20]

The Lords involved in this incident, by opposing the new-fangled, uncourtly, and disruptive clamour of the Commons in their chapter-house to an older, more 'genteel' tradition of intercommuning, were pursuing tactics similar to those of Gaunt in 1376. First, they intended to undermine the collective political clout of the Commons by insisting upon the singular representation by which the Lords expressed their own opinions (as suggested above, if intercommuning appeared to be an equitable practice it was nevertheless to the magnates' advantage because each delegate ultimately represented himself). Second, by proliferating 'clamour', the Commons' official mechanism of consensus, into 'murmur, crye, & noise', the Lords were accusing the Commons of being an illegitimate commonalty, not representative of the collective interests of the community of the whole but rather resembling, in their very insistence on common assent, the *commune vulgus*: the politicized obverse and social incarnation of the community of the whole. By refusing to take part in the Commons' 'murmur, crye, & noise', the Lords were not really accusing the Commons of being common people. They recognized, rather, that the Commons' unprecedented influence stemmed in part from their delicately wrought definition of commonalty, a definition that the Lords sought to destabilize by challenging the Commons' method of deliberation. Or, to put it another way, the Lords were using the rhetorical instability of clamour to undermine commonalty, and in doing so, to break it

---

[20] *Rotuli Parliamentorum*, iii. 36.

down into its constituent parts. By doing so, however, they ended up creating the Commons as a collective construct at once socially distinctive and politically viable.

II. Usk's 'Appeal' and Northampton's 'voys accorde'

Chronologically speaking, it might make sense to turn from the parliamentary rolls to *Piers Plowman,* which, as we will see below, explores in complicated ways the structures on which medieval English politics were founded. Yet Usk's 'Appeal', written eight years after the Good Parliament, usefully extends the commonalty debates from Westminster to London, showing in the process how competing models of commonalty emerged through the exploitation of a nascent political rhetoric. This 1384 document, written while Usk was in the custody of mayor Nicholas Brembre, accuses the former mayor of London, John of Northampton, of trying to rig the 1383 mayoral election. As several scholars have noted, the 'Appeal' is a fascinating document about London factionalism, as well as being an unusual testimony to the ways that documentary culture might be recruited for self-empowerment and absolution.[21] The most pressing issue in the 'Appeal', however, is one that goes right to the heart of late medieval civic politics and parliamentary negotiations: how might the mechanisms of commonalty be distorted to serve interest and, worse, to obscure crucial distinctions between collectivity and social status, distinctions on which civic government ultimately rests? Just as the royal party tried to undermine the Commons by portraying their clamour as the undifferentiated *vox* of a *commune vulgus,* so Usk uses clamour to level his most damning accusation against Northampton. He argues that his former mayor and employer manipulated the common assent of the London council in order to defend his incumbency against Nicholas Brembre, and to incite the city's apprentices and labourers to revolt.

The 'Appeal', in the partly illegible copy in which it survives, begins by describing a secret meeting held in a London tavern in the summer or autumn of 1383. The meeting probably included Northampton, his henchmen, a number of representatives from the crafts, Usk as secretary to 'write thair billes', and a few members of the 'comun conseyl' who

---

[21] For a fascinating account of the relationship between factionalism and vernacular self-actualizing, see Paul Strohm, 'The Textual Vicissitudes of Usk's "Appeal" ', in *Hochon's Arrow: The Social Imagination of Fourteenth-Century Texts* (Princeton, 1992), 145–60.

supported Northampton's policies, the most controversial being the election of the council by crafts rather than by wards. The ostensible purpose of the meeting was to drum up support ahead of the mayoral election so that, at the Common Council, those present at the tavern meeting and their followers 'myghten be on voys accorde vpon the purpos to-forn take', and on that same day they would 'crie ayein [the purpos to-forn take]'.[22] Usk, in other words, was accusing Northampton of manipulating the expression of common assent in the London common council ('on voys accorde', 'crie ayein') to advance his own interests and prevent Brembre's election. The incumbent mayor would make the cry of his supporters, those from the 'craftes that hielden with hym', pass for the unanimous assent of the council.

But, says Usk, Northampton went even further in his attempts to distort commonalty. When the aldermen sympathetic to Brembre had abandoned Northampton, the mayor and his cohorts recruited the 'comun people for to stonde be thes purposes to lyue & to dye' (24). The idea was that, on election day, the common people would drown out and, in effect, replace the common assent of the Common Council, should the Council affirm Brembre's election. As Usk goes on to explain, to draw upon the voice of the common people is to pretend to care for the welfare of community of the whole by acting as if the urban *vulgus* legitimately represents that collectivity: Northampton's men 'vnder colour of wordes of comun profit euer more [charg]ed the people fro day in to other to be redy to stonde be hem in the euel purposed matirs' (29). It is to suggest that the voice of the non-patriciate urban populace represents the common profit through analogy or resemblance to the community of the whole. In fact, the common people are unfit to represent the common profit because they are not of such a social standing that they might represent themselves, nor are they sufficiently experienced in government. As Usk complains, Northampton and his men, perturbed that 'worthy persones wer drawe fro hem for willesful gouernaile & fiebel conseyl', inappropriately recruited 'many craftes & muchel smale people that konne non skyl of gouernaunce ne of gode conseyl' (29). To substitute the voice of the common people for the common assent of the Common Council is to exchange clamour as consensus between individuals for clamour as an undifferentiated vox of the *commune vulgus*, or to exchange an official form

---

[22] R. W. Chambers and Marjorie Daunt (eds.), *A Book of London English, 1384–1425* (Oxford, 1931), 23. Subsequent line numbers will be quoted in the main text.

of commonalty for a subordinate and illegitimate one. And it is at the very moment that an undifferentiated voice claims to have the authority of official consensus that it is regarded as insurgent: the *vulgus* replaces the Council by violent substitution rather than by analogy or extension. According to Usk, Northampton hoped that, by substituting the voice of an urban *vulgus* for the common assent of the Council, his policies would be forever 'meightened ek by myght of the peple', as well as by royal statute. In this way, Usk explains, Northampton's plotting was doubly treacherous: not only did it allow the 'smale people' to usurp the mechanism of common assent, but it also pitted the franchised against the disenfranchised, making 'the pore people' the more 'feruent & rebel a-yeins the grete men of the town' (24). Finally, says Usk, if Northampton hadn't already done enough, on the day that Brembre was elected the ousted mayor sent Usk to John of Gaunt to complain that Brembre had recruited an 'orrible companye of criers'. These criers 'with oute any vsage but strength' had prevented Northampton's supporters from attending the election, and had subsequently paved the way for Brembre to be chosen as mayor. Northampton, suggests Usk, had the audacity to accuse Brembre of the very crime of which he himself was guilty, of replacing the common assent of qualified individuals with the single voice of a threatening crowd.

It is plain to see that Usk's supposed concern in the 'Appeal', that the voices of those elected to affirm the mayoral election might be overwhelmed by the voices of those persons not elected ('smal people', 'pore people'), had as much to with Brembre's new electoral policies as it did with Northampton's abuse of political custom. Usk, by identifying Northampton's followers with the common people, was actually making a case for Brembre's winning platform, that representation by crafts, because it was (marginally) more democratic than representation by wards, was a recipe for disorder. As the parliamentary rolls make clear, commonalty by its very nature threatens to obscure distinctions between the non-noble and the *vulgus,* even if the so-called non-noble participants are actually part of the merchant-patriciate. These distinctions must be preserved, however, in order for an official collectivity to exist at all. It is for this reason that the clamour of an unsanctioned (if civic-minded) electorate was often cited as justification for changes in the electoral process. As one letter-book entry for February 1384 explains, post-Brembre elections were based on wards rather than crafts because 'matters in the Common Council had been carried by clamor rather than by reason and sometimes by members who were not qualified to sit, whereby tumults had arisen'.[23] Similarly, back in August of 1376, when the electorate was still drawn from the crafts, the Common Council, faced with the threat of royal interference, assured the king that 'in order to prevent tumult arising from large gatherings, it had been unanimously decided that whenever the Commonalty met in Common Council of the City, the Council should be chosen by the best men of the Misteries and not otherwise'.[24] The point is that Usk, in order to support his case that Northampton's electoral policies encouraged social disorder, and further, that that disorder was evidenced by the very way in which Northampton contested Brembre's election, had to distinguish between—and to a certain extent, collapse—various forms of clamour: the formal assent of delegates, the approbation or censure of better men, and the insurgent demands of the urban *vulgus*. In doing so, he ran the risk of sacrificing commonalty itself which, as I have said, depended on careful distinctions between the official collectivity, the *vulgus*, and the whole.

In sum, if the structures of guilds served in their totality as 'a grammar of governance', as David Wallace has shown,[25] in Usk's 'Appeal' it is precisely the susceptibility of that grammar, both as narrative and as action, that threatened to elide social distinctions between the collectivity that governs and the collectivity that is governed. The argument that I am making about the 'Appeal' is different, of course, from the one I am making about the parliamentary rolls. In Westminster, at least from the perspective of the parliamentary Lords, collective constructs are suspect the moment they come into being—in that setting, collectivity is understood to be socially inferior by its very nature, and therefore politically suspect; whereas in London, it is the mishandling of collective constructs, of exchanging one for another, that disqualifies political participation. In Westminster, clamour refers to the attempt to authorize or challenge the mechanisms of common assent by defining the relation of collectivity to social status. In London, common assent is not socially problematic in itself; rather clamour comes into view at the moment that common assent is replaced by the insubordinate and homogeneous voice of the *vulgus*. Taken together, however, Usk's 'Appeal' and the 1376 rolls suggest that the

[23] *Calendar of Letter-books Preserved among the Archives of the Corporation of the City of London at the Guildhall, Letter-book H, c.1375–1399*, ed. Reginald R. Sharpe (London, 1907), 227, fo. clxxiii.
[24] Ibid., 36, fo. xliv.
[25] David Wallace, *Chaucerian Polity: Absolutist Lineages and Associational Forms in England and Italy* (Stanford, Calif., 1997), 65–82.

relationship between collectivity and social status was not a given; rather, it came into view within the formulation of a vernacular rhetoric which blurs social distinction in its very fashioning of political structure.

III. Langland's Common Voice

The parliamentary rolls and Usk's 'Appeal' shaped official commonalties (the parliamentary Commons, the Common Council) by testing out the relationship between collectivity and social status in the political realm. Both texts, however, are more invested in political rhetoric, in persuasion and recrimination, than they are in political structure: they use clamour to contest the social meaning and political authority of collective constructs, but they do so primarily to promote the interests of individuals and factions. As I argue in the last part of this essay, disputes about commonalty in Westminster and London also resonate as clamour in contemporary poetry, as best seen in the *Piers Plowman* B Prologue (*c.*1376–9), which also uses clamour to come to terms with the political viability and social status of collective constructs. Yet *Piers Plowman* differs significantly from the Good Parliament records and Usk's 'Appeal', not because it follows them sequentially—it is difficult to determine how the poem *responds* to historical events and legal records—but rather because it deals with the ways that political structure might be worked out *as structure,* and particularly as allegory. The prologues to the B and C texts culminate in spectacular scenes of parliamentary activity, with exhaustive possibilities for referencing royal marriage, John of Gaunt, and power struggles of all sorts. They nevertheless manage to elude topical readings, in part because they are so thickly allusive (e.g. the 'belling the cat' fable), and in part because they interpret topicality itself as poetic form. If we were to ask, in other words, what *Piers Plowman* has to do with political life of the 1370s, we might answer that it is less concerned with reproducing political conflict than it is with modelling political structure. More specifically, in the *Piers Plowman* B Prologue, contemporary debates about commonalty are presented as formal problems about the ways that singular and collective constructs represent and are represented by vernacular allegory. Langland is interested in delineating the forms through which commonalty comes into being, both as allegorical experiment and political problem.

The Prologue opens and closes with a brilliant flurry of activity, a dream-list of occupations in action. In doing so, it anticipates the poem's ethical commitment to labour, but also its poetic investment in 'alle folk', the imagining of a general entity. Guillaume de Deguileville's *Pelerinage de la vie humaine* (French, 1330s–1350s; English 1370s–1420s), an allegorical dream-vision which clearly inspired *Piers Plowman*, similarly imagines a readership of 'alle folk', a readership which is both the inclusive subject of spiritual instruction ('Now cometh neer and gadereth yow togideres alle folk . . . for þis towcheth alle, boþe grete and smale, withouten any owt-taken'), and, by implication, insofar as it excludes poor people, the exclusive subject of Christian salvation ('þe riche mighte not entre [heaven] no more þan a camele miht passe thoruh þe eye of a needle . . . Miche likede me þis passage for þe commune avauntage þat alle folk hadden þere if þei bicumen verrey poore').[26] Langland, however, makes Deguileville's readership the subject of his visionary satire—'I sei3 in this assemblee, as ye shul here after . . . Of alle kynne lybbynge laborers lopen forth somme' (B. 218, 223), and in doing so he commits himself to a poetics of 'alle folk', as well as to the ethics of labour. Significantly, however, although every version of the Prologue begins and ends with the description of 'alle manere of men, þe meene and þe riche | Werchyng and wandrynge as the world asketh' (B. 18–19), in the B text (*c.*1376–9) that description is suspended by several political models featuring different sorts of allegorical experiments: personified abstractions such as Conscience; allegorical beasts such as the mice and rats of the 'belling the cat' episode; historical characters tending toward the symbolic, such as a ploughman, an angel, a lunatic, and a king; and generalized legal-political entities such as the Commons, knighthood, and clergie. These political models date the B text to the 1370s, but they also align the poem's interest in 'alle folk' with the political problem of commonalty or the relationship between collectivity and social status. They relocate to the political sphere that general entity that is the poem's visionary subject. From its very inception, I am suggesting, Langland's dream-vision is radically invested in the political and literary effects of commonalty, and further, that the political models in B and C bring those effects strikingly into focus.

To take the well-known 'three estates' model, for example, Langland capitalizes on the ambiguity of 'commune(s)' to dramatize the interdependence of the three estates in government, food production, spiritual welfare, and law:

---

[26] Guillaume de Deguileville, *Pilgrimage of the Lyfe of the Manhode*, ed. Avril Henry, vol. ii, EETS, os 288 (London, 1985), p. 1, ll. 8–12; p. 3, ll. 85–96.

> Thanne kam þer a kyng, kny3thod hym ladde;
> Might of þe communes made hym to regne.
> And þanne cam kynde wit and clerkes he made,
> For to counseillen þe kyng and þe commune saue.
> The kyng and kny3thod and clergie boþe
> Casten þat þe commune sholde [hire communes] fynde.
> The commune contreued of kynde wit craftes,
> And for profit of al þe people Plowmen ordeyned
> To tilie and to trauaille as trewe lif askeþ.
> þe kyng and þe commune and kynde wit þe þridde
> Shopen lawe and leaute, ech [lif] to knowe his owene.
>
> $(112–22)$[27]

Certainly, as Anna Baldwin and others have argued, the ostensible purpose of this passage is to locate monarchical power within the shifting relations of traditional estates theory, and concomitantly to delimit the social, economic, and political functions of those who might limit the monarch.[28] Because this passage appears to argue for some form of communal sovereignty, it has often been cited as an example of Langland's political radicalism (largely by Reformers), or alternatively, as an example of the way in which a fundamentally conservative poem might be misread by political radicals (for example, by the authors of the rebel letters of 1381).[29] I believe that this passage is preoccupied with monarchical power and communal sovereignty insofar as both are expressed within the idea of commonalty itself. The passage lays the groundwork, in other words, for both political radicalism and political conservatism: it is concerned with the *process* by which collective constructs emerge from non-noble entities, at the same time that it grapples with that process by imagining it as political allegory. Who makes up the entity called the 'communes', this passage asks, and how and what does it represent both as a political construct and as a poetic fiction? What happens when commonalty is broken down into its constituent parts and made legible as poetic practice?

[27] William Langland, *Piers Plowman: The B Version*, ed. George Kane and E. Talbot Donaldson, rev. edn. (London, 1988). All subsequent citations from *Piers Plowman* will be to this edition, unless otherwise indicated.

[28] Anna Baldwin, *The Theme of Government in Piers Plowman* (Cambridge, 1981).

[29] See Larry Scanlon's illuminating discussion of these interpretive traditions in his forthcoming essay, 'King, Commons, and Kind Wit: Langland's National Vision and the Rising of 1381'.

More specifically, collective constructs and relationships that they for-
mulate between social status and political agency, become visible in this
passage as a series of semantic, syntactic, and metonymic substitutions.
For example, Langland first presents the 'communes' rather daringly as a
politicized construct with the phrase, 'might of the communes made hym
to regne' (113), the word 'might' hinting both at the scope of monarchical
power and the coercive agency that Usk ascribes to the *vulgus* that threatens to distort the relationship between official commonalty and the common profit (just as, as Usk says, Northampton was 'meightened ek by
myght of the peple').[30] But the 'communes' are next described in terms of
estate rather than urban or parliamentary politics—as labourers and the
fruits of their labour—and are syntactically subordinated to the other two
estates, which 'casten þat þe commune sholde [hire communes] fynde'
(117). The 'communes' promptly strip themselves of commonalty
altogether: first, by defining themselves as diverse occupations ('The
commune contreued of Kynde Wit craftes' (118)), thus moving from an
amorphous political body to the various constituencies from which that
body might be formed; and next, by re-presenting themselves as near-
allegorical 'plowmen' ('plowman' in some manuscripts), who piously
labour for the communes 'as trewe lif askeþ' (120). These exemplary figures of traditional labour ideology effectively empty commonalty of
its political agency by isolating its least controversial social function—
agricultural production. It is from these pious ploughmen, moreover,
that 'the profit of al the peple' is finally said to proceed, common profit
here cautiously conceived as the alimentary and spiritual rather than the
political well-being of the community of the whole. Finally, at the end of
this passage, Langland once more imagines commonalty as a syntactically
and legislatively empowered entity ('the kyng and the commune . . .
shopen law and leaute I eche lif to knowe his owne' [B. 121–2]), 'commune' by now signifying a dizzying range of collective constructs by
which individual and common profit may be represented.

At this moment the estates model breaks off, revealing itself to be at
once political paradigm and poetic experiment. Despite the fact that this
scene only appears in its entirety in the B Prologue, it seems to advertise a

---

[30] This line is revised in the C text presumably to de-emphasize the political agency of the
'communes': 'Mygt of tho men [i.e. knights] made hym to regne' (140) (*Piers Plowman: A Parallel Edition of the A, B, C and Z versions*, ed. A. V. C. Schmidt (London, 1995)). All subsequent
citations from the C text will be to this edition.

quintessentially Langlandian poetic, in its episodic abruptness, its composite allegories, and its juxtaposition of semantic ambiguity and ideological ambivalence. Yet the formal peculiarities of this passage are sustained or propelled by some of the same concerns operating in the political sphere, as if, in this instance, poetic invention might be directly analogous to current political debates, or as if the topical might be expressed simultaneously through thematic allusion and formal illustration. The project of this passage, I am arguing, is both politically current and characteristically Langlandian: it uses contemporary concerns about the social status of collective constructs to reframe relations between the general and specific, the collective and the singular, and the common and the vulgar. In doing so, it also asks what role commonalty plays within the very structures, and likewise within the material, causal, and conceptual relations that govern poetic form. What happens, for example, when that collective construct called the communes is represented metonymically or allegorically by food, crafts, or the conventional but socially subordinate ploughmen? It is clear, moreover, that to make these kinds of poetic substitutions like so many Russian dolls (the communes with the crafts, the crafts with the ploughmen, the ploughmen with a ploughman), is continually to draw attention to the social underpinnings of collectivities even while rendering them apolitical or singular. That the ploughmen remain politically suspect as a collective construct, for example, is a point possibly addressed by the C Prologue in which 'Plowmen' (or 'plowman') is efficiently replaced with 'a plogh'. 'And for most profitable to þe puple a plogh gonne þei make' (C. 145). It is as if to say that the ploughmen must be replaced by the singular instrument of their labour in order for the political agency of the non-noble to be cancelled out.[31]

In short, what this passage explores is the emergent relationship between collectivity and social status, a relationship that becomes especially critical when depicted as allegory. It becomes critical because the translation of political issues into poetry (and vice versa) always leaves traces of exertion, awarding to abstract political theory the force of contemporary events, but more significantly because allegory—like caricature—exposes the structures of political systems, while attributing to those structures an imaginative agency all their own. (It is for this reason, I would argue, that the passage has attracted radical and conservative readers alike.) The

---

[31] For a summary of the differences between B and C, and the political implications of those differences, see E. Talbot Donaldson, *Piers Plowman: The C-Text and Its Poet* (New Haven, 1966), 85–90, and Anna Baldwin, *The Theme of Government*.

radical imaginative work of commonalty in this passage is highlighted by such verbs as 'casten' and 'contrived' (both meaning 'devised'), words that capture both the relevance of political theory and the structural immediacy of vernacular allegory.

In the political model that follows, a heated debate between a lunatic, angel, and goliard regarding the king's accountability to the law, clamour reveals once more what is finally at stake in commonalty, in the tensions, that is, between collectivity and social status, and between collective and singular constructs. Indeed, in this 'coronation scene', Langland muffles the claims of commonalty by deferring the voice that is its very indication. First, by having an angel argue in Latin on behalf of the common people ('for lewed men ne koude I Iangle ne Iugge þat Iustife hem sholde I But suffren and seruen' (B. 129–31)), he very explicitly marks the voice of commonalty as linguistically and politically abject. He has replaced the 'communes' of the previous scene, in other words, with an apolitical collectivity ('lewed men'), which simply does not know how to vocalize its own profit effectively, either as a corporate body of deliberating representatives or as a uniform mob (theirs is the clamour cited rather than heard by authorities, such as Philip V of France). What is significant in this passage, then, is not just the fact that the common people haven't mastered the techniques of academic debate or clerical diplomacy—unlike the lunatic, for example, they cannot speak 'clergially', and therefore, by a kind of analogy, can't participate in political process—but also that as a 'lewd people' they are sharply distinguished from other collective constructs used to represent the community of the whole.

Second, Langland distributes the excess and cacophony associated with spurious forms of commonalty among the three singular figures who admonish the king: the lean but well-spoken lunatic, the angel 'an hei3', and the aggrieved goliardis who, we are told, is 'a gloton of wordes' (139). These socially elusive figures, which speak from the far limits of the community, speak in some sense like the parliamentary lords, as their proper selves rather than as members of a commonalty or as metonyms of a collective construct.[32] As such, they may legitimately represent the common profit: rather than standing for a collectivity or even for identifiable historical persons, they embody the very act of speaking in the political

---

[32] As David Burnley argues, these figures deliver speeches that are distinctly courtly, not so much because they are concerned with social status, but because they reflect the conflict between 'personal interest' and 'courtly proprieties' (*Courtliness and Literature in Medieval England* (London, 1998), 106–9). As such, I would add, they gesture not just to a mode of courtly speech, but also to the way that speech reveals ideal forms of parliamentary representation and negotiation.

realm. In this way, by assigning speeches to these figures, Langland has replaced commonalty in all of its conflicting forms with the singular representation that characterizes both academic disputation and traditional aristocratic politics.

Third, and perhaps most importantly, Langland defers the much-anticipated noise, the common assent or *vox populi*, to the end of the scene:

> And þanne gan al þe commune crye in vers of Latyn
> To be Kynges counseil—construe whoso wolde—
> *'Precepta Regis sunt nobis vincula legis!'*

When the Commons finally begin to cry at the end of the scene, it is with a safely generalized *vox populi* confirming absolute rule, having been divested of the rhetorical and political agency inherent in representations of the whole.[33] Like the 'three estates' model, then, the thematic subject of the 'coronation scene' is political theory—the divine right of kings, the place of counsel, and so forth—but its formal subject is political structure, the differing claims of singular and collective constructs, and the complex relationship between collectivity and social status. At the centre of the *Piers Plowman* B Prologue, then, is not just the issue of who has political agency but also the formal experimentation that commonalty produces, and which is here articulated as voice.[34] This is not to insist that clamour as an official action in the political sphere means the same thing or achieves the same effects as it does as a literary speech genre, nor is it to claim that formal considerations take priority over ideological ones. It is to suggest instead that the poem's response to institutions or events is essentially a literary investigation into the ways that old political structures are defended and new ones are made. If poetic invention—allegorical puzzles, narrative incoherence, generic shifts—may be considered a type of response to medieval political life, Langland's allegory is itself the very

[33] On the use of the word 'commune' in this scene and throughout *Piers Plowman*, see A. V. C. Schmidt, *The Clerkly Maker: Langland's Poetic Art* (Cambridge, 1987), 119–24.

[34] The scene immediately dissolves, of course, into the 'belling the cat' allegory, in which mice and rats consider the merits of belling an irrepressible cat: 'Wiþ þat ran þer a route of Ratons at ones I And smale mees myd hem; mo þan a þousand I Comen to a counseil for þe commune profit' (ll. 146–8). It would appear that in these lines Langland is finally replacing the indeterminate forms of commonalty of the two previous scenes with a politically legitimate one characterized by deliberation and assent. Yet the term 'common profit', as applied to the rodent council, squeaks with irony from the beginning of this next scene: first, because the 'belling the cat' allegory recounts a story of self-interested counsellors hoping to resist the exactions of the royal party; and second, because it is to those counsellors that Langland immediately ascribes the restless insurgency of the *commune vulgus*: 'wiþ þat ran þer a route of ratons at ones'.

process through which contemporary political structures come into being.[35]

It is instructive to leave *Piers Plowman* by taking a brief look at the end of B.5, a scene that encapsulates the Prologue's movement from the estates model to the coronation scene. Directly following the confessions of the seven sins, Repentance prays Christ to forgive all those repentant, and Hope blows a horn of forgiveness, the sound of which temporarily unifies heaven and earth in prayer. At once, we are told, all the saints began to sing on behalf of sinners, 'alle Seintes [for synful] songen' (508), praising the multiplication of God's mercy among men and beasts. These celestial singers are immediately echoed by 'A þousand of men þo þrungen togideres', who 'cride upward to crist and to his clene moder I To have grace to go [to] truþe—[God leve þat þey moten!]' (510–12). The possibility of universal mercy is thus reflected simultaneously in the harmonious unity of the saints and the *vox* of a throng, the collective nature of which both attests to and calls down the wide dissemination of God's mercy to the community of the poem. These men are the inaudible abject, who in their spiritual crisis can be heard only within the miracle of the poem and in imitation of a heavenly choir: *vox populi vox dei*. But notably, at the very second that these earthly men attempt to join in the cosmic verbal unity, at the very moment that they offer a prayer on their own behalf, they turn into blundering beasts: 'Ac here was wight noon so wys, þe wey þider kouþe I But blustreden forþ as beestes over ba[ch]es and hilles . . .'(513–14). For a collectivity to resonate as voice, even in prayer, is to announce its resemblance to the *commune vulgus*, the crowd whose collective vision has neither the coherence of reason nor the logic of consent. It seems that any collective construct threatens to change the trajectory of the poem from the spiritual to the political. *Piers Plowman*, of course, is rife with similar moments of surprising unity and sudden dispersal or rupture. As Anne Middleton has argued, such moments are characteristic of Langland's episodic form in general.[36] Certainly, too, the ruptured unity between men and saints illustrates a larger moral point, that the bliss of salvation enjoyed by saints is not readily attained by those

---

[35] David Aers, remarking on the absence of the 1381 revolt in Chaucer's poetry, argues that the complexity of that poetry attests to its 'resistant' artistry because it enables the poet to dodge 'determinate situation[s]' while, at the same time, responding brilliantly and unexpectedly to them (Aers, '*Vox Populi* and the Literature of 1381', 444).

[36] Anne Middleton, 'Narration and the Invention of Experience: Episodic Form in *Piers Plowman*', in Siegfried Wenzel and Larry D. Benson (eds.), *The Wisdom of Poetry: Essays in Honor of Morton Bloomfield* (Kalamazoo, Mich., 1982), 81–122.

still wandering the surface of the earth. I am suggesting, however, that in this scene episodic rupture is founded upon the fraught status of collectivity in the first place, both as a political entity and as a poetic formation: at the very moment that a collectivity is expressed as a unified voice it is undercut by the social implications of that act.

I have argued in this essay that commonalty was a major preoccupation of all sorts of texts written in the 1370s and early 1380s, from the records of parliamentary debates and civic trials to allegorical poetry. I have suggested, too, that clamour was the rhetorical means by which commonalty might be attacked and defended; it was clamour that helped poets and politicians negotiate the difficult and under-theorized relationship between collectivity and social status. This argument could just as well have been expanded to include Chaucer's *Parliament of Fowls* (*c.*1382), another allegorical dream-vision featuring a raucous parliament. Chaucer's poem, for example, is clearly interested in the conflict between the singular representation of courtly love and aristocratic politics, on the one hand, and collective representation, on the other. Chaucer consistently portrays this tension as clamour: the birds' noise is initially sympathetic insofar as it reflects the pious complaint of the community of the whole or the harmonious disharmony of the birds assembled for procreation. But once clamour is entertained within the bird's parliament as a principle of commonalty, it becomes immediately associated with the disruptive and uncourtly voice of the *vulgus*, in contrast, say, to the individual speeches of the eagle-suitors or the singular opinions delivered by the nobler birds. Like the *Piers Plowman* Prologue, then, commonalty in the *Parliament of Fowls* is that poem's ideological subject *and* poetic process. It might be possible to claim, then, that Langland and Chaucer were writing on either end of what was simultaneously a political moment and literary tradition, one marked by the discovery of commonalty within political discourse and within an English vernacular poetics.

University of Pennsylvania

Allegory and the Madness of the Text: *Hoccleve's* Complaint

Jeremy Tambling

I. Allegory

In *The Allegory of Love*, C. S. Lewis says about the opening stanzas of Thomas Hoccleve's *The Regement of Princes*, completed around 1411 for the future Henry V: 'here we have a description, much infected with allegory, but still unallegorical, of a sleepless night. . . . [Hoccleve] analyses the state of his emotions during the wakeful night, just as the love poets had analysed the state of the sleepless lover; and Thought personified . . . is recognised as the immediate enemy. . .'[1] While Lewis is equivocal how far Hoccleve's text is allegorical, his description of the power of anxiety provokes a question about the connection between three things: allegory, autobiography, madness. Perhaps Hoccleve is an exemplary case for all three, for the text which brings them all together is his *Complaint*, which is a record of madness.[2]

Hoccleve (*c.*1367–1426) was employed from about 1387 in London, at Westminster, in the Office of the Privy Seal, so that he was a clerk, issuing documents authorized by the king's seal, as well as becoming, in the period after *The Regement of Princes*, a semi-official Lancastrian court-poet, his loyalty showing itself, for instance, in *The Remonstrance against Oldcastle* (August 1415). But Pearsall notes a silence after that: 'for whatever

---

[1] C. S. Lewis, *The Allegory of Love* (Oxford, 1936), 238.

[2] Quotations from *Thomas Hoccleve's Complaint and Dialogue*, ed. John Burrow, Early English Text Society (Oxford, 1999). I quote from the 'Edited text' but omit the mid-line break which Burrow inserts, and have modernized archaic letters. The *Complaint* begins a sequence of linked texts known as the *Series*, beginning with a Prologue leading into a Complaint (both together may be called the *Complaint*). A Dialogue with a Friend follows, leading into the Tale of Jereslaus's Wife, a translation of a text 'Learn to Die' and the Tale of Jonathas. Quotations other than those for the *Complaint* and the *Dialogue* are taken from M. C. Seymour, *Selections from Hoccleve* (Oxford, 1981). Again, I have replaced the archaic letters. I have used the editorial matter of both (Burrow, Seymour plus page reference in the text).

reason, soon after 1415 and by 1419, Hoccleve was looking for a new patron'.[3] The dating is not clear, but it seems that ten years after *The Regement of Princes*, in November 1421, Hoccleve began his *Complaint*—which was to be the first poem in a proposed series whose intention was to produce a new patron, the Duke of Gloucester. The substance of the *Complaint* was Hoccleve commenting on a madness he had endured five years before.[4] Was Hoccleve ever mad or no? The question cannot be answered in that form, and not only because of Polonius's belief that to 'define true madness, what is't but to be nothing else but mad?' (*Hamlet* II. ii. 93–4),[5] nor because there is virtually no evidence on the point outside the text. What is entailed for a text to separate off a period and say that the subject was mad then? If it was mad, how did it know? If the evidence that can be brought is the way the 'I' of the poem thinks that his contemporaries see him, in Westminster, Westminster Hall, and walking the pavements of London (*Complaint* 72, 73, 183–6) how can that be separated from a paranoia, possibly related to city existence, as 'modern' paranoia seems to be city induced?[6] This paranoia might be the very madness itself, though subsequent in date to the madness he thought he had endured. If the text could be taken as an objective account, there might be some point in finding a positivistic form of madness that could be described.[7] But no text, on account of its textuality, can be taken so objectively, and this one firmly draws attention to itself as a text, not least through its quasi-allegorical form, so that it confronts the reader with the madness of writing, which is the madness of thinking that a textual deci-

[3] Derek Pearsall, 'Hoccleve's *Regement of Princes*: The Politics of Royal Self-Presentation', *Speculum*, 69 (1994), 386–410: 410.

[4] John Burrow argues for 1414 as the date of madness throughout his writings on Hoccleve; see 'Thomas Hoccleve: Some Redatings', *Review of English Studies*, NS 46 (1995), 366–72. Seymour argues for 1416, as does Matthew Boyd Goldie, 'Psychosomatic Illness and Identity in London, 1416–1421: Hoccleve's *Complaint* and Dialogue with a Friend', *Exemplaria*, 11 (1999), 23–52: 25.

[5] Shakespeare quotations from *The Riverside Shakespeare*, ed. G. Blakemore Evans (Boston, 1974).

[6] On paranoia and urban culture, see my 'We are Seven: Dante and the Serial Killer', *Paragraph*, 22 (1999), 293–309.

[7] For accounts of Hoccleve's madness see Stephen Medcalf, *The Later Middle Ages* (London, 1981), 108–71; Gordon Claridge, Ruth Pryor, and Gwen Watkins, *Sounds from the Bell-Jar: Ten Psychotic Authors* (London, 1990), 49–70, 144–7; George MacLennan, *Lucid Interval: Subjective Writing and Madness in History* (Leicester, 1992), 15–38. In the *Dialogue* the Friend says the madness was caused by study (*Dialogue*, 302)—a Chaucerian note, reminiscent of the Eagle in *The House of Fame* (e.g. lines 655–8), but with implications for the dominance of the subject by thought—and the Hoccleve of the poem declares it was only sickness (*Dialogue*, 426), which may ignore the text's penitential aspects. Neither view can be regarded as adequate.

sion can be made between madness and reason. The evidence for the madness is in the writing, which is therefore the writing of madness. And that phrase brings together two positions which we might like to keep distinct: that of rational texts which describe madness from the outside, and texts whose being is mad, perhaps because their author is mad. But whether the distinction can be maintained, and which position corresponds to Hoccleve's text, or whether the *Complaint* makes for a confusion of both positions, is a question for this essay.

To return to Lewis's point, the enemy seems to be 'thought'. The *Complaint* compares with *The Regement of Princes*,[8] which also opens autobiographically, with the subject of the poem musing on the world's 'restless business' so that

> As I lay in my bedde upon a nyght
> Thoght me berefte of slepe the force and myght.
>
> (6–7)

The power of thought is associated with death, and perhaps with the death-wish: 'to the deth he wel ny hath me feyntyd' (14). Thought has 'vexed' his 'poore goost' (9) before, so that the text makes two allegorizations, with himself objectified as his spirit, and with a double sense in 'poore'—i.e. in poverty, and an object of pity, the subject for a complaint. Thought has made him consider the lack of surety of anyone living, and he enumerates the dangers of poverty, before returning to the actual night:

> Thus ylke nyght I walwed to and fro
> Sekyng reste, but certeynly sche
> Appeeryd nought, for thoght, my cruel fo,

---

[8] In addition to other references to Hoccleve I specifically cite in the notes, see Jerome Mitchell, *Thomas Hoccleve: A Study in Early Fifteenth Century English Poetic* (Urbana, Ill., 1968); David Lawton, 'Dullness and the Fifteenth-Century', *English Literary History*, 54 (1987), 761–99. On the *Complaint*, see John Burrow, 'Hoccleve's *Series*: Experience and Books', in Robert Yeager (ed.), *Fifteenth-Century Studies* (Hamden, Conn., 1984), 259–74; Burrow, 'The Poet as Petitioner', *Studies in the Age of Chaucer*, 3 (1981), 61–75; Burrow, 'The Poet and his Book', in Piero Boitani and Anna Torti (eds.), *Genres, Themes and Images in English Literature* (Tübingen, 1981); Burrow, 'Hoccleve and Chaucer', in Ruth Morse and Barry Windeatt (eds.), *Chaucer Traditions* (Cambridge, 1990), 54–61; Burrow, '*Thomas Hoccleve*, Authors of the Middle Ages', 4 (Aldershot: Variorum 1994); see further Malcolm Richardson, 'Hoccleve in his Social Context', *Chaucer Review*, 20 (1986), 313–22; Stephen Kohl, 'More than Virtues and Vices: Self-Analysis in Hoccleve's "Autobiographies"', *Fifteenth-Century Studies*, 14 (1988), 115–27; D. C. Greetham, 'Self-Referential Artifacts: Hoccleve's Persona as a Literary Device', *Modern Philology*, 86 (1989), 242–51; Anthony J. Hasler, 'Hoccleve's Unregimented Body', *Paragraph*, 13 (1990), 164–83; Anna Torti, *The Glass of form: Mirroring Structures from Chaucer to Skelton* (Cambridge, 1991), 87–106.

> Chaced hadde hyre and sleepe away fro me.
> And for I scholde not alone be
> Ageyn my lust, wach profrid hys seruyse
> And I adytted hym in heuy wyse.
>
> So long a nyght ne felte I neuer non
> As was that same to my iugement.
> Who so that thoughtys ys, ys woe begon.
> The thoughtful wyght ys vessel of turment.
> Ther nys no gref to hym equypolent
> He graueth deppest of seekenesse alle
> Ful wo ys hym that in swyche thought ys falle.
>
> (71–84)

When Lewis calls this writing unallegorical, he means that it is realist description, the account of someone rendered sleepless by worry, worry about poverty. When saying it is 'infected with allegory', he implicitly makes allegory a sickness, a contagious disease. The point, which is obviously loaded for a poet whose work was written under the shadow of madness, is also present in Angus Fletcher, who takes allegory negatively when he refers to a relationship between contagion, sickness, and allegory; the Latin *infectio* means a dyeing, or staining, just as allegory as a form of symbolic expression is a staining of the subject, while Fletcher quotes from Origen (*Contra Celsum*, IV. xlviii) on making a connection between allegory and a fear of contagion.[9] But before we can take this as a general thought about allegory further, it should be noticed that 'Thought' as a particular instance of an allegorical conception and so an infection, is in this text already a form of sickness; since it is annotated by Seymour as 'anxiety' or 'worry' in a sense the OED dates from *c.*1220. So as soon as self-reflexiveness, self-consciousness, which may also be part of the meaning of 'Thought' enters into allegorical existence, it casts a staining or sickening quality upon the subject, in a way that Hamlet also records in like allegorical manner ('the native hue of resolution I Is sicklied o'er with the pale cast of thought' (*Hamlet* III. i. 83–4) so much so that it appears that modern self-awareness is inseparable from the history of allegorical writing, the allegory which is the subject of Lewis's text (*Le Roman de la rose* dates from that same moment, soon after 1220). Here it seems worth quoting, as supplementary evidence, Louis Sass's comments on schizophrenia—which as a condition was first named as such by Bleuler, around

---

[9] Angus Fletcher, *Allegory: The Theory of a Symbolic Mode* (Ithaca, NY, 1966), 199–209.

1910, which makes it, therefore, another aspect of a modernist condition. Sass, who is opposed to an 'anti-psychiatry' position which sees in schizophrenia an increased affectivity, finds in it 'not an overwhelming by but a detachment from normal forms of emotion and desire, not a loss but an exacerbation of various kinds of self-conscious awareness'.[10] For Sass, schizophrenia is an overwhelming by thought; not a form of emotional hyperactivity but its opposite. If thought, then, is in Hoccleve inherently oppressive, that may in itself be a form of madness—where if madness is a state of alienation, thought is already alien, and the oppression itself. Or, thought may be a symptom of some other cause or problem, perhaps related to self-awareness. In which case, the desire to think allegorically may also be read as a retreat from such awareness, rather than as simply a development of it, since in allegory the subject moves back into abstractions, and sees its mental life in abstract, almost geometric forms. Allegory thus serves a double purpose; and it is not surprising that Lewis should see Hoccleve as allegorical and non-allegorical at once, also double.

Hoccleve's Thought, split off from himself, becomes his cruel foe. As masculine, it chases away the feminine rest and sleep.[11] Wakefulness as a substitute offers its services, and the subject is forced to take him 'in heavy wise'—in a melancholic spirit that recognizes that there is no choice, as there is no resisting a disease. The thoughtful person is 'woebegone', a 'vessel of torment' (a vessel filled with torment, another form of possession by allegory).

This story of the night leads to reflection, which is not based on a specific occasion, and to a desire to be alone:

> What whyght that inly pensyf is, I trowe
> Hys most desyre ys to be solytarie.
> That thys is soth, in my persone I knowe,
> For euere whyl that fretynge aduersarie
> Myn herte made to hymn trybutarie
> In sowkynge of the fresshest of my blood,
> To sorwe soule me thought yt dede me good.

---

[10]   Louis Sass, *Paradoxes of Delusion: Wittgenstein, Schreber and the Schizophrenic Mind* (Ithaca, NY, 1994), 12. Sass's discussion of schizophrenia as modernist appears in his *Madness and Modernism* (New York, 1992).

[11]   Ruth Nissé, '"Our Fadres Olde and Modres": Gender, Heresy and Hoccleve's Literary Politics', *Studies in the Age of Chaucer*, 21 (1999), in contrast reads the 'Thought' as feminine and feminizing. It seems to me that the 'force and myght' of Thought makes the subject feminized rather, by an act of violence.

> For the nature of heuynesse ys thys.
> If yt habunde gretly in a wyth,
> The place eischewyt he where as ioye ys
> For ioye and he not mow acorde aryght.
> As discordant as day ys vnto nyght.
> And honure aduersarie is vnto schame,
> Is heuynes so to ioye and game.
>
> Whan to the thoughtful wyght ys tolde a tale,
> He herit yt as though he thennes were.
> Hys heuy thoughtys hym so plukke and hale
> Hydyr and thyder and hym greue and dere
> That hys eres avayle hym nat a pere.
> He understondeth nothyng what men seye,
> So ben hys wytts fer gone hem to pleye.
>
> The smert of thought I by experience
> Knowe as wel as any man doth lyuynge.
> Hys frosty swoot and fyry hote feruence
> And troubly dremes, drempt al in wakynge,
> My mazyd hed slepless han of konnyng
> And wyt despoylyd, and so me be-iapyd
> That after deth ful often haue I gapyd.

(85–112)

Infection increases from the state of being inly pensive, as opposed to thinking outwardly, in a mode that directs attention away from the interior. Thought, a biting adversary, like a vampire, induces melancholia, called 'heaviness', which as a substantive becomes an allegorical force. Heaviness can be defined (92) and, conjoined with thought in the phrase 'heavy thoughts', has power to pull him about, so that he cannot be spoken to, for his wits have gone forth to play,—which when it returns as a phrase in the *Complaint* (50, 51, to be discussed below), indicates madness. The last verse speaks of the smert of thought, its frosty sweat and fiery hot zeal, where the power of allegorization and the desire for it constructs thought in oppositional binary modes, and refers to troubling dreams, dreamed in a waking state, making sleep impossible.

In the *Complaint*, thought again assails him. The Prologue describes Autumn, where the seasonal change leads him into a depressive state where he returns to the topic of *The Regement of Princes*:

> Sighynge sore as I in my bed lay
> For this and othir thoght which many a day

Before I took sleep cam noon in myn ye,
So vexid me the thoghtful maladie.

(18–21)

In the last reference to thought in the *Complaint*, it is the 'thoughtful disease' (388). Thought as 'anxiety' stains its other meanings, so that in the *Complaint* it cannot be taken other than as a malady, a cause of self-division—as in

As that I ones fro Westmynstre cam
Vexid ful greuously with thoghtful herte
Thus thoghte I 'A greet fool I am . . .'

(183–5)

—where thought possesses him, so that the thoughtful heart produces in the 'I' the activity of thinking, and where to think is to consider oneself a fool (afflicted with madness); followed by:

And thanne thoghte I on that othir syde . . .

(190)

—so that thought induces splitting and the divided self. Personifying thought and its possession of him as melancholia go together. The man of the Prologue recalls his past, how he has been sourged with sickness, how 'the sonne abated and the dirk shour | Hildid doun right on me' (25–6), like the 'black sun' of melancholy Kristeva refers to, whose origins are Dürer's engraving *Melancolia I* as interpreted by Gerard de Nerval.[12] In both Dürer and Hoccleve, melancholia and thinking are interlinked. And in Hoccleve thought is linked to memory, for now it is not his 'wits' which went out to play, as on holiday, in carnival excess, but everything of consciousness, including memory:

But althogh the substance of my memorie
Wente to pleye as for a certein space,
Yit the lord of vertu the kyng of glorie,
Of his hye might and benigne grace
Made it for to retourne into the place

---

[12] Julia Kristeva, *Black Sun*, trans. Leon S. Roudiez (New York, 1989), 139–52. Kristeva quotes from de Nerval's 'El Desdichado', 'le soleil noir de la Mélancolie' which refers to Dürer's engraving of *Melancolia I*: on this, see Raymond Klibansky, Erwin Panofsky, and Fritz Saxl, *Saturn and Melancholy* (London, 1964).

> Whens it cam which was at Alle Halwemesse,
> Was fiue yeer neither moore ne lesse.
>
> (50–6)

This 'nomadic' subject, whose memory seems to have gone out of his body, as with a loss of body boundaries, may be compared with the subject in Deleuze and Guattari in *Anti-Oedipus: Capitalism and Schizophrenia*, as decentred and schizoid. However much Hoccleve despairs over his madness, the potentiality for a form of freedom in going forth to play also seems present. But Hoccleve's poetry shows no encouragement of going forth to play. The conservative remonstrating voice against Oldcastle accuses Lollards of asking such carnivalesque questions of the teaching of 'holy chirche' as:

> Why stant this word heere? and why this word there?
> Why spak God thus, and seith thus elleswhere?
>
> (*Remonstrance*, 156–7)

The context is the influence on Oldcastle of women, 'lewed calates' (147), where the feminine is—as in Deleuze and Guattari—the agent of 'deterritorialization', wherein desire wanders off from fixed categories of perception and meaning. But as God's wits are not to be accused of having gone forth to play, the sacred text must not be thought of as having any play within it.[13] Nomadicism looks for 'lines of flight' which will bring about its deterritorialization and so its freedom from the oppressive and paranoid dominant order, but in the *Remonstrance* and the *Complaint* it returns towards the imaginary centre, to speak its discourse more obediently.[14]

II. Autobiography

Hoccleve for Seymour is 'of course, a minor poet, whose closeness to Chaucer vividly illuminates the narrowness of his achievement' (Seymour, xxxiii), though he could not have anticipated the attention

---

[13] 'Play' is used here in Derrida's sense in 'Structure, Sign and Play in the Human Sciences', in *Writing and Difference*, trans. Alan Bass (London, 1978), 278–93. Hoccleve's poetry would belong to the dream of 'full presence, the reassuring foundation, the origin and the end of play' (292).

[14] For the nomadic subject, see Gilles Deleuze and Félix Guattari, *A Thousand Plateaux*, trans. Brian Masumi (Minneapolis, 1987), 311–423 *passim*, but esp. pp. 380–4.

that has in the past twenty years undone that 'of course' by bringing out the extent of Hoccleve's interest. But to stay with Seymour: minor literature can also speak differently. One characteristic of a 'minor' literature for Deleuze and Guattari—an example is Kafka—is to exist as a deterritorializing space within a major literature, 'appropriate for strange and minor uses'. If Hoccleve may be read as minor in that other way, constituted by his madness as 'a stranger within his own language',[15] it would be because his melancholia made him transgressive within the discourse of the Lancastrian hegemony, where Chaucer was held as poetic father.[16] But the move towards reterritorialization, re-incorporation within the dominant order is present in Hoccleve. A desire towards an assertion of normality could account for the attitude taken up by the sane Hoccleve towards Lollardy. The discourse that judges the heretic also constructs the self as not heretical, not different. If Richard Green is to be followed, Hoccleve had so internalized a dislike of the Lollards that he went further than Henry V in his condemnation of them, and thought of Henry as too likely to fall into compromise with their error.[17]

This minor poet produces autobiographical poetry, and the problematics of autobiography are connected with his subject matter: the madness endured five years previously, making him 'the first . . . to write at length and *in propria persona* of a madness that could be real'.[18] The earlier poem,

---

[15] Gilles Deleuze and Felix Guattari, *Kafka: Towards a Minor Literature*, trans. Dana Polan (Minneapolis, 1986), 17, 26.

[16] For the relationship between Chaucer and his fifteenth-century 'official' status, the Lancastrian hegemony, and the promotion of English as a way of promoting that, see John H. Fisher, 'A Language Policy for Lancastrian England', *Publications of the Modern Language Association of America*, 107 (1992), 1168–80. On the propagandist role of poets such as Hoccleve and Lydgate within the fifteenth-century formation, and under the dominance of Chaucer, see Richard Firth Green, *Poets and Princepleasers: Literature and the English Court in the Late Middle Ages* (Toronto, 1980); and Paul Strohm, in *England's Empty Throne: Usurpation and the Language of Legitimation* (New Haven, 1998) and his chapter, 'Hoccleve, Lydgate and the Lancastrian Court' in David Wallace (ed.), *The Cambridge History of Medieval English Literature* (Cambridge, 1999), 640–61. See Seth Lerer, *Chaucer and his Readers: Imagining the Author in Late Medieval England* (Princeton, 1993), 87–8, on Chaucer as 'father'. But this does not discuss Hoccleve. See also Larry Scanlon, *Narrative, Authority and Power: The Medieval Exemplum and the Chaucerian Tradition* (Cambridge, 1994), 299–322, for Hoccleve's relation to the Lancastrian dynasty, and for his part in the canonization of Chaucer's authority.

[17] Green, *Poets and Princepleasers*, 183–6.

[18] Penelope Doob, *Nebuchadnezzar's Children: Conventions of Madness in Medieval English Literature* (New Haven, 1974), 228. On this view see Seymour, 133. For an overview of medieval madness, see Muriel Laharie, *La Folie au moyen age, xi–xiii siècles* (Paris, 1991), and more generally Liza Veith, *Hysteria: The History of a Disease* (Chicago, 1965), whose ch. 4 is on 'Hysteria in the Middle Ages' (possibly relevant for the *Complaint*, 34–5), and citing Augustine, 'there are no diseases that do not arise from witchery and hence from the mind' (55); Stanley Jackson,

La Male Regle de T. Hoccleve (1405) had invoked 'Helthe', speaking as being out of health both on account of his misrule (*La Male Regle* 56, 90, 290), and for his failure to adhere to 'reuled resoun' (70) or a 'mene reule' (352). Excess is both saturnalian carnival *and* melancholia, the anxieties of 'thought' *and* 'folie' (40). Since 'folie' also means madness, it is evidently impossible to put boundaries round the state of *madness* discussed in the *Complaint*, since:

> Excess of mete and drynke is glotonye;
> Glotonye awakith malencolie;
> Malencolie awakth werre and stryf
> Stryf causith mortel hurt thurgh hir folie . . .

> (*La Male Regle*, 300–3)

Penelope Doob reads this as what Deleuze and Guattari would call reterritorialization, the subject no longer nomad, but returning to known and conventional ground; so she takes the madness of the *Complaint* as perhaps only a 'metaphor for the crippling state of sin which is the real subject of the poem'. In contrast John Burrow has concentrated on Hoccleve's newness in English as an autobiographical writer, while James Simpson finds innovation in his writing, in contrast to the conservatism within his politics, so that the *Complaint* followed by the *Dialogue* is a 'critique of the premises of consolation literature . . . it is deploying literary traditions to undercut the model of personality implicit in the consolatory tradition, and to create new models of personality, unauthorized by literary tradition.'[19] Simpson thinks of the subject being differently created through different forms of writing. His Hoccleve is aware of 'the prison-house of language'—associated with forms of writing he must escape, and in this Simpson sees a tendential modernism, so if modernism is to be taken as a structural position, a recurrent set or approach towards writing and the text (for example, associated with the foregrounding of the split between the signifier and the signified), then this modernism

---

Melancholia and Depression: From Hippocratic Times to Modern Times (New Haven, 1988). On Hoccleve's earlier autobiographical writing, see Ethan Knapp, 'Bureaucratic Identity and the Construction of the Self in Hoccleve's *Formulary* and *La male reglé*', *Speculum*, 74 (1999), 357–76.

[19] James Simpson, 'Madness and Texts: Hoccleve's *Series*', in Julia Boffey and Janet Cowen (eds.), *Chaucer and Fifteenth-Century Poetry* (London, 1991), 26; see also James Simpson, 'Nobody's Man: Thomas Hoccleve's *Regement of Princes*', in Julia Boffey and Pamela King (eds.), *London and Europe in the Later Middle Ages* (London, 1995), 149–80; John Burrow, 'Autobiographical Poetry in the Middle Ages: The Case of Thomas Hoccleve', *Proceedings of the British Academy*, 68 (1988), 115–27.

may perhaps be articulated with the modernism of schizophrenia which Louis Sass has argued for.

Nonetheless, Simpson believes it is Hoccleve the subject who changes those forms of writing. But there is a particular problem highlighted in poetry which is both assumed to be autobiographical *and* taken to be the record of madness. It is exacerbated if it is to be assumed that there is a normative subject about whom the term 'mad' can be used, or who initiates poetic changes or who works with a chronology that assumes the self-validating, continuously self-present subject. Simpson, discussing Hoccleve as someone who makes the rules for himself, puts the subject of autobiography outside the text. But autobiography, a nineteenth-century term, sets up the subject in a particular way and under certain constraints; it produces, in a pattern of blindness and insight, a certain form of subject, who is knowable in one way, and need not be known in another. As a compulsion, this splits the self, since it creates another self that must be known objectively and textually, and which may also be thought of as dead, as finished. While it may *seem* to be the expression of a full sensibility which is summed up in the proper name, which indeed Hoccleve uses of himself, in the subsequent words of the Friend (*Dialogue*, 3), it compels a splitting off, which associates autobiography with two forms of splitting: madness and allegory. Schizophrenia implies the splitting of psychic functions in the individual, who in that state no longer operates as an integrated whole. What happens when the tools to describe a split state both replicate such splitting: autobiography and allegory?

Memory, in Hoccleve's case, has gone forth to play and by doing so it throws everything of the autobiographical possibility into jeopardy. What is an autobiography if it admits that its memory has disappeared? What good is it even if the subject says that its memory has come back? Can it remember not having a memory? To turn to an early autobiographical poet writing in English is to expect to find something of the history of the subject. Much of the recent turn to theory within medieval studies has been premised on the point that the 'early modernists' have neglected the bourgeois subject and its interiority within the fourteenth and fifteenth centuries. 'To write the history of the medieval subject is to write the history of medieval culture,' as Lee Patterson has written.[20] It is

[20] See David Aers, *Culture and History, 1350–1600: Essays on English Communities, Identities and Writing* (London, 1992), 182, quoting Lee Patterson, 'On the Margin: Postmodernism, Ironic History and Medieval Studies', *Speculum*, 65 (1990), 87–108. (The volume was entitled

baffling to turn to a text of autobiography, then, and find in the place of evidence for the existence of the subject marked by interiority, a text marked by its absence, madness. Michel Foucault, so much of an inspiration to New Historicism, and to the project to think in terms of the 'early modern', begins the *Histoire de la folie* with the sixteenth century, and with the possibility that madness could exist in a state governed by reason, that madness and reason could be in dialogue with each other, but here, a century earlier, madness seems to be a ground of exclusion, even from the subject's own speech. This exclusion means that Hoccleve's text disallows writing a history of the subject with the thought that here, the autobiographical desire is also a form of madness, since it cannot access the past, while to read it may also require the reader to listen to madness, in the sense that Shoshana Felman in *Writing and Madness: Literature, Philosophy, Psychoanalysis* means when she defines madness in the literary text as an 'irreducible resistance to interpretation'.[21] The early text which might prove paradigmatic for understanding autobiography is indeed paradigmatic in one of two ways: either the subject says it cannot remember in a form of textual repression, which has willed its own forgetting, or, relatedly, in that its possibility of describing the self is inscribed by the impossibility of knowing whether it remembers or not. Its melancholy is that it cannot remember, and that it cannot remember the extent of its melancholy.

But the subject may be connected with another history. Paul Strohm finds in Hoccleve's poetry for the Lancastrian court 'less wholesome and inauthentic alternative[s]'—he lists 'heresy, effeminate fashion, female practices of reading and introspection, or false speech' regarded by him as 'subversive of Lancastrian practice [which was] stabilized around ideas of the orthodox, the identity of inner and outer'. He adds that 'held at bay is the embarrassing fact of the Lancastrians as a usurping dynasty, and the

---

'The New Philology'.) See also Patterson's attack on adherents to New Historicism (including Francis Barker, Catherine Belsey, Jonathan Dollimore, and Stephen Greenblatt) for an implicit denial of an earlier history of the subject in *Negotiating the Past: The Historical Understanding of Medieval Literature* (Madison, 1987), ch. 2. For an overview of the interrelationships between critical theory and medieval literature, see Sarah Kay, 'Analytical Survey 3: The New Philology', in David Lawton, Wendy Scase, and Rita Copeland (eds.), *New Medieval Literatures*, 3 (Oxford, 1999), 295–326, and in *New Medieval Literatures*, 2 (1998) see Louise O. Fradenburg, 'Psychoanalytic Medievalism', 249–76. See also my 'Dante and the Modern Subject: Overcoming Anger in the *Purgatorio*', *New Literary History*, 28 (1997), 401–20, for discussion of writing the history of the subject.

[21] Shoshana Felman, *Writing and Madness: Literature, Philosophy, Psychoanalysis*, trans. Martha Noel Evans and the author with the assistance of Brian Massumi (Ithaca, NY, 1985), 254.

extent to which issues of misrepresentation and false display reach a crisis-point during their regime. This is the unacknowledged issue around which Hoccleve's public poems revolve, never explicitly admitting the flawed nature of the Lancastrian title.'[22] It means that orthodoxy is the concealment of violence, and that at the centre of everything is a still 'empty' throne, disavowed as such; it leads to the thought that Hoccleve's madness, itself discursively constructed, articulates with a loss of memory, a loss of narrating ability, which is encouraged at the very centre of signification. The madness of Hoccleve, never described, about which hangs a silence, becomes another emptiness to add to the central emptiness of the throne itself.

That absence of memory tilts Hoccleve towards the modern state. The terms to explore this breakdown, impinging both on memory and melancholia, come from Walter Benjamin, whose study of Baroque drama, *Ursprung des deutschen Trauerspiels* (1928), a crucial text of Modernist theory, prompts rethinking about allegory, since he dwells on this not as the art of finding clear equivalents to ideas of the A equals B type, but takes it as writing which knows that there is no more than the ruin and the fragmentary. Allegorical naming, following Benjamin, implies the realization that no statement can be made in terms of another, which would in any case imply the possibility of making a total, ideally complete statement. In allegory, 'every person, every thing, every relation can signify any other'.[23] But this sense of impossibility which comes from the sense of the breakdown of thought, allegory devaluing the appearance of things on the surface, comes from melancholy, where the subject looks below surfaces (e.g. the idea of nature as consolatory) and the appearance of resolution, to awareness of history as the record of the 'untimely' and 'sorrowful'.[24] And that is where the minor poet is found. Such characterization of thought as a melancholic structure is already moving towards its breakdown, into a state which is associated with madness, Foucault's 'absence of work'.[25]

Memory, in this paradigm of the modern subject, cannot be of a

[22] Strohm, *England's Empty Throne*, 185.

[23] Walter Benjamin, *The Origin of German Tragic Drama*, trans. John Osborne (London, 1977), 175. See my 'Dante and Benjamin: Melancholy and Allegory', *Exemplaria*, 4 (1992), 341–63.

[24] Benjamin, *The Origin of German Tragic Drama*, 166.

[25] Foucault's definition of madness as the 'absence of work' comes from the Preface to his *Folie et déraison: histoire de la folie a l'âge classique* (Paris, 1961) p. v; the passage does not appear in the English version, *Madness and Civilization*, trans. Richard Howard (New York, 1973).

consistent, self-validating nature, but is overwhelming, threatening the subject with trauma. Perhaps that appears on the violence of the initial outburst of the *Complaint*, 'And for to preeue I cam of a womman I I brast out on the morwe and thus began' (34–5). That might mean 'to prove I was human' but the gender reference makes the outburst feminine, aligning the subject with the feminine—though noticeably, the Friend will later say that he has offended women (*Dialogue*, 667–700), which would imply a normative anti-feminism, but would also imply another registering of a splitting, as though this implied masculinism was another form of his alienation and a reason for his exclusion. The passage could also mean that his outburst proved, analeptically, that there was a woman in him, or that he felt it identified him with the mother: that was how he read his own outburst, in yet another splitting. The resultant outburst proved the sickness to be that of the presence of the feminine. At such a moment, on this reading, the subject speaks his own self-hatred. Memory of madness, of trauma, is read as memory of an excess which has momentarily split gender difference.

The melancholic subject could not write autobiography: no self-consistent history of subjectivity could emerge from it. Writing, deferral, allegory, and madness all connect. Walter Benjamin contends that 'allegories are in the realm of thoughts what ruins are in the realm of things'.[26] Allegory is the end of thought as something self-consistent and complete and knowing itself; it undoes the power of Thought as a dominating agency, in its tendency towards fragmentation, associated with, and partly concealed by, the act of naming. When Hoccleve makes the Friend give him his proper name, this demonstrates not the end of personification allegory and the beginning of a new, more immediate attention to the subject, but rather an allegorical mode continued in another form of naming, where both forms—whether referring to Thought, or Reason, or a Friend, or Thomas, or Hoccleve, or the name of the text as the *Complaint* (by calling it that, its other qualities are occluded)—are attempts to delineate and to fix. A double movement works within the text: the desire to affirm a substantial unity, which includes an assertion of normality, which the community would accept, and which would make them accept him, and a contrary movement towards the splitting of the subject, which makes the act of writing a form of madness, what Blanchot, in keeping with Foucault on madness, calls *désœuvrement*—

[26] Benjamin, *The Origin of German Tragic Drama*, 178.

worklessness.[27] It is a state ironically split off from the conditions of clerkly work in which Hoccleve—like Kafka, a yet stronger example of *désœuvrement*—laboured for so long. Writing is allegorical, which means it fragments in two different ways. Thought, which in post-Cartesian terms splits the subject into a duality, does so in the medieval text by forcing aspects of the subject into isolation and treating them as wholes. This splitting is part of a constraint on the self to speak itself, as though the one thing the self cannot do is to describe itself, to bring itself out into the open—it being, from the standpoint of normality, an act of folly to describe a state of madness. But it fragments too in that it prevents clear utterance, prevents the self from speaking itself.

Shoshana Felman discusses 'mad writing', whose resistance to interpretation is the text's resistance to reading. Perhaps the *Complaint* illustrates that. She also discusses that form of writing which Foucault in *Histoire de la folie* could not get beyond, according to Derrida's critique: writing about madness.[28] About this she says two things: that to write about madness—as Hoccleve seems to do, whether or not he can say anything about it—is to deny it. 'However one represents madness to oneself or others, to represent madness is always, consciously or unconsciously, to play out the scene of the denial of one's own madness.' That applies, whether the person is sane and writing about the mad, or, like Hoccleve, attempting to put madness into the past. It works by assuming that madness and reason can be seen as binary opposites—a tendency which exists in allegorical thought. Yet Felman adds that 'there still exists in these texts a madness that speaks, a madness that is acted out in language, but whose speaking role no subject can assume. It is this movement of non-totalizable, ungovernable linguistic play, through which meaning misfires and the text's statement is estranged from its performance, that I call . . .

[27] Maurice Blanchot, 'The Essential Solitude', in *The Space of Literature*, trans. Ann Smock (Lincoln, Neb., 1982), 23; see also translator's introduction p. 13. This sense of disappearance within the text needs to be placed against Simpson's contrasted, other emphasis in 'Madness and Texts' on the Series as 'a work peculiarly concerned with the story of its own composition' (p. 18). Robert J. Meyer-Lee, 'Hoccleve and the Apprehension of Money', *Exemplaria*, 13 (2001), 173–214, which, exploring the pathology of his thought, takes Hoccleve's 'anxiety' to be related to the instability of money as a representational system (p. 210). If that sense could be generalized from, it could be said that *désoeuvrement* is writing in the absence of a sense of writing's representational power.

[28] For Derrida's critique of Foucault, as objectifying madness, see 'Cogito and the History of Madness', in Jacques Derrida, *Writing and Difference*, trans. Alan Bass (London, 1978), 31–63, and Foucault's response to Derrida, 'My Body, this Paper, this Fire', *Oxford Literary Review*, 4 (1979), 9–28. On the debate see John Frow, *Marxism and Literary Theory* (Oxford, 1986), 207–35, and Felman, *Writing and Madness*, 33–55.

the madness of rhetoric.'[29] Perhaps such a moment of linguistic play appears in the excess which Hoccleve himself notes when he bursts forth; perhaps such a play may also be noted in describing his memory—or his wits, which are certainly feminine—going out to play.[30] Autobiographical yet attended by memory loss, Hoccleve's writing defeats a chronology which would provide an aetiology of the madness and make it complete.

III. Madness

Even if something within the text defeats the oppression within the madness, yet Hoccleve's madness and the recourse to allegory still bear the marks of a damaged subject. The *Complaint* opens with a Prologue whose autumnal meditation on decay follows on from the opening of the General Prologue to *The Canterbury Tales*, as though writing had to preserve its normalizing quality by staying inside the terms set down by the poet whose status, the more it was elevated in Lancastrian circles, would keep Hoccleve as a 'minor' poet. Burrow comments that Hoccleve 'lacked his master Chaucer's ability to speak in voices other than his own'[31] but he is compelled by his minor status and by his madness to speak at all times in a voice which is 'other' to him—in a Chaucerian voice, including dialogue, the use of the Chaucerian persona, and the notion of linking narratives—which is another way of saying that in one sense he is always compelled to speak allegorically. But at the same time, something within his work makes him speak differently.[32] At the end of this November, he speaks of his melancholia, but this state, with its uncertainty, disconfirms the narrative that puts the madness away from him by five years, and means rather that nothing has changed.

He is in a state of 'languor' (implying *acedia*). Recollection of his grief leads him into the *Complaint*, which opens with the confession—and that means that the text has on it the marks of being forced to acknowl-

---

[29] Felman, *Writing and Madness*, 252. I have dropped the author's use of italics, and her use of quotation marks.

[30] Compare: 'Whan reuled wit and manly hardiness | Ben knitte to-gidre, as yok of mariage | Ther floweth of victorie the sweetnesse'; *The Regement of Princes*, 3991–3.

[31] Burrow (n. 15), 402.

[32] A. C. Spearing writes, with reference to Langland, Margery Kempe, and Hoccleve, that 'those who were driven to find ways of writing their individual life-histories tended to the eccentric, even the unbalanced, who felt their inner selves to be different from those of their neighbours'. He also finds in Hoccleve a 'persistent use of small-scale personification' which he calls non-Chaucerian. See *Medieval to Renaissance in English Poetry* (Cambridge, 1985), 113, 119.

edge a position in relation to normality—of 'the wylde infirmitee | Which
that I hadde as many a man wel kneew | And which me out of myself caste
and threew' (40–2). The *Complaint* acknowledges what he has been, but
it emphasizes that he has recovered his normality. The 'me' of line 42
seems to be identified with the 'substaunce of my memorie'; as he speaks
of 'my wit' having come home again (64). It is self-deprecatory; as though
continuing with the mock self-deprecations which are common to
Chaucer in his personae, so that it complicates the sense that Hoccleve
can be speaking in his 'own' voice, rather than that of another, more
powerful predecessor, whose very power, as now made an aspect of
Lancastrian ideology, may even be a source of madness. This description
of having gone out and come back is repeated later in the image of a drunk
person about whom after his drunkeness 'he . . . cometh to hymsilfe
agein' (229–30). Hoccleve asserts that his wits have come back again, and
so has the 'substance of his memorie', so that he can say the 'soothe' (the
truth):

> The soothe is this swich conceit as I hadde
> And vndirstondyng, al were it but smal,
> Before that my wittis weren vnsadde,
> Thankid be oure lord Ihesu Crist of al,
> Such haue I nowe but blowe is ny oueral
> The reuers wherethurgh moche is my mournynge,
> Which causith me thus sighe in compleynynge.
>
> (253–9)

The first five lines, to the caesura ('nowe'), assert his normality, that his
wits are no longer 'unsadde'—light, or unsteady, or unsettled; but the last
two and a half lines reveal an anxiety that his normality will not be validated by the community. Instead, his madness is 'blown' as if by Fame
or Rumour's trumpet, in a passage recalling Chaucer's *The House of
Fame*.[33] The result is a mourning to add to his melancholia and his 'com-
pleynynge'—both title and substance of his text. A complaint is produced
by an anxious melancholia; it declares that he does not have what he says
he has: i.e. his normality. Autobiography then, is not the statement of a
position but the desire for a position; that is the constraint upon it, that
it is not written from where one would wish to be. It produces a subject

---

[33] The connection between the two texts is made by David Mills, 'The Voices of Thomas
Hoccleve', in Catherine Batt (ed.), *Essays on Thomas Hoccleve* (London, 1996), 107. He quotes
Dialogue, 477–9, as like the timbre of much of *The House of Fame* (e.g. line 1878).

outside the circle—of his wits, and of his friends, and of those who would give him social validation.

The drive towards asserting present normality is both repressive and an impossibility. Using the phrase that a drunk comes to himself again

> Righte so thogh that my wit were a pilgrym
> And wente fer from hoom he cam agayn
>
> (232–3),

he makes himself like the prodigal son of the Bible who came to himself (Luke 15: 17) and returned to his father. This might align Hoccleve's text with the progress of Augustinian confession. But the figure of returning in a circle is what the philosopher Levinas criticizes in Christianity as opposed to Judaism, in which he argues that the prototypical figure is Abraham, who went out he knew not whither. The desire for return forms the basis of what Derrida would see as a logocentrism which is anxious to protect the word—and Derrida opposes to what he sees as its presence in Lacan the concept of 'dissemination', where there can be no return.[34] The pilgrim, 'peregrinos' in Latin, is a stranger, an exile, an alien, and in Hoccleve's seeing his wits as pilgrim there is an obvious allegorization, which again goes further than the accidental, for if allegory is a figure of speaking other, of alien speech, it also associates itself with the figure of the pilgrim. Yet the pilgrim hopes to return home. Hoccleve anxiously fixes the identity of the place where 'the substance of his memorie' came back to, and above all the time—five years ago exactly, 1 November, All Hallows' Day. Returning home denies any value in the experience of madness, in which sense it is potentially repressive; so that the text indeed plays out the scene of denial of the subject's madness by repressing it from memory.

The text, though it tries to close the wound, or *béance* opened by madness, cannot do so, and into that gap, which is the place of trauma, an excess of signification appears to try and show that the subject can indeed think autobiographically, in terms of past and present. The formal elements of allegory—personification—repeat an allegory already in the text, and the text is constructed by a madness, that is, a split state, inseparable from the madness it describes. Hoccleve has described a condition of ecstasy, of his 'me' being outside the 'self'. The allegorical thinking which imported Thought as an outsider, in the *Regement*, has thrown the

---

[34] See on Levinas's article 'The Trace of the Other', Jill Robbins, *Prodigal Son, Elder Brother: Interpretation and Alterity in Augustine, Petrarch, Kafka, Levinas* (Chicago, 1991), 106–10.

'me' of the 'myself' out, but now claims that these two things, aspects of an allegorical language, have come together again. Like saying that his memory has returned, it is impossible—and it will be noted too that, for whatever reason, he says nothing about the state that he was in when he was mad, as though that memory was gone for good. The anxiety in the text is that the friends who made him an object of their scrutiny cannot confirm that he was as he was. But no more can he.

The *Complaint* describes sitting alone in his chamber at home, and nervily jumping up to look at himself:

> I streighte vnto my mirour and my glas
> To looke how that me of my cheere thoghte,
> If any othir were it than it oghte;
> For fayn wolde I if it had nat been right,
> Amendid it to my konnynge and might.
>
> Many a saut made I to this mirour
> Thynkynge 'if that I looke in this maneere
> Among folk as I now do noon errour
> Of suspect look may in my face appeere.
> This contenance I am seur and this cheere
> If I foorth use is no thyng repreeuable
> To hem that han conceits resonable.'
> And therewithal I thoughte thus anoon:
> 'Men in her owne case bene blinde al day . . .'
>
> (157–70)

The dominance of the intrusive thought now becomes something to judge another allegorical quality: his 'cheere'—which Burrow annotates as 'face' or 'expression'. Hoccleve's face is the index to how far he may be thought to be out of a state of melancholia. Further, since he thinks of himself as containing more than his thought, he records what his thought, in a soliloquy (163–8), which is, implicitly, a further fragmentation. This soliloquy is followed by another, which begins at line 169, where his thought has itself split, thought against thought, in a process continued by his thought that the subject is blind, unknowing, about himself. But these forms of splitting are minor in comparison to the major form: of measuring his being by what he sees in the mirror. The skill he wants is to be like the 'they' of Shakespeare's Sonnet 94, who are 'the lords and owners of their faces'. But since the mirror may not be able to tell him what he wants to know about his face, since 'men in hire owne case been blynde alday', the mirror which tells will be the people whose

look will confirm or disconfirm his state. Identity is fashioned not in a
void but under paranoid constraints, not to be 'other' than expected.

In Lacan's essay on the mirror-stage, invoked here for comparison, the
mirror gives an image which confirms a narcissistic sense for the subject
whereby it may feel complete and secure. Narcissism is dependent on seeing the self as not split, as not the *corps morcelé*, the body in pieces, which
is the other fantasy against which the mirror-stage works.[35] The image
must come from the other, from the outside world which acts as a mirror
to the subject telling him what he is. It is evident that no such narcissistic
identification can be made by the subject, and the writing follows the
problem this evokes. A textual aporia about the timing of this repeated
episode of going to the mirror repeats the aporia about the timing of the
Prologue; how, chronologically, does the episode relate to his madness,
and has he recovered or not? The ambiguity is repeated by another: silence
about what he sees in the mirror. It may tell the subject what he is like
inside—where, as Strohm suggested, inner and outer representations
were supposed to correspond. He refers to the 'wylde infirmitee' (40) and
the 'wyldenesse' (107) caused by a grievous venom 'that had infectid and
wyldid my brayn' (235); as he is compared to a 'wylde steer' in a series of
animal or monstrous images evoking him as a wilde man in his 'seeknesse
sauage' (86). He fears that he may have become monstrous: but actually
the monstrosity that he fears is worse than that: it is the state of not being
able to fit his face (index to his cheer, his non-madness) into the social
order, the social body.[36] The face is to be read allegorically, for an allegorical madness. To be different risks having the face read unfavourably.[37]

[35] Jacques Lacan, 'The Mirror Stage as Formative of the Function of the I as Revealed in
Psychoanlytical Experience', in *Écrits: A Selection*, trans. Alan Sheridan (London, 1977), 4.

[36] Compare for its suggestiveness Diderot's definition of a monster, 'a being whose survival
is incompatible with the social order', *Éléments de physiologie*, quoted Michael André Bernstein,
Bitter Carnival: Ressentiment and the Abject Hero (Princeton, 1992), 24. See also Richard
Bernheimer, *Wild Men in the Middle Ages* (Cambridge, Mass., 1952) for contexts for the *sauvage*
or wild man, and Timothy Husband, *The Wild Man: Medieval Myth and Symbolism* (New York,
1980).

[37] To make a modern comparison, illustrating the power of national paranoia, Russell
Berman refers to the fascist Ernest Jünger, who shows his dislike of others by showing he does not
like their faces, because he does not like faces, i.e. the face as the index of an individual personality: Jünger wrote of Weimar artists; 'in Germany one meets this art world . . . in close connection with all those forces on whom a hidden or overt treasonous character is written right across
their faces'—quoted, Russell Berman, *Modern Culture and Critical Theory: Art, Policy and the
Legacy of the Frankfurt School* (Madison, 1989), 100. Meditation on the face should include reference to Levinas on the face of the other as the original site of the sensible: see Sean Hand (ed.),
The Levinas Reader (Oxford, 1989), 82 ff.

In contrast, Arcite's melancholy in the *Knight's Tale* changes him so completely that he resolves to return to Athens:

> And with that word he caughte a greet mirour,
> And saugh that chaunged was al his colour
> And saugh his visage al in another kynde.
> And right anon it ran him in his mynde,
> That sith his face was so disfigured
> Of maladye the whiche he hadde endured,
> He myght wel, if that he bar him lowe,
> Lyve in Athenese everemoore unknowe.[38]

Hoccleve's desire is to live in Athens—the modern Athens, London—unknown, unremarked, uncommented on, like Arcite; but Chaucer's text is different from Hoccleve's in that Arcite's face has changed; it has lost its figure. Hoccleve's face may express nothing exceptional (164–5), beyond the distortions coming from a convex mirror, which make all reflection monstrous. The face conveys nothing of what he has been going through. The aporia is in the absence of description. If the face appears normal, that would imply a further monstrosity; the face *not* marked, the wildness within unrepresented, perhaps unrepresentable, just as the madness is also unrepresented in the text. Autobiography, which continues the narrative of not knowing what to think of his cheer, his face, is the production of the monstrous.

We would like to know what Hoccleve thought his face looked like. He had a regard for Chaucer's face and kept a copy of it, as he tells the Old Man in *The Regement of Princes*: 'the resemblaunce | Of hym hath in me so fresch lyflynesses | That, to put other men in remembraunce | Of hys persone, I haue heere hys lykeness | Don made' (4992–6).[39] The face, belonging to a man ten years dead, seems as important as the poetry: for, as Alberti puts it, 'through painting, the faces of the dead go on living for a long time'.[40] The face gives the illusion of a speaking voice within Chaucer's poetry; it puts a face on it. Chaucer's poetry accords with Chaucer's face. And that suggests the aporia here in discussing Hoccleve's

---

[38] *Knight's Tale* A 1399–1406, *The Riverside Chaucer*, ed. Larry D. Benson (Oxford, 1987), 44.

[39] See Jeanne E. Krochalis, 'Hoccleve's Chaucer Portrait', *Chaucer Review*, 21 (1986), 234–45, discussing late fourteenth-century realism in portraiture. Andrew Martindale, *Heroes, Ancestors, Relatives and the Birth of the Portrait* (The Hague, 1988), 8, says that 'the first recorded portrait in our modern sense—a painted or drawn life-like representation of a face—was produced by Simone Martini in 1336.' Martindale distinguishes between the work as *portraire* (representation) and *contrefais als vif*, a phrase dating from c. 1220: an imitation of living reality.

[40] Quoted, Andrew Martindale, *Simone Martini* (Oxford, 1988), 50.

text as autobiography. The restraints on behaviour that Hoccleve exercised, alluded to, for instance, in lines 176–82, imply that his whole existence since his sickness has been assuming a mask; and that this is continued in the autobiography of the *Complaint*; preparing a face. The face that should look out on him ideally would be that of a normal man, which would be an allegorical image. Desire to have an identity confirmed in the mirror would meet the insuperable obstacle of a face expected to look in one particular way. Can there be a face outside the mask?

It is as though the face in the fifteenth century is being pushed into further visibility—further than the *Knight's Tale* could go. This move is resisted by the text's silence. Discussing a politics of 'faciality', where the body is being brought into a 'molar', single, disciplined form, Deleuze and Guattari say that

the head, even the human head, is not necessarily a face. The face is produced only when the head ceases to be a part of the body, when it ceases to be coded by the body, when it ceases to have a multi-dimensional, polyvocal corporeal code—when the body, head included, has been decoded, and has to be *overcoded* by something we shall call the Face. This amounts to saying that the head, all the volume-cavity elements of the head, have to be facialized.[41]

The emergence of portraiture, by the end of the fourteenth century, may imply a new reading of the subject in terms of 'facializing', making the body more abstract and machine-like and producing the face as the index of individuality, and of the subject's place within sociality. But the face, particularized, must look like every other face. Hoccleve's fear and melancholy take two forms, both implicit: a face that is the same denies him as a subject while it also threatens him with the thought that his experience as mad or as sane and trying to demonstrate this, has gone outside the representable.

Madness as the 'absence of work' is the loss of the subject's sense of self-presence. Near the end of the *Complaint* occurs a *mise en abime*, when Hoccleve turns from himself to describe another complainant, a mirror of himself:

> This othir day a lamentacioun
> Of a woful man in a book I sy
> To whom wordes of consolacioun
> Resoun yaf spekynge effectuelly
>
> (309–12)

---

[41] Deleuze and Guattari, *Thousand Plateaux*, 170.

The *mise en abime* is a reminder of Derrida, for whom the abyss represents the impossibility of the text establishing the subject's presence to himself. In the *mise en abime* appears a 'repetition and the splitting of the self. Representation in the abyss of presence is not an accident of presence; the desire of presence is, on the contrary, born from the abyss (the indefinite multiplication) of representation, from the representation of representation, etc.'[42] The desire is to replicate the self, to give the subject full presence, by doubling its presence by this further example of the mournful man—who is, however, by being mournful, already a shadow, only a figure, as much as he is also only textual. It is as though Hoccleve has taken the Chaucerian persona of *The Parliament of Fowls* who knows not Love indeed, but reads about him in books,[43] and applied it non-ironically; as though denying his own experience and shifting it to that of the woeful man in books. It is another moment where Hoccleve links with what Benjamin says of the Baroque, as the modern: 'the Renaissance explores the universe; the Baroque explores libraries. Its meditations are devoted to books.'[44] The particular book, identified as Isidore of Seville's *Synonyma* or *Soliloquia*,[45] speaks of the 'heuy man woful and angwisshous' who 'compleyned' (316–17) of—as Seymour explains it—'the general willingness to accept rumour without proof and of the need to keep silent in the face of provocation' (Seymour, 135). Like Hoccleve, the woeful man speaks in allegorizations: 'Vexacioun of spirit and torment I Lakke I right noon I haue of hem plentee' (323–4); 'Sorwes so many in me multiplie' (332). Resoun, whose rule appears in *La Male Regle*, responds consolingly over six stanzas in dialogue with him, and gives a clue how the persona can escape his melancholia: 'Wrastle . . . ageyn heuynesses I Of the world troubles, suffrynge and duresses' (342–3). But his speech is distanced from the Hocclevian persona by being framed within a book, and ceasing abruptly:

> Lenger I thoghte red haue in this book
> But so it shoop that I ne mighte naght;
> He that it oghte ageyn it to him took,
> Me of his haaste vnwaar. Yit haue I caght

[42] Jacques Derrida, *Of Grammatology*, trans. Gayatri Chakravorty Spivak (Baltimore, 1977), 163.
[43] Chaucer, *The Parliament of Fowls*, 8–11.
[44] Benjamin, *The Origin of German Tragic Drama*, 140.
[45] See A. G. Rigg, 'Hoccleve's *Complaint* and Isidore of Seville', *Speculum*, 45 (1970), 564–74. For the extent of Hoccleve's reading of this, see John Burrow, 'Hoccleve's Complaint and Isidore of Seville Again', *Speculum*, 73 (1998), 424–8.

> Sum of the doctrine by Resoun taght
> To the man as aboue haue I said,
> Whereof I holde me ful wel apaid.
>
> For euere sythen set haue I the lesse
> By the peples ymaginacioun . . .
>
> (372–80)

The reading is broken, a fragment of a consolation, and Hoccleve speaks of this breaking off as though he were the victim of an unconscious violence, since he says, in what Burrow takes to be a fiction to cover the point that he has got to the end of the anthology in which these extracts were contained, that the book's owner took the book away in haste. It is an instance of where the text's unconscious may speak: the fiction covers a sense that he is a victim of violence—that meted out to the subject who in some way is different. Nonetheless, Hoccleve tries to use the words between Reason and the woeful man as a consolation, stitching it into his own discourse, as in the phrase 'as aboue haue I said', and he then attempts to give to his text closure by taking what Reason says and applying it: 'He [God] yaf me wit and he took it away | Whan that he sy that I it mis despente | And yaf ageyn . . .' (400–2).

But the comparison cannot hold, for while the oppressed man in the book can be spoken to by Reason, Reason has for Hoccleve another valency in comparison to madness, in relation to which it may not be the healthy opposite, but the enemy—that which judges the state of 'madness' as mad; which victimizes it with its own violence, which by using the language of 'monstrosity' even associates Hoccleve, ironically if implicitly, with the heretics, the Lollards. Thought was the oppressive force at the beginning; while now it seems that Reason has become accessible as another imposing force, discretely separate from the subject (there is no dialogue between reason and unreason here). But for Hoccleve to differentiate these two aspects of thinking, which have been so neatly discriminated between as allegorical figures, is not easy. Indeed, the allegory of Reason looks like a poetic closure, where one aspect of melancholic thought has been split off and declared to be sane and with power to impose itself on the subject. Hoccleve attempts to unite the experience of the man in the book with his own in the autobiographical relation he gives about his 'wit' (400–3), which makes for an implicit identification of melancholia with madness, or for an inability to separate the two. Further, as he attributes his madness to the judgement of God, it has entirely rational causes, questioning, indeed, whether the state can be called madness at all. This means that if Hoccleve did indeed suffer from a breakdown, his status as a 'minor' poet, with all that this implies in terms of the power of the Chaucerian/Lancastrian discourse that works in him, prevents him from reading his belief in a rationality that judges him as a form of oppression. He cannot read his own madness, nor see the potential for madness in the way he reads his situation after his recovery, in terms of its production of a further melancholia.

But what is that melancholia? It comes from the subject whose autobiography is also a confession, which works to strip the subject of any narcissism. Freud differentiates mourning from melancholia: 'in mourning it is the world which has become poor and empty; in melancholia it is the ego itself.'[46] This implies how much further melancholia goes than mourning in that it rests upon a failure of narcissism, so that Hoccleve's own crisis of narcissism, noticeable in his anxiety about his face, shows how thought has overthrown his subjectivity, not allowing the establishment of an ego, so that everything in and around the subject must be thought of as ruins—the very condition of melancholy in Benjamin, and the opposite of the stability invoked in poetry which would relate to the court. The subject in ruins cannot achieve the textual closure that is desired for and almost affirmed at the end of the *Complaint*. The text's chronology—its forwards and backwards rhythm, which cannot be assigned to a before and after—prevents the narrative from having such a force, and the text when finished is still called a Complaint in the first line of the *Dialogue*, in which text he declares to the Friend's horror his intention to publish it, so that it remains what it ever was: as much self-justificatory as it is confessional autobiography. And something of the penitential continues in the *Dialogue* (215–16). In a sense, Hoccleve does not leave off the substance of the *Complaint*; this may explain why, as Burrow notes (Burrow, 109), the *Dialogue* has exactly double the number of lines of the *Complaint*, as though he is continuing to argue and has split his identity between himself as the subject of the *Complaint* and a Friend.

Freud links melancholia to the word 'complaint': 'the woman who loudly pities her husband for being tied to such an incapable wife as herself is really accusing her husband', which leads him towards the aphorism that 'complaints are really "plaints" in the old sense of the word'. Freud is in part quoting from Nietzsche, who wrote 'all complaining is accusation'—'Alles Klagen ist Anklagen'.[47] The *Complaint* of Thomas Hoccleve, which incorporates into it the lamentation of another figure who must be instructed by Reason, may also be taken as an accusation, and hence as a record of suffering, which is the trace that madness leaves within the text. This means that it comes from somebody who finds what is around him to be the record of the untimely and sorrowful, and is determined to resist that; so the record of madness is not separable from the sense of his own oppression. The text's two opposing forces means it cannot be interpreted singly; and since the Friend wishes the *Complaint* to be cancelled altogether, there is clearly an element in Hoccleve that wished to exclude all thought of his suffering, but its very repression about a madness it can only speak of indirectly and will not enlarge on, also implies a narrative that belongs within a history which is not just that of the subject, but of the production of the subject. Hoccleve as the mad subject is a casualty of unacknowledged usurpation, replicating in his own absence of work an emptiness elsewhere.

University of Hong Kong

[47] Freud, 'Mourning and Melancholia', 257; Friedrich Nietzsche, *Human, All Too Human: A Book for Free Spirits*, trans. R. J. Hollingdale (Cambridge, 1996), 230.

'Catharism' and the Study of Medieval Heresy

Mark Gregory Pegg

'The most satisfactory answer', for stifling conversation with strangers, W. H. Auden dryly recommended, 'satisfactory because it withers curiosity, is to say *Medieval Historian*.'[1] A universal truth, perhaps, though not in south-western France. There, whether on the 17.22 from Toulouse to Carcassonne, or in a quiet Lauragais café, or at the breezy summit of Montségur in the Pyrenees, such an answer will (nine times out of ten) instantly involve you in lively discussions with Cathar sympathizers, English expatriates hunting for buried Albigensian treasure, or, and this is much more common than one might think, Californians motoring after heterodox enlightenment in the modern *départements* of the Aude (conveniently called the *pays du cathare* on road signs and tourist maps) and the Haute-Garonne. Histories, novels, plays, poems, red wine, television documentaries, troubadour CDs, travel guides, new-age manifestos, cream-filled pastries, academic conferences, www.younameitandthe-cathars.com, redemptive philosophies, gaythers (gay neo-Cathars), snowflake domes, cassoulets, and pamphlets on Occitan regionalism, all celebrate the Cathar *bons hommes* and *bonnes femmes*. The Cathars, promiscuous in their friendships, influencing everything and anything, have been tied to late-antique Manichaeans, Byzantine Bogomils, the Holy Grail, courtly love, the hidden secrets of the Knights-Templars, the magical lodges of late nineteenth-century mysticism, and even the veracity of reincarnation.[2] Occasionally, these fantasies are grafted onto the

This essay refines some ideas previously outlined in M. G. Pegg, *The Corruption of Angels: The Great Inquisition of 1245–1246* (Princeton, 2001), and id., 'On Cathars, Albigenses, and Good Men of Languedoc', *Journal of Medieval History*, 27 (2001), 181–95.

[1] W. H. Auden, 'The Poet and the City', in his *The Dyer's Hand and Other Essays* (New York, 1989), 74.

[2] See, out of a vast and extremely popular literature, especially D. Roché, *Études manichéennes et cathares* (Paris, 1952) and R. Nelli, *Histoire secrète du Languedoc* (Paris, 1978). Roché was the founder of a neo-Cathar group at the turn of this century and of the journal *Cahiers d'études*

anachronistic need to see the good men and good women as Protestants before their time.[3] The epic narrative of the Cathars reached its tragic

cathares. On Roché, see J.-L. Biget, 'Mythographie du Catharisme', *Cahiers de Fanjeaux: Historiographie du catharisme*, 14 (1979), 308–10. Roché also had a curious correspondence with Simone Weil; for example, the latter once wrote—and cited by J. Duvernoy, 'Albigeisme ou Catharisme', in his *Cathares, Vaudois et Beguines, dissidents du pays d'Oc* (Toulouse, 1994), 15— that Catharism was 'la dernière expression vivante de l'antiquité pré-romaine . . .' Weil had more to say about Catharism and Occitanism in her 'L'agonie d'une civilisation vue à travers une poème épique', and 'En quoi l'inspiration occitanienne', in *Écrits historiques et politiques* (Paris, 1960), 66–74 and 75–84. On Weil, see e.g. P. Winch, *Simone Weil: 'The Just Balance'* (Cambridge, 1989), 369, where he considers Weil's notion that Catharism was a descendant of late antique Neoplatonic Christianity to be historically correct; he even argues for Catharism to be the offspring of Gnosticism because (and this is his only evidence) 'of a similarity of ideas'. M. Barber, *The Cathars: Dualist Heretics in Languedoc in the High Middle Ages* (Harlow, 2000), 203–12, is good on Weil, Roché, and the odd Otto Rahn. A. Guirdham, *The Cathars and Reincarnation: The Record of a Past Life in 13th Century France* (London, 1970) documents a fascinating case of an English woman who was convinced that she had experienced a past life as a believer in the good men, a *crezen*, in the early thirteenth-century Lauragais. A southern French travelogue, heavily laced with Cathar fact and fancy, is R. Klawinski, *Chasing the Heretics: A Modern Journey through the Medieval Languedoc* (St Paul, Minn., 1999). S. O'Shea, *The Perfect Heresy: The Revolutionary Life and Death of the Medieval Cathars* (New York, 2000), is really about the Albigensian Crusade and, despite a surprisingly good bibliography, wrong on just about everything. On medieval Languedoc, heresy, and modern southern French politics, see A. Roach, 'Occitania Past and Present: Southern Consciousness in Medieval and Modern French Politics', *History Workshop Journal*, 43 (1997), 1–22. As for Catharism and the Holy Grail, see M. Roquebert, *Les Cathares et le Graal* (Toulouse, 1994). On the innumerable (and usually rather odd) theories about courtly love, *Amour courtois*, and the Cathars, see the excellent critical survey of R. Boase, *The Origin and Meaning of Courtly Love: A Critical Study of European Scholarship* (Manchester, 1977), 77–81. Two recent novels that do little to shake the classic narrative of Catharism are C. Craig, *The Good Men: A Novel of Heresy* (New York, 2002) and S. Burnham, *The Treasure of Montsegur: A Novel of the Cathars* (San Francisco, 2002). Today, the Centre d'Études Cathares at Carcassonne keeps, perhaps unintentionally, the neo-Cathar flame alive. The Centre d'Études Cathares also publishes the serious and learned journal *Heresis*. Now, see the collected papers in J. Berlioz and J.-C. Hélas (eds.), *Catharisme: l'édifice imaginaire: Actes du 7e Colloque du Centre d'Études Cathares/René Nelli, Carcassonne, 29 aoûet–2 septembre 1994, Heresis*, 7 (Villegly, 1998).

[3] Jean Duvernoy, for one, basically sees the Cathars as proto-Protestants in 'Cathares et vaudois sont-ils des précurseurs de la Réforme?' in his *Cathares, Vaudois et Beguines, dissidents du pays d'Oc*, 53–62. In the seventeenth and eighteenth centuries, not surprisingly, such views were quite common amongst Catholic and Protestant thinkers. On these early modern ideas about the Cathars, see A. Borst, 'Neue Funde und Forschungen zur Geschichte der Katharer', *Historische Zeitschrift*, 174 (1952), 17; H. Duranton, 'Les Albigeois dans les histoires générales et les manuels scolaires du XVIe au XVIIIe siècle', *Cahiers de Fanjeaux: historiographie du catharisme*, 14 (1979), 85–118; and A. Friesen, 'Medieval Heretics or Forerunners of the Reformation: The Protestant Rewriting of the History of Medieval Heresy', in A. Ferreiro (ed.), *The Devil, Heresy, and Witchcraft in the Middle Ages: Essays in Honor of Jeffrey B. Russell* (Leiden, 1998), 165–90. Interestingly, under 'Albigenses', the first edition of the *Encyclopædia Britannica or, A Dictionary of Arts and Sciences* (Edinburgh, 1771), i. 75, noted this: 'They [the Albigenses] are ranked among the grossest heretics, the Manicheans, by Roman Catholics; from which charge Protestants generally acquit them, though with some limitations . . . At the time of the Reformation, those of the Albigenses who remained embraced Calvinism.'

crescendo in the bloody violence of the Albigensian Crusade in the first half of the thirteenth century and, thereafter, the relentless persecutions of inquisitors until the heresy disappears, for all intents and purposes, sometime in the early fourteenth century. The Cathars are not only assumed to have had a 'Church' but also to have had what can only be called a distinct ethnicity along with their beliefs, a distinctiveness that therefore makes them a useful past analogy to the systematic destruction of European Jews during the Holocaust or the genocidal violence in the former Yugoslavia.[4] It is because the Cathars are the most famous heretics of the Middle Ages, the vivid paradigms of dissent by which all other medieval heresies are compared and understood, that the fact, fantasy, and fiction about the good men and good women demands rethinking.

Medieval heresies, shaped by a historiography that has barely changed in 200 years, are generally understood to be nothing more than religious attitudes, abstract doctrines, clear philosophies, or elaborate discourses.[5]

---

[4] For example, on the Cathars and the Holocaust, see G. Lerner, 'In the Footsteps of the Cathars', in her *Why History Matters: Life and Thought* (Oxford, 1997), 19–32, and, on the killing of the Albigensians and the massacres in Bosnia, see D. Rieff, *Slaughterhouse: Bosnia and the Failure of the West* (New York, 1995), 27.

[5] This view was explicitly stated by Herbert Grundmann throughout his classic and still deeply influential *Religiöse Bewegungen im Mittelalter: Untersuchungen über die geschichtlichen Zusammenhänge zwischen der Ketzerei, den Bettelorden und der religiösen Frauenbewegung im 12. und 13. Jahrhundert und über die geschichtlichen Grundlagen der deutschen Mystik*, 2nd edn. (Hildesheim, 1961), esp. 396 ff., 503 (trans. S. Rowan, *Religious Movements in the Middle Ages: The Historical Links between Heresy, the Mendicant Orders, and the Women's Religious Movement in the Twelfth and Thirteenth Century, with the Historical Foundations of German Mysticism* (Notre Dame, Ind., 1995), and see esp. R. E. Lerner, 'Introduction', ix–xxv). There is no doubt that Grundmann's approach to studying heresies as religious movements was important, yet what is often forgotten is that he merely shifted the intellectualist methods of *Religionsgeschichte* to the study of heresy. P. Biller, 'Through a Glass Darkly: Seeing Medieval Heresy', in P. Linehan and J. L. Nelson (eds.), *The Medieval World* (London, 2001), 309, is good on Grundmann and his importance. J. L. Nelson, 'Religion in "histoire totale": Some Recent Work on Medieval Heresy and Popular Religion', *Religion*, 10 (1980), 60–85, is still vital on this question about heresy and religion. M. Lambert, *Medieval Heresy: Medieval Popular Movements from the Gregorian Reform to the Reformation*, 3rd edn. (Oxford, 2002), 7–8, acknowledges that his approach to heresy is shaped by Grundmann's scholarship and method. Such idealist assumptions are implicit, as far as Catharism is concerned, in J. Duvernoy, *Le Catharisme: la religion des cathares* (Toulouse, 1976); Duvernoy, *Cathares, Vaudois et Béguines, dissidents du pays d'Oc*; R. Nelli, *La Philosophie du catharisme: le dualisme radical au XIIIe siècle* (Paris, 1978); and A. Brenon, *Le Vrai Visage du Catharisme* (Portet-sur-Garonne, 1988). Now see J. B. Russell, 'Interpretations of the Origins of Medieval Heresy', *Medieval Studies*, 25 (1963), 34, where he emphasized over forty years ago that most modern writers, especially Grundmann, favoured intellectual or moral reasons for medieval heresy and implicitly rejected any thesis that wanted to include the material world. The irony here is not only that Russell's observation is still correct but that the somewhat older Russell, in works such as *Lucifer: The Devil in the Middle Ages* (Ithaca, NY, 1984) or *A History of Heaven: The Singing Silence* (Princeton, 1998), is just as intellectualist, ahistorical, and

This pervasive idealist bias assumes that worlds are made from theories, that cultures are hammered together from discourses, and that the elaboration of a philosophy is all the explanation a scholar need ever give. Anything that is not the stuff of thoughts is either taken for granted or relegated to benign neglect. What is so disturbing about the manner in which heresy is usually studied is that the medieval heretic is taken to be such a coherent and concrete figure in the history of the Middle Ages, particularly in the great scheme of things, that the whys and wherefores of heresy get lost in a kind of intellectual determinism in which certain ideas have an inevitability about them because someone, sooner or later, thought them.[6] Such hindsight applied to the good men and good women, almost always called 'Cathars' since the late nineteenth century, has so predetermined these heretics to be what they supposedly became, that the vital importance of why individuals and communities thought or did things at specific times and places vanishes into generalizations that are either trivially true, the Church feared heterodoxy, or obviously false, there was a 'Cathar Church'. This cultural fatalism, implicit in so much research on heresy and medieval alterity, effectively predestines the Middle Ages to be full of dissent, obsessed with the marginal and, as a consequence, gripped with an immutable need to persecute.

This methodological tendency presupposes that heresies, like religions, have an intellectual purity and theological coherence in which it is possible to neatly sift out other less coherent ideas and, most crucially, it is a technique that effectively ignores historical specificity. The heresy of the good men and good women, for instance, becomes nothing more than a set of stable dualist ideas (good God, bad God, benign spirit, evil matter) lodged in the heads of people—which, if those minds move, so

moralizing, as the historians his younger self had once criticized. A recent learned, passionate, though rather shrill, restatement and defence of the intellectualist approach to religion is B. S. Gregory, *Salvation at Stake: Christian Martyrdom in Early Modern Europe* (Cambridge, Mass., 1999), esp. 1–15, 342–52. On the idealist bias generally in the study of religion, see especially M. Douglas, 'Rightness of Categories', in M. Douglas and D. Hull (eds.), *How Classification Works: Nelson Goodman among the Social Sciences* (Edinburgh, 1992), 239–71; M. Douglas, *In The Wilderness: The Doctrine of Defilement in the Book of Numbers* (Sheffield, 1993), 26–9; M. Douglas, 'Comment: Hunting the Pangolin', *Man*, NS 28 (1993), 161–4. Two much cited anthropological justifications of an intellectualist and idealist attitude towards religion (and so heresy) are R. Horton, 'African Conversion', *Africa*, 41 (1971), 85–108 and C. Geertz, 'Religion as a Cultural System', in his *The Interpretation of Cultures: Selected Essays* (New York, 1973), 87–125.

[6] Cf. Lambert, *Medieval Heresy*, 10, where this cultural determinism overcomes all doubts about the coherent origins of medieval heresy because 'the fact remains that the faint springs in heretical episodes of the eleventh and early twelfth centuries have turned into great torrents by the early thirteenth.'

'Catharism' and the Study of Medieval Heresy   253

too those vacuum-sealed beliefs. The original heresy, no matter how
many different societies rose and fell through the decades, no matter how
great the geographical and cultural differences, stays recognizably the
same.[7] The learned medieval mind (awash with Augustine's descriptions
of Manichaeism, fearful of the timeless nature of evil, convinced of enduring continuities, aware that the new is always revealed in the old)
might classify a twelfth-century heresy as similar to a heterodox creed
from the fourth, or adopt an ancient word to explain a thirteenth-century
belief, or think that Manichaean errors had always lingered in the world,
but these past efforts at explanation should not persuade twenty-first-
century scholars to adopt almost identical approaches.[8] Admittedly, trac-
ing the origins of the heretical good men all the way back to the
Manichaeans of late antiquity, although far less common than a century
ago, can still be found in all kinds of unexpected places.[9] A subtle

[7] S. Runciman's *The Medieval Manichee: A Study of the Christian Dualist Heresy* (Cambridge,
repr. 1982, orig. 1947), esp. 62, 87–8, 171–4, is a famous illustration of this assumption about
being able to delineate original religious intent despite millennia and landscape. H. Söderberg,
La Religion des Cathares: étude sur le Gnosticisme de la Basse Antiquité et du Moyen Âge (Uppsala,
1949), argued for such crystalline continuities. Y. Stoyanov, in his *The Hidden Tradition in
Europe: The Secret History of Medieval Christian Heresy* (London, 1994) and reissued, but heavily
revised, as *The Other God: Dualist Religions from Antiquity to the Cathar Heresy* (New Haven,
2000), assumes the same ability to follow dualist thought through time and space, whether
Mahayana Buddhism, Manichaeism, Bogomilism, or Catharism. On not wishing 'to get mired
in the monotonous and undifferentiated continuities assumed, without reflection, to exist across
the centuries', especially with regard to religion and epitomized by *Religionsgeschichte*, see P.
Brown in 'The Rise and Function of the Holy Man in late Antiquity, 1971–1997', *Journal of Early
Christian Studies*, 6 (1998), 375.
[8] The Cistercian Caesarius of Heisterbach, in his early thirteenth-century *Dialogus miraculo-
rum*, ed. J. Strange (Cologne, 1851), i, V. xxi. 300–3, under the chapter *De haeresi Albiensium*,
compared the heretical tenets of the Languedocian heretics with the heresies of the Manichees.
The Benedictine Wibald of Corvey, writing to Manegold of Paderborn in 1147, deftly stated the
guiding principle of this explanatory technique (medieval and modern) when he noted—in Ep.
167, *Monumenta Corbeiensia*, ed. P. Jaffé, *Bibliotheca rerum germanicarum* (Berlin, 1864), i. 278—
that so much had already been written 'that it is impossible to say anything new (ut nichil iam
possit dici novum)' and that even heretics 'do not invent new things but repeat old ones (non
nova inveniunt, set vetera replicant)'. Three or four years earlier, Eberwin, the prior of Steinfeld's
Premonstratensian abbey, in a letter (Ep. 472, *Patrologia Latina* (*PL*) 182, col. 679) to Bernard of
Clairvaux, described a group of dualist heretics (usually labelled as Cathars) seized in Cologne
who, when brought to trial, defended their beliefs by saying that their heresy had 'lain concealed
from the time of the martyrs even to our own day', and, intriguingly, they went on to say that
these hidden philosophies had apparently 'persisted so in Greece and certain other lands (hanc
haeresim usque ad haec tempora occultatam fuisse a temporibus martyrum, et permansisse in
Graecia et quibusdam aliis terris)'.
[9] See e.g. in the nineteenth century, J. Michelet, *Histoire de France: Moyen Âge* (Paris, 1869),
ii. 317–19; C. Douais, *Les Albigeois: leurs origines, action de l'église au XII' siècle* (Paris, 1879), 1–216;
H. C. Lea, *A History in the Inquisition in the Middle Ages* (New York, 1887), i, esp. 92. In the twentieth and twenty-first centuries see e.g. C. H. Haskins, 'Robert le Bougre and the Beginnings of

variation on this theme has the *gnosis* of Mani being revived in medieval western Europe through the Byzantine Bogomils who, it is tacitly understood, were undoubtedly influenced by this late antique heresy.[10] As for there being any genuine correspondence between the Bogomils and the heretical good men, it is neither obvious nor irrefutable that such a liaison ever existed, even though the assumption of such a connection between the two heresies has become a truism in almost all studies of medieval heterodoxy.[11] For a start, any suggestion that Bogomil preachers were in Europe from the first millennium onwards and that these Bosnian or Bulgarian seers were the cause of almost all eleventh-century heresy

the Inquisition in Northern France', *American Historical Review*, 7 (1902), 440–1; Söderberg, *La Religion des Cathares, passim*, esp. 6, 82, 265–8; H. Sproemberg, 'Die Enstehung des Manichäismus im Abendland', in H. Sproemberg and M. Unger (eds.), *Mittelalter und demokratische Geschichtsschreibung* (Berlin, 1971), 85–102; A. Abel, 'Aspects sociologiques des religions "manichéennes" ', in R. Crozet, P. Gallais, and Y. J. Rion (eds.), *Mélanges offerts à René Crozet* (Poitiers, 1966), I, 33–46; R. French and A. Cunningham, *Before Science: The Invention of the Friars' Natural Philosophy* (Aldershot, 1996), 103, where the 'derivation of Catharism from Manicheeism is almost certainly correct, and on its long journey, chronologically and geographically, the heresy has developed variations'; L. Kaelber, *Schools of Asceticism: Ideology and Organization in Medieval Religious Communities* (University Park, Pa., 1998), 175; implied in J. Oberste, *Der 'Kreuzzug' gegen die Albigenser: Ketzerei und Machtpolitik im Mittelalter* (Darmstadt, 2003), 30–1; and R. Weis, *The Yellow Cross: The Story of the Last Cathars 1290–1329* (London, 2000), esp. xv and 137, where a confused, and confusing, link appears to be made between Catharism and Manichaeism. B. Hamilton, 'The State of Research: The Legacy of Charles Schmidt to the Study of Christian Dualism', *Journal of Medieval History*, 24 (1998), 194–5, implies that a continuity may still be established between the Manichaeans and the Cathars. Interestingly, Charles Schmidt, *Histoire et doctrine des Cathares* (Bayonne, 1849), 253, thought there was no connection between the Cathars and the Manichees. P. Jimenez, 'La Vision médiévale du catharisme chez les historiens des années 1950: un néo-manichéisme', *Heresis*, 7 (1994), 65–96, is a good survey of this issue and many others relating to the historiography of Catharism.

    [10] See e.g. D. Obolensky, *The Bogomils: A Study in Balkan Neo-Manichaeism* (Cambridge, 1948), 109–10, and Antoine Dondaine, 'Aux origines de l'hérésie médiévale', *Rivista di Storia della Chiesa in Italia*, 6 (1952), 78, 'les Cathares occidentaux étaient fils des Bogomils, eux-mêmes héritiers du lointain Manichéisme'.

    [11] On the Bogomils, see F. Šanjak, *Les Chretiens bosniaques et le movement cathare XIIe–XVe siècles* (Brussels, 1976); F. Šanjak, 'Derniéres traces de catharisme dans les Balkans', *Cahiers de Fanjeaux: Effacement du Catharisme? (XIIIe–XIVe S.)*, 20 (1985), 119–34; J. Šidak, *Studije O 'Crkvi Bosanskoj' i Bogumilstvu* (Zagreb, 1976); D. Angelov, 'Der Bogomilismus in Bulgarien', *Bulgarian Historical Review*, 2 (1975), 34–54; and J. Šidak, 'Ursprung und Wesen des Bogomilentums', in W. Lourdaux and D. Verhelst (eds.), *The Concept of Heresy in the Middle Ages (11th–13th C.): Proceedings of the International Conference, Louvain May 13–16, 1973* (The Hague, 1976), 144–56. By contrast, J. V. A. Fine, Jr., *The Early Medieval Balkans: A Critical Survey from the Sixth to the Late Twelfth Century* (Ann Arbor, 1983), 179, notes, '[I]f we are analyzing Bulgarian history as a whole and significant movements and causes of historical developments in Bulgaria, Bogomilism's importance has been tremendously exaggerated in all historical works. In fact . . . one would be justified in writing a history of medieval Bulgaria without the Bogomils at all.' Indeed, in P. Stephenson's recent *Byzantium's Balkan Frontier: A Politcal Study of the Northern Balkans, 900–1204* (Cambridge, 2000), the Bogomils receive no mention.

is simply untenable because this argument rests, with appalling weakness, on the historian simply perceiving a similarity between one set of ideas and another.[12] A more nuanced (and more persuasive) vision imagines

[12] See e.g. the arguments for Bogomil influence in western Europe before the twelfth century by Arno Borst, *Die Katharer: Schriften der Monumenta Germaniae Historica (Dentsches Institut für Erforschung des Mittelalters) 12* (Stuttgart, 1953), 71–80; Runciman, *The Medieval Manichee,* 117–18; Dondaine, 'Aux origines de l'hérésie médiévale', 43–78; Lambert, *Medieval Heresy,* 24–36, 343–8; J.-P. Poly and E. Bournazel, *La Mutation féodale, X^e–XIIe* (Paris, 1980), 382–427 (trans. C. Higgitt, *The Feudal Transformation, 900–1200* (New York, 1991), 272–308); H. Fichtenau, *Ketzer und Professoren: Häresie un Vernunftglaube im Hochmittelalter* (Munich, 1992), 17–53 (trans. D. A. Kaiser, *Heretics and Scholars in the High Middle Ages: 1000–1200* (University Park, 1998), 13–51); M. Frassetto, 'The Sermons of Ademar of Chabannes and the Letter of Heribert: New Sources Concerning the Origins of Medieval Heresy', *Revue Bénédictine,* 109 (1999), 324–40; and C. Taylor, 'The Letter of Héribert of Périgord as a Source for Dualist Heresy in the Society of Early Eleventh-Century Aquitaine', *Journal of Medieval History,* 26 (2000), 313–49. R. I. Moore in 'Heresy, Repression, and Social Change in the Age of Gregorian Reform', in S. L. Waugh and P. D. Diehl (eds.), *Christendom and Its Discontents: Exclusion, Persecution, and Rebellion, 1000–1500* (Cambridge, 1996), 19–46; Moore, 'The Birth of Popular Heresy: A Millennial Phenomenon?' *Journal of Religious History,* 24 (2000), 8–25; and Moore, 'Medieval Europe: Religious Enthusiasm and Social Change in the Millennial Generation', in A. Amanat and M. Bernhardsson (eds.), *Imagining the End: Visions of Apocalypse from the Ancient Middle East to Modern America* (London, 2002), 129–47, 359–63, repeats his nuanced opposition—first articulated in 'The Origins of Medieval Heresy', *History,* 55 (1970), 21–36—to these opinions. Other important arguments against Bogomil influence in the early Middle Ages were made by R. Morghen, *Medioevo Cristiano* (Bari, 1953), 212–86; R. Morghen, 'Problèmes sur l'origine de l'hérésie au moyen-âge', *Revue historique,* 336 (1966), 1–16; H.-C. Puech, 'Catharisme médiéval et bogomilisme', in his *Sur le Manicheisme et autres essais* (Paris, 1979), 395–427; R. Manselli, *L'eresia del male* (Naples, 1963), 118–38; B. Stock, *The Implications of Literacy: Written Language and Models of Interpretation in the Eleventh and Twelfth Centuries* (Princeton, 1983), 98–9, 102–3; G. Lobrichon, 'The Chiaroscuro of Heresy: Early Eleventh-Century Aquitaine as Seen from Auxerre', in T. Head and R. Landes (eds.), *The Peace of God: Social Violence and Religious Response in France around the Year 1000* (Ithaca, NY, 1992), 80–103, and his 'Arras, 1025, ou le vrai procès d'une fausse accusation', in M. Zerner (ed.), *Inventer l'hérésie?: discours polémiques et pouvoirs avant l'Inquisition* (Nice, 1998), 67–85. R. Landes, *Relics, Apocalyse, and the Deceits of History: Ademar of Chabannes, 989–1034* (Cambridge, Mass., 1995), 188–9, argues, somewhat inconclusively, that heretics in the early Middle Ages suffered from this 'Manichaean scapegoating' because such scapegoating 'made sense of a confusing and disappointing world'. Now, without going into the ephemeral problem of millennialism around 1000, which really only exists if one has an intellectualist bias, see R. Landes, 'The Birth of Heresy: A Millennial Phenomenon', *Journal of Religious History,* 24 (2000), 26–43 (which is also a rather angry reply to Moore's 'The Birth of Popular Heresy: A Millennial Phenomenon?'). B. Hamilton, 'The State of Research: The Legacy of Charles Schmidt to the Study of Christian Dualism', 196–8, while not suggesting Bogomil missionaries before the twelfth century, still condemns what he calls 'reductionist' arguments that dismiss the possibility of such Balkan visitors to western Europe. Furthermore, searching within the handful of reported (and persecuted) incidents of heresy in western Europe before the middle of the twelfth century for pre-Catharism or proto-Catharism by simply unearthing what appear to be dualist images, or through recognizing an inherent sameness about heretical anti-clericism between one century and the next, are more exercises in the quixotic than in quiddity. J. Duvernoy, 'Le Problème des origines du catharisme', in his *Cathares, Vaudois et Beguines, dissidents du pays d'Oc,* 39–52; A. Brenon, 'Les Hérésies de l'an mil: nouvelles perspectives sur les origines du catharisme', *Heresis,* 24 (1995), 21–36; and A. Brenon, 'The Voice of the Good Women: An Essay on the Pastoral and Sacerdotal Role of Women in the Cathar Church', in B. M. Kienzle and P. J.

Balkan missionaries only coming to Europe in the twelfth century. In any event, despite allusions to wisdom arriving from the east in the twelfth and thirteenth centuries, as well as the small number of questionable references to heretical holy men journeying from the Byzantine empire to northern France, northern Italy, and, especially, south-western Languedoc with the apocryphal *papa* Nicetas distributing dualist doctrine to an heretical elite, the efforts to truly link the Bogomils and the good men remain unconvincing.[13] (An intimacy between the Paulicians and the good

Walker (eds.), *Women Preachers and Prophets through Two Millennia of Christianity* (Berkeley, Calif., 1998), esp. 115–16, who lean heavily toward searching for, and believing in, proto-Catharism in earlier European heresies.

[13] G. Rottenwöhrer, *Der Katherismus: Die Herkunft der Katharer nach Theologie und Geschichte* (Bad Honnef, 1990), iii. 74–114, 570–1; Fichtenau, *Ketzer und Professoren*, 70–119 (*Heretics and Scholars*, 70–126); B. Hamilton, 'Wisdom from the East: The Reception by the Cathars of Eastern Dualist Texts', in P. Biller and A. Hudson (eds.), *Heresy and Literacy, 1000–1530* (Cambridge, 1994), 38–60, which, it should be pointed out, opens by stating that '[n]o reputable scholar now doubts that Catharism was an offshoot of medieval eastern dualism . . .'; M. Lambert, *The Cathars* (Oxford, 1998), 29–59; and Barber, *The Cathars*, 6–33, are all good, as well as nuanced, recent summaries of the evidence (and scholarship) for missionary and doctrinal connections between the Cathars and the Bogomils. J. and B. Hamilton, *Christian Dualist Heresies in the Byzantine World c.650–c.1450* (Manchester, 1998) is a remarkable collection of translated sources on dualism and has a useful 'Historical Introduction', 1–55. Also, see B. Hamilton, 'Dualist Heresy in the Latin Empire of Constantinople', in C. Hawkesworth et al., *Religious Quest and National Identity in the Balkans* (Basingstoke, 2001), 69–77. The visit by the supposed Bogomil Bishop of Constantinople, *papa* Nicetas, to Saint-Félix-de-Caraman in the Lauragais happened in 1167. The document that records Nicetas's journey is lost and only exists as an appendix to Guillaume Besse's *Histoire des ducs, marquis et comtes de Narbonne, autrement appellez Princes des Goths, Ducs de Septimanie, et Marquis de Gothie. Dedié à Monseigneur l'Archevesque Duc de Narbonne* (Paris, 1660), 483–6. This document, given to Besse by 'M. Caseneuue, Prebendier au Chapitre de l'Eglisle de Sainct Estienne de Tolose, en l'an 1652' (p. 483), is probably (at best) a mid-thirteenth-century forgery by some good men and their followers, a late thirteenth-century collation of a number of disparate documents by an inquisitor in Toulouse, or a seventeenth-century forgery. Also, if it really existed, it probably was preserved until the seventeenth century in the Dominican inquisitorial archives at Toulouse or Carcassonne, where a number of other apocryphal documents supposedly demonstrating eastern links were filed away by inquisitors in the late thirteenth century. B. Hamilton, 'The Cathar Council of S. Félix Reconsidered', *Archivum fratrum praedicatorum*, 48 (1978), 23–53, is generally assumed to have proven the historical validity of Besse's appendix. Now, because so much about this document resembles a *ficción* by Jorge Luis Borges, and because one needs to already believe in connections between Cathars and Bogomils to see the evidence within the text (even though the text itself is the foundational proof underlying this belief about Catharism and Bogomilism), it is more prudent, for the present, to remain unconvinced about its historical veracity. It should also be noted that the elaborate heretical hierarchy imagined in the text would have been culturally impossible in the communities of the Toulousain and Lauragais of the late twelfth century. Further, no person ever questioned by the inquisition from the Lauragais, and thousands were questioned from this small region, ever mentioned the 'council' of Saint-Félix. In support of Hamilton, see e.g. P. Jimenez, 'Relire la Charte de Niquinta—1) Origine et problématique de la Charte', *Heresis*, 22 (1994), 1–26, and her, 'Relire la Charte de Niquinta—2) Sens et portée de la charte', *Heresis*, 23 (1994), 1–28; P. Biller, 'Popular Religion in the Central and Middle Ages', in M. Bentley (ed.),

men, whether through missionaries or through immigration, has never been championed in the same way as that of the Bogomils.[14]) All in all, arguments about the specific influence of the Bogomils upon western European heresy, either in the eleventh century or in the twelfth, rely upon detecting likenesses between ideas irrespective of time and place.

The discovery of seemingly analogous attitudes over the *longue durée*, or between *les vastes espaces*, can never account for medieval predictive or inductive practices. Apparently similar representations, symbols, *mentalités*, dissenting discourses, rituals, or religious *Zusammenhänge*, though undeniably interesting, prove nothing conclusive in themselves. Any exercise in detecting what appears to be homologous ideas through time and space, no matter how learned, is only the beginning of an explanation about the past and not, as is so often assumed, the concluding proof, in and of itself, about why a particular society once thought certain ideas worth thinking.[15] The reasons why someone in the twenty-first century

---

Companion to Historiography (London, 1997), 239–40; Lambert, *The Cathars*, 45–59; and Barber, *The Cathars*, 21–2, 71–3. By contrast Y. Dossat, 'A propos du concile cathare de Saint-Félix: les Milingues', *Cahiers de Fanjeaux: Cathares en Languedoc*, 3 (1968), 201–14, argued that Besse's document was a seventeenth-century forgery (probably by Besse) and was part of a polemic concocted during the seventeenth-century religious wars. This line of thought was recently (albeit tentatively) supported by M. Zerner, 'La Charte de Niquinta, l'hérésie et l'éruditia des années 1650–1660', in (the exemplary collection of articles) *L'Histoire du catharisme en discussion: le 'concile' de Saint-Félix (1167)*, ed. id. (Nice, 2001), 203–48. It has also been argued that Bogomil dualism was secretly carried back by crusaders returning from twelfth-century Outremer. On such heretical transmissions from the Levant, C. Thouzellier, 'Hérésie et croisade au XIIᵉ siècle', *Revue d'histoire ecclésiastique*, 49 (1954), 855–72, was the first to strongly suggest the importation of dualist beliefs by returning crusaders. Along similar lines to Thouzellier, K. Heisig, in 'Ein gnostische Sekte im abendlandischen Mittelalter', *Zeitschrift für Religions- und Geistesgeschichte*, 16 (1964), 271–4, suggested that crusaders brought ancient Gnostic practices back from the East to the Rhineland.

[14] On the Paulicians see esp. N. Garsoïan, *The Paulician Heresy: A Study of the Origin and Development of Paulicianism in Armenia and the Eastern Provinces of the Roman Empire* (The Hague, 1967), esp. 18–21, where she argues against Paulician influence in western Europe in the Middle Ages. Garsoïan, ibid. 186–230, also strongly rejects the Paulicians as descendants of Manichees; rather, she considers the original Paulicians to be nothing more than Armenian Old Believers—an argument that is perhaps as unconvincing, and certainly just as unprovable, as the one she rejects. Bernard Hamilton cannot let go of the notion that there must be some connection between the Paulicians and the Cathars despite the dearth of evidence in his 'The Origins of the Dualist Church of Drugunthia', *Eastern Churches Review*, 6 (1974), 115–24, his 'Wisdom from the East', 50–1, and his *Christian Dualist Heresies in the Byzantine World c.650–c.1450*, 5–25.

[15] Some of the ideas in this paragraph were adapted from N. Goodman, 'Seven Strictures against Similarity', in his *Problems and Projects* (Indianapolis, 1972), 446. See also N. Goodman, 'The New Riddle of Induction', in his *Fact, Fiction, and Forecast*, 4th edn. (Cambridge, 1983), 59–83; N. Goodman, *Of Mind and Other Matters* (Cambridge, Mass., 1984); N. Goodman with C. Elgin, *Reconceptions in Philosophy & Other Arts & Sciences* (Indianapolis, 1988), 446. See also the collected (philosophical) essays on the problem of 'grue' put forward in Goodman's 'The

believes that two things truly resemble each other, or can safely predict certain continuities from today to tomorrow, should never be confused with (or assumed to be the same as) the certainties that men and women in the thirteenth century knew (or attempted to know) about their world. If one were to find, for example, ostensibly matching heresies from the thirteenth century in the very same region in the eleventh, then even with the same words, beliefs, representations, and symbols, the similarity would be, at best, superficial, while the meaning, in any case, could not be the same. To study heresy, or anything else for that matter, as though ideas waft over societies and centuries like loose hot-air balloons, so that the trick is to catch those drifting beliefs which look similar to each other, allows for whatever ideal contextualization, whatever intellectual continuity, an erudite zeppelin-chaser so chooses.

Likewise, explanations which treat heresy as solely a manifestation of economic or material problems, as an expression of social or class discontent, not unlike something from the revolutions of the nineteenth and twentieth centuries, are just as limited as the more prevalent intellectualist arguments from the similarity of ideas.[16] A peculiar irony about these

---

New Riddle of Induction', in D. Stalker (ed.), *Grue! The New Riddle of Induction* (Chicago, 1994), esp. I. Hacking, 'Entrenchment', 193–224, and the collected (historical, philosophical, anthropological) essays in M. Douglas and D. Hull (eds.), *How Classification Works: Nelson Goodman among the Social Sciences* (Edinburgh, 1992).

[16] For example, E. Werner, *Pauperes Christi: Studien zu sozial-religiösen Bewegungen im Zeitalter des Reformpapsttums* (Leipzig, 1957); M. Erbstösser and E. Werner, *Ideologische Probleme des Mittelalterlichen Plebejertums: Die freigeistige Häresie und ihre sozialen Wurzeln* (Berlin, 1960); G. Koch, *Frauenfrage und Ketzertum in Mittelalter* (Berlin, 1962); B. Töpfer, *Das kommende Reich des Friedens: zur Entwicklung chiliastischer Zukunftshoffnungen im Hochmittelalter* (Berlin, 1964); M. Erbstösser, *Ketzer im Mittelalter* (Stuttgart, 1984); trans. J. Fraser, *Heretics in the Middle Ages* (Leipzig, 1984); and M. Erbstösser and E. Werner, *Ketzer und Heilige: Das religiöse Leben im Hochmittelalter* (Vienna, 1986). On this (especially former East German, especially Karl-Marx University of Leipzig) way with history that, despite the Marxist materialism, had many affinities with the medieval vision of a Jules Michelet, see A. Dorpalen, *German History in Marxist Perspective: The East German Approach* (Detroit, 1985), esp. 74–6, 91–2; W. Malecsek, 'Le ricerche eresiologiche in area germanica', in G. G. Merlo (ed.), *Eretici ed eresie medievali nella storiografia contemporanea: atti del XXXII Convegno du studi seilla Riforma e i movimenti religiosi in Italia* (Torre Pellice, 1994), 64–93, esp. 68–75; P. Biller, 'Cathars and Material Women', in P. Biller and A. J. Minnis (eds.), *Medieval Theology and the Natural Body* (Woodbridge, 1997), 75–81; Fichtenau, *Ketzer und Professoren*, 110–13 (*Heretics and Scholars*, 115–19); and Kaelber, *Schools of Asceticism*, 196–202. It was also this East German treatment of medieval heresy and spirituality that Borst and Grundmann—working within the idealist *Religionsgeschichte* tradition, sincere anti-Marxists, and West Germans after World War II—consciously reacted against. An informed observation on this issue is made by Lerner in his introduction to Grundmann, *Religious Movements in the Middle Ages*, xxii–xxv. James Given, stepping outside this historiographic debate, has adopted a subtle neo-Marxist approach in his *Inquisition and Medieval Society: Power, Discipline, and Resistance in Languedoc* (Ithaca, NY, 1997). For further discussions about German historians and heresy, see D. Müller, 'La Perspective de l'historiographie allemande', in Berlioz

theses, tying such dated Cold War Marxist-Leninist approaches to equally dated Victorian Romantic notions, and so elevating both above the level of just curiosity value, indeed an irony permeating much historical thinking about the Middle Ages, is that if the material world is thought to be unchanging, as physical existence in the medieval countryside is especially thought to be, then the beliefs concerned with that world are assumed to be unchanging as well.[17] Rural communities, tied to the soil, trapped in the cyclical movement of the seasons, forever dwelling in an eternal present and so denied the virtues of linear time, never change the way they do things, never change the way they think things.[18] The

and Hélas *Catharisme: l'édifice imaginaire*, 47–64, and for German historians and the Middle Ages, see O. G. Oexle, 'Die Moderne und ihr Mittelalter—eine folgenreiche Problemgeschichte', in P. Segl (ed.), *Mittelalter und Moderne: Entdeckung und Rekonstruktion der mittelalterlichen Welt. Kongreßakten des 6. Symposiums des Mediävistenverbandes in Bayreuth 1995* (Sigmaringen, 1997), 307–64.

[17] See e.g. E. Le Roy Ladurie, *Montaillou, village occitan de 1294 à 1324* (Paris, 1993) (trans. and condensed by B. Bray, *Montaillou: Cathars and Catholics in a French Village 1294–1324* (Harmondsworth, 1981)), where a tendency to romanticize life in the Occitan countryside, and to see it as possessing unchanging qualities, is crucial to his brillant and influential evocation of rural existence from a late thirteenth/early fourteenth-century inquisitorial register. Now, see M. Benad, *Domus und Religion in Montaillou* (Tübingen, 1990), and the collected essays in A. Brenon and C. Dieulafait (eds.), *Autour de Montaillou: un village occitan. Histoire et religiosité d'une communauté villageoise au Moyen Âge. Actes du Colloque de Montaillou (25–26–27 août 2000)* (Castelnaud la Chapelle, 2001). Weis, *The Yellow Cross*, using the same text as Le Roy Ladurie—*Le Registre d'Inquisition de Jacques Fournier, Évêque de Pamiers (1318–1325)*, ed. Jean Duvernoy (Toulouse, 1965, and additional *Corrections*, 1972) and one other, *L'Inquisitor Geoffroy d'Ablis et les Cathares du Comté de Foix (1308–1309)*, ed. and trans. A. Pales-Gobilliard (Paris, 1984)—promotes the same image of an unchanging rural landscape, although this time it is populated with more individuals possessing intensely anachronistic attitudes. The same is true for C. Ginzburg's remarkable, but supremely ahistorical, *Storia notturna* (Turin, 1989) (trans. R. Rosenthal, *Ecstasies: Deciphering the Witches' Sabbath* (Harmondsworth, 1991)), where Ludwig Wittgenstein's notion of 'seeing connections'—from *Bemerkungen über Frazers Golden Bough* (*Remarks on Frazer's Golden Bough*), ed. with revised trans. R. Rees (Atlantic Highlands, NJ, 1979), esp. 8–8e, '[A]n [historical] explanation as an hypothesis of the development, is only *one* kind of summary of the data—of their synopsis. We can equally well see the data in their relations to one another and make a summary of them in a general picture without putting it in the form of an hypothesis regarding temporal development'—and the consequent downplaying of historical change and specificity, justifies the lack of gravity in Ginzburg's universe. P. Anderson, 'Nocturnal Enquiry: Carlo Ginzburg', in his *A Zone of Engagement* (London, 1992), 207–29, thoughtfully, but severely, reviews Ginzburg's unchanging rural world and the materialist assumptions such an idea embraces. W. C. Jordan, in his *The Great Famine: Northern Europe in the Early Fourteenth Century* (Princeton, 1996), 13, has attacked the general prevalence of such timeless notions about the tempo of rural life in the Middle Ages.

[18] A. Gurevitch, for instance, has expressed these views in his *Categories of Medieval Culture*, trans. G. L. Campbell (London, 1985), 98, and *Medieval Popular Culture: Problems of Belief and Perception*, trans. J. Bak and P. Hollingsworth (Cambridge, 1992), 99. Cf. J. Fentress and C. Wickham, *Social Memory* (Oxford, 1992), 100, who dismiss such views of time and memory in rural communities.

overt materialist, in the end, reinforces the idealist bias, and, once more, an anti-gravity world of long duration is imagined, where one can jump about all over the place, from century to century, from the Balkans to the Pyrenees, blithely ignoring temporal and cultural specificity in the proving of a point.

These analytic tendencies have the interesting effect of causing scholars to emphasize the writings of medieval Catholic intellectuals who, without fail, always describe heretical ideas as doctrinally coherent and heretics themselves as never isolated, never unconnected to each other, but always organized, always threatening.[19] This is in stark contrast to the testimonies collected by inquisitors into heretical depravity, especially in Languedoc, where thousands of ordinary men and women confessed to beliefs that were quite malleable, not always opposed to the Church, and distinctly localized. Unfortunately, the records of the inquisition in the thirteenth and fourteenth centuries, mostly a collection of monotonous and fragmented forensic replies interspersed with longer and more vivid confessions, all too often just get concertinaed to fit a priori Cathar-templates, preconceived notions about what a testimony really was saying even if it did not say it.[20] What is so fascinating about this tendency to search for the religious unity of a heresy in the theoretical unity of its ideas is that, somewhat ironically, this was how inquisitors themselves came to understand heterodoxy by the beginning of the fourteenth century. This shift can be followed, quite explicitedly, in the way in which the questions asked by inquisitors in their interrogations change within half a century from an emphasis on what an individual did or would do to what a person thought or would think.[21] This intellectualization of heresy, which affected not only those who persecuted but, and this can never be stressed enough, also those who deliberately chose to resist the Church, necessi-

[19] For example, this is clearly observed in Lambert, *The Cathars.*

[20] For example, Hamilton, 'Wisdom from the East', 57 and n. 93, misreading *et hoc in vulgari* (about a book) in a seventeenth-century copy of an inquisition record (in Paris, Bibliothèque Nationale, Collection Doat 25, fo. 217'.) as *et hoc in Bulgaria.* Coincidently, Lambert, *The Cathars,* 55 n. 29, faults Duvernoy for the same misreading of Doat 25. See also Rottenwöhrer, *Der Katherismus: Die Herkunft der Katharer nach Theologie und Geschichte,* iii. 529. Biller, 'Through a Glass Darkly: Seeing Medieval Heresy', 308–26, is excellent not only on the problems in the use of inquisition documents but also why they must be used if we are to understand the good men and good women.

[21] Pegg, *The Corruption of Angels,* 45–51. See also Pegg, 'Questions about Questions: Toulouse 609 and the Great Inquisition of 1245–1246', in P. Biller and C. Bruschi (eds.), *Texts and Repression of Medieval Heresy* (York, 2002), 111–25.

tates more wariness than is usually given in the general interpretation of the good men in particular and heresy in general.[22]

In the end, however, perhaps the most disturbing irony about Catharism is that almost no one in the Middle Ages used the noun *Cathari* to describe the good men and good women. In eight decades of Cistercian preaching against heresy in the Toulousain, for instance, starting with Bernard of Clairvaux in 1145 and ending with Hélinand of Froidmont in 1229, the only heretics denounced were a grab-bag of 'Manichaeans', 'Arians', 'Publicani', 'Paterini', 'Albigenses', and good men.[23] The noun 'Cathar' (apparently first used in the middle of the

---

[22] B. Hamilton, 'The Cathars and Christian Perfection', in P. Biller and B. Dobson (eds.), *The Medieval Church: Universities, Heresy, and the Religious Life: Essays in Honour of Gordon Leff* (Woodbridge, 1999), 6, where he observes any 'understanding of Cathar spirituality can only be gained through a study of the Cathars' own writings'. These writings are the Occitan New Testament and 'Ritual' edited by L. Clédat in *Le Nouveau Testament traduit au XIIIᵉ siècle en langue provençale, suivi d'un rituel cathare* (Paris, 1897), 470–82; a Latin 'Ritual' edited by C. Thouzellier in *Rituel Cathare* (Paris, 1977); 'The Book of the Two Principles' edited in C. Thouzellier, *Livre des deux principes* (Paris, 1973); a 'Gloss on the Lord's Prayer' and an 'Apologia for the Church of God' found in Trinity College Dublin and edited by T. Venckeleer, 'Un Recueil cathare: le manuscrit A.6.10 de la "collection vaudoise" de Dublin: I "Une Apologie"', *Revue belge de philologie et d'histoire*, 38 (1960), 815–34, and 'Une Glose sur le Pater', *Revue belge de philologie et d'histoire*, 39 (1961), 758–93; a 'Cathar' treatise in the polemic of Durand de Huesca edited by C. Thouzellier in *Un traité cathare inédit du début du XIIIe siècle, d'après le 'Liber contra Manicheos' de Durand de Huesca* (Louvain, 1961); some passages from a lost work of the 'Cathar' Tetricius quoted by Moneta de Cremona, *Adversus Catharos et Valdenses Libri Quinque*, ed. T. Ricchini (Rome, 1743); and a lost 'Cathar' treatise *Stella* mentioned by Salvo Burci of Piacenza in his massive anti-heretical work *Liber supra stella* of 1235 that has been partially edited by I. da Milano, 'Il *Liber supra stella* del piacentino Salvo Burci contro I catari e altre correnti ereticali', *Aevum*, 19 (1945), 307–41 and now expertly edited by C. Bruschi as *Liber Suprastella* (Rome, 2002). Also, see P. D. Diehl, 'Overcoming Reluctance to Prosecute Heresy in Thirteenth-Century Italy', in S. L. Waugh and P. D. Diehl (eds.), *Christendom and its Discontents: Exclusion, Persecution, and Rebellion, 1000–1500* (Cambridge, 1996), 47–66. In favouring these few supposed 'Cathar' writings, in comparison to the thousands of inquisition testimonies, scholars demonstrate the pervasive bias towards ideas in the study of heresy because what they find are ready-made and seemingly articulate 'Cathar' discourses, doctrines, and theology. Yet, it must be obvious that these texts are incredibly problematic in that most are lost and only survive either in Catholic polemical treatises or Catholic (often Dominican) document collections. A further problem is that so many of them are Italian, although they are used to explain Languedoc. Yet, even for Italy, once the surviving inquisition registers are read then the notion of an hierarchical 'Cathar Church' crumbles. See, esp., G. Zanella, *Itinerari ereticali: Patri e catari tra Rimini e Verona* (Rome, 1986). Now, see the vigorous and thoughtful arguments of Julien Théry, 'L'Hérésie des bons hommes: comment nommer la dissidence religieuse non vaudoise ni béguine en Languedoc (XIIe–début du XIVe siècle)?', in *Heresis: hérétiques ou dissidents? Réflexions sur l'identité de l'hérésie au Moyen Âge*, 36–7 (2002), 75–117.

[23] On this preaching, see B. M. Kienzle, *Cistercians, Heresy and Crusade in Occitania, 1145–1229* (York, 2001). It should be noted that Kienzle adopts the classic historiographic narrative of Catharism as the omitted 'truth' distorted in the sermons and, because she starts with this unwarranted preconception, actually misses the remarkable vision of heresy within Cistercian

twelfth century by a group of heretics from Cologne, or so Eckbert of Schönau wrote in his *Sermones contra Catharos* of 1163[24]) is, and always has been, used with such an appalling lack of discrimination by modern scholars that, for all intents and purposes, it is an epithet of confusion rather than clarity.[25] It gets thrown about like so much Cathar-confetti, artfully adorning all sorts of individuals and groups accused of heresy in the Rhineland, England, northern France, northern Italy, Catalonia, and Languedoc, from the eleventh to the sixteenth centuries, whose connections with one another, though worth reflection, are at best problematic.[26]

This relentless renaming of almost all heretics, particularly in the twelfth and thirteenth centuries, as 'Cathars' (with the exception of the Waldensians who were always the *Valdenses*[27]) is not only the product of,

---

preaching. Now, from a somewhat different twelfth-century perspective, see D. Iogna-Prat, *Ordonner et exclure: Cluny et la société chrétienne face à l'hérésie, au judaïsme et à l'Islam, 1000–1150* (Paris, 1998) (trans. G. R. Edwards as *Order & Exclusion: Cluny and Christendom Face Heresy, Judaism, and Islam, 1000–1150* (Ithaca, NY, 2002)).

[24] Eckbert of Schönau, *Sermones contra Catharos*, PL 195, col. 31: 'Catharos, id est mundos'. Yet, it appears that Eckbert of Schönau was merely copying what the canonist Yves of Chartres (d. 1116) had copied in his *Prologue*, ed. and trans. J. Werckmeister (Paris, 1997), 95, § 31, 'his qui nominant seipsos catharos id est mundos,' from a letter of Pope Innocent I (401–17) to the bishops of Macedonia. Théry, 'L'Hérésie des bons hommes', 80, makes this important observation. See also the learned discussion of Uwe Brunn, 'Cathari, catharistae et cataphrigii, ancêtres des cathares du XIIe siècle', in *Heresis: hérétiques ou dissidents? Réflexions sur l'Identité de l'Hérésie au Moyen Âge*, 36–7 (2002), 183–200. Now, see R. I. Moore, *The Origins of European Dissent* (London, 1977), 176–82.

[25] For example, there is little justification for the use of 'Cathar' in the useful (but often overlooked) M. Suttor, '*Le Triumphus Sancti Lamberti de castro Bullonio* et le catharisme à Liège au milieu du XIIe siècle', *Le Moyen Âge*, 91 (1985), 227–64, or in W. Simons's otherwise excellent *Cities of Ladies: Beguine Communities in the Medieval Low Countries, 1200–1565* (Philadelphia, 2001), esp. 11–25.

[26] For example, M. Camille, *The Gothic Idol: Ideology and Image-Making in Medieval Art* (Cambridge, 1989), 211, glossing the *Chronicon universale anonymi Laudunensis (1154–1219)*, ed. A. Cartelleri (Leipzig, 1909), 62–3, labelled, with no evidence at all, a certain 'Nicholas, the famous painter in all of France' a Cathar simply because he was examined and burnt with a group of *infideles* in 1204. Or A. Del Col, *Dominico Scandella detto Mennocchio: i processi dell'Inquisizione (1583–1599)* (Pordenone, 1990), pp. liii–lxxvi, where the ideas of the sixteenth-century miller Mennocchio from Friuli—the same Mennocchio made famous by C. Ginzburg in *Il formaggio e i vermi: il cosmo di un mugnaio del '500* (Turin, 1976)—were clearly derived from thirteenth-century Catharism because, and this is Del Col's only evidence, they were so similar.

[27] On the Waldensians, see the remarkable collection of articles in P. Biller, *The Waldenses, 1170–1530: Between a Religious Order and a Church* (Aldershot, 2001) and his 'Through a Glass Darkly: Seeing Medieval Heresy', esp. 313–14. Now, see the excellent G. Merlo, *Valdesi e valdismi medievali*, 2 vols. (Turin, 1984–91), who argues (in contrast to Biller) that the term 'Waldensianism' (*valdismo*) should be replaced by 'Waldensianisms' (*valdismi*). On the Béguins of Languedoc see J. Given, 'The Béguins in Bernard Gui's Liber sententiarum', in *Texts and the Repression of Heresy*, 147–62, and L. Burnham, 'Les Franciscans spirituels et les Béguins du Midi', in J. Berlioz (ed.), *Le Pays cathare* (Paris, 2000), 147–63.

but the very justification for, the intellectualist approach, in that if the word is used enough times by enough scholars to describe enough heretics in enough places then, in what can only be called a self-fulfilling prophecy, a great heretical 'Cathar Church' with a systematically similar doctrine comes into being.[28] (Intriguingly, historians convinced of Catharism as an institution stretching from the Mediterranean to the North Sea accept that the medieval inquisition into heretical depravity was much more institutional than ever was the case.[29]) This remorseless relabelling also applies to *perfectus*, 'perfect', as a respectful title for a good man, and taken for granted by modern scholarship, but, once again, it is a designation rarely found in the original records of the Languedocian inquisition.[30] Similarly, the *heretici* were never called *Albigenses* in the

[28] For example, Barber, *The Cathars*, and B. Hamilton, 'The Cathars and Christian Perfection', 5–21, stress the existence of a 'Cathar Church'.

[29] B. Hamilton, for example, in his *The Medieval Inquisition* (New York, 1981), argues for the existence of a medieval Inquisition. Even H. C. Lea admitted that there was no comprehensive institutional 'Inquisition' throughout the European Middle Ages. Lea's admission is in his *A History of the Inquisition of the Middle Ages*, i. 397 ff. On Lea's thoughts about the medieval inquisition, see Edward Peters, 'Henry Charles Lea (1825–1909)', in Helen Damico and Joseph Zavadil (eds.), *Medieval Scholarship: Biographical Studies on the Formation of a Discipline* (New York, 1995), 89–100 and his *Inquisition* (New York, 1988), 287–92. Now, see Richard Kieckhefer, 'The Office of Inquisition and Medieval Heresy: The Transition from Personal to Institutional Jurisdiction', *Journal of Ecclesiastical History*, 46 (1995), 36–61: 56–7, and H. A. Kelly, 'Inquisition and the Prosecution of Heresy: Misconceptions and Abuses', *Church History*, 58 (1989), 439–51, for their warnings about not confusing the medieval inquisition with the institutional early modern Inquisition. On the fourteenth-century inquisition in Languedoc see A. Friedlander, *The Hammer of the Inquisitors: Brother Bernard Délicieux and the Struggle against the Inquisition in Fourteenth-century France* (Leiden, 2000). A fascinating variation on this problem occurs in J. H. Arnold's important *Inquisition and Power: Catharism and the Confessing Subject in Medieval Languedoc* (Philadelphia, 2001), where he argues that one can use 'Inquisition' not because it is justifiable historically but rather in the Foucaldian sense of discursive and textual operations of power beyond the individual inquisitor. This seems unwarranted to me, especially as Arnold's somewhat anachronistic notions of power and knowledge—which might be exercised in different forms but their amount, and crucially their quality, remain the same and so oddly ahistorical—also force him to believe in, or rather not to question, what amounts to a 'Cathar Church' as well. Now, see two recent doctoral dissertations about the medieval inquisition and mendicants: C. Caldwell, *Doctors of Souls: Inquisition and the Dominican Order, 1231–1331* (Notre Dame, 2002) and H. Grieco, *A Dilemma of Obedience and Authority: Franciscan Inquisitors and the Franciscan Inquisition in Provence and the Dauphine, 1235–1400* (Princeton, 2003).

[30] Pegg, *The Corruption of Angels*, 18. On the use of *perfectus* see lucid comments of P. Biller, 'Why no Food? Waldensian Followers in Bernard Gui's *Practica inquisition is* and *culpe*', in *Texts and the Repression of Heresy*, 129 n. 10. Weis, *The Yellow Cross*, 2, where the fact that Jacques Fournier's inquisition did not record this title is put down to spite on the part of the bishop-inquisitor. D. Müller, *Frauen vor der Inquisition: Lebensform, Glaubenszeugnis und Arburteilung der Deutschen und Französischen Katharerinnen* (Mainz, 1996), is a nuanced study marred by a tension (largely between footnotes and text) between using terminology like 'perfect', with all that this implies, and the evidence that does not warrant such usage. It seems that *perfectus*, as far as inquisitorial use is concerned, has only survived in the Collection Doat (e.g. Doat 26, fo. 258ʳ–259ʳ). This apparent fact, in contrast to original manuscripts surviving from the thirteenth

registers of the inquisition. Yet, in histories and encyclopedias until the beginning of the last century, 'Albigensian' was almost always the term for the good men and good women of Languedoc. It is only in the last hundred years that *Cathari*, absorbing the more regional designation of *Albigenses*, has become the term of choice amongst scholars.[31]

Crucially, rather than Cathars or Albigensians, the heretics named in the Languedocian inquisition registers surviving from the thirteenth and fourteenth centuries were the 'good men' (*boni homines, probi homines* in Latin, *bons omes, prozomes, prodomes* in Occitan) and the 'good women' (*bone femine, bone domine, bonas mulieres* in Latin, *bonas femnas, bonas domnas, bonas molhers* in Occitan). Persons who admitted to (or were accused of) believing in the heretics were known, rather straightforwardly, as 'believers' (*credentes, crezedors,* or *crezens*).[32] The good men and good women themselves, just to add one more sobriquet to the list, usually referred to each other as the 'friends of God' (*amici Dei, amicx de Dieu*). None of this is simply semantics or philological pendantry. Far from it. All men in the thirteenth-century Toulousain, for example, whether heretic or not, whether noble or peasant, were described in charters, wills, oaths, communal decisions, court appearances, in everything and anything, as 'good men'.[33] This name for a holy person, and so a heretic to the

and fourteenth centuries, should suggest that the seventeenth-century copyists employed by Jean de Doat perhaps took more transcribing liberties than is often realized. On Jean-Baptiste Colbert's commission and Doat's copying, see L. Delisle, *Le Cabinet des manuscrits de la Bibliothèque Impériale*, Histoire Générale de Paris (Paris, 1868), i. 441–2; H. Omont, 'La Collection Doat à la Bibliothèque Nationale: documents sur les recherches de Doat dans les archives du sudouest de la France de 1663 à 1670', *Bibliothèque de l'École des Chartes*, 77 (1916), 286–336; L. Kolmer, *Ad Capiendas Vulpes: die Ketzerbekämpfung in Süd-frankreich in der ersten Hälfte des 13. Jahrhunderts und die Ausbildung des Inquisitionsverfahrens* (Bonn, 1982), 12–15, and his, 'Colbert und die Entstehung der Collection Doat', *Francia*, 7 (1979), 463–89; and C. Bruschi's learned '"Magna diligentia est habenda per inquisitionern": Precautions before Reading Doat 21–26', and 'The "Register in the Register": Reflections on the Doat 32 Dossier', in *Texts and the Repression of Heresy*, 81–110, 209–20.

[31] On the meaning of *Albigenses*, see C. Thouzellier, *Hérésie et Hérétiques: Vaudois, Cathares, Patarins, Albigeois* (Rome, 1969), 223–62, and J.-L. Biget, '"Les Albigeois": remarques sur une dénomination', in M. Zerner (ed.), *Inventer l'hérésie? Discours polémiques et pouvoirs avant l'Inquisition* (Nice, 1998), 219–56.

[32] J. Duvernoy, 'L'Acception: "haereticus" (*iretge*) = "parfait cathare" en Languedoc au XIIIᵉ siècle', in W. Lourdaux and D. Verhelst (eds.), *The Concept of Heresy in the Middle Ages (11th–13th C.): Proceedings of the International Conference, Louvain May 13–16, 1973* (The Hague, 1976), 198–210.

[33] Pegg, *The Corruption of Angels*, 95. Incidently, in a variation on this lack of specificity about nomenclature, even someone as learned as Lambert, *The Cathars*, 62, mistook *bonomios sive bonosios* in Guilhem de Puylaurens, *Chronica Magistri Guillelmi de Podio Laurentii*, ed. and trans. J. Duvernoy (Paris, 1976), 32, as a reference to the '"*Bonosii*", that is Bosnians', and so the Cathars.

inquisitors, drawing upon familiar words of respect, suggests that holiness was understood to be, and embraced as, something decidedly ordinary, as something in which routinely polite words instantly transformed the tiny cosmos of a village. The same cannot quite be said for use of 'good woman' to mean a holy person, as this designation seems to be a deliberate, if not always successful, exercise at imitating commonplace masculine notions of respect and holiness. Further, and something often missed, is how many young girls under 12 were also known as 'good women' when they lived with older matrons in *domus hereticorum*; yet at no time was there ever any implication that these infants were either aware of any heretical ideas or that their holiness was necessarily for life.[34] These basic facts, if nothing else, should shake our complacency about using 'Cathar' and suggest that research into the specific communities questioned by the inquisition will reveal a very different world than the one now taken for granted.[35]

Certainly, the Dominican inquisitor (and former 'heresiarch' at Piacenza) Rainier Sacconi in his *Summa de Catharis et pauperibus de Lugduno* of 1250 did add a tiny appendix about the 'Cathars of the Toulousain church, and those of Albi and Carcassonne' towards the end of his detailed treatise about the *Cathari* of Lombardy, but there is nothing in this brief afterthought except an opinion that the *langue d'oc* heretics were obviously connected to the *langue de si* dualists.[36] Only five years earlier, however, in the largest inquisition of the Middle Ages, by two other Dominican inquisitors, Bernart de Caux and Joan de Sant-Peire, where almost 6,000 men and women from the Toulousain and the Lauragais were questioned in 201 days, not only was 'Cathar' never uttered or an elaborate dualist theology ever expounded, but no international heretical organization, no 'Cathar Church', was discovered by them. Nor will such an entity be unearthed by modern scholars— unless, of course, hundreds of references to *heretici* and *boni homines* are

[34] Pegg, *The Corruption of Angels*, 95, 100–1 for a rare example of two small boys as holy *bons omes*, and 119–20. Hamilton, 'The Cathars and Christian Perfection', 12, incorrectly states that '[m]embership of the Cathar Church was confined to adults'.

[35] Cf. Biller, 'Through a Glass Darkly: Seeing Medieval Heresy', esp. 312–17.

[36] Rainier Sacconi, *Summa de Catharis et pauperibus de Lugduno*, is in the preface of Antoine Dondaine's edition of *Un traité néo-manichéen du XIIIe siècle: Le* Liber de duobus principiis *suivi d'un fragment de rituel cathare* (Rome, 1939), 77. Now, see Christine Thouzellier, *Catharisme et Valdéisme en Languedoc à la fin du XIIe et au début du XIIIe siècle* (Paris, 1966), 19–26, and the more general discussion of Italian heresy (and one which assumes a strong, and obvious, connection to the heretics of Languedoc) in C. Lansing, *Power and Purity: Cathar Heresy in Medieval Italy* (New York, 1998), esp. 4–5, 15–16, 37–9, 188–90.

persistently, and rather unashamedly, translated as referring to 'Cathars' and 'perfects'.[37]

If the scholarship on medieval heresy is to revitalize the sterile and suffocating methods and narrative that it has trapped itself within, a story forever searching for doctrinal origins and ideal articulations, then it must take seriously (rather than just give lip service to) the worlds in which the heretics (and those accused of heresy) actually dwelt and not make doubtful deductions, founded upon idealist predilections, about outside causes, about timeless verities.[38] Such equations, though clean and neat, presuppose a deeply unconvincing passivity on the part of medieval men and women, heretical or not. Ideas and habits do not hibernate, lie dormant, or remain buried in eternal folkways. The mistake is to assume that the good men, good women, and their believers, necessarily went through life with strict dualist structures shaping their minds, determining their actions, to the exclusion of all else. (It is quite easy to argue that there is nothing outside the text when the nothingness framing all discourses is assumed to be unchanging, innate, and essential to the human condition.) Individuals and their societies possess no inherent tendencies, no fundamental hot-wiring, towards any particular theories, towards any particular actions.[39] Dissenting ideas, as far as they were

---

[37] Pegg, *The Corruption of Angels*, esp. 130. The original parchment leaves of Bernart de Caux and Joan de Sant-Piere's inquisition are lost. Two other Dominican inquisitors, Guilhem Bernart de Dax and Renaud de Chartres, had the Lauragais testimonies copied onto paper sometime after October 1258, though no later than August 1263. This copy of 260 folios has been in the Bibliothèque municipal of Toulouse since 1790 and is now catalogued as MS 609. A startling fact about MS 609, and one that can never be forgotten, is that it is only two books, five and four, arranged in that order, out of an estimated ten that Bernart de Caux and Joan de Sant-Piere originally compiled.

[38] For example, such recent revitalizations in the study of the good men and good women can be seen in Arnold, *Inquisition and Power*, P. Biller, 'Medicine and Heresy', in J. Ziegler and P. Biller (eds.), *Religion and Medicine in the Middle Ages*, York Studies in Medieval Theology, 3 (Woodbridge, 2001), 155–175; Biller, 'Cathar Peacemaking', in S. Ditchfield (ed.), *Christianity and Community in the West: Essays for John Bossy* (Aldershot, 2001), 1–13; C. Bruschi's forthcoming *Tales of Travelling Cathars*; Given, *Inquisition and Medieval Society*; and Pegg, *The Corruption of Angels*; and Théry, 'L'Hérésie des bonshommes'. The collected essays in Zerner (ed.), *Inventer l'hérésie? Discours polémiques et pouvoirs avant l'Inquisition* and *Texts and the Repression of Heresy* all suggest new directions in the study of heresy. S. Lipton's brilliant *Images of Intolerance: The Representation of Jews and Judaism in the Bible moralisée* (Berkeley, 1999) eloquently and powerfully suggests the necessity of understanding the converging relationship between heretics and Jews in the twelfth and thirteenth centuries. Cf. N. Berend who artificially (and rather anachronistically) separates heretics from Jews, Muslims, and 'pagans' in her otherwise exceptional *At the Gate of Christendom: Jews, Muslims and 'Pagans' in Medieval Hungary, c.1000–c.1300* (Cambridge, 2001), 58–9.

[39] For example, D. Maybury-Lewis, 'Introduction: The Quest for Harmony', and U. Almagor, 'Introduction: Dual Organization Reconsidered', in D. Maybury-Lewis and U. Almagor (eds.), *The Attraction of Opposites: Thought and Society in the Dualist Mode* (Ann Arbor,

understood, and the beliefs of priests or mendicants, as far as these were understood, frequently lived together, sometimes rudely, sometimes amicably, in the thoughts of medieval persons. It is this seeming paradox which makes the thinking of so many ordinary people in the Middle Ages appear, at least to modern eyes, as often shallow, equivocal, and incoherent.

To all these ahistorical assumptions can be added the equally questionable notion of a modern person adopting an emotional and moral stance towards medieval heresy, that is, acknowledging a sense of mourning about past persecutions or, somehow or other, establishing an affective touch through time, as though reflection upon one's own sensitivity to the marginal, as though openly confessing to having emotions about people being hurt 700 years ago is, in and of itself, an analytic category. Such sentiments, mistaking not only the experience of marginality as being similar through time but also that emotions possess an unchanging quality, tell us an awful lot about an individual scholar but next to nothing about the Middle Ages.[40] Any meditation upon the past that starts

1989), 1–18, 19–32, where each one argues (under the influence of Claude Levi-Strauss) that dualism is inherent in the human perception of the world; and P. Boyer, *The Naturalness of Religious Ideas: A Cognitive Theory of Religion* (Berkeley, Calif., 1994), where religion is natural and innate to human thought. Now, see the interesting philosophical critique of innateness in F. Cowie, *What's Within: Nativism Reconsidered* (Oxford, 1999).

[40] This self-referential creation of an affective connection to the past (sometimes bordering on the sanctimonious), where emotion functions as a rhetorical strategy and analytic category, ultimately discredits, for example, K. Biddick's 'The Devil's Anal Eye: Inquisitorial Optics and Ethnographic Authority', in her *The Shock of Medievalism* (Durham, NC, 1998), 105–34, and C. Dinshaw, *Getting Medieval: Sexualities and Communities, Pre- and Postmodern* (Durham, NC, 1999). Biddick and Dinshaw draw inspiration from Michel Foucault, post-colonial studies (especially the scholars associated with the journal and collective *Subaltern Studies*), and queer studies. Biddick and Dinshaw fail to take seriously Foucault's own doubts about how applicable his intensely subjective philosophy was to understanding the Middle Ages; similarly, each of them uses the subaltern analogy so ahistorically that both post-colonial studies and medieval studies are drained of any historical and historiographic context. On these points see esp. G. M. Spiegel, 'Épater les Médiévistes: Review Essay of Kathleen Biddick, *The Shock of Medievalism*', *History and Theory*, 39 (2000), 243–50, and B. W. Holsinger, 'Medieval Studies, Postcolonial Studies, and the Genealogies of Critique', *Speculum*, 77 (2002), 1195–227. Likewise, the use of Foucault, post-coloniality, and subalternity in Arnold, *Inquisition and Power*, has led authorial self-reflexiveness to be used as a method of research into heresy; paradoxically, this modern subjectivity, where Arnold uses himself as a scholar as an analytic category, frequently limits avenues of research because an emotional stance towards the past is confused as being the same as an insight into it. Now, on Foucault and the intense subjectivity of his philosophy, see the brilliant A. Nehamas, *The Art of Living: Socratic Reflections from Plato to Foucault* (Berkeley, Calif., 2000), esp. 157–88; on emotions, although from a deeply ahistorical perspective, M. C. Nussbaum, *Upheavals of Thought: The Intelligence of Emotions* (Cambridge, 2001); and, in general, S. B. Ortner, 'Resistance and the Problem of Ethnographic Refusal', *Comparative Studies in History and Society*, 37 (1995), 173–93, for an insightful discussion on how frequently inherent (and far from theoretical) assumptions often underwrite self-consciously theoretical scholarship

with the assumption that some things simply are universal in humans or are always just there in human society, never changing, inert, immobile, is a retreat from attempting a historical explanation about previous rhythms of existence.

All of this means turning aside from the bias towards ideas and recognizing that communities actively survive, from one day to the next, from one decade to another, because of an interweaving of thoughts and actions, so individually intimate, so communally strengthening, that the relations a person (or thing) maintains in the material realm entrenches the relations he or she (or it) maintains in the metaphoric, and vice versa. It is only in trying to grasp this deep intimacy through the evocation of a world, at once particular and yet general, at once marginal and yet integrated, and certainly easier said than done, that the experience of heresy in the Middle Ages will be understood as more than just an idealist exercise in imagining the past. What is being argued here is not that metaphors, language, texts, and suchlike merely mirror social structures, habits, and so forth, because this would be no more than a scholar simply noting what he or she finds similar between one set of (usually lively) discourses, ideas, symbols, and one set of (often dull and unchanging) practices, behaviours, routines.[41] Scholars must resist the allure of the intellectualist hall of mirrors, that reflective labyrinth of homologies in which a handful of ideas perpetually gazing at each other, unable to escape the superficial glitter of similarity, do no more than give the illusion of temporal and cultural depth. This is a vicious historiographic circle that, if not broken, will keep circulating within itself.

The scholarship on the good men and good women rests upon almost two centuries of extraordinary learning in a way that has been, and still is, rarely equalled in the historical study of the Middle Ages. Nevertheless, in making these heretics such coherent and concrete figures, in classifying certain individuals and their thoughts as similar to each other, in joining

inspired by Foucault, post-colonialism, and feminism. Now, see the observations on alterity, postmodernism, and medievalism in P. Freedman and G. M. Spiegel, 'Medievalisms Old and New: The Rediscovery of Alterity in North American Medieval Studies', *American Historical Review*, 103 (1998), 677–704, and C. Bynum, 'Miracle and Marvels: The Limits of Alterity', in F. J. Felten and N. Jaspert (eds.), *Vita religiosa im Mittelalter: Festschrift für Kaspar Elm* (Berlin, 1999), 799–818.

[41] Despite my agreement with much of what G. M. Spiegel has to say in her influential 'History, Historicism, and the Social Logic of the Text in the Middle Ages', in *The Past as Text: The Theory and Practice of Medieval Historiography* (Baltimore, 1997), 3–28, the final argument still rests upon a flawed notion of similarity in which texts mirror society and language mirrors social locations.

dissenting dots until we get a pervasive heretical 'Cathar Church', we lose the specificity of what heresy meant at particular times and places, so that even if there were no Cathars, no widespread organized *ordo* of dissent, then something intrinsic to the Middle Ages must have produced them, no matter the evidence to the contrary. Notions of alterity or marginality have actually caused us to mistakely narrow our avenues of research into heterodoxy, to end where we should begin our interpretations of dissent in the Middle Ages. It is not simply at marginal ideas or doctrines that we should look in comprehending heretics like the good men and good women but in the familiar, distinctly mundane, not always articulate, rhythms of medieval existence.

Washington University in St Louis

Analytical Survey 6: Medieval Literature and Cultures of Performance

Bruce W. Holsinger

If 'performance's only life is in the present'; if 'performance cannot be saved, recorded, documented, or otherwise participate in the circulation of representations *of* representations', because 'once it does so, it becomes something other than performance'; if, 'to the degree that performance attempts to enter the economy of reproduction', it 'betrays and lessens the promise of its own ontology'; if the 'document of a performance . . . is only a spur to memory, an encouragement of memory to become present': then, it seems, medievalists who claim to be making contributions to the long history of performance are deluding themselves. For by this logic performance has no history, its putative historiography nothing more than an exercise in sophistry—and I mean 'sophistry' here in one of its narrower denotations, the spectral economy in which rhetorical gamesmanship stands in for *materia*, in this case that of embodied, present-to-the-viewer performance.[1] By this logic, too, every artefact attesting to particular premodern performances—the text of the Greater Passion Play in the Benediktbeuern manuscript, heighted neumes in late Carolingian chant books, copies of Lydgate's mummings—possesses an inescapable belatedness, a twice- or thrice-removedness that is inherent to the form in which it survives.

The scare-quoted claims above come from Peggy Phelan's *Unmarked: The Politics of Performance*, a crystallizing text in the emergence and recognition of performance theory during the early 1990s. A brilliant and far-reaching book, *Unmarked* has nevertheless achieved much of its authority in this interdisciplinary subfield by virtue of its unwavering

I would like to thank the editors of *New Medieval Literatures* for commissioning this survey as well as a number of scholars (acknowledged in the footnotes) for sharing unpublished work in progress with me as I wrote it.

[1] On this sense of 'sophistry', see Copeland 2002.

insistence on generating a 'politics of performance' from the author's experience as a critical observer of art, photography, drama, and film produced, screened, and exhibited over a span of just twelve years (and mostly on a single island). Nearly all of Phelan's theoretical work in *Unmarked*, in other words, springs from her first-hand engagement with modalities of performance staged in urban spaces in her own historical moment.[2] I am uninterested here in taking Phelan to task for a metropolitan parochialism and a narrow synchronism that in fact constitute two of the book's great analytical strengths. What interests me, rather, is the way in which *Unmarked* exemplifies in a particularly direct way the authorizing power of the present in the institutionalized study of performance, whether the performative events in question took place in ancient Athens or two years ago in an adjacent urban borough. The explanatory prestige of the contemporary obtains in the most forward-looking as well as in the most recherché corners of performance studies: if Joseph Roach's *Cities of the Dead* can tease out 'the three-sided relationship of memory, performance, and substitution' (1996: 2) through a series of performative genealogies traced from the writings of the nineteenth-century past to the personally witnessed 'orature' of the present, John Miles Foley's *Traditional Oral Epic: The Odyssey, Beowulf, and the Serbo-Croatian Return Song* (1990) invokes the comparative interpretive authority of Parry and Lord's live recordings of the Balkan *epske pjesme* for the light they shed on an ancient epic tradition because these recordings 'contain no ambiguous elements possibly traceable to written composition and can confidently be classed as oral traditional texts in the truest sense of that rubric' (1990: 3). Even if its personnel have been dead for centuries and its scholarly scrutiny is undertaken by (for example) classicists or early modernists, it often seems that performance can come alive for academic recuperation only through the bodies and voices of the living. This may be explained in

---

[2] The performance objects providing Phelan's analytical focus include a selection of photographs from 1979 to 1989 by Robert Mapplethorpe, Mira Schor, and Cindy Sherman; *The Man Who Envied Women*, a 1985 film by Yvonne Rainer (dubbed 'the Purple Rose of Soho' by a critic in the *Village Voice*) concerned in part with 'the city of Manhattan's proposal to allocate housing funds to artists moving into the Lower East Side' (80); Jennie Livingston's *Paris is Burning* (1991), shot mostly in Harlem's Imperial Elks Lodge between 1987 and 1989; Tom Stoppard's *Hapgood*, premièred on the London stage in 1988; and the tactics of the anti-abortion activist organization Operation Rescue in the years immediately preceding the book's publication. The specific political context of this focus is not lost on Phelan, though its implications remain undertheorized: 'Under the ever-growing shadow of the politically powerful New Right in the United States, I am writing against the perpetual fracturing of disciplines, specializations, and identities progressive political and critical theory has wrought. These fractures make us easy targets for a relatively unified Right' (1993: 27).

part by a common narrative of disciplinary and institutional provenance claimed by performance theory, whose practitioners most often name cultural anthropology and theatre studies (embodied respectively by Victor Turner and Richard Schechner, two of the field's prime movers) as the field's intellectual wellsprings (see e.g. Schechner 1998). While I would not necessarily characterize the unexamined coevalism underlying performance studies as nostalgic (though more often than not it surely is), I do find it curious how the field's rhetoric of inquiry likes to locate its specialists geographically and temporally at the original site of performance: an East Village basement, a New Orleans parade route, a mountain village in Kosovo. As Roach puts it in the most straightforward articulation of this stance I have read, 'The pursuit of performance does not require historians to abandon the archive, but it does encourage them to spend more time in the streets' (1996: xii).

Yet this rhetoric of the contemporaneous has a greater and more disturbing complexity than these observations might suggest. For in the work I have discussed above, the unacknowledged subject of Phelan's 'politics of performance'—the subject that grounds this politics and makes it legible—is, I would propose, history, and history writ quite large. Performance may indeed be lost to us by its pastness, but that 'pastness' is exactly what performance theory so often jettisons from its authorizing strategies. 'Performance occurs over a time which will not be repeated', Phelan (1993) observes, failing to add that the same could be said of reading, eating, sleeping—and, most precisely, history. The 'history of performance' thus becomes a double-edged sword that swipes and cuts with the ironic impossibility of its inscription. Perhaps, then, the modern discipline of history and the contemporary *antidiscipline* of performance theory have much more in common than we might expect. In their purely ontological (*not* epistemological—this is not a claim for relativism) relation to the human lives and actions they seek to body forth, the study of history and the study of performance approach their respective archives with a healthy respect for spectrality for which the historian will try to compensate but which the performance theorist will proffer as her *raison d'être*. In the end, though, as the emergence since the 1970s of self-critical languages in the discipline of history would seem to promise, performance makes claims upon the practice and ethics of historical understanding that may be too strong to elude; conversely, as I have suggested here, the trace of history will always corrode the coevalist allegations rooted in performance. To put it another way before moving on: the Scylla and Charybdis of history and performance coexist metonymically—or better, perhaps, synechdocally and symbiotically. Performance casts in miniature the dilemma of ultimate irrecuperability endemic to historical inquiry, a relation that also foregrounds the strange (indeed etymological) relations between the problematics of theatricality and the theoretical enterprise itself (Puchner 2002).

Performance, finally, is less a knowable phenomenon than a 'way of knowing' in itself (Schechner 1998: 360), a disposition that I hope will guide the following overview of just a few of the many provocations that medievalists in a variety of disciplines have made to the theory and history of performance over the last twenty years. Like the previous analytical surveys published in this journal, these observations will be partial, biased, and inevitably selective, not only because of the capaciousness of the historical phenomenon I will be addressing (premodern cultures of performance), but also because the term performance has in recent years undergone a striking mutation into one of those voracious master categories (much like 'queer' a decade ago) that promises to subsume practically every sphere of human action into its compass; as Schechner himself has recently asked, 'Is there anything outside the purview of performance studies?' (1998: 361). That the probable answer is no can best be appreciated on the terms defined by Andrew Parker and Eve Sedgwick, who identify the expansive grey area separating the performative from performance, or, in their words, the 'oblique intersection between performativity and the loose cluster of theatrical practices, relations, and traditions known as performance' (1995: 3). While this survey will not attempt to do a responsible job covering the proliferation of medievalist scholarship influenced by theories of speech-act performativity, this dimension of performance's life in the Middle Ages will be one of its inevitable and historically unavoidable components. When Victor Turner traced the etymology of performance to the Old French *parfournir*, a verb that connotes a furnishing forth, a completion, or the thorough accomplishment of a task—various forms of *doing*, in other words—he revealed the sense in which the Middle Ages has a rigorously archaeological role to play in defining the terms on which the performance-performativity relation might continue to be examined.[3] Indeed, as James Paxson observes, 'Much contemporary work on medieval grammatical or scholastic cultures continues to assert, ever more strongly, that the semiotic and ideological constitutions of that culture, although textual in documentary

---

[3] Turner 1982: 13; cited in Roach 1996: 3.

form, cohere as performative realities': the 'historionic' and the 'ideologically constitutive' dimensions of medieval performance merge to such an extent that 'the literal performance or performative of the medieval stage becomes as constitutive as the figural performance of the *grammatica*'.[4] The history of medieval preaching, too, was intimately bound up with what Claire Waters has identified as a deep-seated anxiety over the proper relationship between embodied preaching in the world and the citational authority of clerical discourse, a performative conundrum with more than incidental bearing on the genealogy and self-presentation of modern speech-act theory: 'The points of contact between these modern *auctoritates* [of speech-act theory]—the points where Butler draws on Derrida, which in turn mark Derrida's productive disagreements with Austin— are, strikingly, also matters crucial to the medieval debate: the "iterability" or "citationality" of speech, the concept of ordinary versus extraordinary speech-acts, and the problems posed, for both Austin and the preaching theorists, by the "peculiarly hollow and void" speech of acting.' It was just this simultaneous distance and intimacy between the performed and the performative—a simultaneity that will be axiomatic in the observations to follow—that gave rise to the ubiquitous concerns 'over the ownership and origination of speech that plagued medieval theorists as they tried to work through the simultaneous presence and absence of Christ that made the preacher's authority so complicated'.[5]

A few final words of caution: although my own home discipline is English literature, much of what follows derives from my investments and interests in the fields of musicology and liturgical studies, primarily of Christian northern Europe. As a result, given this survey's stated topic, I spend much less time here than most readers might expect (or desire) on drama, and the coverage heavily favours scholarship on English, French, and Latin traditions. It goes without saying that every work listed in the bibliography that follows this survey could be replaced by another, and that any new combination would produce an entirely different narrative of medieval literature in its relation to premodern cultures of performance. The particular combination here arises in part from my sense that literary medievalists tend not to read around much in areas such as musicology and liturgy, which have significantly greater bearing on the

---

[4] Paxson, introduction to Paxson et al. 1998: 2–3.
[5] The citation comes from chapter 1 ('The Golden Chains of Citation') of Waters's forthcoming book from the University of Pennsylvania Press, *Angels and Earthly Creatures: Preaching, Performance, and Gender in the Later Middle Ages* (citation from typescript chapter 1, p. 4).

notions of performance, performativity, and even literature obtaining in our field than we have generally allowed.

I. Oral/Aural: The Text in Action

Easily the most daunting bibliography on the topic of medieval literature and/as performance has emerged from the study of oral cultures and the nature of oral performance. If the oral-formulaic theories of Parry and Lord predominant in the middle of the last century survive largely in their continued rejection, one of the legacies of their work has been an insistence on the historical particularity of discrete cultures of performance and a corresponding methodological flexibility vis-à-vis the categories employed to study them.[6] It is hard to find a general pronouncement on orality and literacy written in the last few decades that does not include a call for a more malleable interpretive approach to these categories, though it is striking how oral-formulaicism and oral-traditionalism remain forceful reminders of the field's origins in an energizing spirit of comparativism. When A. N. Doane identified oral-formulaic studies as 'one of the first bastions of structuralism and . . . one of the last' (Doane and Pasternak 1991: xii), the target was of course the seeming rigidity and even essentialism of its approach to the formal character of the literary artefact. Yet if we reconsider this intellectual genealogy in more capaciously historical terms, we might recognize that in decades past the structuralist impulse in medieval literary studies was less a 'bastion' than (to stick with Doane's military metaphor for a moment) a guerrilla campaign, part of a climate in which an Anglo-Saxonist such as Antoine Culioli, for example, could become a leading figure in the avant-garde revision of linguistics in Parisian academic circles during the 1960s.[7] It might be helpful to conceive of oral-formulaic studies and performance theory as two ends of a methodological continuum—one that also embraces cultural anthropology, ethnomusicology, certain areas within sociology, and many other disciplinary sub-fields—that has largely defined the cultural study of

---

[6] Those medievalists whose work touches on the field of orality-literacy studies will find immensely useful John Miles Foley's on-line annotated bibliography of oral-formulaic scholarship at www.missouri.edu/~csottime/biblio.html, which includes the contents of Foley's printed 1996 bibliography as well as updates originally published in subsequent volumes of *Oral Tradition*.

[7] See Dosse's comments in Dosse 1997: i. 194–5 and 220–1.

performance phenomena in the humanities and social sciences over the last half-century.

For medievalists, one of the most significant points along this continuum has been the theory of 'oral poeticity' generated by Paul Zumthor, which sought its phenomenological basis in the materiality of the voice and the inherence of vocality in the social. It is telling that Zumthor opened his 1983 *Introduction à la poésie orale* (translated as *Oral Poetry: An Introduction*, 1990) with a ground-clearing dismissal of the raw empiricism he perceived in the (much-criticized) work of Ruth Finnegan, who—despite, again, a call for a new flexibility in working definitions of orality—'refuses to theorize', in his view, beyond the 'diverse external classifications' that determine her groupings of oral performance phenomena. If Finnegan put 'the final strokes to a half century of [Anglo-American and Germanic] research into the world of oral poetic traditions', Zumthor contends, we still lack a 'general poetics of orality . . . applicable to the phenomenon of the transmission of poetry by voice and memory, to the exclusion of all other media' (1990: 3). Zumthor's *praeambulum fidei* was the rootedness of voice in body and community as the wellsprings of desire: 'Listening as much as vocalizing overflows speech. These are the primary functions of the libidinal body . . . through which metonymy and metaphor move toward each other. Writing, if by chance it intervenes, neutralizes these ambiguities'; more poignantly, Zumthor suggests, 'The desire for live voice dwells in all poetry, but it is in exile in writing' (1990: 127). Along with John Miles Foley and a number of other medievalists (particularly Anglo-Saxonists) whose work has been central to the critical recovery and study of orality, Zumthor has led a quest (often acknowledged as quixotic even by those who have joined it) to understand what Foley calls 'the unique phenomenology of a text that nonetheless has clear (and nourishing) oral roots' (Foley 1991: 35).[8]

Yet phenomenology can account for only a portion of the intellectual foundations of orality-literacy scholarship. I think the field owes a more profound philosophical debt to Platonism. Only in certain (largely editorial) quarters of early music studies would a comment such as the following be considered an acceptable stance toward the authority of historical performance: 'particular styles of performance could be quite perilous if used in turn to support claims about medieval contexts of performance,

---

[8] For a refreshingly sceptical overview of scholarly investments in the 'lost' oral text (through the lens of *Roland* scholarship), see Taylor 2001: esp. 60–5.

or if given the same weight as the musical identity that a piece of music keeps through extremely different performances . . . for all our work on musical texts and techniques, on performance practice and social context, we merely make music in performance with the raw materials of the notated substance'.[9] Here 'performance' becomes denigration, a particularization of the 'substance' of the (in this case musical) work whose 'identity' exists before or beyond its fall into the vagaries of human community and interaction. For most scholars in orality-performance studies, by contrast, knowledge of these 'extremely different performances' would be a Holy Grail, a desire signalled surprisingly often by the Neoplatonic metaphors that suffuse theoretical reflection in this field. No wonder, then, that one of Father Ong's favourite images was the *integumentum*: writing and print are 'integuments of voice', a 1977 essay on mimesis and irony argued, the veil that must be lifted before the vocal body of performance can be truthfully and honestly viewed (Ong, 'From Mimesis to Irony'). Elsewhere Ong enlists the Platonic language of imitation, diminishment, and separation to capture the deleterious effects of writing on oral Idea: 'Although we take writing so much for granted as to forget that it is a technology, writing is in a way the most drastic of the three technologies of the word. It initiated what printing and electronics only continued, the physical reduction of dynamic sound to quiescent space, the separation of the word from the living present, where alone real, spoken words exist.'[10] The denigration of writing here and elsewhere in orality studies (are scripted words not 'real'?) would seem ripe for grammatological critique had Ong not anticipated such objections decades ago (the appeal of Derrida et al., Ong avows, comes from their 'unreflective, uncritical literacy' (1982: 169) and an unthinking privileging of writing). If I seem to be singling out Ong, I would also make the point that Ong, at least, has been philosophically straightforward about his vision of performance in ways that others in this field and in performance studies more generally have not (and in fact I wouldn't be surprised to learn that Ong's decades-long flirtation with a kind of Christian Neoplatonism has been deliberate and fully conscious).[11] The presentism that guides Phelan throughout *Unmarked*, for example, is an idealism of the

---

[9] Bent 1993: 630–1. I have discussed the language of Platonism as it informs the early music movement at greater length in Holsinger 2001: 347–51.

[10] Ong 1992: iv. 150.

[11] See the essay in Ong 1992, vol. i, 'Orality-Literacy Studies and the Unity of the Human Race': 'although orality-literacy studies are not redemptive, nevertheless such studies can open new depths in our understanding of the work of redemption as known to Christian faith' (218).

first order, one in which the 'economy of reproduction'—diminution from the Idea, in other words—renders performance into 'something other than performance', a formulation that exposes the logical paradox at the centre of so much critical-theoretical work on performance: for if others than its original witnesses cannot perceive or comprehend performance outside its pale imitation, how can we be at all confident in the defeat of its ontology?

A less idealist strain of scholarship has adopted approaches to medieval orality rooted more inductively in the artefacts of material culture, in the histories of diverse textual cultures that maintained varying and often highly idiosyncratic relationships to orality and performance. In *Visible Song*, an investigation of 'transitional literacy' in Old English poetry, Katherine O'Brien O'Keeffe traced the dynamic between the aural and the visual reception of early English verse; while indebted to Ong's notions of textual spatialization and 'oral consciousness', O'Keeffe maintains a high degree of scepticism about the fixity of such categories, developing a from-the-ground-up approach based in the differing proclivities of local reading communities. The ' "literate" reception of Old English verse retained a substantial element of oral processes' (1990: 46), she suggests, an element registered very clearly in the manuscript traditions of such lyrics as Cædmon's *Hymn*. O'Keeffe's refusal to romanticize orality and oral performance was adumbrated in M. T. Clanchy's influential *From Memory to Written Record*; while supporting his more general account of the wide-scale transition in England from the authority of oral testimony to the normalization of 'literate ways of thinking and of doing business', the eighth chapter alone can be read as a mini-history of political and documentary performance in medieval England. From the performative language and milieux of twelfth-century charters (which often begin with the formulaic address to 'all who shall hear and see this charter') to bilingual recitations of royal and papal letters before audiences in Westminster and the 'auditing' of monetary accounts in Benedictine abbeys, Clanchy describes a culture in which 'the reader [remained] a specialist in the spoken word' even while documentary modes were achieving unmatched heights of prestige and viability.[12]

Evelyn Birge Vitz, in a chapter on the 'orality of the octosyllabic couplet' in French romance, postulates a 'medieval performance "spectrum" or continuum' (1999: 164), one that embraced simultaneously a number of performative modalities in the twelfth and thirteenth cen-

---

[12] Clanchy 1993: 1 and 293; for later developments in legal orality see Green 1999.

turies, including the so-called aurality of the medieval literary text: the reception of (mostly) poetry among late medieval (and thus ostensibly 'literate') reading communities accustomed to hearing read more than reading the French and English romance tradition and the works of such writers as Machaut and Chaucer. The nature and variety of these public reading performances receive rigorous treatment in Joyce Coleman's *Public Reading and the Reading Public in Late Medieval England and France*, a remarkably provocative investigation of 'the medieval sense of literature's embeddedness within . . . a community of hearers' (1996: 178). The situatedness of the literary text, Coleman shows, is never simply (or even, perhaps, primarily) codicological at base, for its diffusion depended on the unique pleasures and interpretive possibilities afforded by collective aural reception: '[M]edieval readers chose to share their experience of literature because they valued shared experience. For them, a book read aloud came alive not only with the performer's voice but with the listeners' reactions and responses, with their concentration, their tears and applause, their philosophical or political debates, and their demands that the page be turned' (1996: 221). Nor should public reading, as previous scholarship often assumed, necessarily be imputed to such canards (in Coleman's view) as transitional literacies, the survival instincts of the minstrel class, or supposed 'deficiencies' resulting from widespread illiteracy and lack of books (1996: 80–1). Though our manuscript-obsessed field has not yet accorded Coleman's book the influence it merits, the author has done a real service to the study of medieval literature by providing an ethnography of performative reading that powerfully revises many received views of the social character of premodern literary cultures.[13]

It should be mentioned here, though, that Coleman's laudable resistance to what she sees as hard-and-fast divides in the study of orality and literacy often forces her to disregard subtleties in previous scholarship that might have helped her build an even more convincing case for the significance of aurality-as-performance in the late Middle Ages. This tendency is especially apparent in her dismissal of Brian Stock, who, she alleges, perpetrates 'the fallacy of equating the presence of books with the

---

[13] Compare the view of Taylor: 'Just as the very possibility of extended oral poems of quality is difficult to comprehend within a literate culture, whose images of aesthetic achievement are deeply grounded in the fixity of writing, so is the fragmentation of minstrel performance. If it was only rarely that listeners could hear a complete version of a poem, and then only when it was supported by the authority of a book, how could the story become a common point of reference for predominantly illiterate societies?' (2001: 64) While Taylor is writing primarily about the twelfth and thirteenth centuries, this view perfectly illustrates Coleman's point about literacy-based assumptions and their misrecognition of aurality.

extinction of "orality"' (1996: 22). Yet in *The Implications of Literacy*, Stock had insisted emphatically on the extreme malleability of 'oral' and 'written', suggesting that performance may in fact play a mediating role in negotiating the boundaries of and between these categories. 'Written texts are continually being re-performed, offering continuities to human behaviour over time' (1983: 13), Stock suggested. Indeed, the very notion of 'textual communities', in his enormously influential phrase, virtually defined itself in terms of what Coleman would call aurality: in Stock's words, 'the textual community was not only textual; it also involved new uses for orality. The text itself, whether it consisted of a few maxims or an elaborate programme, was often re-performed orally' (1983: 91). Stock's textual communities not only make room for the liminal character of 'a literate's orality' (1983: 91), in other words, but presuppose an avowedly *non-residual* oral element at their very core.[14]

II. Performance and the Book

This recognition of the oral, performative impulses subtending even the most institutionally privileged modes of literacy may go a long way toward explaining such strange phenomena as the medieval neuming of the Latin classics. It will probably come as a surprise to most readers that passages from Horace, Virgil, Lucan, Juvenal, and a number of other Roman poets surviving in dozens of manuscripts are accompanied by musical notation (both unheighted and diastematic), a practice that seems to have peaked from the ninth to the twelfth centuries. As Jan Ziolkowski argues in several recent essays as well as a forthcoming monograph that will become the standard work on this subject, the neuming of the classics served manifold purposes in various contexts of reception: as a mnemonic technique, as a mode of rhetorical embellishment (an aural equivalent of decoration or excessive rubrication, perhaps), as a heuristic device for rehearsing the metrical and syntactical forms of Latin prosody, as a means of heightening the drama of pivotal moments in a narrative or the pathos of particular passages of direct speech (for example several of Dido's

---

[14] Much of this misrepresentation arises from Coleman's reliance on Gabrielle Spiegel's review of Stock's more recent collected essays, *Listening for the Text: On the Uses of the Past* (in *Speculum*, 66 (1991), 480–2), in which Spiegel makes a more generous and subtle point about Stock's reliance on past models of orality-literacy in an earlier decade when they were still prevalent. A useful work for comparison that relies very much on notions of residual and 'secondary' oralities is Gellrich 1995.

speeches in the fourth book of the *Aeneid*, some of the most frequently neumed passages in these manuscripts), and perhaps even as an implicit recognition of the performative power of women's laments in the vernacular. That the classics were neumed in highly lettered and elite clerical subcultures—subcultures possessing all the accoutrements that Ong originally imputed solely to literacy—suggests the ubiquity of aurality in myriad performance genres throughout the Middle Ages.

It also points to what medievalists have recognized in varying ways as the performativity of the book itself, the various modes of excitation that the codex enjoined, inspired, and reconstituted for individual readers and diverse reading communities. The signal study here remains Sylvia Huot's *From Song to Book* (1987), which defined a domain of codicological inquiry aimed at taking seriously the physical layouts, scribal idiosyncrasies, and decorative conventions of medieval books as integral to the social and aesthetic performance of their texts among various readerships and audiences. The medieval illuminated manuscript, Huot observed, 'has a certain theatrical—at the risk of anachronism, one might even say cinematic—quality; it does not merely describe events but, rather, stages them' (1987: 3). The same could be said of many (if not most) unilluminated manuscripts, of course, which create what Zumthor famously identified as the fundamental *mouvance* shaping any book's social performance in eras before print (Zumthor 1972). For John Dagenais, the manuscript tradition of Juan Ruiz's *Libro de buen amor* exemplifies the ways in which medieval material texts functioned as 'acts of demonstrative rhetoric that reached out and grabbed the reader, involved him or her in praise and blame, in judgments about effective and ineffective human behavior' (1994: xvii; see also Amsler 2001). Olivia Holmes applies Huot's methods to the corpus of Italian lyric from Guittone d'Arezzo to Dante, suggesting that the anthologizing of author-ordered, first-person lyric cycles in the thirteenth and fourteenth centuries distinguishes them from contemporaneous French and Occitan collections, which tended to reflect the greater cultural capital of orality and performance in these more northern traditions. Italian vernacular poetics was 'born under the sign of Latinity, and of writing', Holmes avows; 'there is little evidence of its oral transmission or musical performance' in its earliest incarnations (2000: 47).

This bookish facet of medieval performance studies has received particularly rigorous treatment at the hands of musicologists concerned with the history of musical notation and its phenomenological implications for those books that were 'performed' in the most doggedly literal historical sense (i.e. performed *from*). Several now-classic articles by Leo Treitler adapted the work of various theorists of orality and literacy to study the nature of medieval musical notation as a sign system profoundly dependent on oral process at various points in its history, which had often been cast as a straightforward evolution toward modern staff notation. Plainchant and even some polyphonic notation systems should be seen less as 'blueprints for the performers' (1981: 473) than as complex *representations* of performance; in the Middle Ages, Treitler argues, musical notation was 'a depiction of the voice moving through the sound-scape as it declaim[ed] the syllables of a text' (1985: 153), representing 'the chant as performed, that is, as event rather than as object—and particularly not as object comprising sequences of pitches' (162). This readjustment in thinking about the purpose and role of musical notation has implications as well for our understanding of the utility of the human senses during this period; as Treitler put it over twenty years ago, ' "hearing" should be broad enough to include the situation in which a cantor, compiling a book for his own use, sings—aloud or to himself—from written exemplars and writes down a version of what he has assimilated from his singing' (1981: 484). A different though I think complementary approach to the historical particularity of medieval notation is adopted in the work of Timothy McGee, who has collected dozens of overlooked passages from theoretical treatises and practical handbooks testifying to the performance conventions entailed by various notational systems. Medieval descriptions of how certain liquescent, repercussive, and ornamental neumes should be performed can often be quite quirky, writers going out of their way to find the most appropriate analogy (gargling, shaving, thumping, choking, and so on) to convey the ideal relationship between written neume and performed sonority.

The concern with the materiality of the medieval book in relation to its performance has reached its musicological apogee in Emma Dillon's groundbreaking *Medieval Music-Making and the 'Roman de Fauvel'*. The central problem Dillon addresses is that of positioning music within the 'visual, non-sounding aesthetic' of the codex, and in particular of assessing 'what status the written text of music had in [the] material aesthetic of the book' (2002: 44). While musicologists have long been concerned with the codicological contexts of musical production as keys to its chronology, institutional provenance, patronage, and so on, what Dillon has achieved is a full-scale and mutually challenging integration of medieval musicology and the history and theory of the book. As she shows, music may be intimately involved in such centrally important rhetorico-critical practices as *compilatio*; creative and interpretive decisions about musical texts not only figured crucially in the making of books, then, but exerted a uniquely musical pressure on the visual and verbal aesthetic predominant in the period's scribal cultures. In the case of the *Roman de Fauvel*, Dillon shows with remarkable precision 'how, in putting music into the text of the *roman*, the creators were exploring the material space occupied by song as an extension of its expressive and poetic power' (2002: 216). And as *Medieval Music-Making* demonstrates with numerous examples (including the provocative and convincing suggestion that Guillaume de Machaut may have come into contact at some point with the *Fauvel* manuscript itself), throughout the later Middle Ages 'the "making" of a song might include its material setting as a vital dimension of its expressivity' (281) as well as its unique survival in its culture's collective memory.

III. Performance and the Rhetorical Turn

At first glance, the workings of individual memory would seem to abnegate the very category of performance, which most would insist depends definitionally on audience and display—on the presence of more than one person, in other words. Yet memory necessarily involves the ongoing re-performance of individual and communal pasts; the medieval art of recollection or *anamnesis*, as Mary Carruthers describes it in *The Book of Memory*, resembles less the reproduction of a discrete bit of information than the reactivation of 'a personal event, with full phenomenological status' (1990: 61). The memorial interplay of senses and emotions was an intensively spatialized practice in medieval intellectual cultures, in which a certain kind of pedagogical performance was responsible for constructing an *arca sapientiae* in the mind of every medieval student (1990: 44); it is no accident that one of the most ancient analogies for memorial process, according to Carruthers, was the 'theater of memory' (1998: 291). For the rhetorical tradition, at least, memory, not necessity, is the mother of invention. Medieval mnemotechniques have foundational bearing as well on performance practices in numerous other aesthetic and institutional contexts; memory functions as performative process not only in theological, devotional, and literary spheres, but also in the domains of musicality and visuality. Anna Maria Busse Berger's work on Notre Dame polyphony, for example, illustrates the interplay among mnemonics, notation, and performance that inspires this repertory; as she explains, 'The written page might have triggered the memory of the melodic and rhythmic outline of the piece, a piece which the performers already knew . . . If they had memorized the piece once with the help of the written page, they would always use it as a mnemonic device when singing by heart' (1996: 297).

It is rhetoric's fifth and final canon that has begun to uncover perhaps the most intriguing pathways into the study of specific performance traditions in premodern eras. Due in large part to the work of Jean-Claude Schmitt (*La Raison des gestes dans l'occident médiéval*, 1990) and particularly Jody Enders (*Rhetoric and the Origins of Medieval Drama*, 1992), we are now in a position to recognize that in its energetic inscription of *actio* or delivery, the Roman rhetorical tradition bequeathed to the Middle Ages a voluminous legacy of critical reflections on the role of the body— gesture, facial expression, vocal inflection and timbre, costume, even foot position—in the coherence and meaning of public discourse: a voluminous legacy, in other words, of performance theory. In Cicero's *De oratore*, Quintilian's *Institutio oratoria*, and many other foundational texts in the rhetorical tradition, *actio* achieves the status of a kind of master-discourse of performative expression that surpasses even the achievements of *inventio* and *dispositio* in the rhetor's presentation; in Quintilian's words, 'it matters less what sorts of things we have composed within ourselves than how we utter them' (*Institutio*, 11.3.2). Though long neglected by historians of rhetoric, law, liturgy, and theatre alike, delivery has the potential not only to transform our understanding of the rhetorical underpinnings of such performance traditions as liturgical drama, the quodlibetal debates, and fifteenth-century mystery plays, but also to reshape our comprehension of the anti-generic impulse conditioning the premodern history of performance writ large, and to allow for the reintegration of vast fields of performative knowledge that modern disciplines have generally kept rigidly separated. This is not to suggest that the rhetoric of delivery promotes an 'anything goes' approach to performance; to the contrary: delivery in its classical embodiments demanded a rehearsed, self-critical, and at times (as anyone who has read Quintilian knows very well) quite regimented protocol for the individual cultivation of forensic performance.

Actio in this broadly conceived sense thus has important bearing on a number of other performance milieux, beginning most obviously with that of the *ars praedicandi*, the medieval 'art of preaching'. If James Murphy's pioneering *Rhetoric in the Middle Ages* identified the 'homiletic revolution' of the early thirteenth century that gave rise to 'a complete new rhetorical genre' (1974: 310) devoted to the invention and arrangement of effective sermons, more recent scholarship has revealed that the physical delivery of predicatory rhetoric (a topic treated only tangentially by Murphy) possessed a controversy-ridden history all its own. Thus Rita Copeland views Chaucer's Pardoner as a recursive instantiation of the troubled history of rhetoric itself, exemplifying rhetoric's 'compulsion to perform its disciplinary instabilities by performing the exposure of its own vices'; the Pardoner's Prologue thus becomes 'a consummate performance of rhetoric's self-exposure of its transgression and counterfeit' (1994: 151). Claire Waters has emphasized the extent to which, for medieval theorists of the *ars praedicandi*, preaching was inherently 'a physical performance, and thus the problems raised by the preacher's body had to be addressed'; medieval treatments of the preacher's performed persona 'demonstrate the doubleness inherent in the very activity of preaching, a doubleness that was both essential and potentially devastating to the preacher's activity and role'. Indeed, despite its attempts to control the physical and ethical content of predicatory speech, the corpus of writings devoted to the arts of preaching 'inadvertently highlighted the preacher's own hybridity and his inevitable participation in a world of partialness, appearances, and duplicity'.[15]

The widespread development of self-conscious vocabularies and conventions addressing bodily performance in other written genres—what J. A. Burrow has called 'the disciplines of decent gesture' (2002: 1)—necessarily raises the question of the extent of their debt to classical rhetorical writings as mediated through medieval contexts of reception. It seems clear, for example, that the vocabulary of *actio* stands behind early Christian notions of the music of the flesh, the organological understanding of the 'tuning' of the body to accommodate the self to the demands of devotion and morality.[16] As Brian Stock shows, Augustine's intricate theorization of reading in *De magistro* (clearly influenced by the Ciceronian tradition of delivery) offers the utility of *gestus* (along with writing) as one of the means by which 'signifying takes place in the absence of [spoken] words' (1996: 152). Burrow's own *Gestures and Looks in Medieval Narra-*

[15] Waters 2002: 81. I was unable to consult the new collection edited by Carolyn Muessig (2002) by the time this survey went to press; several advertised titles from the collection, however, promise to shed much-needed new light on the medieval sermon in its performative contexts. See in particular Augustine Thompson, 'From Texts to Preaching: Retrieving the Medieval Sermon as an Event'; Phyllis Roberts, 'The *ars praedicandi* and the Medieval Sermon'; Blake Beattie, '*Coram papa*: Preaching and Rhetorical Community at Papal Avignon'; Beverly Mayne Kienzle, 'Medieval Sermons and their Performance: Theory and Record'; and Muessig, 'Audience and Preacher: *ad status* Sermons and Social Classification'.
[16] On this understanding see Holsinger 2001: *passim*.

tive, which assesses the literary significance of bodily gestures and looks in the writings of Chaucer, Dante, Mallory, the *Gawain* poet, and others, grounds its approach in the *De doctrina christiana* of Augustine, a figure well schooled in Roman rhetorical traditions; Burrow has very little to say about delivery *per se*, however, which clearly influences the medieval literary discourse of gesture to a much greater (and I think complicating) degree than he allows.[17] There may even be classical underpinnings to the medieval tradition of monastic sign language currently being excavated by the historian Scott Bruce: in his tenth-century *Life of Odo*, John of Salerno describes this disciplinary practice among the monks of Baume-les-Moines in the precise vocabulary of 'somatic language' found in Quintilian, who imagined delivery as a kind of eloquence of the body: 'Whenever it was necessary for them to ask for something, they made it known to each other through various signs, which I think grammarians would call *notas* of fingers and eyes.'[18]

Quintilian was most specifically concerned with the public performance of lawyers at court, of course, and the Roman tradition of forensic oratory has an interesting lineage in the widespread medieval imbrication of theatricality and legality.[19] The legal cultures of the Middle Ages played host to an extraordinary variety of forensic performances while developing a sophisticated battery of protocols aimed at regulating the form, content, and delivery of legal speech. Here again Clanchy provides a rich point of departure in an overview of the personnel and procedures involved in legal narrative and its oral delivery, from the Anglo-Saxon *forspeca* to the dramatic dialogues recorded in the Year Books of Edward I to rhetorical handbooks (such as *The Court Baron*) providing scripts for hypothetical courtroom situations.[20] What fascinates in such materials is the etymological and conceptual intimacy—and thus the often quite tenuous generic distinctions—between law and literature as performed recitations of events and inventions of character. The earliest surviving collection of pleas at common law, the *Brevia placitata* (mid-1200s), describes the words of the pleaders as 'les contes en romancees'. A person's lawyer was his or her *narrator* or *conteur*, the content of the plea itself a

[17] A revealing exception to Burrow's (2002) curiously disabling neglect of *actio* in this short book occurs on p. 69, where the opening paragraph and first footnote explicitly invoke the canon of delivery yet leave its important implications for his subject unaddressed.

[18] Cited in Bruce 2001: 197.

[19] Some of the more important studies in this area are cited in the notes accompanying the useful overview that begins Lipton 2002: 115–17.

[20] Clanchy 1993: 272–8.

narratio or *conte*, for the 'professional oral remembrancer' such as the *for-speca*, the discipline of *ryhtracu* (enunciation) had a central role in the effective delivery of legal discourse (Clanchy 1993: 274). And Emily Steiner's recent study of what she terms 'documentary poetics' illustrates the extent to which modes of documentary performance figure centrally in the formal, rhetorical, and poetic strategies of late medieval English writing, whether in the vernacular lyric tradition, the alliterative fabric of *Piers Plowman*, or the testimony of the Norwich Lollards (Steiner 2003).

Intriguing, too, are those public forums designed with the performance of legal conflict and spectacle explicitly in mind; the most famous example here is the theatre of the Basoche, a kind of initiation programme for new lawyers that thrived between 1450 and 1550 in France, 'exemplif[ying] the time-honored confusion between acting and oratory and perpetuat[ing] the dramatization of the law'.[21] A similar agonistic impulse inspires courtroom scenes in late medieval English drama; Emma Lipton (2002) reads the N-Town *Trial of Mary and Joseph* not as a simple re-enactment of medieval trials, but as a self-conscious exploration of the social consequences of legal language and action that recruits a host of other performative modes (liturgy, sacrament, the ordeal) in staging its dramatic argument. Legal and liturgical performance often go hand in hand as well, the vocabulary of liturgical *actio* intermingling with forensic lexicons that embrace the ethics and deportment of the lawyer arguing at court or the clerk writing in chancery; the overlay of liturgy and legality results in some strange experiments in vernacular making in which the relation between the two performative domains is both theorized and disputed (see Holsinger 1999 and 2002). Helen Solterer has uncovered a vital aspect of the literary history of legal disputation in the genealogy of the 'woman's response' within and in relation to medieval clerical culture, a tradition of feminine speech in which the 'cardinal criterion available . . . is the idea of injurious language: words in and of themselves can cause harm to the public'.[22] '[F]or much of medieval culture', Solterer shows, 'injurious language was an article of faith' (11), a faith registered in a series

---

[21] Enders 1992: 134; on the Basochiens more generally, see pp. 129–61; and the classic study by Harvey (1941). For a very useful consideration of conflict, *quaestio*, and *disputatio* as rhetorical models for early modern drama, see Altman 1978, particularly the first two chapters.

[22] Solterer 1995: 11. Here again performativity and performance merge within the constraints and expectations shaping a particular literary genre: 'By attributing a role from the disputation to a female figure, I do not assign to them any particular definition of femininity. Nor do I assume them to be women. In this study, the medieval figure of a woman disputant is a role that can by played by anyone. This is already evident in the disputation, since its performative quality allows participants to take on a number of different roles' (18).

of literary and legal *disputationes* that powerfully anticipate twentieth-century theories of the performative injuriousness of language (see e.g. Butler 1997 on 'hate speech'). Jody Enders goes so far as to propose a 'medieval theater of cruelty' that unites the history of stagecraft and the juridical history of torture, a union in which 'the numerous beatings, tortures, and ordeals of medieval and Renaissance drama' foreground 'the hermeneutic difficulties of theater and violence' negotiated and rehearsed throughout the history of drama, law, and rhetoric alike (1992: 218).

IV. Performance, Genre, and Ritual

As the examples discussed so far in this survey illustrate, the rhetoric of performance broadly conceived enlivens cultural production in the Middle Ages across forms, languages, institutions, and centuries; practically all genres of medieval writing exhibit some investment in the performative as a mode of engagement with the social. Suydam and Ziegler, the editors of a collection titled *Performance and Transformation* (1999), argue for a fairly direct application of performance theory (reviewed for medievalists by Suydam in primer form as the collection's first chapter) to the domain of medieval spirituality, though subsequent chapters (including Suydam's own) tend to exhibit more interpretive flexibility and theoretical give-and-take than the volume's rather clunky premise implies. Walter Simons suggests that the *vitae* of Beguines in the Low Countries functioned as theatrically self-conscious scripts of the women's visionary performances, in which 'bodies give external expression to experiences of mystical transport which spoken or written language did not and could not articulate' (1994: 13). As John Ganim argued in *Chaucerian Theatricality* (1990), more properly 'literary' texts are similarly suffused with various modes of performative self-consciousness. Chaucer's preoccupation with theatricality and spectatorship is now well known, though as Seth Lerer has provocatively suggested (perhaps in an implicit response to Ganim), the *Canterbury Tales* may be understood to be animated as well by a sophisticated critique of theatricality—'not a criticism as such', Lerer specifies, 'but an ongoing query, almost a setting up on trial, of competing forms and structures of public drama operating in the last decades of fourteenth-century England'. One of the effects of Lerer's analysis is to expose Chaucer's self-conscious relation to dramatic 'making' as one of the primary literary agons operative in his own moment: 'Ricardian spectacle, guild play, and rural rebellious theatrics define the backdrops against which Chaucer stages his own authorial self construction—one continually striving to adjudicate between the patron and the reader, the historically immanent and the transhistorically literary' (1998: 76). Middle English alliterative romance, by contrast, understands its relation to performance alongside a keen recognition of romance's own generic recuperations of the past and the audience it projects for its own future; as Christine Chism suggests, the 'performed archaism' promoted in these romances allows them to 'distinguish themselves from other fourteenth-century poetic traditions in the provocative spectacularity of their historic consciousness, their reinvention of insular metrical and romance traditions, and the ways they perform and constitute poetic voice and audience' (2002: 39). The scholastic theory of authorship provided yet another cultural medium in which various notions of authorial performance could be worked out. As A. J. Minnis shows, medieval etymological associations between *auctor* and verbs such as *agere* (to act or perform), *augere* (to grow), and *auieo* (to tie) lent even the academic arena of writing and *auctoritas* a performative vogue; thus, an 'auctor "performed" the act of writing. He brought something into being, caused it to "grow" . . . poets like Virgil and Lucan were *auctores* in that they had "tied" together their verses with feet and metres' (1984: 10). Rita Copeland suggests that academic theory of translation in the Middle Ages depends on a notion of *inventio* as 'hermeneutical performance', a process of *translatio* whereby 'hermeneutical moves transform themselves into rhetorical performances [by] locat[ing] invention within the operations of exegesis' (1991: 177).

Medieval lyric, too, bears a fluid relation to the music that it describes and to which it was (imaginatively or actually) performed. The scholar who has made the most provocative use of literary production as evidence of musical performance practice is Christopher Page, who has defined a rigorous historical relationship between medieval music and literature that fundamentally challenges the assumptions underlying John Stevens's (1986) *Words and Music in the Middle Ages* (the one book that literary medievalists are most likely to know and cite as authoritative on the performance and aesthetics of medieval music). Already in *Voices and Instruments of the Middle Ages* (1987), Page exposed the fallacy that literature provides straightforward testimony to medieval musical practices (the approach adopted in Wilkins's *Music in the Age of Chaucer*, 1995), revealing instead the dialectical relation between the two mediums and the resultant interpretive demands placed on their modern exegetes for careful attention to the particularities of genre, institution, chronology, and readership. As Page showed in regard to Roger Dragonetti's so-called *grand chant courtois*, for example, the elevated courtly style seemingly ideally suited to elaborate musical display may in fact have been among the least likely to receive a musical setting; indeed, 'a song was less appropriate for instrumental accompaniment the more it lay claim to self-conscious artistry' (1987: 38). This attention to the complexities of the relationship between literary artifice and musical performance carries over into Page's *The Owl and the Nightingale: Musical Life and Ideas in France 1100–1300* (1989), an imaginative cultural history of medieval music within historical milieux ranging from tensions between monastic and scholastic institutions and sensibilities to the emergence of proto-nationalism in the thirteenth century. Another of Page's books, *Discarding Images* (1993), pays titular hommage to C. S. Lewis while arguing polemically for the intellectual rigours of performance *practice* as an indispensable component of performance *study*. One of Page's consistent points of reference has been the motet, a musical genre little studied by literary historians but which, as Sylvia Huot's *Allegorical Play in the Old French Motet* has shown, depends for much of its performative expression within both courtly and ecclesiastical settings on the 'juxtaposition of sacred and profane discourse and the allegorical and parodic readings that emerge from [its] hybrid structure' (1997: 1).

Court culture more generally has proved fertile ground for literary scholars exploring the intersection of literary production and the performance of secular ritual. Louise Fradenburg's *City, Marriage, Tournament* demonstrates vividly the power of spectacle and display in the production of political identities and the formation of royal sovereignty in fifteenth- and sixteenth-century Scotland. Poetry played a vital role in constituting and remembering a culture of performance in which 'arts of rule and of embodiment (tournament, peripatetic kingship) were being reimagined, in coexistence with newer forms (capital, elaborate nuptial pageantry) that tried to lay claim to the past and thereby to conceal their historicity and consequently their vulnerability' (1991: xv). Peter J. Arnade's *Realms of Ritual* (1996) makes similar points about the public rituals of the upper Burgundian aristocracy, whose members invented a self-conscious 'theater of power' that helped them negotiate their relation to the urban polity of Ghent. Susan Crane's *Performance of Self* presents a wide-ranging study of the literature and spectacle of courtly ritual in England and France during the Hundred Years War. One of Crane's historical tenets is the 'conviction of medieval elites that identity exists in social performance' (2002: 5), and that important aspects of material culture—

clothing, costume, armour, heraldry, and so on—have been neglected by medievalists focused on the body (not to mention religiosity) as the privileged ground of self and identity. Various forms of performance across gender, class, and even species (Maying rituals figuratively identifying women as Flower and Leaf, for example) reveal the medieval sense in which the 'concretely visible—the courtier variously costumed, masked, liveried, cross-dressed, and disguised—is crucial to establishing identity and asserting its worth' (2002: 9). And Gordon Kipling's comprehensive study of the medieval royal entry emphasizes a similar obsession with display and self-representation in the court cultures of the later Middle Ages, demonstrating that the often improvisational interplays of liturgy, ritual, and drama effected in the entry tradition created what he aptly terms 'the "metaphysical theatre" of the civic triumph' (1998: 47). All of these studies focus on the later Middle Ages, though the role of secular ritual in early medieval culture is equally fascinating and worthy of much more scrutiny in relation to the literary than it has yet received. Philippe Buc's chapter in *The Dangers of Ritual* (2001) on texts and events in the ninth century, for example, demonstrates the central role of textual self-consciousness in mediating between consensus and violence in Carolingian ritual performance.

V. The Liturgical Challenge

The bibliography on medieval religious ritual is of course too massive even to attempt a position statement, let alone a responsible overview; I'll let a cautionary prescriptive suffice here: the study of medieval vernacular literatures will need to reckon much more comprehensively than it yet has with the liturgy, site of the most enduring, expensive, elaborate, widespread, and influential cultures of performance in the premodern West. It is no accident that Eamon Duffy's *Stripping of the Altars* (1992) inspired such fierce resistance from scholars of late medieval literature, who saw in its account of 'traditional religion' a homogenizing portrait of the historical relation between literary practice and theology. Yet the reaction to Duffy's book cannot be explained as an effect solely of its perceived ecclesiastical conservatism; the more one reads *The Stripping of the Altars*, in fact, the clearer it becomes that the unacknowledged challenge the book represents to the historiography of Middle English literature lies in its implicit argument that the sphere of vernacular literary production constitutes a quite small (and, truth be told, comparatively insignificant and elite) cultural excrescence when set alongside the immensely diverse cycle of devotion, learning, building, collecting, and daily living entailed by lay participation in the liturgy ('Any study of late medieval religion must begin with the liturgy,' Duffy writes at the opening of chapter 1, 'for within that great seasonal cycle of fast and festival, of ritual and observance and symbolic gesture, lay Christians found the paradigms and the stories which shaped their perception of the world and their place in it' (1992: 15)). While this is an argument many would find hard to accept—and Duffy's notorious sidestepping of Lollard writings crystallizes this point (Hudson's *Premature Reformation* does not appear in the book's bibliography)—it remains undeniable that the analytical pressure of the liturgy could be felt much more keenly than it has been in recent models of literary historicism. Though medieval literary studies has generally (and particularly in the last twenty years) relegated it to an eccentric corner of the discipline, liturgy was never simply a static body of doctrinal and theological tradition passively reflected in vernacular making, but an all-consuming dimension of medieval life that almost inevitably draws those who study it with any comprehension into a quicksand of totalization.

This may help explain the unfortunate bifurcation of liturgical studies from the mainstream of medieval studies over the last half-century, a period in which most scholarship on the western Middle Ages (with the important exceptions of certain quarters of the history of religion, musicology, and, as we shall see, drama, which has always kept a foot or two firmly planted in liturgical waters) largely abandoned the serious study of liturgy as a cultural practice inseparable from other aesthetic and social spheres. Liturgical studies evolved its own journals (*Studia liturgica, Liturgical Arts*, and so on) or got folded into the study of patristics (as represented by publications such as *Sacris erudiri*), and it was only rarely that this central component of medieval religious and social practice was treated as a significant intepretive factor for medievalists in all fields of study rather than an isolated discourse safely delegated to the purview of obsessive specialists. Yet as many of its most agile modern students have recognized, medieval liturgy constitutes an inherently antidisciplinary field precisely resistant to such specialization, embracing music, literature, theology, the visual arts, dance, drama, costume, pageantry, agriculture, and numerous other dimensions of medieval civilization in a material practice that impinges on nearly every aspect of cultural production. As Margot Fassler describes it, liturgy represented 'a fabric of interwoven human efforts' (1993: 16) for its participants, a site of enormous cultural variation, creativity, and embellishment. In Fassler's *Gothic Song*, a study of liturgical change and its implications for the religious and institutional history of the Augustinian canons in twelfth-century Paris, liturgy merges exegesis, spirituality, and politics into an arena of cultural negotiation and memory founded on collective traditions of performance. Studies of specific liturgical manuscripts as well as the liturgical traditions of particular localities have revealed the extent to which liturgy was instrumental in the formation of what Pierre Nora termed *lieux de mémoire*, 'places of memory' constituted by the books, artefacts, and performances that together fabricate the institutional and public lives of their inhabitants (see, among many others, Curran 1984; Stanton 2001; Camille 1998; Gibson et al. 1992; Donovan 1991; Hamburger 1990). Liturgical modes of pedagogy, too, have received provocative treatment at the hands of musicologists and literary historians alike; Susan Boynton, for example, observes that the liturgy 'was in many ways a school within the monastery', and that musical education was 'part of a broader liturgical formation in which reading, singing and writing were fully integrated' (2000*a*: 16 and 7). Katherine Zieman's ongoing work on liturgy and literacy in late medieval England is excavating the role of song schools in the formation of particular models of literate practice that had remarkable influence on the writings of such centrally canonical vernacular writers as Chaucer and Langland.

Far from exhibiting the uniformity and institutional hegemony so often imputed to it, then, liturgy in fact enabled historically diverse experiences of performance, learning, humour, and even self-protection. Boynton has used the phrase 'performative exegesis' to get at the sense in which liturgical drama works hermeneutically through the multiple levels of meaning in the commentary tradition; in the case of the Fleury *Interfectio puerorum*, the 'entire play exists within a liturgical time that encompasses the temporal levels created by the senses of Scripture (historical, allegorical, eschatological, and tropological) in individual sections of the play' (1998: 60). Like the genre of the motet, the liturgical and 'mock-liturgical' musics interpolated into the *Roman de Fauvel* manuscript expose how often and creatively liturgical chant could be enlisted to serve the purposes of parody and satire (Rankin 1994; Dillon 2002: 230–6). Lester Little (1993) has unearthed a fascinating tradition of liturgical cursing prevalent among the Benedictines of northern France and the Low Countries in the eleventh and twelfth centuries; specially designed prayers called 'clamours' were inserted into the mass calling down the wrath of God onto the perpetrators of offences of various sorts

('May they be cursed in the head and the brain. May they be cursed in their eyes and their foreheads'). That this bizarre custom was employed in large part as a means of participating in informal disputes over property rights points to the extreme malleability of liturgical ritual, which could be adapted to numerous entirely practical ends even within institutions organized around long-standing traditions of liturgical performance. The appearance of several research guides and historical overviews of liturgical traditions intended for a general readership among medievalists (e.g. Heffernan and Matter 2001; Hughes 1982; Fassler and Baltzer 2000) suggests that the study of liturgy may be gaining ground in medieval cultural studies; this is as it should be, for as Kathleen Ashley, C. Clifford Flanigan, and Pamela Sheingorn describe it, liturgy needs to be understood as a central mode of 'social performance' for medieval culture, as an 'arena of intense communication of cultural values and negotiation of power within social formations at given historical moments' (2001: 714).

VI. From Liturgy to Drama

The one sub-field of medieval literary studies that has maintained traditionally close ties with liturgical studies, of course, is the history of drama. Honorius Augustodunensis was not the last to make interpretive hay from the expressive connection between the classical tragedian and *tragicus noster*, the priest performing the liturgy. The now-famous passage from the *Gemma animae* (*c.*1100) describing the 'theatre of the Church' was foundational for O. B. Hardison's revisionist conception of the Christian mass as 'sacred drama', complete with all the agonism, dramatic reversal, and dramatic catharsis endemic to the history of theatre; at the hands of liturgical commentators like Honorius and Amalarius of Metz, Hardison showed, the liturgy became 'an elaborate drama with definite roles assigned to the participants and a plot whose ultimate significance is nothing less than a "renewal of the whole plan of redemption" through the re-creation of the "life, death, and resurrection" of Christ' (1965: 39). The mimetic impulse at the heart of Christian religiosity was not confined to the *Quem quaeritis* interpolations and the emergence of so-called liturgical drama, then, but was inherent to the embodied performance of liturgical worship, ceremony, and prayer. In one stroke, Hardison (without the benefit of Victor Turner (1982)) extended the domain of drama and theatre into the realm of ritual and sacrament, in the process introducing medievalists to the neglected genre of liturgical commentary that enabled subsequent work by Fassler, Enders, and others treating the mimetic interrelations among rhetoric, theology, and music in the premodern era.

Hardison's vision of medieval liturgy as a 'living dramatic form' (1965: 41) has not won universal acceptance, though most objections to it have come about due to a misunderstanding of its subtleties. A recent example here is Lawrence Clopper's *Drama, Play, and Game* (2001), a book that I want to pause over for a moment given its broad historical scope and its intended implications for the study of premodern theatricalities. Clopper frames the central question pursued in this book as follows: 'How was it possible for drama, especially biblical representation, to appear in the Christian West given the early church's aversion toward and condemnation of the *theatrum* of the ancient world?' Hardison's answer, of course, was appropriation or *translatio*: the Church adapted the rhetoric of the classical theatre to its own liturgical ends, and the mass became the theatrical body of Ecclesia, continually reborn and renewed through liturgical performance. For Clopper, however, theatre and liturgy lived separate lives during the Middle Ages, and thus one has to read the book's historical argument as part of a thoroughgoing rejection of Hardison: 'The allusion to *theatrum* in later medieval documents is not a sign that the *theatrum* or things associated with it continued to exist in any real way, but that *theatrum* was a ready metaphor for the things perceived by individuals within the church not to be of the church. Theatrical metaphor is a rhetoric of abuse' (50); in short, as the introduction proclaims, 'liturgical representations . . . differ from drama in most, perhaps all, ways' (1965: 3).

These are very strong claims to make in the face of Hardison's *Christian Rite and Christian Drama* and the decades of scholarship on liturgy and theatricality that has followed in its wake; in order to refute this intellectual tradition (for it surely is one) persuasively, Clopper would need to include some extended engagement with the corpus of medieval liturgical commentary and other materials on which this work has been based. Yet the more carefully one reads *Drama, Play, and Game*, the more it begins to appear that Clopper has decided to treat the whole issue of liturgical spectacle and theatricality as an inconvenience. The consequences of this decision emerge immediately in the first chapter, which contains the book's single discussion of liturgical commentary, the medieval genre in which the liturgy-theatre analogy is most richly elaborated over the course of several centuries, from Amalarius of Metz to the *Lay Folks' Mass Book*. Here Clopper reads the familiar passage from Honorius as evidence *against* Hardison's claim that the Middle Ages 'recognized the dramatic element in the mass, knew that liturgy was a drama' (2001: 53), basing his objection solely on the verb choices in Honorius' Latin. Once he has un-packed this single passage from just one treatise, Clopper moves on, over-looking the remaining entirety of the tradition and basing all of his subsequent arguments on the writings of blatant aesthetic conservatives such as Aelred of Rievaulx, whose infamous objection to histrionic and effeminate liturgical performance in the *Speculum caritatis* reveals that 'theatrical metaphor is a rhetorical weapon' (2001: 54).

But only in certain hands. For as it turns out, this objection was antici-pated and fully worked through by Hardison himself, who reads the *very same passage* from Aelred in pointing out that 'the clergy frequently trans-lated Mass allegory into histrionic action'; in fact, as Hardison showed quite clearly, the entire tradition of liturgical mimesis adumbrated by Amalarius was already meeting with fierce resistance by the twelfth cen-tury. The antitheatrical prejudice against the classical *theatrum* that Clop-per presents as evidence that clerics performing the liturgy 'did not understand themselves to be creating dramas' (2001: 51), in other words, is precisely *internal* to the theatrical understanding of the liturgy outlined by Hardison. It competed for centuries with the Amalarian theatricaliza-tion of the liturgy, and the two tendencies cannot be understood apart from one another.[23]

If in 1990 Theresa Coletti could observe that the field of medieval drama studies 'seems caught in a methodological vacuum' (252), the last decade has witnessed a small explosion of innovative approaches to the politics, religiosity, and, again, phenomenology of the theatrical cultures of the Middle Ages. Coletti's comments were made in the context of an extended critique of the vision of history promoted in the Records of Early English Drama (REED) project, a vision 'underwritten by a

---

[23] See the discussion of this tension in Rainer Warning's 1974 book *Funktion und Struktur: Die Ambivalenzen des geistlichen Spiels*, recently translated as *The Ambivalences of Medieval Reli-gious Drama* (2001), 27–44, as well as the comments in Warning's afterword to the English trans-lation: 'The religious drama never became an institution that could have enjoyed undivided theological approval. On the contrary: from the beginning there was dispute. Amalarius of Metz's allegorization of the Mass, with which everything began in the eighth century, immedi-ately encountered bitter resistance from Florus of Lyons, who could not comprehend making the liturgy into a performance. According to him, only an idiot, to whom Christ is already present in the sacrament, would nonetheless prefer to concentrate on the shadow rather than the sub-stance of the *veritas corporis* already at hand. True, theology desires the body but as a symbolic substance. And as soon as an attempt was made, however circumspectly, to interpret the gestural provisions of the liturgy mimetically—for example, to proceed from the *corpus verum* to an *imaginatio corporis*—dogmatic gravity registered an objection' (250).

powerful set of assumptions about the nature, conduct, and goals of historical scholarship' which, in Coletti's view, drastically limited the methodological revisionism promised by the project's editors and contributors. Suggesting that REED may serve to 'obscure rather than clarify relationships between dramatic record and dramatic text' (1990: 281), Coletti pointed to the anxiety of fragmentation subtending the project's archival method, a process by which the REED volumes 'enact a deliberate and systematic creation of their own metafragments as they excise references to dramatic activity from their host documents and reconfigure them according to the principles established by the series' (1991: 3). What is not included in the REED volumes was often just as central to the history of dramatic practice as what is included, and even the edited documents reflect and are mediated by 'editorial procedures intended to ensure the stability and authority of the whole picture the project will one day realize' (1991: 3; for another perspective see Badir 1997).

For better or worse, most of the recent studies by scholars affiliated with or heavily dependent upon the archival labours and editorial assumptions of REED do not respond with any directness to Coletti's critique; other scholarship in early English drama, such as Anna Lancashire's magisterial new study of London civic theatre (2002), suggests that the courageous synthesis of these very archival 'metafragments' may in fact hold the greatest potential for revising the basic historical assumptions of theatre history. Yet the field of early theatre studies seems nevertheless marked (as perhaps it has always been) by an awareness of the somehow enabling persistence of the fragmentary, the partial, the incomplete: as Meg Twycross and Sarah Carpenter put it in the introduction to *Masks and Masking in Medieval and Early Tudor England* (2002), 'neither evidence nor contexts are transparent. Records of medieval masking are partial and often uncertain, distorted not only by chance and time but by the biases and preconceptions of the recorders as well as by our own assumptions and cultural attitudes. All interpretations of these records need to be questioned and tested in the light of whatever can be recovered of their linguistic, cultural, religious, and political contexts' (2002: 4). Even here, however, the rhetoric of inquiry seems unable to clarify what precisely separates 'interpretation' from 'context' when it comes to the history of early drama, registering a more general analytical 'paralysis', as Maura Nolan describes it, deriving in part from the uniquely alienating processes of reconstruction demanded by the writing of theatre history. Nowhere is this scholarly alienation felt more keenly than in that supposed no man's land between 'original' performance and surviving script, a conceptual space that has done untold amounts of damage to the phenomenology of dramatic writing. While Nolan's particular focus in the following passage is the mummings of John Lydgate, her insistence on the complex historicity of the *scripted form* of dramatic texts should be considered axiomatic for critical approaches to all putatively 'performative' texts that exist 'in a world of other texts', past, present, and future:

[T]he turn to the cultural 'field'—in which a series of interrelated observations by the critic come to constitute the ground of analysis—must not obscure the extent to which the dramatic text understands itself to be a central and distinct object made for a specifically readerly gaze . . . [A]s a result, notions like 'containment' and 'subversion'—or, as recast in recent years, 'ritual practice' and 'social conflict'—ultimately prove limiting in a basic historical way. They substitute for the particularity of the object or text a vision of *function*, of 'resolution' or 'negotiation' which appears, deceptively, to fulfill a felt need for historical specificity and local analysis . . . But even an assemblage of the most specific details, derived from the most authoritative sources, cannot by itself produce a reading that is genuinely historical in form as well as content. Such a reading requires in the first instance an almost obsessive gaze upon the singular object under consideration, one whose primary concern is to grasp the means by which its historicity declares itself, by which it is suffused with meaning, through which it signifies in the past and in the present.[24]

    This formal, inscribed historicity embraces as well the physical appearance of dramatic texts as they survive in manuscript books: books which, as Carol Symes has forcefully argued, may yield many more surviving plays than the 'gravely flawed' criteria used to locate, classify, and edit the artefacts of premodern theatre have traditionally allowed; in Symes's words, 'the artifacts upon which the study of medieval drama has hitherto been based are preserved in manuscript books alongside an array of materials usually classified as "nondramatic", yet the plays share the formal characteristics of those materials. In most cases, then, the ambiguous appearance of a given text may have little to do with whether or not it was performed or regarded as a play' (2002: 778). In the historiography of drama, this generic confusion will hold true for archive as well as script: as Catherine Sanok suggests in regard to pageants and plays for St Katherine in late medieval England, 'we might know so little about most saints' plays because—perhaps only implicitly, even inadvertently—they challenged political and ecclesiastic institutions in ways that made their

---

[24] Cited from Maura Nolan's manuscript, *The Making of Public Culture, 1422–1432*; see also Nolan 2004 on the 'performance of the literary' as a category for historical understanding.

textual inscription more difficult and less likely' (2002: 270). Another way of articulating this paradox might be to say that any pre-scripted medieval performance may bear within itself the seeds of its script's demise.[25]

As we have seen a number of times thus far in this survey, the history of performance creates its own particular generic demands for what Caroline Walker Bynum has termed a 'comic' approach to historical understanding, a critical stance 'aware of contrivance, of risk', of the choices entailed in 'telling a story that could be told in another way' (1991: 25). Sanok's essay (2002) on the performance of feminine sanctity in parish guild plays exemplifies the revisionist possibilities for the history of medieval drama (as for practically all fields of medieval studies) afforded by critical attention to the intertwined stories of gender, sexuality, and the body. Coletti's work on figurations of female corporeality in the mystery cycles and in the Digby plays shows how drama participated in defining localized notions of women's labour and social roles; 'the class consciousness, market transactions, and charitable ideals' embodied in the Digby vision of the Magdalene 'are as central to her characterization in this text as they were to the self-conception of late-medieval landed classes and urban society' (2001: 376), while the infancy plays from the cycles employ the 'image of the pregnant, virginal body of Mary' to dramatize 'domestic disputes over gender roles, the impact of a transgressed virginity on family and community, and the inevitable links between women's reproduction and the household economy' (1993: 86; see also Kinservik 1996). As Kathleen Ashley has shown, moreover, dramatic performance participated as well in the gendered discourses of conduct, even functioning as scripted and embodied 'conduct books' for women in a variety of social classes and vocations (Ashley 1987). The overlay of class and gender politics in medieval performance cultures receives extended and illuminating treatment in Claire Sponsler's *Drama and Resistance: Bodies, Goods, and Theatricality in Late Medieval England,* which surveys a wide array of cultural productions—morality plays and Corpus Christi dramas, but also Robin Hood ballads, sumptuary laws, the literature of conduct, morris dancing, even books of hours (which produce what she terms the 'self-consuming subject')—in an attempt to recover the variety and creativity inspiring performative cultures of resistance during the fifteenth and sixteenth centuries; 'within the licensed space of the theater', Sponsler

---

[25] Compare the assessment of John Alford: 'It is a truism that reading a dramatic script is like reading a musical score. Whatever impression may be conveyed by the printed page, the only measure of worth that matters ultimately is performance' (1995: 1).

argues, 'official scripts for living could be rewritten—not matter how fleetingly or contingently—to explore alternate possibilities of action and being' (1997: xv).

One such alternative possibility was explored through the device of cross-dressing, a ubiquitous practice in the Middle Ages given the confinement of both liturgical and secular 'acting' nearly exclusively to men.[26] Yet with some rare exceptions, the Middle Ages seem not to have problematized dramatic cross-dressing as Renaissance antitheatricalists did, though as Robert Clark and Sponsler argue, lack of polemic does not imply a corresponding lack of cultural complexity (1995; see also Hotchkiss 1996). Medieval transvestisms performed a variety of cultural work, from the seemingly deliberate transgression of gender boundaries to the negotiation of categories of racial and ethnic difference (Clark and Sponsler 1999). For Ruth Evans, the 'style' of medieval dramatic production was intimately related to the economics and ideologies of spectatorship and consumption: 'the styles of the text and of bodies in performance enlist their audiences in the processes of representation, invite them to take up positions and elicit their desires. Understood in this way, style is not something transparent to go through in order to arrive at a "reality" beyond it, but something to be arrested by' (1997: 196). It is the possibility of such 'arrests' in medieval dramatic spectatorship that inspires a series of essays by Garrett Epp (1997 and 2001) exploring the theatricality of male homoeroticism in European passion plays and in the morality play *Mankind*, which explicitly thematizes sodomy as both deadly sin and performed provocation to theatrical delectation.[27]

Yet perhaps it is medieval vernacular drama's ubiquitous propensity to 'do theological work' (Beckwith 2001: xvii) that most distinguishes its social resonance from that of early modern dramatic forms and genres. This is not to deny that, for example, Shakespeare was uninvested in difficult theological conundrums (witness Greenblatt's *Hamlet in Purgatory*, 2001), nor that the *commedia dell'arte* tradition in its various national forms avoided ridiculing the Church at times; in England the mystery plays survived into the Elizabethan period in any case, and of course a thriving Reformation drama existed for a good part of the sixteenth century. Nevertheless, as scholarship of the past fifteen years or so has

[26] An exclusivity that of course makes those rare exceptions all the more remarkable; one such exception was Hildegard of Bingen's *Ordo virtutum*, on which see Fassler 1998, as well as the essays collected in Davidson 1992.
[27] For a provocative perspective on the homoerotics of medieval cross-dressing from a literary perspective, see Sautman 2001.

suggested, there seems to be an uncanny fit between the dramatic impulses and the incarnational religiosity of the pre-Reformation Church that extends well beyond Honorius' understanding of liturgy as theatricality as taken up by Hardison. Gail McMurray Gibson's *The Theater of Devotion*, which rigorously explored the rootedness of particular dramatic and literary artefacts in a single locality, proposed that an 'incarnational aesthetic' was largely responsible for making East Anglia into such a thriving centre of religious performances of various kinds in the fifteenth century—performances by no means limited to or even inevitably impelled by the laity (as Gibson writes, 'It is one of those curious and unconsidered stereotypes of our patchwork history of early drama that we acknowledge that Christian drama began in monastic churches, assume that the service books of Benedictine churches spread dramatic elaborations of the liturgical ritual, and yet reject the notion of monastic involvement in medieval vernacular drama').[28] Yet if the vernacular drama of late medieval England featured a remarkable investment in the social and corporeal instantiation of its religiosity, the plays themselves were also very much *about* theology as an ideological problem: they may in fact be understood as 'staged interpretations', in Ruth Nissé's felicitous phrase (1998). As Nissé shows, fifteenth-century English dramatic texts 'take up a series of contests over who could legitimately interpret scripture—men or women, clerics or lay people; rulers or subjects, Christians or non-Christians—and stage them for a wide audience' as part of a broader 'interplay of textual hermeneutics and spatial politics' operative throughout the later Middle Ages.[29] Antitheatrical writings are themselves deeply aware of the theological gyrations of vernacular religious drama; a work such as the Lollard *Tretise of Miracles Pleyinge*, for example, understands that Corpus Christi drama 'reverses discipline', as Nissé suggests (1997), by disrupting the proper order of biblical hermeneutics and resisting the metaphoricity of the body in favour of a transgressive literalness.

Nowhere do the theological and the dramatic merge more seamlessly than in the work of Sarah Beckwith, whose *Signifying God* will surely transform our understanding of the very ontology of what we call 'medieval drama'. Beckwith's notion of 'sacramental theater' locates the incarnational aesthetic postulated by Gibson within a cultural formation that intimately conjoined dramatic performance and performative utter-

---

[28] Gibson 1989: 108; compare the observations of Clopper 2001: 204–34.

[29] The citations come from 'Drama after Chaucer', the introduction to Ruth Nissé's forthcoming book *Defining Acts: Drama and the Politics of Interpretation in Premodern England*.

ance to the point of indistinguishability. As Beckwith writes at the beginning of this book on the York plays, 'I understand the plays as sacramental theater. How we present ourselves to each other (the classical domain of theater) and how we are present to each other (the domain of the sacrament) become, I argue, vital theological as well as theatrical resources in the York plays. In them theater and sacrament become profound investigations of each other's opportunities and limits' (2001: xv). What is most startling about sacramental theatre as Beckwith defines it is that it allows us to specify precisely how the theological work and, indeed, transformation accomplished by medieval theatre actually took place. Just as the vernacular in late medieval England becomes a contested yet uniquely appropriate medium for the writing of certain kinds of theology, so theatre (which, we need to recognize, has been a virtually exiled category for recent scholarship on 'vernacular theology') bears an uncannily mimetic and adequating relation to sacramentality: not simply to its performance, but to its instantiating *logic*. This, it seems to me, is the sort of revelation that promises a fundamental shift in critical thinking about dramatic mimesis as such; as medievalists we can only hope that it achieves the impact on the history of drama that it deserves.

Beckwith frames her study of medieval Corpus Christi drama with an extended scrutiny of its modern revivals during the post-war Festival of Britain (1951) as well as in contemporary film, fiction, and theatre. Beckwith investigates this twentieth-century revivalism not for the interpretive authority it provides, however, but for its role in a dialectic of historical understanding that refuses to eschew the 'present of things past' entailed in the study of performance and performativity in premodern eras. If this returns us full circle to my opening comments on the authorizing strategies of performance studies, we might also want to recognize that medieval studies has been responsible for some of the more sceptical appraisals of this coevalist tendency. I want to conclude, in fact, with a few sentences from Katherine Bergeron's inspiring study of the revival and 'invention' of Gregorian chant at the Benedictine monastery at Solesmes, *Decadent Enchantments*, a book with important lessons to teach those of us who make it our life's ambition to visit 'the imaginary landscapes that form history's invisible core' (1998: xiv). What Bergeron says of music and song applies equally well to performance in general, and what she has to say about the imaginative origins of musicology could easily be said of performance studies or, indeed, medieval studies, which derives significant branches of its materialist genealogy from early musicologists like the nineteenth-century monks of Solesmes. For these liturgical makers and performers, Bergeron suggests, history sings of and from the past, its own performance in modernity realized in the artefacts and manuscripts that 'would define the image of the repertory for many generations to come, an image of lost time that functioned, in turn, to shape the very idea of music history. If such acts of putting chant into the modern imagination constitute the origins of our discipline, then musicology comes into being, in a very literal sense, through the enchantment of history. It is this enchantment that my own historical narrative attempts to restore, listening into those places where history may not be able to speak, but only sing' (1998: xiv).

University of Colorado-Boulder

List of Works Cited

ALFORD, JOHN A. (ed.) (1995), *From Page to Performance: Essays in Early English Drama. In Memory of Arnold Williams* (East Lansing, Mich.).

ALTMAN, JOEL (1978), *The Tudor Play of Mind: Rhetorical Inquiry and the Development of Elizabethan Drama* (Berkeley, Calif.).

AMSLER, MARK (2001), 'Affective Literacy: Gestures of Reading in the Later Middle Ages', *Essays in Medieval Studies*, 18: 83–109.

ARNADE, PETER J. (1996), *Realms of Ritual: Burgundian Ceremony and Civil Life in Late Medieval Ghent* (Ithaca, NY, 1996).

ASHLEY, KATHLEEN (1987), 'Medieval Courtly Literature and Dramatic Mirrors of Female Conduct', in Nancy Armstrong and Leonard Tennenhouse (eds.), *The Ideology of Conduct: Essays on Literature and the History of Sexuality* (New York), 25–38.

—— FLANIGAN, C. CLIFORD, and SHEINGORN, PAMELA (2001), 'The Liturgy as Social Performance: Expanding the Definitions', in Heffernan and Matter 2001: 695–714.

BADIR, PATRICIA (1997), 'Playing Space: History, the Body, and Records of Early English Drama', *Exemplaria*, 9: 255–79.

BECKWITH, SARAH (2001), *Signifying God: Social Relation and Symbolic Act in the York Corpus Christi Plays* (Chicago).

BENT, MARGARET (1993), 'Reflections on Christopher Page's *Reflections*', *Early Music*, 21: 625–33.

BERGER, ANNA MARIA BUSSE (1996), 'Mnemotechnics and Notre Dame Polyphony', *Journal of Musicology*, 14: 263–98.

BERGERON, KATHERINE (1998), *Decadent Enchantments: The Revival of Gregorian Chant at Solesmes* (Berkeley, Calif.).

BOYNTON, SUSAN (1998), 'Performative Exegesis in the Fleury *Interfectio Puerorum*', *Viator*, 29: 39–64.

——(2000*a*), 'Training for the Liturgy as a Form of Monastic Education', in Carolyn Muessig and George Ferzoco (eds.), *Medieval Monastic Education* (Leicester), 7–20.

——(2000*b*), 'Liturgy and History at the Abbey of Farfa in the Late Eleventh Century: Hymns of Peter Damian and Other Additions to BAV Chigi C.VI.177', *Sacris Erudiri*, 39: 253–80.

BRUCE, SCOTT (2001), 'The Origins of Cistercian Sign Language', *Cîteaux: Commentarii cistercienses*, 52: 193–209.

BUC, PHILIPLE (2001), *The Dangers of Richal: Between Early Medieval Texts and Social Scientific Theory* (Princeton).

BURROW, J. A. (2002), *Gestures and Looks in Medieval Narrative*, Cambridge Studies in Medieval Literature, 48 (Cambridge).

BUTLER, JUDITH (1997), *Excitable Speech: A Politics of the Performative* (New York).

BYNUM, CAROLINE WALKER (1991), *Fragmentation and Redemption: Essays on Gender and the Human Body in Medieval Religion* (New York).

CAMILLE, MICHAEL (1998), *Mirror in Parchment: The Luttrell Psalter and the Making of Medieval England* (Chicago).

CAMPBELL, THOMAS P. (ed.) (1981), 'Liturgy and Drama: Recent Approaches to Medieval Theatre', *Theatre Journal*, 33: 289–301.

CARRUTHERS, MARY (1990), *The Book of Memory: A Study of Memory in Medieval Culture* (Cambridge).

——(1998), *The Craft of Thought: Meditation, Rhetoric, and the Making of Images, 400–1200* (Cambridge).

CHISM, CHRISTINE (2002), *Alliterative Revivals* (Philadelphia).

CLANCHY, M. T. (1993), *From Memory to Written Record: England 1066–1307*, 2nd edn. (Oxford).

CLARK, ROBERT L. A., and SPONSLER, CLAIRE M. (1995), 'Queer Play: The Cultural Work of Crossdressing in Medieval Drama', paper delivered at Cultural Frictions: Medieval Cultural Studies in Post-Modern Contexts (Washington, DC). Posted at http://www.georgetown.edu/labyrinth/conf/cs95/papers/clark.html.

——(1999), 'Othered Bodies: Racial Cross-Dressing in the *Mistere de la Sainte Hostie* and the Croxton *Play of the Sacrament*', *Journal of Medieval and Early Modern Studies*, 29: 61–88.

CLOPPER, LAWRENCE (2001), *Drama, Play, and Game: English Festive Culture in the Medieval and Early Modern Period* (Chicago, 2001).

COLEMAN, JOYCE (1996), *Public Reading and the Reading Public in Late Medieval England and France* (Cambridge).

COLETTI, THERESA (1990), 'Reading REED: History and the Records of Early English Drama', in Lee Patterson (ed.), *Literary Practice and Social Change in Britain, 1380–1530* (Berkeley, Calif.), 248–84.

——(1991), 'Fragmentation and Redemption: Dramatic Records, History, and the Dream of Wholeness', review of David N. Klausner (ed.), *Records of*

Early English Drama: Herefordshire/Worcestershire (Toronto, 1990), *Envoi*, 3: 1–13.

—— (1993), 'Purity and Danger: The Paradox of Mary's Body and the Engendering of the Infancy Narrative in the English Mystery Cycles', in Linda Lomperis and Sarah Stanbury (eds.), *Feminist Approaches to the Body in Medieval Literature* (Philadelphia), 65–95.

—— (2001), '*Paupertas est donum Dei*: Hagiography, Lay Religion, and the Economics of Salvation in the Digby Mary Magdalene', *Speculum*, 76: 337–78.

COPELAND, RITA (1991), *Rhetoric, Hermeneutics, and Translation in the Middle Ages: Academic Traditions and Vernacular Texts* (Cambridge).

—— (1994), 'The Pardoner's Body and the Disciplining of Rhetoric', in Sarah Kay and Miri Rubin (eds.), *Framing Medieval Bodies* (Manchester), 138–59.

—— (2002), 'Sophistic, spectrality, iconoclasm', in Jeremy Dimmick, James Simpson, and Nicolette Zeeman (eds.), *Images, Idolatry, and Iconoclasm in Late Medieval England* (Oxford).

COX, JOHN D. (2000), *The Devil and the Sacred in English Drama 1350–1642* (Cambridge).

—— and KASTAN, DAVID SCOTT (eds.) (1997), *A New History of Early English Drama* (New York).

CRANE, SUSAN (2002), *The Performance of Self: Ritual, Clothing, and Identity during the Hundred Years War* (Philadelphia).

CURRAN, MICHAEL (1984), *The Antiphonary of Bangor and the Early Irish Monastic Liturgy* (Blackrock).

DAGENAIS, JOHN (1994), *The Ethics of Reading in Manuscript Culture: Glossing the Libro de Buen Amor* (Princeton).

DAVIDSON, AUDREY (ed.) (1992), *The Ordo Virtutum of Hildegard of Bingen: Critical Studies* (Kalamazoo, Mich.).

DILLON, EMMA (2002), *Medieval Music-Making and the 'Roman de Fauvel'* (Cambridge).

DOANE, A. N., and PASTERNACK, CAROL BRAUN (eds.) (1991), *Vox intexta: Orality and Textuality in the Middle Ages* (Madison).

DONOVAN, CLAIRE (1991), *The de Brailes Hours: Shaping the Book of Hours in Thirteenth-Century Oxford* (London).

DOSSE, FRANÇOIS (1997), *History of Structuralism*, trans. Deborah Glassman, 2 vols. (Minneapolis).

DUFFY, EAMON (1992) *The Stripping of the Altars: Traditional Religion in England 1400–1580* (New Haven).

ENDERS, JODY (1990), 'Vision with Voices: The Rhetoric of Memory and Music in Liturgical Drama', *Comparative Drama*, 24: 34–54.

—— (1992), *Rhetoric and the Origins of Medieval Drama* (Ithaca, NY).

—— (1999), *The Medieval Theater of Cruelty: Rhetoric, Memory, Violence* (Ithaca, NY).

EPP, GARRETT P. J. (1997), 'The Vicious Guise: Effeminacy, Sodomy, and *Mankind*', in Jeffrey Cohen and Bonnie Wheeler (eds.), *Becoming Male in the Middle Ages* (New York), 303–20.

——(2001), 'Ecce Homo', in Glenn Burger and Steven F. Kruger (eds.), *Queering the Middle Ages* (Minneapolis), 236–51.

EVANS, RUTH (1997), 'When a Body meets a Body: Fergus and Mary in the York Cycle', *New Medieval Literatures*, 1: 193–212.

FASSLER, MARGOT (1993), *Gothic Song: Victorine Sequences and Augustinian Reform in Twelfth-Century Paris* (Cambridge).

——(1998), 'Composer and Dramatist: Melodious Singing and the Freshness of Remorse', in Barbara Newman (ed.), *Voice of the Living Light: Hildegard of Bingen and her World* (Berkeley, Calif.), 149–75.

——and BALTZER REBECCA, (eds.) (2000), *The Divine Office in the Latin Middle Ages: Methodology and Source Studies, Regional Developments, Hagiography. Written in Honor of Professor Ruth Steiner* (Oxford).

FOLEY, JOHN MILES (1990) *Traditional Oral Epic: The Odyssey, Beowulf, and the Serbo-Croatian Return Song* (Berkeley, Calif.).

——'Orality, Textuality, and Interpretation', in Doane and Pasternack, 1991: 34–45.

FRADENBURG, LOUISE (1991), *City, Marriage, Tournament: Arts of Rule in Late Medieval Scotland* (Madison).

GANIM, JOHN (1990), *Chaucerian Theatricality* (Princeton).

GELLRICH, JESSE (1995), *Discourse and Dominion in the Fourteenth Century: Oral Contexts of Writing in Philosophy, Politics, and Poetry* (Princeton).

GIBSON, GAIL MCMURRAY (1989), *The Theater of Devotion: East Anglian Drama and Society in the Late Middle Ages* (Chicago).

GIBSON, MARGARET, HESLOP, T. A. and PFAFF, RICHARD W. (eds.) (1992), *The Eadwine Psalter: Text, Image, and Monastic Culture in Twelfth-Century Canterbury* (London).

GREEN, RICHARD FIRTH (1999), *A Crisis of Truth: Literature and Law in Ricardian England* (Philadelphia).

GREENBLATT, STEPHEN (2001), *Hamlet in Purgatory* (Princeton).

GREENFIELD, PETER H. (1991), '"But Herefordshire for a Morris-daunce": A Response to Theresa Coletti', *Envoi*, 3: 14–23.

HAMBURGER, JEFFREY (1990), *The Rothschild Canticles: Art and Mysticism in Flanders and the Rhineland circa 1300* (New Haven).

HARDISON, O. B., JR. (1965), *Christian Rite and Christian Drama in the Middle Ages: Essays in the Origin and Early History of Modern Drama* (Baltimore).

HARVEY, HOWARD GRAHAM (1941), *The Theatre of the Basoche* (Cambridge, Mass.).

HEFFERNAN, THOMAS J., and MATTER, E. ANN (eds.) (2001), *The Liturgy of the Medieval Church* (Kalamazoo, Mich.).

HOLMES, OLIVIA (2000), *Assembling the Lyric Self: Authorship from Troubadour Song to Italian Poetry Book* (Minneapolis).

HOLSINGER, BRUCE (1999), 'Langland's Musical Reader: Liturgy, Law, and the Constraints of Performance', *Studies in the Age of Chaucer*, 19: 99–141.

——(2001), *Music, Body, and Desire in Medieval Culture: Hildegard of Bingen to Chaucer* (Stanford, Calif.).

——(2002), 'Vernacular Legality: The English Jurisdictions of *The Owl and the Nightingale*', in Emily Steiner and Candace Barrington (eds.), *The Letter of the Law: Legal Practice and Literary Production in Medieval England* (Ithaca, NY), 154–84.

HOTCHKISS, VALERIE R. (1996), *Clothes Make the Man: Female Cross Dressing in Medieval Europe* (New York).

HUGHES, ANDREW (1982), *Medieval Manuscripts for Mass and Office: A Guide to their Organization and Terminology* (Toronto).

——(1993), 'Liturgical Drama: Falling between the Disciplines', in *The Theatre of Medieval Europe: New Research in Early Drama* (Cambridge), 42–62.

HUOT, SYLVIA (1987), *From Song to Book: The Poetics of Writing in Old French Lyric and Lyrical Narrative Poetry* (Ithaca, NY).

——(1997), *Allegorical Play in the Old French Motet: The Sacred and the Profane in Thirteenth-Century Polyphony* (Stanford, Calif.).

JAMES, MERVYN (1983), 'Ritual, Drama and Social Body in the Late Medieval English Town', *Past and Present*, 98: 3–29.

KINSERVIK, MATTHEW J. (1996), 'The Struggle over Mary's Body: Theological and Dramatic Resolution in the N-Town Assumption Play', *Journal of English and Germanic Philology*, 95: 190–203.

KIPLING, GORDON (1998), *Enter the King: Theatre, Liturgy, and Ritual in the Medieval Civic Triumph* (Oxford).

LANCASHIRE, ANNA (2002), *London Civic Theatre: City Drama and Pageantry from Roman Times to 1558* (Cambridge).

LERER, SETH (1998), 'The Chaucerian Critique of Medieval Theatricality', in Paxson et al. 1998: 59–76.

LIPTON, EMMA (2002), 'Language on Trial: Performing the Law in the N-Town Trial Play', in Emily Steiner and Candace Barrington (eds.), *The Letter of the Law: Legal Practice and Literary Production in Medieval England* (Ithaca, NY), 115–35.

LITTLE, LESTER K. (1993), *Benedictine Maledictions: Liturgical Cursing in Romanesque France* (Ithaca, NY).

McGEE, TIMOTHY J. (1998), *The Sound of Medieval Song: Ornamentation and Vocal Style According to the Treatises* (Oxford).

——(1996), with Rigg, A. G., and Klausner, David N., *Singing Early Music: The Pronunciation of European Languages in the Late Middle Ages and Renaissance* (Bloomington, Ind.).

McLAUGHLIN, MEGAN (1994), *Consorting with Saints: Prayer for the Dead in Early Medieval France* (Ithaca, NY).

MINNIS, A. J. (1984), *Medieval Theory of Authorship: Scholastic Literary Attitudes in the Later Middle Ages* (London).

MUESSIG, CAROLYN (2002), *Preacher, Sermon, and Audience in the Middle Ages* (Leiden).

MURPHY, JAMES J. (1974), *Rhetoric in the Middle Ages: A History of Rhetorical Theory from St. Augustine to the Renaissance* (Berkeley, Calif.).

NISSÉ, RUTH (1997), 'Reversing Discipline: The *Tretise of Miraclis Pleyinge*, Lollard exegesis, and the Failure of Representation', *Yearbook of Langland Studies*, 11: 163–98.

——(1998), 'Staged Interpretations: Civic Rhetoric and Lollard Politics in the York Plays', *Journal of Medieval and Early Modern Studies*, 28: 427–52.

NOLAN, MAURA (2004), 'The Performance of the Literary: Lydgate's Mummings', in James Simpson and Larry Scanlon (eds.), *John Lydgate: Poetry, Culture and Lancastrian England* (Notre Dame, Ind.).

O'KEEFFE, KATHERINE O'BRIEN (1990), *Visible Song: Transitional Literacy in Old English Verse* (Cambridge).

ONG, WALTER J. (1976), 'From Mimesis to Irony: Writing and Print as Integuments of Voice', *Bulletin of the Midwest Modern Language Association*, 9: 1–24.

——(1982), *Orality and Literacy: The Technologizing of the Word* (London).

——(1992), *Faith and Contexts*, ed. Thomas Farrell and Paul Soukup, 4 vols. (Atlanta).

PAGE, CHRISTOPHER (1987), *Voices and Instruments of the Middle Ages: Instrumental Practice and Songs in France 1100–1300* (London).

——(1989), *The Owl and the Nightingale: Musical Life and Ideas in France 1100–1300* (Berkeley, Calif.).

——(1993), *Discarding Images: Reflections on Music and Culture in Medieval France* (Oxford).

PARKER, ANDREW, and SEDGWICK, EVE (eds.) (1995), *Performativity and Performance* (New York).

PAXSON, JAMES, CLOPPER, LAWRENCE, and TOMASCH, SYLVIA (eds.) (1998), *The Performance of Middle English Culture: Essays on Chaucer and the Drama in Honor of Martin Stevens* (Cambridge).

PHELAN, PEGGY (1993), *Unmarked: The Politics of Performance* (New York).

——(1997), *Mourning Sex: Performing Public Memories* (London).

PUCHNER, MARTIN (2002), 'The Theater in Modernist Thought', *New Literary History*, 33: 521–32.

RANKIN, SUSAN (1994), 'The Divine Truth of Scripture: Chant in the *Roman de Fauvel*', *Journal of the American Musicological Society*, 47: 203–43.

RASTALL, RICHARD (1996), *The Heavens Singing: Music in Early English Religious Drama*, vol. i (Cambridge).

——(2001), *Minstrels Playing: Music in Early English Religious Drama*, vol. ii (Cambridge).

ROACH, JOSEPH (1996), *Cities of the Dead: Circum-Atlantic Performance* (New York).

SANOK, CATHERINE (2002), 'Performing Feminine Sanctity in Late Medieval

England: Parish Guilds, Saints' Plays, and the *Second Nun's Tale*', *Journal of Medieval and Early Modern Studies*, 32: 269–303.

Sautman, Francesca Canadé (2001), 'What Can They Possibly Do Together? Queer Epic Performances in *Tristan de Nanteuil*', in Sautman and Pamela Sheingorn (eds.), *Same Sex Love and Desire among Women in the Middle Ages* (New York), 199–232.

Schechner, Richard (1998), 'What Is Performance Studies Anyway?' in Peggy Phelan and Jill Lane (eds.), *The Ends of Performance* (New York), 357–62.

Schmitt, Jean-Claude (1990), *La Raison des gestes dans l'occident médiéval* (Paris).

Simons, Walter (1994), 'Reading a Saint's Body: Rapture and Bodily Movement in the *Vitae* of Thirteenth-Century Beguines', in Sarah Kay and Miri Rubin (eds.), *Framing Medieval Bodies* (Manchester), 10–23.

Solterer, Helen (1995), *The Master and Minerva: Disputing Women in French Medieval Culture* (Berkeley, Calif.).

Sponsler, Claire (1997), *Drama and Resistance: Bodies, Goods and Theatricality in Late Medieval England* (Minneapolis).

Stanton, Anne Rudloff (2001), *The Queen Mary Psalter: A Study of Affect and Audience* (Philadelphia).

Steiner, Emily (2003), *Documentary Culture and the Making of Medieval English Literature* (Cambridge).

Stevens, John (1986), *Words and Music in the Middle Ages: Song, Narrative, Dance and Drama 1030–1350* (Cambridge).

Steward, Pamela D. (1986), *Retorica e mimica nel 'Decameron' e nella commedia del Cinquecento* (Florence).

Stock, Brian (1983), *The Implications of Literacy: Written Language and Models of Interpretation in the Eleventh and Twelfth Centuries* (Princeton).

—— (1996), *Augustine the Reader: Meditation, Self-Knowledge, and the Ethics of Interpretation* (Cambridge, Mass.).

Suydam, Mary A., and Ziegler, Joanna E. (eds.) (1999), *Performance and Transformation: New Approaches to Late Medieval Spirituality* (New York).

Symes, Carol (2002), 'The Appearance of Early Vernacular Plays: Forms, Functions, and the Future of Medieval Theater', *Speculum*, 77 (July), 778–831.

Taylor, Andrew (2001), 'Was there a Song of Roland?' *Speculum*, 76: 28–65.

Treitler, Leo (1974), 'Homer and Gregory: The Transmission of Epic Poetry and Plainchant', *Musical Quarterly*, 60/3 (July), 333–72.

—— (1981), 'Oral, Written, and Literate Processes in the Transmission of Medieval Music', *Speculum*, 56 (July), 471–91.

—— (1985), 'Reading and Singing: On the Genesis of Occidental Musical Writing', *Early Music History*, 4: 135–208.

—— (1992), 'The "Unwritten" and "Written Transmission" of Medieval Chant and the Start-up of Musical Notation', *Journal of Musicology*, 10: 131–91.

Trexler, Richard (1987), *The Christian at Prayer: An Illustrated Prayer Manual Attributed to Peter the Chanter (d. 1197)* (Binghamton, NY).

TURNER, VICTOR (1982), *From Ritual to Theatre: The Human Seriousness of Play* (New York).

TWYCROSS, MEG, and CARPENTER SARAH (2002), *Masks and Masking in Medieval and Early Tudor England* (Aldershot).

VITZ, EVELYN BIRGE (1999), *Orality and Performance in Early French Romance* (Cambridge).

WARNING, RAINER (2001), *The Ambivalences of Medieval Religious Drama*, trans. Steven Rendall (Stanford, Calif.).

WATERS, CLAIRE (2002), 'Holy Duplicity: The Preacher's Two Faces', *Studies in the Age of Chaucer*, 24: 75–113.

—— (2004), *Angels and Earthly Creatures: Preaching, Performance, and Gender in the Later Middle Ages* (Philadelphia, forthcoming).

WILKINS, NIGEL (1995), *Music in the Age of Chaucer*, 2nd edn. (Cambridge).

ZIOLKOWSKI, JAN (2000), 'Nota Bene: Why the Classics Were Neumed in the Middle Ages', *Journal of Medieval Latin*, 10: 74–114.

ZUMTHOR, PAUL (1972), *Essai de poétique médiévale* (Paris).

—— (1990), *Oral Poetry: An Introduction*, trans. Kathryn Murphy-Judy (Minneapolis).

Index